Caring Capitalism

Companies are increasingly championed for their capacity to solve social problems. Yet what happens when such goods as water, education, and health are sold by companies – rather than donated by nonprofits – to the disadvantaged and when the pursuit of mission becomes entangled with the pursuit of profit? In *Caring Capitalism*, Emily Barman answers these important questions, showing how the meaning of social value in an era of caring capitalism gets mediated by the work of "value entrepreneurs" and the tools they create to gauge companies' social impact. By shedding light on these pivotal actors and the cultural and material contexts in which they operate, *Caring Capitalism* accounts for the unexpected consequences of this new vision of the market for the pursuit of social value. Proponents and critics of caring capitalism alike will find the book essential reading.

EMILY BARMAN is an associate professor of sociology at Boston University. She received her PhD in sociology from the University of Chicago. Her first book, *Contesting Communities: The Transformation of Workplace Charity* was awarded the 2007 Association of Fundraising Professionals' Research Prize. Her articles have appeared in *American Journal of Sociology, Social Forces, Journal of Management Studies, Nonprofit and Voluntary Sector Quarterly*, and *Social Science History*.

Caring Capitalism

The Meaning and Measure of Social Value

EMILY BARMAN

Boston University

CAMBRIDGE
UNIVERSITY PRESS

CAMBRIDGE
UNIVERSITY PRESS

32 Avenue of the Americas, New York, NY 10013–2473, USA

Cambridge University Press is part of the University of Cambridge.

It furthers the University's mission by disseminating knowledge in the pursuit of education, learning, and research at the highest international levels of excellence.

www.cambridge.org
Information on this title: www.cambridge.org/9781107088153

First published 2016

A catalog record for this publication is available from the British Library.

Library of Congress Cataloging in Publication Data
Names: Barman, Emily, author.
Title: Caring capitalism : the meaning and measure of social value / Emily Barman.
Description: New York : Cambridge University Press, 2016. | Includes bibliographical references and index.
Identifiers: LCCN 2015043521 | ISBN 9781107088153 (Hardback)
Subjects: LCSH: Nonprofit organizations. | Capitalism–Moral and ethical aspects. | Social responsibility of business. | BISAC: SOCIAL SCIENCE / Sociology / General.
Classification: LCC HD62.6 .B367 2016 | DDC 658.4/08–dc23 LC record available at http://lccn.loc.gov/2015043521

ISBN 978-1-107-08815-3 Hardback

Contents

Figures

Tables

Acknowledgments

This book was too long in coming and therefore, it is of no surprise that I must give thanks to a large number of people who helped me along the way. I owe a tremendous debt of gratitude to those individuals who took the time and energy to give me their thoughtful feedback on and encouragement with this book as it made its slow and winding journey toward publication. These include Malin Arvidson, Claudio Benzecry, Elizabeth Popp Berman, Patricia Bromley, Joanne Carman, Curtis Child, Nitsan Chorev, Elizabeth Clemens, Kate Cooney, Alnoor Ebrahim, Renuka Fernandez, Joe Galaskiewicz, Stine Grodal, Neil Gross, Chao Guo, Matthew Hall, Emily Heaphy, Victoria Johnson, Monika Krause, David Lewis, Wes Longhofer, Fergus Lyons, Heather MacIndoe, Paul-Brian McInerney, Andrea Mennicken, Yuval Millo, Michael Moody, Konstanze Senge, Steven Rathgeb Smith, David Suarez, and Zsuzsanna Varga.

Colleagues in the Department of Sociology at Boston University, including Nicole Aschoff, Cati Connell, Susan Eckstein, Zophia Edwards, Ashley Mears, Sigrun Olafsdottir, Emily Philipp, David Swartz, and Itai Vardi, made everyday life much more enjoyable than it would have been otherwise and offered their much appreciated thoughts and encouragement on the book project. I am indebted to the BU Department of Sociology's endlessly efficient and indefatigable Anna Bakanova and Keryn Egan for their assistance. Finally, I am thoroughly grateful and always cheered by the friendship of Zarena Aslami, Jessica Berger Gross, Bart and Kristina Bonikowski, Brian Carey, Dino Christenson, Andrea and Chris Davis, Gavin Froome, Filiz Garip, Erin Graves, Kiri Gurd, Erin Holmes Christenson, David and Yaminette Linhart, Jody Rayher, Mert Sabuncu, and Mary Lass Stewart.

Sections of the book or related papers from it were presented at annual conferences of the American Sociological Association, Academy of Management, Association for Research on Nonprofit Organizations and Voluntary Associations, Eastern Sociological Society, European Group for Organizational

Studies, Social Science History Association, and The Society for the Advancement of Socio-Economics, as well as in presentations at Boston University, TSRC Birmingham University, Stockholm Center for Organizational Research, University of Washington, Brown University, University of Michigan, University of Southern California, University of Notre Dame, University of Hamburg, and Emory University. I am grateful for the valuable comments, critiques, and suggestions that I received from participants and audience members at those events.

A very special and indebted thanks to those individuals who took time from their busy schedules to talk with me about their work. Without you, this book would not be possible, and I have done my very best to represent your thoughts and opinions accurately in this text. The reviewers of the book manuscript provided extraordinarily thorough, sound, and useful comments; I hope they can see their influence in this final version. Robert Dreesen, my editor at Cambridge University Press, provided unstinting patience and support as this manuscript worked its way toward publication.

My parents, Jean and Roderick Barman, two academics, never ceased to provide both familial love and scholarly support to me. As always, thank you so much; I am eternally grateful to you for everything. My brother, Rod, and my sister-in-law, Dominique, served as admirable models of good humor and hard work. My son, Oliver Go, arrived just as the book project began – he was a welcome distraction from scholarship as only an adorable small child can be. This book is dedicated with all my love and gratitude to my favorite colleague, closest friend, and dearest husband, Julian Go.

I

Introduction

In 2008, at the World Economic Forum, Microsoft founder Bill Gates famously called for nothing less than an entirely new form of the global economy. This was to be a form of capitalism where the "reach of market forces" would mean "that more people can make a profit, or gain recognition, doing work that eases the world's inequities." He was articulating a vision of a new more caring version of the market where corporations pursue both money and mission. Such a dual emphasis on firms making the world a better place while also making a profit is increasingly common. Multinational corporations achieve this by the adoption of inclusive business models and by the sale of socially beneficial goods. Unilever (2010:3), a global consumer goods conglomerate, proclaims a desire "to develop new ways of doing business which will increase the positive social benefits arising from Unilever's activities." Poverty is to be addressed by market actors: local firms can provide new entrepreneurial and employment opportunities, microfinance can deliver financial services to the economically disadvantaged, and a growing type of financial investor evaluates companies not just for their production of shareholder return but also for their capacity to effect social change.

I term this newer, supposedly kinder vision of the economy "caring capitalism." The idea seems simple enough: companies can pursue social impact and they can make profit in so doing.[1] Firms do well and do good at the same time. Caring capitalism thus represents a departure from how we have traditionally understood the societal division of labor. It upends the recent belief, one that dominated the global economy for much of the late twentieth century, that businesses should focus on shareholder value while nonprofits should work on social value, and government should deliver public value. Now, what are termed "social purpose organizations," – private, nongovernmental entities who claim in all or in part to address social inequities – include not only traditional nonprofits, like CARE, Salvation Army, and the United Way, but also "compassionate companies," which seek not only money but also mission.

Caring capitalism contains a world of possibilities and promises but also raises a host of beguiling and potentially troubling questions. Foremost, what happens to the project of social value – actors' concerted efforts to address social inequities – when companies take up this mantle?[2] What is the consequence when social goods are no longer donated by NGOs to the disadvantaged, both here in the United States and in the global South, but now are sold by firms on the market to paying customers? And what happens to our understanding of social good when it is subject to companies' quest for economic profit and investors' desire for shareholder return? Given both commonsense concerns and scholarly expectations over the negative effects of the market on moral action, how does the meaning of social value get modified when the pursuit of mission becomes entangled with the pursuit of money?

Based on an extensive array of data, including interviews, field research, document analysis, and secondary scholarship, this book addresses these questions and concerns. It examines the effect of the rise of caring capitalism for the meaning and measure of social value. Common sense, as well as one strand of academic theory, would make dire predictions. It would lead us to expect that caring capitalism does little else than marketize social value. Money and its pursuit take over, subsuming the very definition of social good to its unwieldy power. But as we will see, what I find is not as simple nor as calamitous in its effects. This book shows that caring capitalism has not resulted in the wholesale marketization of social value. By and large, compassionate corporations are not evaluated by the use of market indicators – to succeed in changing the world has not categorically meant such efforts are monetized and nor are they subject to the criterion of economic profit or shareholder return. And even when these expected outcomes occur, they do not always subjugate the pursuit of social value to that of only monetary gain. To make sense of the unexpectedly limited impact of caring capitalism on social value requires attention to the work of a group of actors I call "value entrepreneurs." We need to understand their attempts to create tools and techniques for measuring social value and the cultural and material constraints that they face in their efforts. Only in this way can we account for the complexities of caring capitalism and its consequences for the meaning and measure of social value in the market.

THE TURN TO CARING CAPITALISM

In his clarion call for companies to take up the mantle of social welfare, Bill Gates was not alone. His comments illustrated a larger movement in the global economy (Roy 2010; Porter and Kramer 2011; Blowfield and Dolan 2014). Beginning in the late 1990s, a growing number of powerful public and private actors (including multilateral organizations such as the United Nations and the World Bank, charitable foundations like the Bill and Melinda Gates

Foundation and the Omidyar Foundation, and governments in the global North through their development aid agencies) have proposed that market actors, including investors and firms, can produce social value through their business practices as a means to both economic gain and to produce a more just and sustainable society. These proponents of caring capitalism have offered up a number of different envisionings of the project of social value, with each constituting a distinct field.[3] First, like Unilever, PepsiCo, and Dell, multinational corporations can organize their production processes and governance policies to ensure their social and environmental responsibility, including respect for the rights of stakeholders, as a means to shareholder value. Responsible Investment (RI) is an emerging financial industry that views firms' social, environmental, and governance behavior as a strategy to reduce costs, eliminate risks, improve brand appeal, and create new business opportunities for companies (World Economic Forum 2005; Hebb 2012). Alternatively, multinational corporations, often called Inclusive Businesses, purposively can include the poor in the developing world as suppliers, workers, distributors, and include customers in their value chain in ways that both alleviate poverty and increase shareholder return (Prahalad 2004; UN Global Compact 2012). Coca Cola, for example, not only sells its typical products, including Coke and Fanta Orange, to the rural poor in India, but now also sells Vitingo, an orange drink fortified to address the common problem of iron deficiency (Coca Cola India 2014).

In the developing world, novel types of local companies pursue social change by facilitating individuals' access to the market and by growing the regional economy. These market-based solutions to poverty are promoted and funded by actors in the global North. A new financial market called Impact Investing has arisen to facilitate innovative investment in this range of double bottom line–entities (Bugg-Levine and Emerson 2011). These investment opportunities include microfinance vehicles that provide financial services to low-income clients – individuals to whom traditional financial institutions have been unwilling to offer banking services. Customers then invest their loans in an entrepreneurial opportunity and repay it to the bank with interest. Most famously, Muhammad Yunus founded the Grameen Bank in 1983 in order to provide microcredit to the poorest residents of Dhaka, Bangladesh (Yunus 1999; Roy 2010). Similarly, Impact Investing can be directed to "small and medium enterprises" (SMEs) – locally owned firms in developing regions. In the development literature, and as championed by scholars, policy makers, and funders, SMEs are deemed key to a nation's economic growth because they provide entrepreneurial and employment opportunities that can mitigate poverty (Halberg 2000; Ferranti and Ody 2007). One instance of an SME is Escopil International in Mozambique. Formed in 1998, Escopil is a locally owned company that provides industrial maintenance services to the nation's technology market and that employs over 200 people (Escopil 2013).

Together, these different fields that make up caring capitalism constitute a small but significant portion of the global economy. Over 8,000 businesses in 145 countries have signed on to a United Nations pledge to incorporate socially responsible practices as of 2013 (UN Global Compact 2014).[4] In 2012, the last year for which data was available, over 30 trillion investment dollars worldwide were committed to firms with a social purpose and, in the United States, $3.74 trillion in that same year were oriented around investment in companies with a double or triple bottom line of economic, social, and/or environmental return (US SIF 2012). The provision of "good" has become big business.

These market-based solutions to social problems are heralded as innovative precisely because they undermine traditional expectations about the division of labor in society across the public, private, and nonprofit sectors in terms of each space's core responsibility. For much of the last century, government and the voluntary sector have been perceived as the primary deliverers of social goods in the United States, while companies have been largely concerned with the pursuit of economic profit or pursued social betterment outside of their business model through corporate philanthropy. Intensifying in the 1980s and 1990s with the growth of a finance economy, firms were asked to refrain from a concern with social welfare altogether in the pursuit of shareholder value (Davis 2009; Mizruchi 2013).[5] In contrast, government has been viewed either as a caring welfare state that provides public goods to all citizens or as a vehicle serving the interests of competing social interest groups (Alford 1994).[6] And the primary task of the nonprofit sector has been to deliver needed goods and services to clients and communities. Nonprofits are private organizations granted tax-exempt status by the government in exchange for delivering programs that benefit the public interest while withholding the distribution of profits to members (Frumkin 2002).[7]

Yet, a number of broader societal changes have disrupted those expectations and paved the way for caring capitalism. For one, a marked decline of public funding of nonprofits in the 1980s led to the formation of new types of mixed, hybrid organizations to pursue the public good. Emerging out of the nonprofit sector in the 1990s, social enterprises employ market methods in order to ensure clients' equitable participation in the economy while relying on sales revenue for income. Typically, social enterprises ensure the fair procurement of supplies, the employment of disadvantaged populations, and/or the sale of socially beneficial products and services to underserved customers (Kerlin 2009). One case of a social enterprise is iCater, a firm run by Pine Street Inn, a nonprofit in Boston with a social mission to end homelessness in the community. As an affiliated catering business, iCater offers job training and employment skills in food service and preparation to its employees and it also provides needed income for the nonprofit's additional programs (Pine Street Inn 2014).

In the private sector, the social responsibility of firms in the United States came under scrutiny in the late 1960s and on. Consumers, investors, civil society actors, and the media criticized corporations for the social harm caused by their business practices and sought to mitigate those ill effects for consumers, employees, and society. In part, a new form of investing arose, called Socially Responsible Investing (SRI), whereby investors were encouraged to direct their investments for both social and stockholder return. Through the tactics of community investment, shareholder activism, and social screening, proponents of SRI viewed financial activity as a means to minimize firms' sale of harmful products (e.g., the sin stocks of cigarettes, alcohol, and firearms), to divest from businesses operating in countries with human rights abuses, and to facilitate corporations' adoption of beneficial personnel policies, beyond those required by government guidelines (Bruyn 1991; Schueth 2003). A second and distinct critique of firms' social responsibility began in the 1990s with the growth of the global economy. The outsourcing of much of American corporations' manufacturing to developing countries resulted in low wages, human rights violations, and unsafe working conditions for migrant workers and workers in the global South. Corporate Social Responsibility (CSR) emerged as a strategy by which civil society actors sought to convince multinational corporations to equitably treat its stakeholders, including employees, customers, and suppliers, in their global value chains, through the threat of media attention and consumer boycotts (Bartley 2007a; Soule 2009).

In striking contrast, the embrace of caring capitalism over the last decade has seen firms increasingly heralded as the best providers of social goods. Drawing from one long-standing strand of economic thought dating back to Adam Smith's (1776/2012) belief in the benefits of the "invisible hand" of the free market for societal well-being, the idea of caring capitalism has been based on the claim that companies are equally effective, if not superior, to charity or government agencies in their ability to deliver needed social goods. The assumption of caring capitalism is that firms will pursue the same benefits as nonprofits and government, just in a more successful manner due to their economic self-sufficiency and greater potential scale of delivery. C.K. Prahalad, the author of the highly influential 2004 book, *The Fortune at the Bottom of the Pyramid*, saw in the market an attractive alternative to nonprofits' efforts to aid the poor. "Charity might feel good," he wrote, "but it rarely solves the problem" (Prahalad 2004:16). The turn to caring capitalism resulted from efforts by a coalition of groups, including market enthusiasts responding to criticisms of the neoliberal agenda in the global economy, actors working to redress the aftermath of the spectacular 2008 crash of the finance market, and those members of the international development arena seeking to end world poverty as part of the United Nation's Millennium Development goals.

VALUING COMPASSIONATE COMPANIES

The growing embrace of caring capitalism by powerful global actors raises countless new questions about its possible effects and efficacy; its possibly cynical motivations or incredulous claims. But a crucial set of questions also emerges around the question of meaning and measure. Detractors might and should question whether corporations can ever do the job of "doing good" properly.[8] But even that denunciation rests upon a notion of how to define and gauge "doing good" in the first place. How do we know when companies are not just making profit but also addressing social inequities? To judge whether caring capitalism "can work," we need to be able to measure its impact. And this is precisely what is happening now. In each and all of these different forms and practices both inside and outside of the market – Inclusive Businesses, locally owned firms, double bottom line–investments, social enterprises, and nonprofit organizations – social purpose organizations are being asked to demonstrate their results.

In facing this growing pressure to value their efforts, social purpose organizations are not alone; actors, objects, and activities of all types increasingly are being subject to valuation through formal tools and techniques (Power 1994; Porter 1995; Espeland and Stevens 2008). In the case of baseball, for instance, the use of statistics has replaced scouts' judgments of a player's ability (Lewis 2004). Think "Moneyball." Similarly, in the field of education, standardized testing, as spurred on by the Common Core requirements, has superseded teachers' subjective estimation of a student's capacity (Elmore 2007). This wider turn to performance measurement is commonly understood to result from the dominance of neoliberalism in the private sector and the doctrine of New Public Management in the public sector (Espeland and Sauder 2007; Lamont 2012).

Similarly, compassionate companies, as well as other types of social purpose organizations, have been held to a growing and widespread requirement to show the results of their efforts, often by reference to the term of "social value." Even though this effort is seen as particularly challenging if not impossible given that social value is deemed ambiguous to define and slippery to measure, this move to valuation for social purpose organizations has definitely occurred, as evidenced by the growth of multiple and competing measuring devices of such beguiling and seemingly technical nature as "Outcome Measurement," the "B Impact Ratings System," the "Global Impact Investment Ratings System (GIIRS)," the "Global Reporting Initiative (GRI)," and "Social Return on Investment (SROI)," among others.[9] In all, over one hundred and fifty different types of tools, techniques, and technologies were available to any organization seeking to assess its social value in 2014.[10]

THE BOOK'S PURPOSE

So, what does it mean to "do well at doing good"? Given the complexity of setting the meaning of social value and the recognized difficulty of appraising it, the first purpose of this book is to identify the types of measuring devices present for social purpose organizations as a lens to understand the question of social value. How is the concept of social value defined and gauged by a field's prevailing tools, tests, and techniques? Secondly, employing a comparative and historical perspective, this book seeks to determine how the rise of caring capitalism has affected the valuation of social good. What happens to the meaning and measure of social value when it is no longer produced just by nonprofit organizations but now also by a range of hybrid or for-profit actors committed to market-based solutions to social problems? Finally, this book seeks to explain when and why different measuring devices – varying in their use of market indicators such as money and shareholder return – come to prevail across this assortment of social purpose organizations. What factors determine whether and when the pursuit of social value gets subsumed to the pursuit of economic value?

ON SOCIAL VALUE

To date, we know markedly little about how compassionate companies, or indeed other types of social purpose organizations, seek to demonstrate their social value. In order to investigate this topic, it will be helpful to further explore the meaning of the concept of social value. The concept "social value" brings together two terms, each with a long-standing history in the social sciences. The term "social" has been used to refer to a distinct societal space or to a particular orientation of action. And the term "value" has been employed to reference either the possession of a criterion of worth or the assessment of an entity's merit. More recently, the idea of social value has been employed to describe the distinctive contributions of social purpose organizations to society. Crucially, scholars disagree as to how to define social value, despite its increasingly widespread usage in scholarly discourse and in popular culture.

Take the term "social" first. This term has several different, albeit related, meanings, in the social sciences (Calhoun 1998; Mansbridge 1998; Krause 2014). To begin, the concept of social refers to a specific societal space, contingent upon both the horizontal and the vertical partitioning of society. One definition of the term social, emerging in the early nineteenth century, conceives of society as composed of three different realms: the economy, the government, and the social, with the last defined as a realm of autonomous, voluntary interactions among individuals and groups – what also is called "civil society" (Steinmetz 1993). In this view, as in the example of the "social sciences," the social also invokes the notion of a collectivity that stands distinct from and analytically above its constituent members. The social refers to the properties of this third space. It does not constitute an aggregation of individuals' interests or values but rather possesses autonomous qualities and characteristics of its own (Durkheim 1895/2014; Etzioni 1999).

Relatedly, the term social is often used, as in the instances of "social security" or "social welfare," to refer to an orientation of action. Drawing from a view of the social as the presence of relationships among individuals (e.g., "social networks"), the social can reference action with positive intent toward and/or beneficial consequences for the well being of others, as opposed to the expectation of individuals' rational and self-interested behavior in the market. The concept of "social capital" refers to the composition and strength of networks among actors that positively affect individuals' and groups' capacities (Coleman 1990; Putnam 2000). Similarly, the social is frequently used to describe the quality of an actor's relationship with others, as with the example of labeling someone as "anti-social" when they do not enjoy others' company (Owens 2013).

Finally, the notion of the social also can refer to organized efforts, historically by government but also (and predominantly in the United States) by private actors like nonprofits or corporations, to improve the lives of individuals, communities, and/or society. Examples include the concepts of "social welfare" and the "social state," the latter a term synonymous with the welfare state in Europe. Here, the assumption is that individuals' material well being is not determined by their own biography or characteristics (e.g., their religious beliefs or moral character) but rather shaped by structural, macro-level conditions, such as the absence of sanitation or education, that cause wide-scale troubles for a community's residents and so require organized intervention to address (Steinmetz 1993; Foucault 1994).

As the second dimension of the concept of "social value," the term "value" comes with its own genealogy in the social sciences. Value encapsulates both a decision about quality and an act of assessment (Dewey 1939; Stark 2011). In their appraisal of the world around them, actors must make a choice about what criteria is of salience for an entity in a specific situation. This is the question of "what counts." To make a claim about what is of value, actors can select from a range of different qualities available to them. Broadly speaking, an order of worth (also called an "institutional logic" or "regime of justification") constitutes a claim about the quality by which the merit of the entity should be assessed. Multiple orders of worth exist and each specifies what criterion is of fundamental worth. An emphasis on market value, for example, stresses the primacy of monetary gain, while an aesthetic order of worth underscores the quality of physical beauty, and a concern for religious value is based on faith and spirituality (Lamont 1992; Stark 2011; Boltanski and Thévenot 2006)

Given these options, actors must determine what type of order of worth is salient for the object in question. Contra economics and its attention to the utility function, economic sociology has emphasized that the choice of a salient order of worth is not fixed, but rather shaped by societal context and the process is not always straightforward. Often the selection of the relevant quality results from dialogue or even contestation between actors with different social positions, moral values, and material interests (Stark 2011; Boltanski and Thévenot 2006). Take the simple example of the family heirloom: a piece of jewelry or furniture perhaps. While some members of a family may view the inherited item solely in terms of its economic worth on the market, others may view it as priceless and gauge its merit solely in regard to its sentimental value. Market value confronts sentimental value – and the two may or may not marry happily.

To complicate matters further, "value" refers not just to the issue of what counts but also the act of *how* to count. Any order of worth contains within it a claim about the criterion of value and also a claim about how to gauge entities according to that criterion. To assess the worth of an entity, actors can either engage in their own personal estimation or they can employ or create a measuring device – a test, tool, or instrument – that contains within it an objective claim about the prevailing order of worth and the appropriate type of information to be used as proof. Measuring devices, such as rankings, ratings, and ratios, perform the act of calculation by assigning a value to an entity on behalf of the actor employing the instrument (Callon 1998; Boltanski and Thévenot 2006; Espeland and Sauder 2007; Karpik 2010).[11] Any new car, for example, is subject to multiple assessments of its worth: it is not only allocated a price by the car company, but it is also ranked numerically in its segment by JD Powers and Associates, and rated on a scale from one to a hundred in its class by Consumer Reports.

These are helpful ways for thinking about the nature of the social and the question of value but they are limited for addressing the question of *social value*. The literature on the concept of the social explores how "the social" gets defined and enacted in society but tells us little about it as an order of worth for social purpose organizations. For its part, social science research on the concept of value has been largely discussed in terms of how and why economic value gets assigned to goods in the marketplace and has overlooked how the organized pursuit of social good is defined and assessed.[12]

So what about *social value*? Existing scholarship tells us little, even as the discourse of social value proliferates in organizational practice and popular memes. On the one hand, as shown in Figure 1.1, the term "social value" is increasingly employed by scholars to describe a particular type of quality of worth in society. On the other hand, despite the growing popularity of this term, there is strikingly little theorization of the term. When it is discussed, there is marked semantic and conceptual disagreement and little attention to its actual use by those engaged in the production of social value (Auerswald 2009; Mulgan 2010).

As with the concept value more broadly, social value is understood as both a noun and a verb.[13] Take social value as a noun. Here scholars offer two main ways to define the concept of social value, each of which draws from existing definitions of the idea of the social. In one case, social value is based on the identity and social location of the organizations that produce it. Social value occurs when nonprofit organizations, located in a "third" sector distinct from the public actions of government and from the market's production of private benefits for individuals, seek to address social inequities. (Auerswald 2009). Here, social value has been defined as the "value that

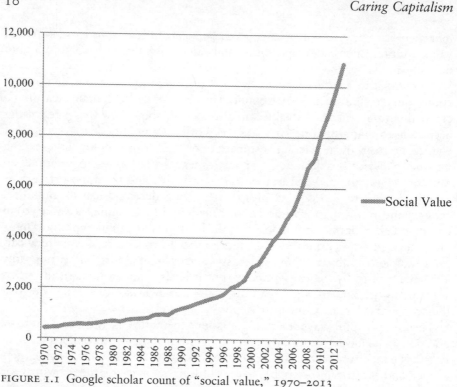

FIGURE I.I Google scholar count of "social value," 1970–2013

nongovernmental organizations (NGOs), social enterprises, social ventures, and social programs create" (Mulgan 2010:38).

Another approach to social value as a noun views social value as consisting of different types of benefits and recipients than that of economic or public value, regardless of the location of the actors who produce it. Most centrally, in this literature, the pursuit of social value is opposed to the pursuit of economic value.[14] Social value concerns actors' purposeful production of collective well being for others. In contrast, economic value is derived from action intended to generate utility for the individual supplier or consumer of a good (Anderson and Dees 2006; Martin and Osberg 2007). And, social value also is often contrasted with "public value" – governmental actors' efforts to identify and pursue the preferences of the collectivity in order to meet the needs of the median voter (Moore 1995).[15]

If disagreement exists about how to define social value, even more uncertainty surrounds the question of how to measure it. Here we come to social value as a verb. Defined in terms of action, social value is perceived of as an inherently challenging task, due to the problems of measurement. The frequently cited challenge is how to assess organizations, situations, or goods in terms of their social worth. One observer has described the goal of assessing a nonprofit's social value as one of "measuring the unmeasurable"

(Forbes 1998). The task of measurement typically is understood to consist of two decisions: conceptualization (the definition of the term to be studied) and operationalization (the selection of procedures used to assign a value to cases).

Several challenges are commonly noted as central to the problem of gauging social value. First, the ambiguous and complex nature of social good makes the task of conceptualization difficult. Different stakeholders in an organization may define the meaning of its social value in different ways (Kanter and Summers 1987). As Sawhill and Williamson (2001:371) propose: "Imagine an organization whose mission is to alleviate human suffering. How can you measure such an abstract notion?" This challenge of conceptualization, secondly, is complicated by the recognized difficulties of operationalization. Among other measurement challenges, many commonly recognized social goods are characterized by "information asymmetry." These products are hard to evaluate for their worth by consumers, including services that are difficult to judge in terms of their quality (such as education or health care), programs where the typical customer is not in a position to provide such judgment (such as care of the elderly, children, or the mentally disabled), and assistance provided at great distance from the resource provider (such as in international development) (Hansmann 1980). In result, even if consensus is reached about the meaning of social value, gauging the amount of social good an organization produces remains difficult.

While a genealogy of the concept of social value provides rich empirical insights into how scholars have sought to define the goals of social purpose organizations and how to assess their merit, social scientists have not applied the tools of their trade to make sense of how the criteria of "social value" is actually defined and deployed in practice.[16] Further, this literature has yet to investigate the question of how the rise of market solutions to social problems has affected the meaning and measure of the pursuit of social value. These are the issues I take up in the chapters that follow.

THE BOOK'S APPROACH

This is a book about the effect of the embrace of market-based solutions to social problems on the meaning and measure of social value. The goal is explanatory, not normative or policy-oriented in nature. Rather than critiquing the assumptions of caring capitalism or evaluating its causal efficacy in solving social inequities, the book's focus instead is on accounting for the consequences of caring capitalism for how we think about and seek to capture the worth of social purpose organizations as they strive to address societal problems. The study, of course, has normative implications. It also can help policy-makers. But its foremost task is to address the basic underlying questions about the meaning and measure of social value in a time of caring capitalism.

To do so, my methodological approach is to examine the act of valuation (of how social purpose organizations are judged for social value), rather than to examine the question of value (the decision as to which quality is of worth), by analyzing the measuring devices that are present in the fields of study in order to gauge the social value of social purpose organizations. The analysis of the formal tools, techniques, and technologies that are used to count these organizations' social value allows me to delineate how the rise of caring capitalism has affected what types of social change get to count as social value and by what metrics and indicators they can be counted. A measuring device is central to the allocation of value in any situation because it recognizes and rewards one particular meaning of value over all others. In the study of value, measuring devices are particularly important because they contain both a description of and a prescription for action (Callon 1998; Callon and Muniesa 2005; McKenzie and Millo 2003; Espeland and Sauder 2007).[17] Their existence and employment shapes the social world around them. From a technical perspective, a measuring device contains within it a claim about the type of quality that counts, thereby facilitating some lines of action while constraining others. The presence of a measuring device also shapes what is valued in a field because it creates reactivity. In the social sciences, reactivity is the "idea that people change their behavior in reaction to being evaluated, observed, or measured" (Espeland and Sauder 2007:1).[18] Actors seek to perform well according to the logic of the measure in order to establish legitimacy and obtain resources.[19]

A measuring device does all of this work by incorporating within it several decisions. First, it requires the selection of a quality of worth as salient for evaluation, thus excluding or rendering invisible other logics or qualities. It then creates a metric – a uniform scale with regular intervals, so that an entity can be assigned a value on that scale. The construction of a scale permits commensuration – the comparison of different objects according to a single and common metric.[20] Finally, a measuring device also includes a claim about what type of evidence or proof counts. It necessitates the employment of particular kinds of measures or indicators to gather data and the collection of specific type of data in order for evaluation to occur (Power 1994; Porter 1995; Espeland and Stevens 1998). Consider the challenge of how to assess the health of a nation's economy: a number of measuring devices exist to identify and so allow for comparison across countries, including GDP, employment statistics, the inflation rate, and so on.

A focus on the measuring device/s that are in place to gauge social value across different fields of social purpose organizations moves the study of social value away from other methodological approaches to this topic – away from an analysis of how people on the ground understand the idea of social value (of how actors define the project of social good), away from the study of their enactment of social value (of how actors implement their morals or interests through specific practices), and away from the study of their everyday enactment of measurement and valuation (how actors either subjectively or informally try to estimate their own worth or that of others). This book's attention to measuring devices shifts the analysis of social value toward a concern for

TABLE 1.1 *Sectoral location and market orientation of fields of study*

	Sectoral Location	
Market Orientation	Nonprofit Sector	Market
Embrace of Market	Social Enterprises	Responsible Investment, Inclusive Business, Impact Investing
Non-Market/ Critique of Market	Nonprofit Organizations	Socially Responsible Investing, Corporate Social Responsibility

what types of goals, strategies, and justifications are recognized and rewarded as social value in a particular setting via a prevailing measurement tool, technique, or technology (Callon 1998; Callon and Muniesa 2005; Smith 2007; Fourcade 2011).[21]

To specify the precise effect of caring capitalism on the meaning and measure of social value requires the use of comparison. It necessitates placing side by side and examining not only the measuring devices used in the project of caring capitalism but also those tools employed in other societal arenas, such as the nonprofit sector, and earlier efforts in the private sector to have firms consider their social and environmental obligations, prior to the growth of caring capitalism.[22] The book analyzes the meaning and metrics of social value present in the measuring devices that prevail across a range of these fields, including nonprofit organizations, social enterprises, SRI, CSR, RI, Inclusive Business, and Impact Investing. As shown in Table 1.1, these fields are all composed of social purpose organizations that share a commitment to the pursuit of social value but they differ along two critical, theoretically-salient dimensions: their sectoral location relative to the economy and their normative orientation toward the use of market methods to solve social problems. It is only through the employment of the comparative method (both across space and across time) that a determination can be made of the precise consequence of caring capitalism – as a site of both morals and money – for the meaning and measure of social value.

As a whole, I was interested in both the content of these measuring devices and in their history or biography – how and why these material objects came to be constructed by specific actors out of all possible meanings and measures of social value (Kopytoff 1998; Goede 2005; Espeland and Stevens 2008).[23] To identify and to account for the construction of the measuring device/s that dominate in each field, I draw on a range of materials, including expert interviews, field research at conferences, document analysis of publications, websites, and media sources, archival research, and secondary data, gathered over a four-year period from 2010 to 2014. I conducted semi-structured interviews with sixty-seven professional experts (including respondents from resource providers, intermediaries, and social purpose organizations) involved with one or more of the fields of study. I engaged in field research at practitioner-oriented conferences held by trade and member associations in each field in order to understand the configuration of each field (Garud 2008). I engaged in textual analysis of a range of publications and media sources. I reviewed all available documents, reports, and websites produced by each respondent's affiliated organization and by other organizations central to the history of the field and/or to the formation of its dominant measuring device/s. I also conducted document analysis of popular advisory texts in each of the fields, the largest trade publications in each field, and mainstream media sources. To supplement this assortment of primary data, I drew from secondary research. The data from these multiple sources was analyzed using the central tenets of grounded theory (Glaser and Strauss 1967). A more detailed outline of the book's data and methods can be found in the appendix and a summary of the data sources employed can be found in individual chapters.

TURNING TO THE LITERATURE

How then does the turn to caring capitalism affect the meaning and measure of social value? How does the growing embrace of market-based solutions to social inequities shape what gets to count as social good and how it gets counted? While the literature has yet to address these questions, we can turn to past studies that provide us with possible expectations for what might be found. These predictions can be thought as oscillating between two poles characterized by an emphasis on the effect of market on society versus an attention to the influence of actors' morals on the market.

The market and society

One long-standing strand of scholarship emphasizes the distinct and colonizing nature of the contemporary economy for social action (Radin 2001; Sandel 2012). In one version of this approach, each sphere of society is characterized by its own logic – a place-based understanding, shared by members of that space, of actors' desired goals and appropriate strategies of action. In the private sector, a "market logic" prevails, where actors are expected to be driven by the pursuit of self-interest and the profit motive (Friedland and Alford 1991; Glynn and Lounsbury 2005). This market logic is often opposed to the dominant logics of other societal spaces. In the study of social value, a market logic is often contrasted by scholars to a mission logic, located in the space of the nonprofit sector, which is characterized by voluntary exchange and the pursuit of social good as an end in itself (Battilana and Dorado 2010; Galaskiewicz and Barringer 2012).

The expectation here would be that the measure of social value would be contingent on sectoral location. For nonprofits, the tools used to gauge organizations' social value would reflect actors' values-based beliefs about how best to achieve social good. For compassionate companies, in contrast, money should be the proposed metric of social value. And, as with corporations more broadly, the measure of social value should become subject to the criteria of shareholder return, given its status as the "privileged metric for assessing corporate success," with potential implications for what gets to count as social value in the market (Krippner 2005, 2011:7; Davis 2009).

A second theoretical perspective rejects the view that only the private sector is characterized by a market logic. Instead, these scholars see contemporary society as inherently a "market society," one diffused throughout with the action orientation and institutions of the economy (Polanyi 1944; Sandel 2012). There is "nothing but" the economy in all places in a society (Zelizer 2009). A market society is defined as the subordination of "the substance of society to the laws of the market" (Polanyi 1944:71).[24] Similarly, organizational scholars emphasize the growing isomorphism of actors in contemporary society around market-based rationales and practices (Meyer and Rowan 1977; DiMaggio and Powell 1983). These social scientists have sought to demonstrate how actors located outside of the private sector employ the logic of the market as an orientation of action (Binder 2007; Battilana and Dorado 2010). As one scholar of the nonprofit sector has concluded: "the market seems to pervade every facet of our lives today" (Eikenberry 2009:582). As proof, we can think of relatively few goods that cannot be bought and sold; a dwindling assortment of items are exchanged based on the alternative means of redistribution or reciprocity, as witnessed by the existence of markets for breast milk, queuing, and human organs, among others (Healy 2006; Sandel 2012).[25] Relatedly, almost any good or activity can be assigned a monetary value (Fourcade 2011). The measure of money is our lingua franca of worth and we think nothing of placing a dollar figure on such disparate items as old growth trees, totem poles, and an indigenous community's DNA.

The implications of this perspective for the book's argument are straightforward. This viewpoint suggests that, regardless of sectoral location, market indicators (e.g., money and profit) will be used to gauge the social value of all types of social purpose organizations, with ensuing consequences for what types of activities and outcomes get counted as being in the social good.[26] When economic gain is privileged, other orders of worth (such as those based on equality or collective welfare) are always crowded out. As the philosopher Michael Walzer (1983:119–120) concluded, "money is insidious, and market relations [tend to] transform every social good into a commodity." For example, a comparative study of blood donation in the United States and the United Kingdom found that the sale of blood – as opposed to its altruistic donation – was detrimental to the quality of the blood, to the moral orientation of action, and to the collective identity of communities (Titmuss 1971).

Morals and the market

However, a second set of scholars rejects this view of the market as an autonomous force that is causally deterministic of social relations and the pursuit of values, either within the economy or in the broader society. Here, authors instead emphasize the capacity of actors to enact their morals as members of the market and as they engage in economic exchange across an array of societal settings. One approach is wary of the effect of the economy on the pursuit of morally oriented behavior (Titmuss 1971; Carruthers and Espeland 1998). The "hostile worlds" perspective emphasizes that actors may resist the move of sacred or intimate goods, such as body parts, children, and care work, into the private sector (Turco 2012; Rossman 2014). The market is opposed to other societal sectors that are characterized by values-oriented activity and where exchange is based on redistribution or reciprocity. This expectation of hostility exists in part because the use of money to value goods is expected to have detrimental effects on actors' ability to pursue their values.

Here, actors might seek to resist the growth of caring capitalism and might try to prevent the valuation of social goods in the market using the metric of money and/or the criterion of shareholder value. Based on the realization that only those types of social goods that can be monetized and that contribute to financial gain will become deemed of worth, some will question the capacity of compassionate companies to pursue social value as an end in itself and they will contest the extension of a market logic to the valuation of social goods.

A final approach in contrast emphasizes the capacity of actors to draw from multiple orders of worth in order to enact their goals through economic exchange, regardless of sectoral location. Rather than see the market as a "straightforward, irresistible force that reprocesses whole tracts of society into the commodity form" (Fourcade and Healy 2007:11), these authors instead investigate how actors' selection from among multiple logics are historically constructed, negotiated, and can be realized in and through economic activity. While the market exchange of goods is commonplace in contemporary society, this perspective emphasizes that individuals are capable of constructing a "moral market," whereby members engage in economic exchange as a means to enact their values (Zelizer 1985, 1997, 2009).[27] Individuals actively work to relationally create "connected lives" (Zelizer 2009), where a transaction is constructed based on shared understandings, practices, and media via a symbolic boundary. In this way, the use of money (as a form of payment, metric of valuation, and so forth) does not spoil or crowd out its intended values-based meaning, given that money can take a variety of meanings (Healy 2006; Bandelj 2012). For instance, while some are critical of the exchange of sex for money between a man and a woman in the case of prostitution, we are far less wary of a man's expenditure of resources on a valuable ring for a woman as a condition of marital engagement. Although both exchanges involve the exchange of money for intimacy, the latter is deemed morally acceptable, and is governed by a set of accepted rules and expectations (Zelizer 2009).

For our purposes, this perspective holds that the rise of caring capitalism constitutes an effort to create a moral market, where actors can engage in economic exchange and employ market indicators, including money as a metric of worth, as a legitimate means to pursue social value. However, the successful establishment of any measuring device, whatever its form and content, must be located in a social relationship characterized by shared understandings among members of a field of its specific moral purpose and its symbolic boundaries from other types of economic exchange.

THE BOOK'S ARGUMENT

This book will show that these theoretically derived expectations – those opposing emphases on the causal priority of the market or morals – are not adequate to account for the meaning and measure of social value in a time of caring capitalism. As we will see, caring capitalism has meant the diffusion of social value into the private sector and, correspondingly, the marketization of the project of social value. Caring capitalism has entailed the proliferation of new meanings of social value, with each field characterized by proponents' construction of a moral market in which economic exchange can be legitimately employed in a particular way to pursue social and financial ends. Yet, at the same time, caring capitalism has not resulted in the wholesale employment of market indicators to measure firms' social value. By and large, with one exception, the tools, technologies, and techniques created to assess the worth of compassionate companies do not employ the metric of money and they do not draw from shareholder return as a criterion of value. And, even when market indicators are employed, they sometimes but not always restrict social value to those aspects that produce economic gain.

How can we account for this discrepancy between the meaning and measure of social value in an era of caring capitalism? Making sense of this puzzle constitutes the empirical task of this book. In part, the issue, as we will see, is that existing theoretical expectations – with their attention to the role of the market or morals – suffer from the "reflection assumption." By this assumption, I mean the notion that the instruments used to perform the act of valuation reflect a particular criterion of value, driven either by the institutional pressure of the market or a particular moral belief. In this "reflection" view, a measuring device is constructed to allow for tests of entities according to the meaning of value held by the predominant actors in a situation or field. A measuring device here incorporates and instantiates a particular belief about the nature of value – of what counts and how it should be counted (Callon 1998; Boltanski and Thévenot 2006; Espeland and Sauder 2007). Each order of worth "entails its own metrics and standards of evidence for proving the value of any object or idea" (Kaplan and Murray 2010:111).[28] Thus, understanding how actors understand the question of value is sufficient to account for what ultimately gets to count and how it gets counted by the salient measuring device.

In contrast, the theory put forward in this book does not presume that value drives valuation. In other words, what counts in terms of how actors envision social value (and how central a market logic is to that definition) necessarily does not determine how it gets counted in the act of valuation (in terms of the presence of the market indicators of money and shareholder value in a measuring device). By examining the construction of these measuring devices, the book is able to account for the presence of distances or disjunctures between the meaning of social value held by actors and the tools, techniques, and technologies that are developed to gauge the social world according to that quality of worth. As I will show, actors hold varying understandings of the meaning of social value – an envisioning of a social project that encompasses what societal problems need to be addressed, by what means, and toward what ends. The rise of caring capitalism has meant not only the embrace of companies as the preferred vehicles to deliver social value, but also entailed the proliferation of new, market-based articulations of social value. But attention to actors' varied understandings of the project of social value in a field, whether it be located in the economy or not, is not adequate to explain the types of measuring devices that are constructed to conduct the act of valuation. Instead, analytical attention also must be given to the work of value entrepreneurs who are charged with developing a tool, technology, or technique in order to gauge the social world according to a specific order of worth. These value entrepreneurs are constrained in their efforts by the communicative purpose of the device and by their professional expertise.

Let me further outline my thesis. To begin, take how social value is defined and understood by actors in different fields of study. Members of a field, particularly early or powerful proponents, articulate what I call a "social project" which includes a definition of social value. A social project consists of the identification of a social problem to be solved, the specification of an intervention to solve the problem (including a claim about what types of actors should provide the intervention), and a cause and effect claim about how the proposed solution produces social value – understood as a particular kind of benefit or improvement to society (Ferguson 1990; Schneider and Ingram 1993; Krause 2014).[29]

Despite a shared concern for social value, the fields of study vary markedly in terms of the precise configuration of their social projects. First, these social projects diverge in terms of the societal problem or challenge to be targeted. While some fields pursue an array of subjectively identified challenges (e.g., gender inequality, race/ethnicity issues, health disparities, and so forth), others focus solely on the problem of economic inequality. And, in this latter group, the solution to the problem of economic inequality occurs either by facilitating inclusion of the economically disadvantaged into the market or by ensuring companies' equitable treatment of a company's stakeholders.

These visions of social value across fields also differ in terms of the centrality of a market logic in their articulation of a social project. Social projects differ in the type of organizational vehicle that can best deliver the desired intervention. Some rely on nonprofits given that these types of social purpose organizations cannot distribute profit to members and that they are recognized by the state as in the public interest. Other social projects specifically critique businesses for failing to consider their negative impact on society and these actors seek to mitigate firms' adverse societal consequences. And, as cases of caring capitalism, actors embrace businesses as the optimal purveyors of social good. Firms are championed because their reliance on market revenue produces a greater scale of delivery and leads to economic self-sufficiency, in contrast to nonprofits dependent on philanthropy. Proponents of some social projects also view market-based interventions as a means to social value by facilitating local economic development, in the form of wages for employees, income or capital for small business owners, and tax revenue for the local government. Finally, these social projects diverge in terms of who is claimed to benefit from the proposed activity – is it individuals, communities, government, and/or shareholders? In caring capitalism, the pursuit of social value through market-based solutions to social problems is proposed not only to best address social inequities but also to produce shareholder return for investors, thus increasing the likelihood that business can be sustainably harnessed for social good.

How does the content of a social project affect how a field's measuring device then defines and gauges social value? As outlined earlier, extant literature on the role of the market in society provides two competing expectations. Either the definition of a social project, as a criterion of worth, should shape the meaning and metrics of a field's measuring device or the irresistible force of the economy, either wholesale or as the sectoral site of the social project, should lead to the privileging of market metrics. Yet, the measuring devices present in and across fields contradict these expectations. As shown in Table 1.2, these tools, techniques, and technologies unexpectedly vary in the presence of market indicators, including their use of money as a metric and their incorporation of shareholder value as a criterion of worth.

TABLE 1.2 *Market indicators and measuring devices*

	Money as Metric	
Measure of Shareholder Value	Absence of Money	Presence of Money
Absence of Shareholder Value	Nonprofits, Corporate Social Responsibility, Impact Investing, Inclusive Business	Social Enterprises
Presence of Shareholder Value	Socially Responsible Investing	Responsible Investment

First, these measuring devices are not consistent across locales and nor do they map neatly onto sectoral location. Money is used as a measure of social value in only a small number of fields and the monetization of social value – when it does take place – has occurred in fields both internal and external to the private sector. Perhaps more surprisingly, the content of these measuring devices does not necessarily reflect the premises of a field's social project. Even when located in the private sector, the incorporation of multiple dimensions of a market logic in the envisioning of a social project can but need not entail the use of market indicators to evaluate the worth of organizations in that field. For instance, the production of economic development benefits through the provision of market inclusion to the poor, while easily monetized, is only counted in the currency of money in one field of caring capitalism. And while a number of fields as examples of caring capitalism are committed to the pursuit of social value as a source of shareholder value, only one possesses a measuring device that can evaluate compassionate companies in terms of their production of return on investment.

In other words, as shown in Table 1.3, measuring devices display a degree of autonomy from either the institutional pressures of the market or the envisioning of social value in a field as a criterion of worth. Striking disjunctures exist between the content of a field's social project and that of its measuring device in many of the cases under study, thus departing from scholarly predictions about the relative causal force of morals or the markets. Sectoral location is immaterial here in explaining the use of money or shareholder value, thus contradicting the theoretical expectation that the market is either a colonizing force in society (Sandel 2012) or exists as a distinct societal space (Friedland and Alford 1991; Glynn and Lounsbury 2005). And, the moral market thesis – in its claim that actors are capable of employing economic indicators and measures to pursue moral goals through economic exchange – cannot explain the marked absence of money as a mode of valuation in many fields of caring capitalism (Zelizer 2009; Fourcade 2011).

To make sense of this unexpected relationship between the rise of caring capitalism and the meaning and measure of social value, I argue that measuring devices are socially and relationally constructed in ways that existing literature cannot account, given their reliance on the "reflection" thesis of value and valuation, in that the performance of valuation is presumed to follow from the determination of value. This book's simple claim is that it is the work of "value entrepreneurs" that holds the key for apprehending the precise measures and meanings of social value that are on offer across these fields. Value entrepreneurs are those actors who produce, justify, and disseminate the measuring device that performs the assessment of social value in a field (Reinecke and Ansari 2012). Value entrepreneurs constitute one type of "institutional entrepreneur": an individual who constructs and diffuses a new organizational form, category, practice, or field (DiMaggio 1988; Beckert 1999; Maguire, Hardy and Lawrence 2004). It is through attention to the work of value entrepreneurs

TABLE 1.3 *Sectoral location, market logic, and measuring devices*

		Nonprofit Organizations	Social Enterprises	Socially Responsible Investing	Corporate Social Responsibility	Responsible Investment	Inclusive Business	Impact Investing
Measuring Device	Money as metric	N	Y	N	N	Y	N	N
	Shareholder value	N	N	Y	N	Y	N	N
Social Project of Field	Shareholder value produced for investors	N	N	Y	N	Y	Y	Y
	Economic development value produced for individuals and/or community	N	Y	N	N	N	Y	Y
	Sustainability and scale of market revenue	N	Y	N	N	N	Y	Y
	Equitable market inclusion	N	Y	N	Y	Y	Y	Y
Sectoral Location	Market	N	N	Y	Y	Y	Y	Y

that we can make sense of the conjunctures and disjunctures between the social project of a field (and what is identified to be of value) and the type of value represented in and rewarded by a measuring device (and how valuation is to take place). And attention to the constrained creativity of value entrepreneurs helps us to understand why social projects that embrace the promise of compassionate companies to produce social and shareholder value do not then necessarily entail the use of market measures to capture those businesses' financial worth.

First, we might expect that value entrepreneurs matter because they impose their own values and understandings onto a measuring device. The absence of both money as a metric and the criterion of shareholder return in many fields might be due to these actors' moral discomfort over assigning a dollar value to social goods or an ethical distaste for joining the pursuit of social good to the pursuit of financial gain. To explain the disjuncture between a social project and a measuring device would be to focus on the agentic capacity of value entrepreneurs to resist the forces of marketization, as one instance of the "hostile worlds" perspective (Zelizer 1983; Turco 2012; Reich 2014). Yet, as I will show in the following chapters, value entrepreneurs in these fields were not morally resistant to the varying social projects that together constitute caring capitalism. These actors sought to produce measuring devices that precisely reflected the desire to employ market-based solutions to social problems. They were, if and when asked to do so, willing to develop a technique to monetize an organization's social value or a tool to demonstrate the financial worth of a socially beneficial business model to shareholders.

But, as captured in Figure 1.2, value entrepreneurs' quest to produce a measuring device that accurately captured their field's view of social value was limited by two factors: the communicative purpose of the measuring device itself and these actors' own professional expertise. First, drawing from critical accounting literature (Ansari and Euske 1987; Hopwood and Miller 1994), I recognize that any measuring device is commissioned to serve a communicative purpose.[30] Valuation entrepreneurs create a measuring tool or technique in order to convince a targeted audience about the merit of the field's social project. Measuring devices, in this sense, are inherently relational in nature in that they are critical to actors' attempts to create particular types of networks, ties, and exchanges with others (Zelizer 2009). As a whole, a measuring device's communicative purpose matters because it determines what dimensions of the field's social project, including the presence of a market logic,

FIGURE 1.2 Theoretical model

are incorporated into and which are omitted from the valuation tool itself and therefore how social value itself gets counted and so defined.

Measuring devices in the case of social value serve one or more of three communicative purposes. A valuation instrument can establish focal actors' legitimacy. It can be employed, as predicted by institutional theory, to show that those organizations conform to their constituents' expectations of good governance (Meyer and Rowan 1977; Porter 1995; Hwang and Powell 2009). Actors with the goal of altering others' behavior, secondly, can commission a measuring device. A measuring device can be critical to a larger project of "governing by numbers" by gathering knowledge about others in order to influence their activities (Foucault 1979, 1994; Power 1994; Miller 2001). And, finally, a measuring device can be utilized in the justification of a new field. It can demonstrate the relative worth of a new social project compared to existing projects or it can solve the value problem in a new market (Beckert 2009; DeJean, Gond, and Leca 2004).

To achieve any one of these three communicative goals, value entrepreneurs are commissioned to develop and diffuse a new measuring device of social value in the field. But, these actors are constrained in their capacity to do so by their professional expertise.[11] Here, I draw from the sociology of professions and employ the concept of expertise as a shorthand term to convey the scope and manner of knowledge possessed by an actor or group as a result of their professional education, training, and employment background (Abbot 1988; Eyal 2013). The type of expertise held by value entrepreneurs matters because it provides those actors with a valuation repertoire that they can draw from to create a new measuring device in accordance with the field's social project and the valuation tool's communicative purpose.

In the social sciences, the concept of repertoire refers to the norms, conventions, and tools available to an individual or group in a specific setting. The analytical purchase of the concept has been to show that actors' lines of actions are not driven solely by their values or interests but that their existing repertoire provides a limited range of strategies of action, containing a set of possible practices and meanings (Swidler 1986; Tilly 1986; Clemens 1993; Boltanski and Thévenot 2006). Any effort to change existing societal arrangements is fundamentally structured by the actors' existing repertoire of strategies and tactics at their disposal. With some exceptions, these scholars have focused largely on cases where actors have successfully transposed and recombined existing items in their repertoire in order to enact the desired change (Sewell 1992; Clemens 1993; Johnson 2008).

In the cases under study here, value entrepreneurs rely on their valuation repertoire in the formulation of a new measuring device. They transpose, extend, and synthesize existing tools in order to create an appropriate valuation instrument. In some fields, these actors are facilitated by their knowledge of an assortment of tools, techniques, and technologies (and their attendant conventions) they then can draw from to create a new measuring device that suits the content of the field's social project and fits with the tool's intended communicative purpose. In other cases, value entrepreneurs are constrained by the limited nature of their valuation repertoire and are unable to construct a valuation tool that embodies and so reproduces the social project of the field, due to the difficulty, knowledge, and capacity inherent to and required for creating a new measuring device. This failure, as noted by scholars, occurs because the construction of the material tools of valuation requires both skill and is a form of "work": the assignment of numerical worth to items requires "enormous organization and discipline" (Espeland and Stevens 1998:315; Helgesson and Muniesa 2014).

In all, the book's main argument is that it is the value entrepreneurs' communicative purpose and professional expertise that explains the presence of conjunctures and disjunctures between the social project of a field and the meaning and metric of social value embedded in a measuring device. That is, rather than seeing measuring devices as following from and embodying a specific understanding of value, these tools and techniques must be analyzed as discrete social objects that are constructed by specific actors in particular relational contexts. The existence of a measuring device – and the precise ways in which it counts social value and so determines what gets to count as social value – requires a sustained effort on the part of value entrepreneurs with not only a commitment to a specific meaning of social value to guide them, but also the interests and ability to convey the worth of that social project to others.

OVERVIEW OF THE BOOK

The book has three parts. The two chapters of Part I focus on the question of social value for social purpose organizations outside of the market. In the 1990s, nonprofit organizations and a newly emerging category in the sector of "social enterprises" were both subject to pressures to demonstrate their social worth. In both cases, value entrepreneurs in the field promulgated a specific measuring device.

Chapter 2 analyzes how outcome measurement – the counting of positive program change in a charity's clients – came to dominate members of the nonprofit sector. Contrary to popular explanations that place its origins in nonprofits' emulation of firms, value entrepreneurs, consisting of consultants and academics, instead selectively drew from their own expertise with measuring devices prevalent in the public sector to gauge social programs. They innovatively refashioned those existing practices in order to generate a new measuring device that was to be used by key funders in the field who faced accountability demands and sought to assert their legitimacy.

Chapter 3 examines the field of social enterprises. Emerging in the 1980s and 1990s, social enterprises were a new type of nonprofit organization that used market means to achieve social value. Here, one charitable foundation sought to grow the field of social enterprises by developing its own measuring device that could capture social enterprises' economic and social value. "SROI" was distinct from outcome measurement in that it entailed the monetization of social good and the assessment of a social enterprise in terms of cost benefits for funders. Despite its use of finance discourse and money as a metric, SROI was intended to positively demonstrate the success of social enterprises in achieving social value via the innovative use of market solutions for economically disadvantaged clients.

The book then turns to the study of the meaning and measure of social value in the private sector prior to the emergence of caring capitalism. Chapters 4 and 5 of Part II focus on market monitors: civil society actors who sought to privately regulate corporations to hold them accountable for the social consequences of their products and production processes. In both the fields of SRI (in the 1970s and 1980s) and of CSR (in the 1990s), early value entrepreneurs developed ratings of companies' social and environmental performance in order to engender the desired behavior from firms. They did so as a form of market incentive but they varied in terms of their specification of the economic value of firms' social behavior, either for the local community or for shareholders.

Part III takes up the case of caring capitalism. Chapters 6 and 7 look at different fields of caring capitalism to account for why and when firms' production of social and shareholder value is assessed using the market indicators of money and shareholder return. In Chapter 6, I consider the case of RI, where a company's ESG performance – how a firm conducts itself in terms of its environmental impact, its social consequences, and its model of governance – is understood as a positive determinant of long-term shareholder value. Advocates of RI sought to develop a measuring device for ESG performance that could be integrated with ease into mainstream financial analysis. The result is that the meaning of social good has become contingent upon its financial materiality as part of financial analysts' fundamental equity valuation of a stock.

In contrast, Chapter 7 focuses on two other fields of caring capitalism where firms pursue both money and mission, but where market indicators are not used to value their social worth. Inclusive Businesses are multinational corporations whose business models alleviate poverty in the developing world while creating shareholder value. However, the prevailing measuring device of social value focuses only on positive social changes for individuals in a business' value chain and omits the monetization of firms' production of economic profit or shareholder value. This disjuncture occurred because proponents of Inclusive Businesses sought to develop a measuring device for social value in order for companies to obtain license to operate from stakeholders, as constrained by value entrepreneurs' expertise only in the fields of international and sustainable development.

Alternatively, in the case of Impact Investing, value entrepreneurs have sought to create a new industry based on investment in local companies in developing countries that pursue both mission and money. As part of their effort to create this new market, as with RI, proponents worked to create a measuring device that paralleled that of mainstream investing. Yet, these value entrepreneurs faced two challenges: the pool of potential investors held varying expectations concerning the desired balance of financial versus social return and they possessed different meanings of social value. Value entrepreneurs responded by creating a new measuring device that allowed for investors to engage in the contingent assessment of a firm's social and/or financial value with the goal of customized commensurability.

The final chapter summarizes the constituent argument made in the book. It then traces out the pragmatic implications of these competing and intersecting accounts of social value for social purpose organizations across different societal settings. Chapter 8 concludes by highlighting how these findings speak not only to our theoretical understanding of social value and the broader study of value and valuation but also to debates concerning the relationship of morals and the market. An appendix lays out the data and methods used herein.

Notes

1. This new vision of capitalism also has been called "creative capitalism" (Gates 2008), inclusive capitalism (Hart 2005), and conscious capitalism (Mackey and Sisodia 2013).

2. Here, the concept of social value differs from its use in other empirical fields and scholarly debates, such as social psychology's use of the term of "social value orientation" to describe individuals' other-oriented tendencies (Kramer, McClintock, and Messick 1986). And its use in the analysis of societal welfare departs from the tendency in economics to view the social good of an object as deriving from its relative worth to others (Zuckerman 1999).

3. Drawing from organizational literature (DiMaggio and Powell 1983; Fligstein and McAdam 2012), I employ the concept of "field" in this book to refer to a "group of individuals and collective actors who orient their behavior to one another and see themselves as playing the same game" (Berman 2012:181).

4. Similarly, as of 2011, over three-quarters of the world's largest companies by revenue were members of the GRI, in which corporations voluntarily report on their economic, governance, social, and environmental impacts (KPMG 2013).

5. Admittedly, the recent emphasis on shareholder value departs from a long-standing view of firms that stresses their role in generating social benefits through individuals' pursuit of self-interest in the market (Smith 1776) and an ongoing debate in the United States over the social responsibility of firms (Bowen 1953; Davis 2009).

6. For a discussion of the state as a provider of public goods, see Samuelson (1954) and Olson (1965). For an overview of scholarship on the state as serving the interests of specific groups (e.g., the pluralist, class-analytic, or power-elite perspectives), see Alford (1994).

7. Of course, such a simple portrait of this societal division of labor overlooks long-standing intersections and mutual dependencies across the three sectors.

The government, for instance, provides the regulative framework for activity in the market and the nonprofit sector. This simple tri-sector understanding also omits a consideration of how different sectors have been involved in the definition and growth of other societal arenas (Polanyi 1944; Hall 1992). Take the case of corporate elites in the early twentieth century who worked diligently to create the central funding vehicles of the nonprofit sector (i.e., the Community Chest) precisely in order to prevent the expansion of the welfare state (Barman 2006).

8. See, for example, critiques of the constituent claims of caring capitalism made by Karnani (2007), Shamir (2008), and Soederberg (2009).

9. For an overview of the range of valuation practices available to social purpose organizations, see Foundation Center (2014).

10. The Foundation Center (2014) operates a website called TRASI which serves as a database of available "tools and resources for measuring social impact."

11. While some measuring devices are based on the objective criteria of the entities to be assessed, others rely on the subjective assessment of intermediary actors, such as critics, experts, or consumers, to determine the quality of the good in question (Karpik 2010).

12. Scholarship on orders of worth identifies six dominant regimes of evaluation in contemporary society: inspired (creativity), domestic (tradition), fame (reknown), industrial (efficiency), market (competition), and civic (collective good) (Boltanski and Thévenot 2006). Yet, the civic order of worth focuses on the public sector and elides a distinct discussion of private efforts toward collective good. And literature on the related concept of institutional logics emphasizes the sectoral spaces of the market, professions, the state, family, and religion, and their internal set of institutions and conventions, and omits recognition of the nonprofit sector as a societal sector, with an accompanying orientation of action (Thornton, O'Casio and Lounsbury 2012).

13. The use of the term "social value" is not new. It was often used by proponents of the scientific charity movement in the early twentieth century to capture the broader, societal benefits of organized efforts to rationalize philanthropy beyond those produced for individual clients (Devine 1911; Parmelee 1920).

14. A related perspective on social value views it as limited to those "public goods" that cannot be produced by the market due to their non-rivalrous (where the good's consumption does not diminish the amount available to others) and non-excludable (where it is impossible to exclude consumption by others besides the buyer) nature. In result, these types of goods cannot be produced for profit and must be offered by the public or nonprofit sectors, where actors are not reliant on profit for their revenue (Samuelson 1954; Weisbrod 1977). Examples here include lighthouses, roads, and a community's defense system. However, given the rise of market-based actors aiming to produce social value, the delimitation of social value to this notion of public goods is no longer feasible.

15. In other cases, the terms of social value and public value are used interchangeably, often by considering the public and nonprofit sectors as a single, coherent societal space or set of actors with shared interests in effecting social welfare (Moore 1995).

16. Economic sociology largely has limited the study of social value to the analysis of how this order of worth shapes the assignment of monetary worth to goods in a market. How do ethical consumers, for example, incorporate the increased equity and justice of the production process used to create such goods as fair-trade coffee

or chocolate into their purchasing decisions (Gourevitch 2011)? In all, this approach tells us surprisingly little about the criteria or quality of social value in and of itself, separate from its role in the economic valuation of goods in a particular market.

17. "Even though from a *theoretical* point of view human actors encode things with significance, from a *methodological* point of view is the things-in-motion that illuminate their human and social context" (Appadurai 1986:5).

18. The concept of reactivity is similar to other scholars' emphasis on the performative capacity of calculative tools to shape the social world in its model (MacKenzie and Millo 2003; Callon 2007).

19. Alternatively, a measuring device can have an unintended reactive effect that departs from its intended purpose. In the case of a state unemployment agency, Blau (1955) studied how performance measurement expectations affected the work of staff whose job was to assist clients in finding work. At the organizational level, their success was measured as the number of job placements achieved; the unintentional result was that the interviewers ended up emphasizing any type of job placement, despite the suitability of clients for those positions.

20. A measuring device permits objects to be evaluated and compared in terms of their possession of more or less of that quality. Alternatively, a measuring device can entail the specification of a performance standard that sets a minimal threshold or goal. Here, entities can be gauged against a benchmark.

21. It also moves the study of measuring devices away from the assumption that such objects necessarily are only ceremonial in nature in that they serve to convey the presence of rationality to other actors (Meyer and Rowan 1977; Hwang and Powell 2009).

22. The comparative case study method consists of the purposeful selection of cases so that differences in the outcome of interest can be explained by reference to differences in the configuration the fields under study, employing both a deductive approach to test existing expectations and the inductive method to note emerging causal patterns.

23. The approach extends work on the "social life of things" (Appadurai 1998): a perspective originating in the study of commodities that views objects as having biographies of their own that provide insights into their use and meaning.

24. In this account, many Western societies shifted at some point in the mid-to-late twentieth century to an economy organized around capitalism. In a traditional society, an economy based on reciprocity and redistribution existed to serve the purposes of social relations (e.g., the family, religion, civil society, and the government). In a market society, in contrast, the logic of the economy (the self-interested pursuit of gain via monetary exchange along with an accompanying set of supporting institutions) instead comes to govern all social relations as a result of the commodification of land, labor, and money (Polanyi 1944). This move to a market society has been exacerbated by the rise of shareholder capitalism and the spread of a neoliberal ideology in the global economy (Harvey 2005; Davis 2009).

25. Similarly, social actors (including both individuals and organizations) often are expected to make key decisions based on instrumental rationality (the systematic and reasoned selection of the most efficient means to an end) as an orientation of action, rather than based on the criteria of tradition or personal values (Kalberg 1980). For example, universities no longer assess the merit of faculty research based

on the yardstick of the production of academic knowledge but rather have begun to commodify it, due to encouragement from government and the growing realization that technological innovation fosters economic growth (Berman 2012).

26. While social value might be widely understood to be difficult to quantify, economic valuation methods for incommensurable, nonmarket goods (like environmental or heritage sites) based on consumers' preferences have become commonplace. Based on the assumption that price is the best estimation of a good's worth, this technique derives an item's monetary value from consumers' preferences (Champ, Boyle and Brown 2003; Fourcade 2011).

27. The market mediation thesis emerged out of the study of intimacy, largely in response to the marketization of activities like sex and childcare in the domestic sphere. In her study of the domestic care industry, for example, Zelizer (2009) demonstrated how individuals are able to maintain intimate and authentic ties to others, despite those relationships being mediated by monetary value. The approach has been extended to other social spaces, where the viability of sacred goods and the presence of morally oriented action are supposedly at stake in the process of commodification, including the cases of organ donation (Healy 2006) and life insurance (Chan 2012).

28. In this view, measuring devices follow from and represent material instantiations of an order of worth regardless of the origins of that prevailing justification – whether it results from struggles between agents over capital (Bourdieu 1993; Emirbayer and Johnson 2007), from battles between institutional entrepreneurs to define a field (Kaplan and Murray 2010), or from efforts by actors to govern by numbers (Foucault 1979, 1994; Power 1994; Miller 2001).

29. Here, I draw theoretically from literature on the study of institutional change (Strang and Meyer 1993; Tolbert and Zucker 1996; Greenwood, Suddaby, and Hinings 2002). In order to effect change, actors must engage in the act of theorization, where they diagnose a problem and justify their proposed solution in ways intended to both discredit an existing institution and to frame the new innovation to meet key audiences' expectations and interests.

30. This approach to accounting rejects the assumption that accounting (defined here as a technique or technology that seeks to count and classify) reflects technical needs and rational considerations and instead views accounting as a social and institutional practice (Hopwood and Miller 1994).

31. Given that I study only those measuring devices that have become accepted as dominant in a field, my argument does not extend to the understanding of why some measuring devices, rather than others, become institutionalized, and so omits a concern for value entrepreneurs' networks, social position, and/or access to resources in accounting for the diffusion of a measuring device in a field (DiMaggio 1988; Fligstein 2001; Battilana 2006).

PART I

MISSION AND METHOD

2

In the public benefit

Nonprofit organizations

> "It seems that now, more than ever, everyone wants to know about outcomes: What changes are occurring because of nonprofit programs and services?"
>
> (Hatry and Lampkin 2001:1)

The nonprofit sector long has been considered a place in American society where individuals and groups are able to come together to generate social good – by pursuing their collective interests, bettering the lives of their communities, enacting their morals, and strengthening democracy. Whether in churches, political groups, bowling clubs, or knitting circles, "Americans of all ages, all conditions, and all dispositions constantly form associations," as Alexis de Tocqueville (1835), the French political philosopher, wrote about nineteenth-century America. Not much has changed: the United States today has a large and vital nonprofit sector, with over 1.8 million organizations drawing in over $1.9 trillion in revenue and relying on over 64.5 million volunteers (Pettijohn 2013).[1] In the United States, the nonprofit sector is typically understood as the societal space both historically and theoretically tasked with the production of social value – distinct from the public value created by government and the private value created by the market. This chapter and the next seeks to approach the question of social value by taking a close look at the dominant measuring devices present for social purpose organizations in the nonprofit sector – first for public charities and then for social enterprises. In result, this first section of the book allows for an understanding of the meaning and measure of social value in fields outside of the market and prior to the rise of caring capitalism.

To investigate this question, the chapter focuses on the question of how nonprofits are valued for their worth. While there is no question that members of the nonprofit sector – individual and institutional donors, intermediaries, and charities themselves – all engage in a range of subjective estimations of the impact of nonprofit organizations, I examine the valuation tool of "outcome measurement," which for two decades has prevailed as the central methodology by which nonprofit organizations have been assessed for, and by which nonprofits demonstrate, their social value. This measuring device seeks to determine the beneficial consequence of a charity for society by quantifying the amount of desired change produced by a nonprofit's program in its clients, without reference to its monetized value or its relationship to economic profit. The presence of outcome measurement allows us to not only consider what social value looks like – how it is defined and demarcated – in the contemporary nonprofit sector, but also to begin the task of specifying the consequence of caring capitalism for the meaning and measure of social value. And asking the question of how and why outcome measurement came to prevail in the non-profit sector also permits for the investigation of how the determination of social value in a field is driven by both ideational and material considerations – the question of not only what should count as social value but also the question of how it can be counted via the construction of a specific valuation tool.

THE SOCIAL PROJECT OF THE NONPROFIT SECTOR

To understand the origins of outcome measurement requires attention to the social project of the nonprofit sector. In the United States, the nonprofit sector is commonly defined as the space outside the market and the government (Frumkin 2002).[2] The nonprofit sector's project of social good is legally recognized, economically incentivized, and regulated via the assignment of nonprofit status by state governments and by the allocation of tax-exempt status by the federal government. Therefore, an understanding of social value in the nonprofit sector begins by examining the regulatory determinants of this societal sphere. The government's assignment of tax-exempt and/or nonprofit status to organizations is based on a particular justification of their worth. Government agencies categorize organizations as members of the nonprofit sector based on their non-distribution of profit, their distinct ownership form, and the classification of their activities as having public or mutual benefit (Hopkins 2011).

First, an organization must be "nonprofit" – it must operate under the "non-distribution constraint" (Hansmann 1980). To qualify as a nonprofit, a charity can legally be reliant on charitable donations, government grants, and/or the sale of good or services. In 2011, the last year for which data was available, nonprofits in the United States obtained almost half of their total revenue from the sale of goods and service, with only 12.6% of all revenue generated from philanthropic donations, and government funding providing the remaining third (along with investment and other income) (Pettijohn 2013). Examples of nonprofits that rely on "fees for services and goods" include hospitals, universities, and museums.

Legally, what distinguishes nonprofits from businesses is that any resulting surplus from the sale of goods and services cannot be distributed to board

members, directors, officers, staff, or other constituents. In order to receive
exempt status, the IRS forbids "private benefit and inurement," in that an
organization is "prohibited from allowing its income or assets to accrue to
insiders" (Internal Revenue Service 2014a). Unlike a business, any economic
profit generated by a charity instead must be either returned into the organization itself or dispersed in the pursuit of its mission.[3] Secondly, a nonprofit
organization is defined as an independent, private entity that is essentially
"ownerless." Unlike the government, nonprofits are not accountable to
resource providers or clients and, in contrast to firms in the market, nonprofits
are not legally responsible in their fiduciary duty to owners or shareholders.
Instead, nonprofits are uncharacterized by "unclear lines of ownership and
accountability" and are subject to demands from resource providers, clients,
community, staff, and members of the board of directors (Frumkin 2002:5).
Most state governments initially bestow nonprofit status when an organization
files an article of incorporation: while state laws vary in specifying the rules of
operation for a nonprofit corporation, most usually require a board of directors
and officers.[4] Similarly, the IRS encourages, but does not require, particular
governance practices, including a board of directors, for many exempt organizations. The governing board of a nonprofit sector is tasked with fiduciary
duty of the nonprofits to the public (Hopkins 2011).

Finally, to be recognized as a nonprofit, an organization must have a
purpose or "mission" that is deemed by the government to be of a collective
nature — either providing public or mutual benefit. A multitude of different
types of tax-exempt organizations exist, as shown in Table 2.1. The most
prevalent members of the nonprofit sector are 501(c)(3)s or what are called
"public charities" because they provide goods and services for the greater good
beyond the generation of value for their own members. Based on an act of
Congress, the IRS recognizes an organization as a public charity if it pursues
one from among a broad range of missions. It must operate "exclusively for
religious, charitable, scientific, literary, or educational purposes, or to foster
national or international amateur sports competition ... or for the prevention
of cruelty to children or animals" (IRS 2014b). Churches and other religious
organizations also qualify as 501(c)(3)s, although they are not required to
register or file returns with the IRS. The wide variety of public charities present
in the American nonprofit sector also is evident in the categories of the National
Taxonomy of Exempt Entities (NTEE), developed by the National Center for
Charitable Statistics to classify all tax exempt organizations, as shown in
Table 2.2. In 2011, almost 1 million public charities filed with the IRS, accounting for more than three-quarters of the nonprofit sector's revenue and expenses
(Pettijohn 2013).

If an organization meets all three requirements of the non-distribution
constraint, proper governance and reporting practices, and a mission that
serves a public benefit, it is able obtain nonprofit status from the local state
government and is eligible to obtain tax-exempt status as a public charity and

TABLE 2.1 *Tax-exempt organizations by Internal Revenue Code Section*

Code	Description of Organization
501(c)(1)	Government Instrumentality; corporations organized under Act of Congress
(2)	Title-holding corporations for exempt organizations
(3)	Religious, educational, charitable, scientific, or literary organizations; testing for public safety; prevention of cruelty to children or animals; fostering national or international amateur sports competition
(4)	Civic leagues, social welfare orgs, and local employee associations
(5)	Labor, agricultural, and horticultural organizations
(6)	Business leagues, chambers of commerce, real estate boards, and like
(7)	Social and recreational clubs
(8)	Fraternal beneficiary societies and associations
(9)	Voluntary employees' beneficiary associations
(10)	Domestic fraternal societies and associations
(11)	Teachers' retirement fund associations
(12)	Benevolent life insurance associations, mutual ditch or irrigation companies, mutual or cooperative telephone companies, and like
(13)	Cemetery companies
(14)	State-chartered credit unions and mutual insurance or reserve funds
(15)	Mutual insurance companies or associations other than life, if written premiums for the year do not exceed $350,000
(16)	Corporations organized to finance crop operations
(17)	Supplemental unemployment benefit trusts
(18)	Employee funded pension trusts (created before June 25, 1959)
(19)	Posts or organizations of past or present members of the armed forces
(20)	Group Legal Services Plan Organization
(21)	Black Lung Benefit Trusts
(22)	Withdrawal liability payment funds
(23)	Associations of members of the armed forces founded before 1880
(24)	Trusts in sec 4049 of Employee Retirement Income Security Act of 1974
(25)	Title-holding corporations or trusts with no more than 35 shareholders or beneficiaries and only one class of stock or beneficial interest
(26)	State-Sponsored High Risk Health Insurance Organizations
(27)	State-Sponsored Workers' Compensation Reinsurance Organizations
501 (d)	Apostolic and Religious Organizations
501 (e)	Cooperative Hospital Service Organizations
501 (f)	Cooperative Service Organizations of Operating Educational Orgs
501 (k)	Child Care Organizations
501 (n)	Charitable Risk Pools
521(1)	Farmers; Cooperative Associations

Source: Internal Revenue Service (2014)

to receive tax-exempt contributions from donors. The justification offered for tax-exemption of these organizations is that they are serving the greater social interest and, in consequence, they are duplicating activities that the government would have to provide via tax collection and government expenditure

TABLE 2.2 *National taxonomy of exempt Entities*

   I. **Arts, Culture, and Humanities**
     A. Arts, Culture & Humanities
  II. **Education**
     B. Education
 III. **Environment and Animals**
     C. Environment
     D. Animal-related
 IV. **Health**
     E. Health Care
     F. Mental Health & Crisis Intervention
     G. Diseases, Disorders, and Medical Disciplines
     H. Medical Research
  V. **Human Services**
     I. Crime & Legal-related
     J. Employment
     K. Food, Agriculture, & Nutrition
     L. Housing & Shelter
     M. Public Safety, Disaster Preparedness, & Relief
     N. Recreation & Sports
     O. Youth Development
     P. Human Services
 VI. **International, Foreign Affairs**
     Q. International, Foreign Affairs
 VII. **Public, Societal Benefit Major Groups**
     R. Civil Rights, Social Action, & Advocacy
     S. Community Improvement & Capacity Building
     T. Philanthropy, Voluntarism, and & Grant-Making Foundations
     U. Science & Technology
     V. Social Science
     W. Public & Societal Benefit
 VIII. **Religion Related**
     X. Religion Related
 IX. **Mutual/Membership Benefit**
     Y. Mutual/Membership Benefit
  X. **Unknown, Unclassified**
     Z. Unknown, Unclassified

Source: National Center for Charitable Statistics (2014)

(Frumkin 2002; Hopkins 2011). In addition, the IRS recognizes almost thirty additional types of organizations as tax-exempt and in the nonprofit sector given that they also serve the public interest, but donors must pay taxes on their donations to those entities. Drawing from the political philosophy of pluralism, these other groups are characterized either by the pursuit of members' specific interests (and so provide "mutual benefit") and/or they engage in political advocacy (IRS 2014b). Examples here include civil leagues and social welfare organizations (501(c)(4)s), labor organizations (501(c)(5)s), trade associations/business leagues (501(c)(6)s), social clubs and fraternal societies, and political organizations (527s), among others (Frumkin 2002; Hopkins 2011).

Surprisingly, there has been remarkably little clarification offered by the federal government as to what characterizes those charities it recognizes as serving the public interest (Hall 1992; Hopkins 2011).[5] However, scholars have worked to define the nature of those missions, emphasizing either the instrumental or the expressive benefits that are produced by nonprofit organizations for society (Gordon and Babchuk 1959; Frumkin 2002). The first perspective focuses on the public benefits derived from nonprofits' offering of goods and services, including health, human services, and education, among others, to clients and to local communities.[6] These types of service-based programs are often called "instrumental" goods. The YMCA, for example, offers childcare and early learning programs to members of the local community. Alternatively, some observers have noted that the nonprofit sector is where another type of societal benefit called expressive goods is produced. Here, the nonprofit sector allows individuals and groups via membership in nonprofits and voluntary associations to freely express their personal values in areas such as religion, politics, and culture, in ways that are not possible in the public or private sectors (Kramer 1981; Mason 1996). These benefits can be produced in and through participation in public or mutual benefit nonprofits. In one study of faith-related organizations involved in the provision of human services via Charitable Choice, for example, the import of religiosity for these organizations was not found in the ability to evangelize with clients, but rather in the capacity of welfare provision as a means to enact faith for its members as one type of expressive good (Campbell 2002).

In sum, no single and shared social project characterizes the nonprofit sector. Member organizations vary in their diagnosis of the social problem to be solved (including the question of which populations are to be targeted for assistance), the type of intervention – in the form of a service or program provided to clients – to be employed to be address it, and the rationale offered to justify their effort. Nonprofits may rely on donations, government grants, and/or market revenue; their only restriction is that any profit generated by their activities cannot be distributed to members. The only shared characteristic of these social projects is the embrace of the nonprofit organization (as distinct from the firm or government agency) as the optimal vehicle by which to address the problem deemed to be at hand and recognition by the relevant government agency that the organization's purpose is in the public interest.

NONPROFITS AND OUTCOME MEASUREMENT

Given such an understanding of the varied and almost infinite social project of public charities in the nonprofit sector, how then are these social purpose organizations evaluated for success? For the last two decades, one measuring device has prevailed, one that is commonly known as "outcome measurement."[7] Outcome measurement consists of the quantitative assessment of an organization's effectiveness. It necessitates the tracking of "the events, occurrences, or changes in conditions, behavior, or attitudes that indicate progress toward achievement of the mission and objectives of the program" (Hatry 1999:15). Or, as a senior staff member of one large, national nonprofit I spoke with explained, "outcome measurement is not measurement of units of service, but rather a measurement of the difference made in people's lives." To engage in outcome measurement, nonprofits gather information from a program's clients (such as individuals, organizations, or communities) to measure the relevant characteristic/s targeted for improvement by the program. Data on outcomes is employed to determine if the provision of a program has been successful. To do so, nonprofits either can use the outcome data to compare the level of that particular attribute before and after the program has been offered, or to compare the result to a standard or to peer organizations. Nonprofits then are meant to demonstrate their social value (what is often called their "social impact") through the use of outcome data (Morley, Vinson, and Hatry 2001).

Examples of outcome measurement vary across nonprofits, depending on the type of programs or services offered. Hospitals, for example, might measure a decrease in patients' level of pain after a medical treatment (Siha 1998); charities offering financial literacy counseling might quantify positive changes in clients via both a short-term outcome, such as increased financial literacy, and the long-term outcome of an increase in home ownership rates (Madan 2007); and, for libraries offering after school story time, parents have been asked to report whether their children demonstrated an increased interest in reading at home after participating in the program (Holt and Elliott 2003).

Outcome measurement has diffused across the nonprofit sector and has become institutionalized as a dominant measure of social value (LeRoux and Wright 2010; Smith 2010; Benjamin 2012).[8] In a comprehensive review of valuation methodologies in the nonprofit sector, the World Economic Forum (2003:48) concluded that: "most systems for measuring impact share the same fundamental paradigm, that Outcomes = Results." National associations, such as the Urban Institute and the Independent Sector, have recommended and facilitated the use of outcome measurement (Hatry and Lampkin 2001; Morley, Vinson, and Hatry 2001; Panel on the Nonprofit Sector 2005) and national and state nonprofit accreditation agencies, such as Interaction, the Minnesota Council of Nonprofits, and Maryland Nonprofits, require it as a condition of certification. Watchdog organizations like CharityNavigator and Guidestar, long committed to evaluating nonprofits according to their financial efficiency, have begun to implement outcomes into their ratings criteria.[9] Nonprofits also have been facilitated in the employment of outcome measurement by the development of tailored software programs, such as Social Solutions and Sales Force.[10] Accordingly, studies have found outcome measurement to be the most prevalent gauge of social value used by nonprofits (Zimmerman and Stevens 2006; Carman and Fredericks 2008; Thomson 2010; Barman and MacIndoe 2012).[11] And, when nonprofit managers are asked to define "effectiveness," they list outcomes first (Mitchell 2012) and members of nonprofits' boards of directors similarly report that their most pressing responsibility is to monitor outcomes (Marx and Davis 2012).

OUTCOME MEASUREMENT AND SOCIAL VALUE

How then does this prevailing measuring device actually define and demarcate social value? As outlined in Chapter 1, any measuring device contains within it a claim about the salient criteria or quality of worth by which entities are to be evaluated (Espeland and Stevens 1998; Espeland and Sauder 2007). Curiously, however, this tool's definitional work in setting the meaning of social value for nonprofits is both clearly apparent and surprisingly absent. On the one hand, outcome measurement is premised on a particular notion of social value. It limits the concept of social value to those positive changes that result from the effects of a nonprofit's programs or services on clients and a local community. Social value, in other words, follows from the product or output of a social purpose organization. However, outcome measurement does not capture the social value produced by how that program or service is created by the nonprofit. Outcome measurement omits a concern for the social value that results from the ways in which a social purpose organization treats its stakeholders (its suppliers, employees, and/or the local community in which it is located) in the sourcing and making of its programs and/or services.

This conception of social value in outcome measurement has had critical implications for what gets to count in practice as social value in the nonprofit sector. By requiring a nonprofit to generate a numerical count of client change, outcome measurement privileges a particular and limited range of all the types of social goods potentially offered by members of the nonprofit sector – valorizing those that produce short-term change and those are easily quantifiable. Specifically, as scholarship has shown, nonprofits intending to serve an expressive function for members by allowing them a free space to voice their openings and enact their values as an end in itself often find the use of outcome measurement difficult. Similarly, charities that pursue longer-term and/or community-based change (often involving political advocacy and citizen engagement) have difficulty demonstrating their effectiveness via outcomes, as do environmental nonprofits that work to produce long-term change (Smith 2010). As two scholars have emphasized: "It is hard to measure whether a church has done well at nurturing the community's sense of good-heartedness or whether a political advocacy organization has effectively spread its message against racism" (Knutsen and Brower 2010:601). Similarly, one early and influential participant in the creation of outcome measurement noted regretfully in an interview that "while OM has done a lot to help clarify and recognize the value of the sector, it has – even I will recognize – made it difficult for some kinds of nonprofits – those with broader or more long-term visions of a better society – to demonstrate their impact. Yes, so there's that. [pause]. Hmm, [laughs] what can I say – no one's perfect."

On the other hand, beyond delimiting social value to the effects of a non-profit's products on clients, outcome measurement does not contain within it any set meaning of social value. Instead, it relies on a subjective and so idiosyncratic notion of social value. Recall from social science literature, as outlined in Chapter 1, that any measuring device should entail the specification of a quality of worth and the development of an accompanying scale. The result is the ability to engage in comparison across similar goods or to a universal standard, thus – in situations of ambiguity or value complexity – privileging one criterion of value over others. In contrast, as a measuring device, outcome measurement does not specify the single salient quality of merit for nonprofits. In and of itself, it is unable to gauge the value of entities, as it carries no assumptions about a defining criterion of worth. Instead, the use of outcome measurement relies on a focal actor's selection of the desired type and unit of social change. It is up to those that implement outcome measure-ment to decide what type of change constitutes a desired social good, and how that desired client change is to be assessed. In result, the meaning of social value in outcome measurement becomes inherently subjective and so idiosyncratic in nature.

The result of this subjective notion of social value is that outcome measure-ment produces a particularly limited capacity for comparison of nonprofits and their programs. A traditional understanding of valuation (as occurs in eco-nomic sociology's study of the market) emphasizes that commensurability is made possible by the establishment of a measuring device. Actors' assessment of the value of a good is made possible by the creation of a tool that transforms different qualities into a single and universal scale. The amount of that salient attribute in a good is then gauged via the use of that scale. The most common example is money – where any objects can be compared in terms of their dollar figure (Callon 1998; Espeland and Stevens 1998). In contrast, outcome meas-urement does not construct commensurability. Instead, it creates what I call "customized commensurability." Customized commensurability is defined as the ability of multiple actors to engage in valuation based on his or her own subjective and idiosyncratic definition of value through the use of a single measuring device. In other words, the use of that measuring device does not necessitate the presence of a single order of worth inherent to that tool. In result, outcome measurement is unable to answer the question of how to assess the worth of one type of nonprofit or program (producing one kind of change in clients) relative to other nonprofits or programs (that produce other kinds of change in clients). At its core, outcome measurement cannot tell us which organizations or programs in the nonprofit sector produce the most social value.

THE TURN TO OUTCOME MEASUREMENT

Why has social value become assessed through the use of outcome measurement as the prevailing measuring device in the nonprofit sector? Many, if not most, accounts of the rise of outcome measurement trace its history to the growing marketization of the nonprofit sector (Speckbacher 2003; Woolford and Curran 2011).[12] While charities historically were dependent largely on philanthropy and government revenue, nonprofits have increasingly been reliant on market-based revenue. They now obtain just under half of their revenue from commercial income (via the sale of their goods and/or services or from unrelated business income) (Pettijohn 2013). In addition, nonprofits in "mixed industries," such as hospitals, fitness centers, nursing homes, and educational institutions, compete with firms for clients. And many nonprofits have relied on venture philanthropists as funders, who seek to apply the principles of the finance industry to improve the efficiency and effectiveness of the nonprofit sector (Letts, Ryan, and Grossman 1997; Young and Salamon 2002).

This perspective posits that nonprofits have responded to these various types of marketization by employing business models of operation and governance in order to improve their efficiency and/or to demonstrate legitimacy, including the implementation of market-based measures of performance (Eikenberry and Kluver 2004; Moxham and Boaden 2007).[13] As a long-time scholar of the nonprofit sector concluded: "if non-profits were becoming serious competitors for societal resources, they needed to measure up to the standards of business" (Young 2003:7). Similarly, other observers have posited, "social pressures to appear efficient in their use of funds and donations may further induce nonprofits to emulate the "businesslike practices" of their for-profit competitors (Schlesinger, Mitchell, and Gray 2004:673). In this account, the onus has been on nonprofits to function and look like companies, according to market principles. They have done so by implementing measurement tools taken from the corporate world so that they would be able to generate the date needed in order to engage in performance measurement and to demonstrate conformity with businesses.[14]

This is a compelling explanation – one that traces the rise of outcome measurement to nonprofits' emulation of firms. This empirical narrative parallels one theoretical perspective within sociology, an approach that sees contemporary society as inherently a "market society," as detailed in Chapter 1. A market society is dominated throughout with the dominant assumptions and practices of the economy (Polanyi 1944; Marx [1867]1992; Simmel 1907 [1990]; Zelizer 2009). The market is characterized by the exchange of goods based on money and the use of economic criteria to assess value, among other characteristics. In the market society thesis, these economic practices tend to govern other spaces and so to structure a wide variety of types of social relations, replacing other action orientations, forms of exchange, sources of value, and media.

Measuring devices and the demonstration of legitimacy

Yet, as I will show later, the move to measuring social value via outcomes resulted from the efforts of an entirely different set of actors seeking to defend their conformity with an entirely distinct set of external pressures. Here, outcome measurement constituted a case of the use of a measuring device as a defensive tactic that can create legitimacy for an actor by demonstrating their performance. Instead of fulfilling a technical purpose – for example, facilitating market exchange or expediting performance measurement – some measuring devices constitute a "political solution to a political problem" (Porter 1995:x). Here, a measuring device is created in order to demonstrate an actor's worth to critics. It is a strategy employed by an actor to achieve legitimacy in the pursuit of credibility (Meyer and Rowan 1977; DiMaggio and Powell 1993; Suchman 1995).

In social science literature, the adoption of a measuring device as a defensive maneuver to address external critiques can take various forms. Some scholars have emphasized that almost all organizations in contemporary society adopt appropriate routines and scripts to signal to others that they are a bureaucracy. The presence of a measuring device a tool, technology, or technique – in an organization's formal structure, along with the adoption of other expected policies and programs, is intended to convey to audiences that the organization is governed by the necessary criteria of technical rationality (Meyer and Rowan 1977; Meyer, Scott, Strang, and Creighton 1984).

Others have worked to show how external actor's criticisms can take particular and varying forms depending on the case under study, with implications for a measuring device's intended purpose. For example, in moments of distrust, the generation of numbers sometimes occurs as part of a group's attempt to demonstrate its objectivity to others. The production of numbers, and the supporting material infrastructure necessary to produce them (such as a measuring device), conveys "mechanical objectivity": the group's compliance with impersonal rules and calculations rather than personal beliefs and biases (Porter 1995; Espeland and Stevens 1998). And yet other social scientists, as discussed earlier, emphasize that actors' adoption of a measuring device is intended to demonstrate their suitability in a field dominated by a market logic. To be deemed legitimate, organizations must act like businesses by adopting the infrastructure necessary to pursue cost efficiency (Hwang and Powell 2009).

In this case, the rise of outcome measurement resulted from key resource providers in the public and nonprofit sectors, specifically, the federal government and the United Way of America, seeking to communicate their worth to external critics. Their audience members held specific institutional expectations that the federal government and the United Way of America were compelled to address. To understand how and why outcome measurement came to dominate the measure and meaning of social value in the nonprofit sector, we need to turn our attention to the efforts of two powerful actors in this sphere in the early

1990s – first, the federal government, and then the United Way of America, as they faced critical challenges and sought to demonstrate their value to external critics in the public and nonprofit sectors. The development of a new measuring device in the form of outcome measurement was central to their efforts.

The federal government and the GPRA

Beginning in the 1990s, multiple governments in the global North, including the United States, the United Kingdom, and Australia, became subject to a new model of governance, one that is typically called "New Public Management" (Hood 1991). New Public Management is commonly understood as one expression of the broader ideology of neoliberalism that was widespread beginning in the 1980s. As an orienting logic for society, neoliberalism is premised on a faith in the capacity of the free market to deliver economic growth and ensure social welfare (Somers and Block 2005; Prasad 2006). Neoliberalism "holds that the social good will be maximised by maximising the reach and frequency of market transactions, and it seeks to bring all human action into the domain of the market" (Harvey 2005:3). Drawing from liberalism as one long-standing strand of political philosophy (Hayek 1960; Friedman 1962; Smith 1776/ 2012), neoliberalism believes that a free, unfettered market has multiple societal benefits: it prevents tyranny and ensures freedom, it fosters creativity and innovation, and it is the best vehicle for the efficient distribution of scarce resources (Hirschman 1982; Fourcade and Healy 2007).

Arising in the 1980s, first in the United States under Ronald Reagan and in the United Kingdom under Margaret Thatcher, the ideology of neoliberalism has taken several forms. Initially, the neoliberal project focused on the weakening of the welfare state in developed nations as a regulatory actor in society, including the dismantling of government's oversight of the market, the attenuation of public sector spending and taxation, and a reduction in social welfare programs. While the neoliberal model of governance in the 1980s had been about retrenchment and privatization, New Public Management in the 1990s constituted a continued neoliberal effort to increase the efficiency and effectiveness of government. It viewed the public sector via the lens of the market and the expectations of economics, particularly in its emphasis on holding government accountable to taxpayers. As a philosophy of governance, New Public Management entailed cutbacks in government spending and the outsourcing of government programs to other actors in the private and non-profit sectors, accompanied by a new governance model for the public sector oriented around "government at a distance" (Rose 1993; Power 1994).[15]

In the United States, the "Reinventing Government Movement" was the primary embodiment of this governance model of New Public Management (Osborne and Gaebler 1992). Theoretically and normatively, the central premises of the Reinventing Government Movement were taken from the disciplines of economics and management. Government was viewed in the frame of the free market model. The cost of government should be low, competition was valued as a means to cost-savings, and taxpayers were framed as customers. To achieve those goals, the Reinventing Government Movement criticized the traditional, bureaucratic model of governance and instead suggested that public offices be modeled after the practices and management strategies of for-profit organizations. In particular, government agencies should seek to improve their cost efficiency by using performance measurement techniques, such as Total Quality Management, taken from the for-profit sector (Kettl 1997). The administrative agents of governance needed to become more "mission-driven or bottom-line oriented" (Thompson and Riccucci 1998: 236).

In practice, the emphasis in the Reinventing Government Movement was on measuring performance not only as a way to improve cost efficiency and government planning but also as a way to demonstrate accountability to external actors. In an era where big government was critiqued and the market was heralded, the idea was to show to outside critics and audiences that government dollars were being spent wisely. Government agencies could do so by engaging in "managing by results" –the use of real-time, ongoing objective knowledge of agencies' accomplishments compared to their goals to inform decision-making (Radin 2006).[16] Managing by results was considered a superior replacement to prior efforts to monitor government performance, including Planning-Programming-Budgeting-System (PPBS) under President Johnson (which compared the cost of alternative methods to achieve an intended goal), Management by Objectives under President Nixon (which sought to hold government employees accountable to specified goals), and Zero-Based Budgeting under President Carter (which specified the effect of alternative budgetary decisions on policy) (Wholey and Hatry 1992; US General Accounting Office 1997).

According to proponents, those prior efforts had focused on a federal agency's inputs, activities, or outputs. They often had focused on efficiency, but they had omitted the measure of government's actual performance or effectiveness in terms of creating intended changes in clients and communities. The intended purpose of the Reinventing Government Movement was to create an infrastructure whereby elected officials could monitor the results of funded agencies, to employ that data to inform budgeting decisions, and, most importantly, to provide accountability to the American public as taxpayers (Wholey and Hatry 1992; Radin 2006).

Led by Vice-President Al Gore, this move to change government practices according to the Reinventing Government Movement culminated in the passing of the Government Performance and Results Act in 1993 (the "GPRA" or the "Results Act"). The GPRA's stated goal was a federal government that "works better and costs less" (US National Performance Review 1993). When signing the law, President Clinton noted, "The law simply requires that we chart a course for every endeavor that we take the people's money for, see how well we are progressing, tell the public how we are doing, stop things that don't work, and never stop improving the things that we think are worth investing in" (Gore 1998:2).

First implemented by the federal government in 1997, the GPRA required almost all federal departments and agencies to develop five-year strategic plans, linked to annual performance plans that specified "objective, quantifiable, and measurable goals" and performance indicators for each program, and to publish annual performance program reports. To begin this process, agencies were requested to seek stakeholder input as to the goals of each program. Once goals were identified in a concrete, quantified manner, agencies were asked to specify their inputs, throughputs, outputs, and outcomes, with outcomes defined as "performance measures that demonstrate to someone outside the organization whether or not intended results are being achieved" (US General Accounting Office 2004:36). Outcomes could be immediate or long-term in nature. Data on a program's outcomes were to be used as indicators of a program's success to increase internal efficiency, to make budgeting decisions, and, perhaps most critically, to demonstrate results to external constituents and critics. Outcomes were at the core of "managing by results" (US National Performance Review 1993).[17]

Importantly, the GPRA's requirement for program accountability via performance measurement by outcomes held for not only government agencies, but also for independent nonprofit organizations. As had occurred for some time, the federal government relied on charities to deliver a substantive portion of its publicly funded services. Beginning in the 1960s with the growth of government entitlement programs under President Lyndon Johnson's Great Society (such as the Economic Opportunity Act in 1964, the Housing and Urban Development Act in 1965, and the Model Cities Act in 1996 and the Title XX changes to the Social Security Act), a large percentage of government-funded services has been provided by nonprofit organizations, many of who had been created solely to provide these specific government-funded services (Hall 1992).

This move was intensified under President Ronald Reagan and again under President Bill Clinton, when the federal government engaged in "privatization." As another key tenet of a neoliberal ideology, privatization consists of the government's decision to no longer have publicly subsidized programs and services provided by public sector agencies but instead by private, contracted organizations (Milward and Provan 2000). Concretely, any publicly provided welfare services were to be privatized via paid delivery to clients by private nonprofit and commercial actors, premised on a belief that government would reap the benefits of market competition among those entities. The contracting out of services to non-governmental entities was presumed to result in lower costs and greater flexibility, thus improving the effectiveness and efficiency of the government's provision of programs. Following this logic, government agencies at the federal, state, and local levels in the 1980s and 1990s had opened up the provision of services via grants or contracts to both nonprofit and for-profit entities (Smith and Lipsky 1993).

In 1996, for example, President Clinton signed the Personal Responsibility and Work Opportunity Act, which replaced the Aid to Families with

Dependent Children program, as the primary means of provision of welfare to the unemployed with dependents. While AFDC provided cash transfers to those out of work, the new program entailed a work development component, where receipt of welfare assistance was conditional upon participation in the Temporary Aid to Needy Families (TANF), a new welfare-to-work initiative. Much of TANF's service delivery was contracted out to private organizations, including both for-profit and non-profit. America Works is a corporation that began to successfully bid for welfare-to-work contracts with municipal governments starting in the 1990s (Bernstein 1996). And Goodwill Industries, a large non-profit with a long-standing focus on workforce development, also began to secure TANF government contracts at the local level as well (Handler and Hasenfeld 2007).

Thus, while the use of outcome measurement as part of the Reinventing Government Movement was intended as a way for the federal government to demonstrate accountability to its critics, one critical effect of the passing of the GPRA also was felt by nonprofit organizations. From 1993 and on, those charities that contracted with public agencies to provide government funded health and human services increasingly were required to engage in outcome measurement as a condition of the receipt of grants or the awarding of purchase of service contracts. This process of privatization and performance measurement also then became popular at the state and local levels of government (Melkers and Willoughby 2005). In each case, the data on outcomes gathered from nonprofits were also to be used, alongside data on public sector agencies, as part of a government's effort to inform decision-making and to convey efficiency and accountability to its stakeholders.

The United Way of America and program outcomes

At about the same time, alongside a new reality of expanded government funding of nonprofits, another large resource provider of nonprofits also separately began to demand that recipient charities engage in outcome measurement. Beginning in 1996, the United Way of America, a national association for over 1,300 local United Ways that in 2012 distributed over $4.25 billion, began a concerted effort to have the member agencies of its local United Ways implement outcome measurement (*Forbes* 2013). As with the federal government, the United Way of America engaged in outcome measurement as a proactive effort in a moment of crisis to demonstrate its value to its key stakeholders, including funders. These resource providers to the United Way system were primarily large corporations that both made donations of its own to the United Way but also permitted United Ways to solicit their employees and executives via an annual workplace campaign.

Historically, each United Way – composed of staff and volunteers with a member of local charities – has existed at the level of a town or city. In each locale, it has provided the critical role of gathering donations through payroll deductions from the region's workplaces. Employees would sign up to have a percentage of their paycheck automatically deducted by the firm and directed to the United Way. In addition, local firms would make contributions to the United Way, either as stand-alone donations or through their corporate foundation. The United Way would then distribute those resources to its membership of local charities such as the YMCA, Boy Scouts, and the Salvation Army, based on a discourse of the assessment of community needs. The model of the United Way originated in the late nineteenth century and quickly diffused across the majority of towns and cities in the United States. By 1948, over 1,000 United Ways had been formed, and the United Way system constituted the biggest and most successful philanthropic institutions in the US nonprofit sector. In the 1970s, the national association for local United Ways expanded its role and sought both to consolidate corporate and union support for United Ways and to highlight the contribution of local United Ways to their community, adopting the new name of the "United Way of America" (Barman 2006).

By the early 1990s, however, the role of the United Way as an intermediary between donors and local nonprofits in a community was put into serious question. First, while once the United Way system had been one of the largest single funder of social services in the United States, it now represented a small and declining percentage of all resources for charities in the health and human services. Instead, nonprofits were increasingly reliant on government funding and on the receipt of income from the sales of services. Government support, by the mid-1970s, had grown from one-third to one-half of total annual revenue for the nonprofit sector (Salamon 1987). Consequently, nonprofits' reliance on the United Way for funds had declined. In addition, the federal government was empowering a local, grassroots approach to social change. These shifts introduced new groups and constituencies to community planning, different from the business leaders and social service representatives that had previously led the provision of aid to the local community through the United Way (Barman 2006).

Secondly, the United Way of America suffered from a financial scandal. In 1992, the president of the United Way of America, William Aramony, was accused of fraud and financial mismanagement and in 1995 was convicted of defrauding the charity of $1.2 million (Hendricks, Plantz, and Pritchard 2008). The effect on local United Ways' legitimacy and fundraising capacity was serious: the United Way of Massachusetts Bay, for example, experienced a decline of nearly twenty percent over the next few years in result (Stone, Hager, and Griffin 2001). Third, the new social movements of the 1960s and 1970s – the environmental, civil rights, consumer rights, and women's movements – had put into question the United Way's traditional mode of fund allocation. Historically, United Ways had distributed the majority of their funding to a relatively small set of large, generalist charities, including the YMCA, Boy Scouts, and the Salvation Army. These core agencies were notable in that they were large and well-established nonprofits largely limited to the provision of health and human services for the middle-class (Barman 2006). Yet, this pattern of funding to long-time member agencies became challenged in the 1960s and 1970s when local United Ways were accused of being unresponsive to the changing composition of the nonprofit sector and the growth of smaller nonprofits targeted around a single issue. As Peter Hall (1992:304) notes in his comprehensive history of the US nonprofit sector, "as communities became more pluralistic and as previously unempowered constituencies, especially blacks and women, became more insistent in their demands for community services – United Way found it increasingly difficult to serve their needs."

The result of these challenges was that the United Way of America, under new leadership, felt that its legitimacy with and support from the corporate community was on shaky ground. To respond to its external critics, as in the case of the federal government, the United Way of America moved to implement a valuation tool – one based around outcome measurement – in order to demonstrate the accountability of the United Way model to its funders. To do so, the United Way of America sought to supplant other measuring devices present in the nonprofit sector at the time. Up until the 1990s, nonprofits had been subject to two dominant gauges of good performance. Beginning in the Progressive Era, charities first had been asked to annually count their outputs in terms of the number of program services that they offered or the number of clients that a program had served. This count of outputs formed part of the larger project by social welfare reformers, like the Charity Organization Society movement, in the early twentieth century to employ "social statistics" to not only demonstrate the community-level nature of social problems but also to highlight the role of charities in addressing these challenges (Clapp 1926; Frankel 1926; McMillen 1930). At the same time, nonprofits began to publish annual yearbooks or reports that presented their mission, staffing, and governance, level and sources of support, and program activities (Solenberg 1909; Ralph 1915). In these publications, charities listed the numbers of those people they had served and/or the number of services provided in order to demonstrate their aptitude/success in the task of community change (Cutlip 1965). The 1916 yearbook for the Salvation Army of America serves as an example of this effort. One section of the yearbook provides an overview of the Women's Social Work department. Under the category of "midnight work," statistics are given that include the number of "girls" spoken with on the streets, in their own homes, or in workhouses; the number of girls interviewed at officers' quarters; and the number brought to Salvation Army homes, sent to friends, or otherwise assisted (Salvation Army 1916).

Nonprofits also were evaluated for their worth based on their financial efficiency. Driven by scrutiny from the popular media and by the work of independent third-party watchdogs, such as the National Information Bureau and the Better Business Bureau, which rated nonprofits for the purported benefit of donors, nonprofits were judged for their success based on their "overhead ratio" – the percentage of the donation used for fundraising and administrative costs, as listed in their annual reports or tax filings (Cutlip 1965). Above a certain percentage – sometimes as little as ten percent of a dollar of a donation – charities were deemed inefficient and, in consequence, illegitimate.[18] This emphasis on overhead costs as a measure of nonprofits' social value continues today, and is used both by the media and by online ratings agencies, like Charity Navigator and Guidestar.

In its efforts to demonstrate accountability to its various stakeholders, the United Way of America sought to replace those existing measuring devices with a new tool. It deemed them "inadequate" (to quote from one retired United Way of America staff member who participated in the construction of outcome measurement). In one publication, for example, staff at the United Way of America concluded that while traditional measures of organizational perform-ance (focusing on fundraising or a count of clients) "show how much effort has been generated for how many individuals, they reveal nothing about whether this effort has made any difference – whether anyone is better off as a result of the service" (Plantz, Greenway, and Hendricks 1997:15–16). Similarly, I interviewed one long-time United Way of America executive who had been involved in the generation of outcome measurement. As he summarized: "the goal was to get rid of anything that couldn't convey all the good we were doing in local communities."

The United Way of America worked to develop and implement a new measuring device that could be used to better demonstrate the social value of United Way's funded nonprofits. The United Way of America began this effort to generate a new measure of its social value by creating a 31-member commit-tee in 1995, spending nearly $2.4 million over the next five years in develop-ing its strategy (Hendricks, Plant, and Pritchard 2008). Similar to the federal government, the committee's final recommendation was that local United Ways should encourage recipient nonprofits to track the outcomes of any programs funded – in whole or in part – by the United Way of America. In short, measuring clients served and/or measuring financial efficiency as indicators of nonprofits' social value was to be replaced by the use of outcome measurement. In 1996, the United Way of America began its push to disseminate the measuring device of outcome measurement to local United Ways, by publishing a manual on outcome measurement, accompanied by a video and training kit that provided concrete guidelines to member agencies on how to identify the intended goals of a program and then to develop measur-able indicators of change in clients (outcomes) that reflected the program's intervention. The national association's goal was to have United Ways require affiliated nonprofits to report their outcomes for aggregation and dissemina-tion to other stakeholders by the local United Way and by the United Way of America (Hatry, van Houten, Plantz, and Greenway 1996; United Way of America 1996).

ACCOUNTING FOR OUTCOMES

In all, in a relatively short amount of time, nonprofits involved in health and human services were subject to demands by two key funders to demonstrate their social value based on the use of outcome measurement. This emphasis by both the federal government and the United Way of America on outcomes as an indicator of social value merits further investigation. Both resource intermediaries sought to adopt a new emphasis on monitoring funding recipients as part of a move to defend themselves against external criticisms, with the ultimate goal of communicating their own value to key constituents. But, given that shared intent, how did both funders, in two different societal sectors, come to employ the particular measuring device of outcome measurement? As I will show later, the move to outcome measurement resulted from analogous factors at work at the same time for both sets of actors. This was not a case of the United Way of America mimicking the federal government's efforts or a matter of interlocked elites who participated in both organizations and who diffused a particular practice.[19] Instead, the similarity of the two efforts resulted from two related causes: first, the particular nature of the institutional expectations facing these organizations that led to their adoption of outcome measurement as a tactic of defense and, secondly, the work of one cluster of academics and consultants – as an example of an "epistemic community" – hired separately by both funders as value entrepreneurs to develop a measuring device that could serve that communicative purpose.

Institutional expectations towards accountability

One key insight of sociological theory is that social actors face not only technical requirements but also institutional expectations. These institutional expectations consist of broader, external understandings of the appropriate goals and means of action for members of a field. Institutional pressures exist distinct from the technical criteria of rationality, whereby actors should choose a line of action in order to most efficiently pursue their goals (Weber 1922/1978). Instead, organizations must respond to institutional pressures by implementing expected practices and structures in order to be deemed legitimate by others. Thus, understanding why organizations look and act as they do requires attention to the broader institutional context in which they are located (Meyer and Rowan 1977; DiMaggio and Powell 1983).

In the case of the federal government and the United Way of America, both were subject to the same sets of institutional pressures during the early 1990s. To begin, both actors faced external criticisms of their performance, based in part on the historical moment but exacerbated by their respective role in their field. Like other organizations at the time, the federal government and the United Way of America were subject to critiques characterized by the dominance of the accountability movement or what more broadly has been called an "audit society" (Power 1994). Present across a range of societal arenas, such as the public sector, the field of education, the market, and the nonprofit sector, the accountability movement is typically understood as the call for actors to report their performance to their key stakeholders for the purpose of control via external assessment and self-discipline (Edwards and Hulme 1995; Townley 1997). The accountability movement drew from the logic of agency theory in finance, where principals (those who own or fund the entity) and agents (those to whom principals have delegated control and decision-making) are assumed to be in conflict. Examples of principals and agents include corporations' shareholders and managers, taxpayers and government, and government and private service providers of publicly funded services. Principals are assumed to be distrustful of agents' willingness to act in the best interests of principals and so must monitor their behavior through ongoing, data-driven evaluation and respond accordingly (Jensen and Meckling 1976).

Given the neoliberal embrace of the market as a preferred vehicle for the delivery of goods in the 1980s and 1990s, agency theory then diffused beyond finance as proponents' successfully applied its key tenets to different societal arenas, including corporate management, policing, and education (Peters and Waterman 1982; Bratton 1998; US Department of Education 1998). In each setting, a range of measuring devices arose to address the separation of ownership and control, including the accounting audit, performance measurement tools, achievement tests, and others. Each measuring device was intended to facilitate principals' scrutiny of agents by providing ongoing, real-time data, to facilitate evaluation, and to induce agents' own self-monitoring as well.

In result, when the federal government and the United Way of America attempted to respond to external criticisms about their value, their response was fundamentally structured by the institutional expectation of accountability, as exacerbated by the parallel nature of their intended purpose and location in their field. Both the federal government and the United Way of America held a similar position in their respective field. Each actor served as a funding and coordinating intermediary that received resources from others but then was responsible for determining the distribution and purpose of those goods as they passed those resources on, along with guidance and oversight, to affiliated organizations that provided the funded services to address the targeted problem. Each was then accountable to their funders for the proper distribution of resources to service providers (Stone et al. 2001).

Both the federal government and the United Way of America, in these intermediary positions, each developed outcome measurement as a means to address external critics. The federal government faced neoliberal critiques of the public sector as bureaucratic and inefficient when compared to the market, as discussed earlier. And the United Way system was viewed as potentially corrupt, as unnecessary, and as outdated in its system of fund distribution. In both cases, the institutional expectation of accountability fundamentally structured their reply. First, both actors needed, in their role as agents, to provide the necessary data on their effectiveness as intermediaries to resource providers who constituted their principals. Yet, the expectations of accountability and "managing by results" also required them – as principals – to demand appropriate data from funded organizations in their role as agents, so that the federal government (and other government actors) and the United Way system (including the United Way of America and local United Ways) could show that as principals they were monitoring their fundees' performance (Milward and Provan 2000). It is no surprise then that, Joseph Wholey, one of the recognized "architects" of the 1993 GPRA, noted that the act's reliance on performance measurement, with a focus on quantifying outcomes, was developed to permit government agencies to "interact with people who control resources to demonstrate what the program accomplished, so they commit the resources to keep the program running." Or, in the words of public policy scholars, public sector managers "must communicate the value of what they are doing" (Cavanaugh and Haggard 1998). Similarly, as one research respondent who had been involved in the formation of the GPRA told me in an interview, "given the climate of the times, it was strongly felt by everyone on board that it is was only through accountability by results that the GPRA could work to increase public trust in government."

Evaluation professionals as an epistemic community

Facing challenges to their legitimacy, the federal government and the United Way of America sought to demonstrate their value in ways that reflected the institutional expectation of accountability. To do so, they turned to an "epistemic community" with knowledge-based expertise in this area by looking to evaluation experts. An epistemic community is commonly understood as a group of professionals whose expertise is considered authoritative and thus used to set formal policy.[20] The rise of epistemic communities as influential actors in the public sphere over the last few decades is traced to the growing devolution of government policy away from internal staff and towards independent experts and authorities (Haas 1992).

While initially used in an international context, the concept of epistemic community also describes the central role of evaluation experts in the federal government and United Way of America's turn to outcome measurement. Here, both actors realized the need to implement a measuring device that could produce the required performance data on funded entities in order to demonstrate accountability to their resource providers. Each actor then turned for advice to the same epistemic community – a cluster of evaluation professionals with a background in setting policy and advising government actors on the matter of program effectiveness. They consisted of a network of evaluation scholars and consultants, many of whom had had an affiliation with the Urban Institute, a Washington DC think tank founded in 1968 in order to generate independent research for use in formulating and implementing public policy at multiple government levels. Chief among this epistemic community was Joseph Wholey, who served as director of program evaluation studies at the Urban Institute from 1968 to 1978 and who went on to work for the federal government and in academia, and Harry Hatry, who had directed the Urban Institute's Public Management Program since the early 1970s. Both were long-time proponents of performance measurement for government agencies, and each had advised, consulted for government offices and nonprofit organizations, and published (both alone and together) on the topic.[21] For example, in an article co-authored just prior to the passing of the GPRA entitled "The Case for Performance Monitoring," Wholey and Hatry (1992:605) concluded that, "in the absence of adequate attention to service quality and program outcomes, government too often becomes wasteful, ineffective, and unresponsive and government credibility sinks ever lower."

Wholey and Hatry are generally recognized as "founders of the GPRA" (Straf 1996) and as having played "key roles in the performance measurement movement" in that they each worked for or advised the federal government and the United Way of America (Evaluation Exchange 1998). Joseph Wholey served as senior advisor to the deputy director for Management at the US Office of Management and Budget, and so was involved in the development and implementation of performance measurement techniques for the GPRA. He then also served in an advisory capacity to the United Way of America in formulation of its policy of outcome measurement (Hatry et al. 1996; Miller and Caracelli 2013). Similarly, while working at the Urban Institute, Harry Hatry had sought to have state and local governments employ performance measures in their planning and budgeting processes from the 1970s and on (Hatry 1977, 1978; Wholey and Hatry 1992; Epstein 1992). Hatry and his colleagues at the Urban Institute then led the United Way of America's move to define nonprofits' performance by the measurement of program outcomes (Hatry et al. 1996).

The role of the valuation repertoire

The members of this epistemic community were charged by funding intermediaries with developing a new measuring device, one that would allow those actors to communicate their legitimacy to external critics at a moment in which they faced institutional expectations towards accountability. This group of experts already had been involved in the construction and employment of a range of measurement tools in order to gauge the worth of government programs and agencies from the 1960s and on. As evident from the analysis of professional publications, interviews with members of this group, and secondary data, this epistemic community developed outcome measurement as a measuring device for the federal government and the United Way of America by combining two prior tools with which they were familiar and which had been present in the US public sector from the 1960s and on: program budgeting and program evaluation. They transposed these methods to a new setting and modified them in order to fit within a culture of accountability – as guided by the collection of ongoing, real-time data on performance – so as to demonstrate and defend the legitimacy of the federal government and the United Way of America.

Similarly, in the social science literature, actors engage in the act of transposition when they apply existing schemas (ranging from formal rules to informal prescriptions for action) in their repertoire to new situations (Swidler 1986; Sewell 1992; Boxembaum and Battilana 2005). In this view, the contents of an actor's repertoire "can be used not only in the situation in which they are first learned or most conventionally applied. They can be generalized – that is, transposed or extended – to new situations when the opportunity arises" (Sewell 1992:8). Elisabeth Clemens (1993, 1997), for example, has shown how early women's groups, otherwise disenfranchised from the political process, managed to successfully transpose existing organizational repertoires in order to effect the desired change in the political sphere. In this view, actors are easily able to engage in transposition – "knowledge of a rule or a schema by definition means the ability to transpose or extend it – that is, to apply it creatively" (Sewell 1992:18) and they are only limited in doing so either by the limited content of their salient repertoire and/or by the perceived legitimacy of their use of a particular schema given their social position (Swidler 1986; Clemens 1993).

The need for performance measures: program budgeting

The construction of outcome measurement first can be traced to these value entrepreneurs' historical familiarity with program budgeting. Many members of this epistemic community began their professional career in the midst of the US federal government's turn to a new method of cost-based, program budgeting in the 1960s, formally called PPBS (Hatry 1961; Wholey 2012). This valuation tool stemmed from early efforts at the RAND Corporation in the post-World War II period to develop the methodology to determine when and how governments should engage in nuclear war. RAND developed "systems analysis" – an effort to identify the benefits, costs, and risks of different alternatives to war in order to select the most optimal strategy (Hitch and McKean 1960). Systems analysis was then picked up, under the new label of PPBS, for budgeting use by the United States Defense Department under Robert McNamara in 1961. PPBS required a department or agency to engage in a planning process by which it identified its program goals, compared and identified the most cost effective means to implement the program, and set a corresponding short-term and long-term budget to put in place the resulting program. PPBS is commonly perceived to be a form of centralized policy making which rests authority in the technical rational authority of policy experts (Mintzberg 1994).

In 1965, at the recommendation of RAND experts, President Johnson then extended this valuation technique for use by other federal agencies, including the Department of Health, Education and Welfare, the Office of Economic Activity, and the Bureau of the Budget. His broader goal was to centralize decision-making and to evaluate the effectiveness of the new social welfare programs at the heart of his Great Society initiative, including the War on Poverty, Medicaid and Medicare, Job Corps, and Head Start, among others (Novick 1967). As before, PPBS was to be employed in order for staff to determine how to select programs to best achieve each agency or department's goals. In addition, in the case of the Department of Health, Education, and Welfare, newly developed programs were to be assessed for their effectiveness in achieving their goal in order to inform future planning, programming, and budgeting. One related challenge for the staff at the Department of Health, Education, and Welfare was to generate performance measures for their programs. They quickly realized that data did not exist to gauge the potential worth of competing social welfare alternatives or to identify the actual worth of newly implemented programs: new measures would need to be developed (Hatry 1970).

However, while the "whiz kids" at RAND and then at the Defense Department had devoted extensive amounts of time and money to create the methodology needed to identify and compare the relative merit of competing defense department strategies, the Department of Health, Education, and Welfare did not possess the staff, expertise, or the time to produce parallel measures to estimate the social benefits of the Great Society's programs and so to allow for comparisons across different policy possibilities (Botner 1970). Most famously, Alice Rivlin, an economist who had served as Assistant Secretary for Planning and Evaluation in the Department of Health Education and Welfare, published her overview of the challenges involved in extending PPBS to social welfare efforts in 1971. In the book's concluding remarks, she highlighted the need to develop performance measures to improve government effectiveness in this domain. She wrote:

It therefore seems to me that analysts who want to help improve social service delivery should give high priority to developing and refining measures of performance. Relatively little effort has gone into devising such measures so far, despite their importance and the apparent intellectual challenge of the task. Performance measures for social services are not, of course, ends in themselves. They are prerequisites to attempts both to find more effective methods of delivering social services and to construct incentives that will encourage their use (Rivlin 1971:141).

And it is precisely out of this problem of developing performance measures to engage in PPBS that members of the epistemic community trace the initial appeal of outcome measurement. At its core, the tool of outcome measurement is centered on the articulation of measurable indicators of an organization or program's consequences. In our interview together, one member of this epistemic community deemed PPBS the "great, great grand daddy" of the concept of outcome measurement. Similarly, Joseph Wholey (2012:264) located his interest in assessing program effectiveness through attention to outcomes to his early work under Alice Rivlin in the US Department of Health, Education, and Welfare in the late 1960s and in that office's search for "cost-effective solutions to social problems."[22]

Theorizing outcomes: program evaluation

Yet, while the implementation of PPBS revealed the need for performance measures of social programs, it also resulted in a second critical influence on the formation of outcome measurement in the 1990s. Specifically, the task of assessing the success of Great Society social programs was the remit of the staff at the Department of Health, Education, and Welfare. Searching around for a method to determine the causal impact of these new programs, government actors settled upon the use of "program evaluation," a methodology initially formulated by social scientists to demonstrate the causal validity of a theoretical claim (Campbell and Stanley 1963; Suchman 1967). Program evaluation is focused around the development of discourse and devices that can gauge the success of an organization's specific intervention by producing data that can be used to compare a program's actual outcomes (in terms of creating desired change) to its intended outcomes. One critical part of the summative version of program evaluation is in determining whether the program actually caused the change in participants or whether the change was caused by other factors. A program's causal effect on participants ideally is proven via the use of the experimental method – comparing results for those who participated in a program versus those who did not participate, either via the random assignment of cases or by the matched pairing of cases (Campbell and Stanley 1963; Suchman 1967).

As part of its use of PPBS, staff in the federal government turned to a growing epistemic community of evaluation scholars to design the application of the growing assortment of social programs and to determine their effectiveness (Poland 1974; Rossi, Lipsey, and Freeman 2004). In 1968, for example, the Income Maintenance Experiments began in order to determine the efficacy of replacing the government's provision of cash and in-kind benefits to the poor with a negative tax income instead. Following the tenets of program evaluation, families in a number of communities were randomly assigned to groups receiving different amounts of benefits and tax rates, in order to determine their effect on work effort (Kershaw and Fair 1977).

After the demise of the Great Society era, program evaluation continued to be employed at various levels and locations of the public sector, albeit with a different purpose. Many attributed the inefficacy of the War on Poverty not to any of the programs' inherent weaknesses but to an "implementation gap" – to problems of their management (Pressman and Wildavsky 1973). In result, the purpose of evaluative techniques in the public sector changed from policy analysis (the search for the most cost-effective way to identify and put in place new programs) to public management (the pursuit of the most effective way to manage an existing policy). This new challenge of gauging and improving the performance of existing programs was solved again by the use of program evaluation research and the expertise of that epistemic community, who again included Joseph Wholey and Harry Hatry, among others later involved in outcome measurement (Weiss 1972; Wholey 1979, 1983, 2012; Hatry, Winnie, Fisk, and Blair 1981).

The construction of outcome measurement

In the 1990s, at the behest of the federal government and the United Way of America, members of this epistemic community of evaluation experts developed outcome measurement as a measuring device that drew from both program budgeting's emphasis on measuring results and program evaluation's attention to performance measures as one component of evaluation, but modified and combined them in ways necessary to meet the specific communicative needs of their clients who faced the broader embrace of performance management in the 1980s and 1990s (Wholey 1979; Miller and Caracelli 2013). This sentiment was reflected in a conversation I had with one respondent who had been a long-time member of this epistemic community before her retirement. As she recounted the feeling of herself and her colleagues at the time, "what we needed to do was develop a way for government agency managers to show they were making progress towards the public's goals."

First, while an attention to performance measures came out of the PPBS era, the specific gauge of outcomes (the measure of changes in clients) as a measure of program success was taken from the theory of program evaluation but altered for a new communicative purpose. In the traditional practice of program evaluation, outcomes data are gathered on a one-time basis in order to retrospectively determine the effect of a program, as conducted by an external evaluation professional. Now, in contrast, outcomes were to be gathered repeatedly by staff members on an on-going basis for purposes of performance management and budgeting, and – perhaps most importantly – for resource providers (like the federal government and the United Way of America) to demonstrate accountability to external audiences (Blalock 1999).

With outcome measurement, secondly, the methodology to demonstrate the causal impact of a program changed. Causal attribution no longer needed to be proven by the use of an experimental design (i.e., with the use of randomized control trials), but rather could be inferred from the specification of a program's logic model, as specified by Joseph Wholey in a number of publications (Wholey 1979, 1983).[23] In so doing, these professionals drew from a more recent strand in evaluation scholarship that emerged in the 1970s called "program theory" (Weiss 1972; Wholey 1979). Program theory requires an organization to outline how a program is intended to effect change.

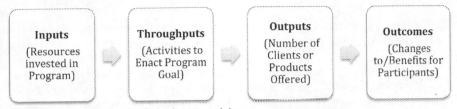

FIGURE 2.1 Evaluation and the logic model

First, a "theory of change" posits a cause and effect claim about the program's activities and how it will effect the desired result in beneficiaries. It requires the identification of the assumptions that underlie a program, including the specification of the social problem to be solved, the presumed cause of the problem, and how the program intervention is understood to correct the problem.

Alongside the articulation of a theory of change, organizations must also specify a logic model to outline how the organization's resources are being employed to achieve that end. As shown in Figure 2.1, a logic model is visually represented through a diagram that shows an organization's inputs (the resources a nonprofit uses to accomplish a program's goals – employees, hours worked, and money spent), throughputs (the activities involved in the provision of the program/service), outputs (the amount of programs and/or services provided, the number of clients assisted), outcomes (changes in clients), and impact (longer-term change in the community or society). An organization would then gather data to measure appropriate indicators of outcomes in order to demonstrate the successful implementation of a program's logic model, with measures of outcomes and/or impact taken as evidence of its effect (Weiss 1972; Wholey 1979). Taken together, this strand of evaluation experts asserted that an organization's articulation of a theory of change and a logic model was adequate to demonstrate a program's causal impact to external audiences and negated the need to employ the experimental research design. Proponents of program theory, which included Joseph Wholey and other experts responsible for the creation of outcome measurement, thus argued for the use of outcomes alone as proof of a program or organization's social value.

With its origins in program budgeting and program evaluation but as transposed by an epistemic community of evaluation experts to a new context, outcome measurement was then put in widespread use by the federal government and the United Way system. Outcome measurement suited the communicative purposes of these actors at that particular historical moment. In its capacity for customized commensurability, outcome measurement reflected and reproduced the varied and subjective meaning of the project of social value in the public and nonprofit sectors. As a quantified gauge of an organization's effectiveness, outcome measurement also allowed these intermediaries to demonstrate accountability to their external audiences by serving as an indicator of these funders' use of real-time, ongoing decision-making to improve their efficacy.

Notes

1. The United States has the largest nonprofit sector in the world by total size, but it is not the largest in terms of its relative proportion of total employment (Salamon 2012).

2. Such a definition by necessity simplifies the ambiguous and complicated nature of defining and bounding the space of the "nonprofit sector." It also signals the variety of ways actors have sought to specify the boundaries of the nonprofit sector. For a discussion of the complexities and challenges of defining and delineating this "third space," see (Corry 2010).

3. With corporations, in contrast, owners or shareholders possess full rights to direct, profit from, and/or sell ownership of the firm and government agencies legally are owned by the electorate and its representatives (Powell and Steinberg 2006).

4. State laws vary as to the specific legal form an entity must take to be recognized as a nonprofit: most register as a nonprofit corporation, but some states recognize charitable trusts, limited liability corporations, and unincorporated nonprofit associations also to be recognized as nonprofit (Hopkins 2011).

5. One exception is the US Supreme Court's statement in 1970 that "the State has an affirmative policy that considers those groups as beneficial and stabilizing influences in community life and finds this classification (exemption) useful, desirable and in the public interest" (*Walz* v. *Tax commissioner*, 397 US 664, 673 (1970), as quoted in Scrivner 2001:127).

6. In this approach, derived from economic theory, the nonprofit sector produces particularistic "public goods" – public goods which the market cannot produce and for which there is demand by some citizens but which the public sector does not provide given that it must only meet the needs of the "median voter" (Weisbrod 1978, 1988). One commonly cited example of a particularistic public good is religious education – while the government provides access to schooling, religious minorities have formed nonprofits in order to educate their own members (James 1993).

7. Other valuation devices are present in the nonprofit sector, but the majority of these focus either on financial efficiency, good governance, or organizational capacity or combine all three dimensions, with one example of the latter being the Balanced Scorecard (Foundation Center 2014).

8. The Foundation Center, with the participation of McKinsey & Co., developed the website, "Tools and Resources for Assessing Social Impact" (TRASI), which serves as a searchable compendium of all devices and discourses surrounding the determination of social value for nonprofit organizations. It identifies eighty-five different methods and tools by which nonprofits may be evaluated for effectiveness; of that total, eighty percent involve the use of outcomes, either alone or in combination with other valuation techniques (Foundation Center 2014).

9. CharityNavigator has begun a process to include the presence of a charity's use of outcome measurement (although not data on outcomes themselves) in their criteria for evaluation of nonprofits. To date, it has used a nonprofit's Form 990 filing to generate a rating based on the organization's financial health and accountability. Now, CharityNavigator, along with the Independent Sector and the Hewlett Foundation, the BBB Wise Giving Alliance and GuideStar, has initiated the Charting Impact Project, an online website that seeks to facilitate nonprofits' specification of

their outcomes for incorporation into ratings as an additional dimension of nonprofit performance, as discussed by a senior executive at a conference that I attended (Guidestar 2014).

10. Social Solutions, for example, developed "Efforts to Outcomes Fundamentals" to allow nonprofits to easily capture data on outcome indicators (and is a partner in the development of the Outcomes and Effectiveness Portal) and SalesForce also offers software to nonprofits that includes the option of outcome measurement, alongside traditional measures of program finances and organization inputs and outputs (Salesforce 2012; Social Solutions 2012).

11. In comparison, a 1991 survey of a sample of funding agencies and national representative organizations about the evaluation activities of their members, affiliates, or grantees found that outcome measurement was rarely employed, as did a 1996 exploratory study of nonprofits (Taylor and Sumariwalla 1993; Sheehan 1996).

12. A competing theory for the rise of outcome measurement attributes its emergence to nonprofits' efforts to address a lack of confidence in their ability to provide social goods and attendant calls for accountability and transparency (Bradley, Jansen, and Silverman 2003; Christiansen 2003). The United Way of America scandal in 1992, frequently cited as a prominent example, was just one of 115 criminal cases occurring between 1995 and 2002 in the United States (Fremont-Smith 2004). While scandals may have contributed to calls for nonprofits' accountability, this explanation cannot account for the specific content of performance measurement in the 1990s – the turn to outcomes as a measure of social value.

13. While the embrace of outcome measurement has seeming affinities with new models of philanthropy based on business practices that appeared in the 1990s – for example, "effective philanthropy" or "venture philanthropy," this new type of giving was not responsible for the diffusion of outcome measurement. For one, the timing is wrong – the first seminal articulations of this new conception of philanthropy occurred after outcome measurement appeared in the nonprofit sector (e.g., Letts et al. 1997). Secondly, venture philanthropy explicitly called for less attention to performance metrics of "program efficacy" (e.g., evaluation and outcomes) – and for more concern to the long-term capacity of nonprofits as a whole, directly contrary to the point of outcome measurement (Letts et al. 1997:38). See Chapter 3 for a more detailed discussion of venture philanthropy and its effect on social valuation for social purpose organizations.

14. This explanation often includes the assertion that nonprofits turned to Total Quality Management (Cairns, Harris, Hutchison and Tricker 2005) and the Balanced Scorecard (Kaplan and Norton 1992) as examples of new performance management philosophies premised on the idea that financial measures were not adequate alone to assess firms' performance. In result, these measures fit with the dynamics of the nonprofit sector – and the complexity of measuring social value – because the emphasis was not solely on the financial but rather a multi-dimensional measure of performance. Yet, despite this resonance, research has shown that nonprofits have not implemented TQM and the Balanced Scorecard to nearly the same extent as outcome measurement (Carman and Fredericks 2008).

15. Under President Ronald Reagan, the Republican Party cut the federal government's provision of public services; for example, federal support to nonprofit organizations, not including Medicare and Medicaid, declined by twenty-five percent in real dollars terms in the 1980s (Abramson, Salamon, and Steuerle 1999).

16. As Lohmann (1999) points out, this move to efficient governance via objective performance measurement data has a long history in the United States dating back to the Progressive Era. The repeated goal has been to eliminate decisions by politicians (seen as partisan, corrupt, and uninformed) with the work of professionals who employed objective and scientific data to examine the relative merit and impact of different programs. However, those earlier attempts to impose rationality in budgeting decisions were typically ignored by those policy-makers who sought to differentiate the Reinventing Government Movement in the United States from prior efforts, as I discuss elsewhere in this chapter.

17. However, the policy makers behind the Reinventing Government Movement were not the first to incorporate performance measurement techniques into governance practices. They drew from existing efforts by government actors at multiple levels to implement new performance measurement strategies. By 1992, three states (Florida, Illinois, and Texas) had already passed laws entailing the use of performance measurement techniques by their agencies. And, at the federal level, the Governmental Accounting Standards Board earlier had pushed for adoption of outcome measurement, including the publication of "Service Efforts and Accomplishments Reporting: Its Time Has Come" (Epstein 1992).

18. The argument here was that a nonprofit that kept too high a portion of donations for themselves (as opposed to being used for the pursuit of mission) was either grossly amateur or quite possibly fraudulent (Cutlip 1965). As one 1958 publication by a watchdog organization warned: donors should "know the financial need, usefulness, and prudence of organizations to which you give. Your contribution goes to an organization, not a cause – and organizations are good, bad, and indifferent" (National Information Bureau 1958).

19. In contrast, the United Way of America insisted that its focus to outcome measurement "pre-dated" the federal government's move to outcomes in the GPRA (Hendricks et al. 2008).

20. More specifically, an epistemic community is defined as a "network of professionals with recognized expertise and competence in a particular domain and an authoritative claim to policy-relevant knowledge within that domain or issue-area" (Haas 1992:3).

21. Examples include Hatry (1970), Hatry, Blair, Fisk and Kruimie (1976), Wholey (1979, 1983) and Wholey and Hatry (1992).

22. Similarly, Harry Hatry (1961), another core member of this epistemic community, had worked in the Technical Military Planning Operation at General Electric and had early published on systems analysis before turning his attention to public management in his position at the Urban Institute.

23. As specified in the Results Act, the causality of programs would be assessed by the use of formal evaluation as needed. "The Results Act recognizes the complementary nature of performance measurement and program evaluation, requiring a description of previous program evaluations used and a schedule for future program evaluations in the strategic plan, and a summary of program evaluation findings in the annual performance report" (US General Accounting Office 1997:7).

3

Mission and market

Social enterprises

It is morning on the second day of a national conference for social enterprises – a type of social purpose organization that uses market methods to achieve social value by ensuring equitable economic participation for clients and by relying on sales revenue. The first panel's topic is "Best Practices for Social Enterprises" – a title that to me promises discussion of social value.[1] About thirty audience members listen to speakers who range from the staff of a prominent foundation to a social enterprise consultant and to a private investor in social enterprises in developing countries. After the speakers have finished, questions are welcomed from the audience. The first question directly concerns the question of measuring the social value of social enterprises. A middle-aged woman identifies herself as the head of a social enterprise in a Rust Belt city. She asks for advice on how her organization, which provides workplace training to disadvantaged youth, can best demonstrate that they are achieving "economic success with their clients" as a sign of "social return" – something her organization has struggled with for a while. The speaker from the foundation is the first to reply. She nods vigorously and notes that this is a frequent concern for social enterprises. Her reply is definitive – "Well, you really only have one option: 'Social Return on Investment (SROI)' is really the gold standard for social enterprises. Of course, it has its strengths and weaknesses, its proponents and its detractors, but for now that's your best option." The other panel members express agreement with this point, and the session moves on to another question.

This chapter takes the speaker's statement as a starting point for an investigation into how social value has been defined and demarcated for social enterprises, a form of social purpose organization that emerged out of the US nonprofit sector to become a field of its own starting in the 1980s. Yet, despite a shared sectoral origin (and often a shared legal form), social enterprises are commonly understood to be distinct from traditional nonprofits – as outlined in

Chapter 2 – in terms of their embrace of market-based solutions to social problems. Social enterprises seek to rely on sales revenue or "earned income" as their primary source of income in order to achieve economic viability and they provide equitable access to the economy for disadvantaged populations as their mission. So, when social enterprises have been subject to pressure to demonstrate their social impact, the challenge of valuation for them has been different and more complex than nonprofits – they are accountable for a range of different kinds of social and economic value.

The speaker's point confirmed what became apparent during the course of my research on the field of social enterprise. While not without its critics, one prevailing measuring device present for social enterprises to gauge their performance has been "SROI."[2] SROI is a valuation method that seeks to demonstrate social enterprises' economic and social value in a single measure. To do so, it generates a ratio of the amount of resources provided to a social enterprise (in terms of donations, government funding, and/or financial investments) to the sum of a social enterprise's economic value (its profit) and its socioeconomic value (a monetized count of the government savings generated by the social enterprise through its work with clients). For example, a SROI for a social enterprise of "1:3" means that one dollar of financial support resulted in three dollars of total desired financial and social value.[3] In this formula, the social value produced by social enterprises is measured in monetary terms, the organization is evaluated by the criteria of return on investment, and its social value is aggregated with and inseparable from the social enterprise's amount of profit. Clearly, despite the historical origins of social enterprises in the nonprofit sector, SROI differs markedly in its measure of social value from that of outcome measurement for traditional nonprofit organizations.

How did the tool of SROI come to dominate the field of social enterprise? And how did the social project that characterized the field of social enterprise shape how social enterprises are valued – what counts and how it is counted – via SROI? For many in the field, SROI has meant the triumph of a market logic over a mission logic with its use of money as a metric and its concern for the criteria of investors' financial return. Yet, drawing from expert interviews, document analysis, and field research, I show that the case of SROI constitutes an example of the moral market's approach by showing how actors can employ market indicators in order to pursue their values. Value entrepreneurs in this new field developed SROI as a case of the communicative purpose of justification.[4] SROI was intended to generate data to demonstrate the relative superiority of the social project of social enterprise in addressing homelessness, as compared to traditional nonprofits and government agencies, in order to generate key audiences' support for this new organizational form. Drawing from their professional expertise across multiple fields, these value entrepreneurs transposed the tools and conventions from the world of finance, including the metric of money and the use of the return on investment ratio, in order to capture the precise social value of social enterprises in ways appealing to stakeholders. Yet, this transposition was not entirely seamless, resulting in a disjuncture between the kinds of social value that value entrepreneurs acknowledged were produced by social enterprises and the kinds of social value incorporated into and so valorized by the tool of SROI.

THE CASE OF SOCIAL ENTERPRISES

While the definition of "social enterprise" is varied, one dominant approach sees social enterprises as organizations that embrace market solutions to social problems.[5] In the words of the national trade association for social enterprises, social enterprises are "where mission meets the marketplace" (Social Enterprise Alliance 2012).[6] Social enterprises employ market methods in their pursuit of social value in several regards. First, these organizations hold social missions that address the problem of individuals' inequitable participation in or lack of access to the market. Social enterprises begin with the realization that various groups in the United States and elsewhere either are excluded from employment opportunities (examples include ex-offenders, the physically or mentally challenged, or immigrant groups) or are unable to obtain fair access to trade as producers. In result, the task of social enterprises is to provide equitable economic opportunities for disadvantaged beneficiaries.

Social enterprises, as shown in Table 3.1, produce social value by providing market access to their beneficiaries or clients and thus generating social value in the form of economic development benefits. They do so via the equitable procurement of supplies, the employment of disadvantaged populations, or the sale of socially beneficial products and services to deserving customers (Dees and Anderson 2003). The first market method by which a social enterprise might seek social betterment is by the just sourcing of goods via the Fair Trade model (Stiglitz and Charlton 2005).[7] Tracing back to the post-World War II period, the intention of the Fair Trade model is to develop fair compensation for Southern producers of goods (typically food, crafts, jewelry, and clothing) and their communities by changing production and trading conditions, as well as by engaging in advocacy work. One example of this type of Social Enterprise is Equal Exchange, the largest fair trade company in the US.

TABLE 3.1 *Typology of sectoral differences*

	Market	Nonprofit sector
Nature of exchange	Monetary	Voluntary
Source of economic support	Market revenue: sales & investment	Donations & government grants/contracts/sales & investment
Beneficiary/Beneficiaries	Self	Others
Measure of success	Profit	Meeting of mission

Source: Galaskiewicz and Barringer (2012)

Social enterprises also may pursue social good via the provision of paid employment and/or job training to disadvantaged populations. Historically, these social enterprises have focused on providing employment and training opportunities for those at the "end of the labor queue, including formerly incarcerated adults, homeless people, at-risk youth, developmentally disabled individuals, folks in recovery from substance abuse, welfare recipients, and the general underemployed, low-income population" (Cooney 2011:186). Greyston Bakery, for instance, is a company located in Yonkers, NY, that provides equitable employment opportunities, including fair wages and benefits, and training, via the production and sale of baked goods. Its motto is "We don't hire people to bake cookies. We bake cookies to hire people" (Greyston Bakery 2012).

Finally, social enterprises may have a mission to sell socially beneficial products to consumers who otherwise lack access to those goods, often providing them at cost (Dees and Anderson 2003). One innovative example of this type of social enterprise is HopeLab, a nonprofit social enterprise begun by the Omidyar Foundation that delivers technology products to "improve the health and quality of life of young people with chronic illness," including the product of Re-Mission, a video game designed to improve treatment adherence for youth with cancer (HopeLab 2012). This last type of social enterprise also might sell financial services to disadvantaged communities, intended to promote the grassroots, physical redevelopment of low to moderate-income neighborhoods and communities and to address the historical exclusion of these groups from the finance market in the United States (Narain and Schmidt 2009).

Alongside providing market access to disadvantaged beneficiaries, social enterprises are often proclaimed by field proponents to be the optimal vehicle for social value because of their economic viability. By their very nature, social enterprises are expected to produce enough profit to be self-financing.[8] As an organizational model, social enterprises rely on the sale of goods and/or services in the private sector in order to generate revenue. These goods and/or services may be sold to the social enterprise's clients (in the case of serving disadvantaged customers) or to customers (in the cases of Fair Trade and workplace development). The reliance of social enterprises solely on sales revenue for income is understood to be in marked contrast to the revenue flows of government and nonprofit actors, as shown in Table 3.1.[9] Public sector agencies that provide similar goods and services as social enterprises draw from tax dollars while proponents of social enterprise argue (often erroneously given many charities' actual dependence on market revenue) that nonprofits rely on charitable donations and/or government grants and so lack financial self-sufficiency (Dees 1998; Battilana, Lee, Dorsey and Walker 2012).[10]

Yet, while social enterprises are viewed as drawing on income from the sales of goods and services and engaging in market methods to produce social value, social enterprises do not need to take the form of a for-profit entity.

Instead, with their mixed emphasis on market and mission, social enterprises historically have not been recognized by the government in the United States as a distinct legal type, and can take the form of either a nonprofit or a nonprofit-affiliated business (Dees and Anderson 2003). Studies of the social enterprises in the US, while limited in number, have found the majority of organizations that claim an identity as a social enterprise are either nonprofit organizations or are businesses' owned and managed by a charity (Battilana et al. 2012; Graddy-Reed, Trembath, and Feldman 2012; Child 2015).[11]

THE EMBRACE OF SOCIAL ENTERPRISE

Social enterprises have a long history in the US and elsewhere but they became particularly popular in the United States in the 1980s and 1990s (Cooney 2011).[12] Their growth in number and popularity at that particular historical moment can be traced to the efforts of nonprofit actors to respond to challenges to the funding flows and to the mode of exchange that had traditionally characterized the sector.[13] As part of the broader neoliberal project to construct a free and unfettered free market economy in the US, the 1980s was characterized by a sharp decline in government funding to nonprofits and a growing embrace of market-based solutions to social problems. This turn to neoliberalism, typically defined as the intentional embrace of the free market, involved a number of key and interrelated components. As we saw in Chapter 2, one central component of neoliberalism was the intentional reduction of the role of government in society in order to liberate a free, unregulated market economy.

This purposeful dismantling of the public sector happened via two routes. One strategy was to cut government funding to social services, which included slashing social welfare programs, many of which historically had been provided by nonprofits since the 1960s. Starting under President Ronald Reagan, charities in the US began to face declining revenue from government, one of their traditional sources of funding for the second half of the twentieth century (Young 2003). Between 1980 and 1994, federal spending cuts to social welfare programs outside of the healthcare field alone totaled $38 billion (Eikenberry and Kluver 2004:133).

A second strategy to minimize big government in the neoliberal project was to reconfigure the public sector along the lines of the market to improve its effectiveness and efficiency. Beginning in the 1960s and 1970s, public sector agencies had frequently provided grants to nonprofits in exchange for their provision of social welfare programs. In contrast, beginning in the 1980s, government agencies implemented the neoliberal belief that market competition resulted in greater efficiency and effectiveness. As discussed in Chapter 2, federal, state, and local governments increasingly engaged in the privatization of publicly funded service provision, such as health and human services. Rather than provide services themselves, instead government agencies contracted with nonprofit and commercial non-governmental actors, thus allowing "citizen-clients" also to have free market relationships with those organizations (Harvey 2005; Hasenfeld and Garrow 2012). The justification here was that "the state, like the private sector, provides services. It is, in this sense, a producer. The citizen pays for those services when he or she purchases a service from a provider ... The purchaser is entitled to the best deal, and it can only be obtained in nonmonopolistic, competitive conditions" (Suleiman 2013:51). The result of privatization was the growth of both nonprofits *and* for-profits providing government services (Salamon 1993; Smith and Lipsky 1993). For example, in mixed industries in the field of human service delivery (including family services, childcare, residential care for the elderly, and job training), the number of for-profit providers increased by over 200 percent from 1977 to 1997, as compared to a growth of 125 percent for traditional nonprofits (Frumkin 2002).

In the nonprofit sector, the aggregate consequence of both decreased government spending and increased privatization was the restructuring of resource flows for many public charities in the health and human services. Facing reduced income from government (in the form of grants/contracts), a growing number of nonprofits considered or turned to the model of social enterprise to generate the market-based income they now needed to survive. They either increasingly relied on fee-for-service income by selling rather than donating their goods or services to clients, they competed with other charities or for-profits for government purchase of service contracts, and/or they created affiliated for-profit social enterprises. By 2011, the most recent year for which data are available, public charities as a whole received just under half their income from fees for services and goods from private sources (Pettijohn 2013).

While nonprofits turned to the sale of goods and services in order to obtain needed resources, other powerful actors in the nonprofit sector also embraced the market as an optimal method by which to deliver social goods. In this view, individuals are best able to realize their capacity via participation in the private sector – through paid employment, the production and/or sales of goods, and/or the purchase of needed goods and services. Social enterprises are heralded for their ability to provide beneficiaries with these market-based opportunities from which they are otherwise excluded or disadvantaged (Dees 1998). In other words, "market engagement may often be the most effective way to address a non-profit organisation's mission" (Young 2003:67). In addition, as noted earlier, due to their reliance on market revenue, social enterprises were understood to be financially viable, and hence would not have to rely on philanthropic support or government grants for their livelihood, as with traditional nonprofits (Dees and Anderson 2003).

In consequence, a number of traditional institutional funders of charities, such as charitable foundations, began to promote social enterprises as their preferred vehicle for social change in the 1980s and on. Charitable foundations are a form of legally recognized nonprofit organization that provides grants to stand-alone charities, individuals, or activities for charitable purposes in the name of the public good. They are of two types: a private foundation, like the Ford Foundation, derives its income from a single source (an individual, family, or corporation) while a public foundation, such as the Boston Foundation, relies on donations from multiple organizations or actors. In the case of social enterprises, many long-standing foundations, including the Rockefeller Foundation and the Jessie Smith Noyes Foundation, had traditionally funded nonprofits that donated goods and services to clients. In the 1990s, these organizations instead also sought out opportunities to fund nonprofits' engagement in the market as social enterprises (Reis 2003). For example, the Pew Charitable Trusts (along with the Yale School of Management and the Goldman Sachs Foundation) launched the Partnership on Nonprofit Ventures in 2001, which provided online support, tools, and research to nonprofits investigating commercial ventures (Massarsky and Beinhacker 2002).

These traditional institutional funders of the nonprofit sector were joined in their embrace of social enterprise by a new group of donors in the 1990s – many of whom self-identified as "venture philanthropists." Venture philanthropy borrowed the investment techniques used by investors to nurture start-up firms in the economy in order improve foundations' giving practices – specifically, the relationship between foundations and their nonprofit recipients (Letts, Ryan, and Allen 1997). Proponents of venture philanthropy believed it would "revolutionize grantmaking and the nonprofit sector" (Moody 2008:324). And many venture philanthropists were committed to the explicit purpose of extending market methods to the nonprofit sector with the intended goal of improving its effectiveness, including supporting the growth of social enterprises. This new group of funders included Roberts Enterprise Development Fund (REDF), New Profit Inc., the Acumen Fund, and Investors' Circle (Reis 2003).[14] For example, Good Capital – a venture capital fund located in San Francisco – operates the Social Enterprise Expansion Fund, which provides investment capital to social enterprises. Good Capital explicitly restricts recipients to companies that "deliver social benefits as part of their business model and often incur a structural cost of doing good" (Good Capital 2012).

MEASURING THE WORTH OF SOCIAL ENTERPRISES: SROI

As we have seen earlier, proponents of social enterprise offered a specific justification for this new social project. When it came to addressing societal issues of economic disadvantage, social enterprises were superior to traditional charities based on their use of market methods to both ensure clients' equitable participation in the economy and to thrive as a self-sufficient and scalable type of social purpose organization. This envisioning of the social project of social enterprise then departed from the traditional imagining of the social project of charities. Rather than being reliant on donative support, social enterprises drew from market revenue gathered from the sale of a good or service. And rather than giving away goods and services to the targeted population, social enterprises engaged in economic exchange with their clients by sourcing from them, hiring them, or selling a needed good to them.

Here, the question of value and valuation for social enterprises, as a distinct social project that originated in the nonprofit sector but that drew from a market logic to define the concept of social value, was pressing. As the category of social enterprise became established and as the field grew in number and became institutionalized in the 1980s and 1990s, a growing body of voices – funders, consultants, and scholars – asked whether and how social enterprises could develop a gauge of value specific to the field (Letts et al. 1997; Dees 1998). To be considered legitimate and in order to demonstrate that they did indeed pursue a double bottom line of money and mission, the claim was that social enterprises needed to develop their own tools, techniques, and technologies in order to assess their double bottom line performance and to demonstrate the legitimacy of this new organizational form. The question was how – would the use of metrics of a firm's financial success alongside the employment of philanthropy's traditional tools of outcome measurement suffice or would an entirely new, blended measure be needed? In one illustrative interview, I spoke with Robin, an early proponent of social enterprises through her consulting work in the 1980s and 1990s with charitable foundations. She recounted how she would often encourage foundations to fund social enterprises as a new and financially sustainable (i.e., in her words, "cheaper") way to "effect social impact." Frequently, she told me, one type of reply from foundations concerned the "question of how the funders could know if social enterprises could succeed, because they needed to work as businesses and as charities at one and the same time."

In 2000, an answer to that question of value for social enterprises emerged with the appearance of "SROI" (REDF 2000). Recall that SROI consists of the calculation of a ratio of the total "investments" (including donated funds) in a social enterprise to the amount of total value that it produced, estimated over a 10-year period. This total value, what is sometimes called "socio-economic value" or "blended value," is measured as the sum of the monetized amount of social value produced by the social enterprise (in terms of government savings resulting from a social enterprise's efforts with clients) and it is combined with the firm's economic value (its profit rate) to estimate its total value.

As a way to assess social purpose organizations, SROI is contingent upon and produces a particular definition of social value. First, similar to outcome measurement, SROI only counts the products (or outputs) generated by social enterprises, in that it focuses on changes to clients, and omits a concern for how a social enterprise produces that social benefit in terms of its treatment of stakeholders, such as its own staff, the local community, or suppliers.

However, unlike outcome measurement that can quantify a range of client changes as being in the public interest, SROI, as with the social project of the field more broadly, delimits the meaning of social value only to social enterprises' production of equitable access to the market for disadvantaged beneficiaries and only to those results that can be counted in the form of government savings.

Unlike outcome measurement, SROI allows for commensurability – the comparison of social enterprises according to a common scale of value. No matter what the particular program employed by a social enterprise, its results can be compared to other social enterprises based on the relative cost of a universal indicator of social value (monetized societal benefits in the form of governmental cost savings). In result, as expressed by some respondents and as voiced by participants in conferences during my field research, SROI produces one likely reactive effect – if a social enterprise seeks to generate a positive SROI ratio, it must choose a program and select clients that are most likely to produce monetary benefit for the public sector while involving minimal cost expenditures in terms of its work with beneficiaries.

Finally, in its relationship to the logic of the market, SROI presents an example of a new type of measuring device, as compared to outcome measurement. As outlined in Chapter 1, a market logic contains within it two consequences for the assessment of social value: social value will be assigned a monetary value and social value will be subsumed to the production of shareholder value. With SROI, as shown in Table 1.2, we see only one indicator of the market logic present: money becomes the currency by which to count a social enterprise's production of social value. SROI does not entail the calculation of a social enterprise's generation of shareholder return for investors, despite its use of the language of "return on investment."

From its first, much publicized appearance in 2000, SROI has become widely synonymous with the question of value for social enterprises.[15] It is frequently discussed, as was the case at the conference that I attended, as the archetypal means by which to assess the worth of social enterprises, and a similar elision of social enterprise and SROI took place in many of my interviews and can be found in academic and advisory literature on this field (Tuan 2008; Antadze and Westley 2012). Further, SROI has diffused in its use to a number of actors – including multiple funders, nonprofits, and consultants – in the fields of social enterprise and nonprofits. For example, SROI has been taught in many management schools, such as UCLA and Harvard Business School (Javitz 2008).[16] SROI, albeit in a modified form with an emphasis on stakeholders' estimations of social value, also has become popular outside the United States, where various proponents in the UK, Canada, Australia, and Europe have embraced SROI for both social enterprises and nonprofits (New Economics Foundation 2007). In 2008, for instance, the UK government began promoting state-funded nonprofits' use of SROI to measure their impact (Nicholls, Lawlor, Neitzert, and Goodspeed 2009).[17]

SROI: MARKET INDICATORS TO MEASURE SOCIAL VALUE

But while SROI became the first widely diffused measuring device for social enterprises, it has been considered to be much more than just a neutral tool that would allow practitioners and proponents of social enterprise to identify and demonstrate the worth of this new type of social purpose organization. For many in the field, SROI – with its use of money to count social impact, the inclusion of economic profit as a criterion of success, and its emphasis on a social enterprise's return on investment as a gauge of worth – constituted a repudiation of the origins of social enterprises in nonprofits' quest for additional financial support to pursue their mission. In one interview that I conducted with a consultant who had publicized the use of SROI to nonprofits, the typical response by audiences was described by her as: "they didn't want to understand what we were saying because they just viewed it all as just, you're trying to make us more business-like and we don't want to be business like, we're here for the children." Another respondent, an early proponent of SROI who later came to be a critic of the tool, told me: "if you posit that social return is all about a monetized value, then you're only going to be looking at monetary value, you know? [But] these organizations are doing things that are helping people but that are not monetizable. But, because of the monetization issue, SROI leaves out those other kinds of value. That is a problem. We eventually came to see that."

In other words, as also was the case with outcome measurement for public charities almost a decade earlier, SROI was a symbol to many in the field of social enterprise and in the broader nonprofit sector that the pursuit of profit – the business side of social enterprise (a reliance on earned income and the use of market methods) – was triumphing over the nonprofit origins of social enterprise (the pursuit of mission, with benefits for clients and community) (Eikenberry and Kluver 2004; Galaskiewicz and Barringer 2012).[18] Similarly, this perspective on SROI embodies one conventional social science expectation – the "hostile worlds" view that the use of market indicators makes difficult the pursuit of value-based ends, where the pursuit of money and morals are assumed to be opposed in nature, as outlined in Chapter 1. The concern is that only those types of social goods that can be monetized and that can contribute to an organization's bottom line will be deemed as of worth, omitting others that cannot be given a dollar value or that do not generate economic return.

Yet, these understandings of SROI omit a consideration of how and why value entrepreneurs created SROI in the first place and how they imbued the use of market indicators with moral significance and intent. While the precise formulation of SROI did indeed transpose tools used to gauge the financial value of firms to the case of social enterprise, SROI was purposefully designed by its creators to communicate the superior amount of *social* value that social enterprises – one defined by the production of economic value, economic development value, and public value – to stakeholders in this new field.

REDF AND SROI

In the case of SROI, the salient value entrepreneur behind its formation was a charitable foundation called REDF (an acronym for "The Roberts Enterprise Development Fund") who first employed SROI in 2000. At the time, REDF was a relatively new foundation located in San Francisco.[19] Formed in 1986 by George Roberts – the co-founder of the global leverage buyout firm, Kohlberg Kravis Roberts & Co – and his wife, Leanne Roberts, The Roberts Foundations (as REDF was initially called) was created to fund nonprofits across multiple fields in San Francisco. In 1990, The Roberts Foundation became the "Homeless Economic Development Fund," with a specific focus on helping nonprofits that ran for-profit social enterprises – specifically, workforce development firms – to address the problem of homelessness in the Bay area (Emerson, Tuan, and Dutton 1998). These firms offered paid employment and training to clients, with the goal of preparing them for success in the labor force. They relied on market-based revenue from the sale of goods and services, along with charitable support from REDF and other philanthropic funders, as their main revenue streams. Rubicon Bakery, for instance, is a social enterprise that received funding from REDF. Rubicon Programs, a Bay Area nonprofit, formed Rubicon Bakery in 1998 as a wholesale bakery that provides "quality entry-level jobs for disadvantaged community residents in the food service industry" (REDF 2000:1).

But the goal of REDF was much larger than simply distributing funds to local nonprofits and their affiliated workforce development social enterprises with the hope of combatting homelessness in the region. Instead, reflecting George Roberts' success with KKR in the finance industry, the Roberts Foundation worked actively to extend the principles of venture capital to its philanthropic work with the ultimate goal of fundamentally improving the efforts of charitable foundations to use their resources to produce social value. In embracing venture capital as its organizing principle, REDF is seen as an early proponent of the model of "venture philanthropy," along with the Robin Hood Foundation in New York City, formed in 1988 by the hugely successful hedge fund manager, Paul Tudor Jones.[20]

REDF wanted to alter the traditional method by which foundations provided philanthropic grants to social purpose organizations in two ways: through its diagnosis and solution to social problems and through its relationship with funded entities. First, REDF sought to champion social enterprises as a new and optimal solution for the problem of homelessness, replacing foundations' and government's historic funding of nonprofit organizations. It was explicitly committed to a "vision of a 'free enterprise' approach to homelessness" – of social intervention premised on capitalism (Emerson and Twersky 1996:i). As companies, these social enterprises corrected for the lack of "economic opportunity" available to their disadvantaged clients in the market; they did so not by the charitable provision of housing and/or money (which the

Roberts Foundation claimed was government and nonprofits' traditional mode of assistance) but instead by extending paid employment and training to clients so that they could then succeed in the private labor market. Each social enterprise then also sold related products to generate revenue. By relying on the sustainability of commercial income (rather than uncertain, short term support from foundations or government agencies), social enterprises were deemed capable of providing meaningful, long-term employment opportunities to clients (Emerson et al. 1998; Tuan and Emerson 1999; Tuan 2002).

Secondly, over the course of the 1990s, REDF also concluded that foundations' traditional philanthropic method of resource allocation to charities was not effective. It began to model its philanthropic ties to recipients on the conventions of venture capital, in direct opposition to and in pointed critique of foundations' typical practices of making sporadic, short-term donations – "small, hands-off grants to nonprofits were not working" (Tuan 2002). The goal was to develop the same type of long-term, multi-dimensional, and hands-on relationships with fundees as the ones that existed in the market between venture capitalists and their for-profit investees. As, Jed Emerson, the founding director of REDF stated, "the REDF is founded upon the belief that a Social Venture Capital approach to philanthropy is both qualitatively and quantitatively better than traditional approaches to philanthropy" (Emerson et al. 1998:20). In its new configuration, REDF made substantive annual investments in a portfolio of only ten, carefully selected nonprofit organizations that ran one or more social enterprises, as well as providing recipients with capacity-building grants, technical support from a business analyst, REDF staff, local industrial experts, and business school interns; and access to a REDF-sponsored local business network (REDF 2000).

SROI AS A TACTIC OF JUSTIFICATION

Once it had settled upon its social project and its relationship to funded entities, by the early 1990s REDF then sought to demonstrate the worth of its efforts, to generate legitimacy both for itself (and its new method of philanthropy) and to generate support for the broader project of social enterprise. Staff wanted to show that social enterprises did indeed provide a superior solution to the problem of homelessness than existing vehicles. The question was precisely how they should do so.

Here, the efforts of REDF in this regard form an example of the concept of "justification" in organizational theory. In this approach, any concerted effort to generate a change is reliant on the efforts of its proponents, those actors who are often called "institutional entrepreneurs." As institutional entrepreneurs, advocates of a new institutional project – such as a novel organizational form, role, or practice – must engage in several key tasks if they are to succeed in institutionalizing it. First, they must offer up a critique of the existing social arrangement that they seek to replace by identifying a problem and providing critiques of existing efforts to address the problem. Institutional entrepreneurs must then also justify their proffered alternative by framing the new arrangement in ways that align with the interests and expectations of potential constituencies (Greenwood, Suddaby, and Hinings 2002; Suddaby and Greenwood 2005). The new project must be argued to be superior to current arrangements. To that end, institutional entrepreneurs must not only discursively assert the advantage of their proposed alternative but they also may seek to materially demonstrate the benefits of the new institutional innovation to others (Reay, Golden-Biddle, and German 2006; David, Sine, and Haveman 2013).

Similarly, once its social mission was selected and its funding strategy settled, REDF's next task was that of justification. As repeatedly emphasized by staff members present at the time and in publications, the nonprofit sought to demonstrate the worth of social enterprises relative to other vehicles employed by funders to address homelessness (Emerson, Wachowitz, and Chun 2000; Gair 2002). REDF (as with other actors in the field) believed social enterprises' distinctive source of social value, as compared to nonprofits and government agencies, was the production of economic value, economic development value, and broader social value (or "public value"). Johanna, an early proponent of workforce development social enterprises at REDF, summarized this view in one interview. "With social enterprises, social value creation and economic value creation go hand in hand. That's the beauty of them. It's not a zero sum equation."

The goal was to convince stakeholders of the worth of social enterprises. In one publication that outlined the history of SROI, the author asserted "How can we test and convince others of what we believe to be true: that for each dollar invested in our portfolio agencies' efforts, there are impressive, quantifiable resulting benefits to individuals and to society?" (Gair 2002:2). A staff member at REDF in the 1990s similarly recounted how the development of SROI largely was motivated by the need to demonstrate the distinct worth of social enterprises to others. She noted:

And the big question was, all right, if we think that social enterprises run the most successful potential strategy, can we actually demonstrate that that's true? From a financial standpoint – are they sustainable businesses? And then from a social standpoint, once that individual's hired and keeping with these businesses, are they really improving their lives? [Can we] demonstrate it to ourselves, to George [Roberts], and to the field? Because there had been a history in the community development space, of organizations trying to create these businesses to employ homeless people, that had really failed, and failed quite spectacularly."

The demonstration of the worth of social enterprises had the purpose of justification – it was deemed critical to gain funders' support and so to grow the nascent field of social enterprise. "What makes a difference," recalled one early REDF advisor, "is being able to go to funders – you know, foundations, individuals, or whatever, and say, we know our programs are working and to be able to show it." For REDF staff, resource providers needed proof of the success of their efforts in order to provide funds. A 2000 publication by REDF staff likewise noted that, "many of the returns created by social purpose enterprises (and many tax-exempt nonprofit organizations) go undocumented. They are therefore largely under-appreciated by practitioners, funders, and policy makers" (Emerson and Cabaj 2000:10). If REDF could demonstrate the value of social enterprises, then funders might be compelled to provide financial support to them. In one early publication, senior managers at REDF proposed that showing social enterprises' worth then "argues for the justification of the use of charitable dollars for the support of business creation efforts by non-profit organizations" (Emerson and Twersky 1996:8).

What then would this effort at justification look like for REDF? In part, REDF was guided by the social project of social enterprise and by its own identity as a venture philanthropist (one who extended the principles of finance to the nonprofit sector) but, in part, staff was aware of the need to present social enterprises' value in ways that appealed to their intended audiences. For REDF, these perceived stakeholders included a range of local actors involved in the goal of ending homelessness in the Bay Area, including George Roberts (the founder of REDF), government agencies, and charitable foundations. They thus included current and potential funders of social enterprises. One long-time staff member told me: we wanted to "demonstrate [the social impact of social enterprises] to ourselves, to George, and to the field." Another recalled: "we had our funder, George Roberts, who kept asking, "Well, how do I know that something good is happening from this? How do I know?""

Similarly, REDF staff viewed government agencies as a potential funder of social enterprises (Emerson, Wachowicz, and Chun 2000). Recall that, at the time, social enterprises were considered a new means by which a social purpose organization could generate sustainable financial support and provide assistance to disadvantaged populations. And the federal and local governments were engaging in the marketization of welfare services as part of its broader privatization of the public sector, increasingly turning to firms to deliver government-funded social service programs. Thus, REDF hoped to highlight the capacity of social enterprises to deliver publicly funded services to address homelessness. When asked to recount the origins of SROI, a senior executive outlined, "I thought, "Who's actually the market for this information?" And I thought, "I bet government agencies are the best market." Finally, REDF believed other charitable foundations with a mission to end homelessness could be convinced of the merit of social enterprises (Gair 2002). In its initial effort to detail a SROI methodology, REDF members proposed that "we describe a quite different way of looking at both the costs and benefits of the same business ventures – this time looking at them from the viewpoint of public policy – an approach that can inform both government and foundation decision-makers" (Emerson and Twersky 1996:191).

In all, the hope of REDF's staff was that social enterprises might be able to access both philanthropic and public funds aimed at assisting the homeless population in the Bay Area. As suggested by the literature on justification, these institutional entrepreneurs look to the interests and expectations of key stakeholders in order to craft the framing of their proposed change (Greenwood, Suddaby, and Hinings 2002; Suddaby and Greenwood 2005). Focusing on the perceived interests of these audiences possessed several implications for how REDF could justify the unique value of social enterprises. Foremost, REDF staff believed that these current and potential funders of social enterprises viewed their investments through the language, tools, and expectations of financial investment. For one, even more than just achieving social impact, funders wanted to know that their resources were achieving results in excess of their cost (Emerson et al. 1998). In other words, funders were assumed to be in interested in "cost savings." "We just thought," recalled a REDF executive, that "if you could show that there was value being created for, and or cost savings being realized by doing something, wouldn't that be appealing to a wider swath of the community?" The goal for REDF was to appeal to donors by showing that a "dollar invested in the social mission of a nonprofit today generates future economic and social returns in excess of the initial value of that dollar" (Emerson et al. 2000:135).

For another, REDF believed that many of these funders already employed the metrics and measures of finance to consider the impact of their philanthropic support (Emerson et al. 1998). REDF staff was particularly struck by how George Roberts sought to understand the impact of his financing of REDF. "As it's true with a lot of business people," said one respondent, "he didn't find [philanthropy] super-compelling because there was no way to track performance and there is no logic to whether one group gets 50 or 500 million dollars, right? So, we started some conversations on 'how could you bring more of an investor mind-set to philanthropy.'" Similarly, drawing from their interactions with charitable foundations in the Bay Area and from broader professional discourse at the time (Letts et al. 1997), REDF staff believed that many foundations, especially other venture philanthropists, also framed the return on their charitable donations through the metaphor of investment. "These new donors speak not only of 'measurement' and 'outcome funding,' but rather of 'social return' and the ability to document the 'added-value' of their philanthropic investments," stated one REDF publication at the time (Emerson et al. 2000:132). Thus, to demonstrate the value of social enterprises, REDF staff believed they needed to use the assumptions and tools of financial investment. "We would adapt business formulas for return to this world," recalled an early REDF executive in our interview together.

Given these perceived expectations of funders, REDF viewed traditional tools of valuation, as they existed in the nonprofit sector, as inadequate to convince stakeholders of the merit of social enterprises. REDF staff believed, based on their past experience with nonprofits, that the organization should not rely on long-standing techniques in philanthropy that were used to demonstrate nonprofits' social impact. Foundations relied on nonprofits' qualitative stories and narratives of impact, lacking the necessary rigor to allow for systematic comparison across potential recipients (Emerson and Twersky 1996; Emerson et al. 1998). One early REDF publication proclaimed: "In the for-profit sector, one speaks of Price/Earnings Ratios and Portfolio Fund Performance. Indeed, at the close of every day one knows exactly what financial returns have been generated by 'the market.' By contrast, nonprofit organizations have no equivalent metrics by which to lay claim to the value created through their labor" (Emerson et al. 2000:132). Another publication concluded that there exists an "absence of appropriate measures by which the value created by nonprofit organizations may be tracked, calculated, and attributed to the philanthropic and public "investments" financing those impacts" (Emerson and Cajan 2000:10).[21] Noted one early senior staffer at REDF: "I felt that the way that non-profits and foundations were using metrics was really for . . . eh, shit."

Given the goal of justification and the lack of appropriate tools, REDF began the process of constructing a measuring device, what would eventually become – after much trial and error – SROI, to count and so to demonstrate the social value of REDF's funded portfolio of social enterprises. To create this new tool, value entrepreneurs transposed existing instruments and conventions from the field of finance to that of social enterprise in ways that largely, but not completely, captured the social project of the field. As defined in Chapter 2, transposition consists of the extension of existing schemas (such as logics of actions, habits, objects, and practices) by actors from an initial setting to a new situation, thus allowing them to successfully navigate the social world (Swidler 1986; Sewell 1992; Clemens 1993).

The ability of REDF to engage in this transposition resulted not only from the organization's communicative need to do so but also from the foundation staff's possession of the necessary expertise to do so. Staff drew from their own professional knowledge and background, resulting in access to a wide and diverse valuation repertoire. Unusually for a charitable organization, all of those actors at REDF who were seminal in the formation of SROI had received or were receiving MBAs in finance, as discovered in the course of the interviews. Some had backgrounds in venture capital. But, as evidenced by their employment at REDF, these were individuals who also were committed to social change, particularly via the hybrid vehicle of social enterprise, and many had experience in the public and nonprofit sectors.

The first Executive Director of REDF, for example, held a Master's in Social Work and had an extensive professional background as a leader of several nonprofits that worked with the homeless population in the Bay Area. When Jed Emerson first was hired by REDF, the foundation paid the tuition for him to obtain a MBA degree from a local university. Similarly, a senior executive at the time recalled: "I had, I had a background in social action, and then, and then had the odd – at that time, the odd twist of going to business school and going into business. And, for a long time, I had been looking for a way to combine the skills that I had learned in business with my desire to improve the world."

In addition, REDF consulted both with the leaders of the nonprofits in its portfolio and with finance and economics professors at several local universities in order to ensure that the formulation of SROI could demonstrate social enterprises' multiple forms of value. In other words, the architects of SROI were fluent with the multiple meanings of value present in and the assortment of tools, technologies, and techniques of valuation that existed across a range of societal sectors.

As one early leader of REDF concluded about how he drew from his MBA education to develop SROI:

You're given this set of assumptions with regard to the role and purpose of business, which have to do with maximizing the performance of capital and the return to shareholder, but if your framework is a wrap-around relative to community and social performance elements, then the first thing you ask is 'how do you think about this from the ability to track what I care about?' And you have to ask 'well, how would you think about this from a social perspective? What are the equivalent metrics that you would use?'

We can see these two key aspects of justification – the demonstration of the specific value of social enterprises through the skilled transposition of the tools of finance to appeal to stakeholders – in several aspects of REDF's formulation of SROI as a valuation methodology. Recall that SROI involves a number of calculations in order to estimate the worth of a social enterprise, including the monetized numerator of investments, the specification of a denominator of socio-economic value, and a ratio of the two figures based on the criterion of return on investment, as measured by the metric of money. In each of these cases, a conscious effort was made by REDF staff to present the value for social enterprises through the lens of financial tools and conventions in ways that represented this social purpose organization's distinctive production of multiple types of economic value (including firm profit and economic development benefits) as a means to social value. As one early senior manager of REDF summarized the foundation's goal: "if we are rejecting traditional non-profit practice and rejecting traditional business practice, then the third way is an integrated ... an integrated framework about what value is and how companies create value."

SROI & Return on Investment

As already noted, REDF wanted to create a measuring device that drew from the conventions of financial investment in order to capture the worth of social enterprises. While various metrics were available to them, they settled on the transposition of Return on Investment to make their case. "We know how to do a financial return on investment," recalled a REDF executive, "what is the SROI look like? And how about a social return for a philanthropic investment?" Similarly, a staff member in the 1990s recounted that, "when Jed said, we want to create this methodology – something like what the financial sector has, in terms of an ROI measure … and manipulate it in some way to demonstrate that there was a public benefit to society."

By the 1990s, Return on Investment was a long-standing measure of corporate performance. It was initially developed for use by the new multi-divisional, vertically integrated firms that emerged in the US economy after World War I (Chandler 1977). Executives at the DuPont Company first devised Return on Investment in 1919 as the company expanded from the manufacturing only of explosives into the diversified production of a range of chemicals. The use of ROI allowed DuPont management to evaluate and compare the performance of its corporate divisions and to decide on asset allocation across divisions based on a comparison of financial efficiency. ROI shortly was picked up for similar use by GM and has become commonplace in corporate finance (Horrigan 1968). The measure of Return on Investment was later extended for use in the burgeoning finance industry in the form of the formula of (gains-cost)/cost. Using this ratio, an investor can then compare investment opportunities based on their ability to generate future economic return (Drake and Fabrozzi 2010).

With SROI, REDF altered the formulation of the metric of Return on Investment to focus instead on "SROI" – to estimate the social benefits that followed from a philanthropic or public contribution to a social purpose organization. Here, REDF consciously sought to construct SROI so that it would resonate with an existing tools and conventions of value in the public sector in order to increase its viability with those stakeholders (Emerson and Twersky 1996; Gair 2002). Given the familiarity of key REDF staff with the public, nonprofit, and private sectors based on their job experience and education, these value entrepreneurs were able to take the public sector tool of cost-benefit analysis (CBA) and to see its fit with the financial language of return on investment. Similarly, in scholarship on the transposition of existing schemas to new settings, actors often consider the extent of fit of a proposed change with their intended audience's existing practices and expectations (Clemens 1993; Maguire, Hardy, and Lawrence 2004). When an early REDF leader spoke about the history of SROI, he emphasized the centrality of CBA to the quest for a market-friendly way to capture the value of social enterprises. He recounted the genealogy of this search: "the closest thing that I had seen to this goal from my grad school days was CBA … And so, I thought, that is what social return framework would look like, basically do a similar thing." Similarly, in a 1996 publication that contains REDF's initial formulation of SROI, for example, the report's authors write that they are going to "describe a quite different way of looking at both the costs and benefits of the same business ventures – this time looking at them from the viewpoint of public policy – an approach that can inform both government and foundation decision-makers" (Emerson and Twersky 1996:191).

As a formal measuring device, CBA typically has been understood to create a financial calculation of the merit of different policy alternatives by identifying the monetary costs and the monetary tangible and intangible benefits of each program alternative over a set period of time through the use of a discount rate. A program's monetary benefits can be operationalized as the economic value of the net positive gains that result from the project for the public. These public gains are measured either as the aggregate of individual level benefits (using market-based measures of economic value such as increased wages) and/or as the cost savings that accrue to government (such as the generation of additional taxes or via lowering the need for program expenditures) in result. CBA can be used in two ways: programs whose benefits outweigh costs are viewed favorably and alternative policy options can be compared and ranked by creating a ratio of the cost of the program and the dollar value of the resulting social benefits (Wildavsky 1966; Porter 1995).

CBA has been a long-standing method of policy analysis in the US public sector, particularly in terms of water resource management and other environmental policy decisions. CBA has its origins in welfare economics, as initially articulated in the 1840s by a French economist. In the United States, CBA was first employed in the 1930s by the federal government to evaluate the public worth of water resource projects. During the 1960s, it was then employed in a limited range of policy arenas amenable to the monetization of benefits, including the Man Power training program and disease control programs, as part of President Lyndon Johnson's embrace of program budgeting (Buxbaum 1981). It was not, however, employed for the development of policy initiatives for majority of the Great Society programs (Rivlin 1971).[22] In the 1970s, CBA became employed as a tool by private and public funders of international development, particularly in terms of large-scale infrastructure projects. More recently, President Ronald Reagan mandated CBA at the federal level as the required metric to evaluate the worth of new regulatory initiatives (Mishan and Quah 2007).

SROI & investment

As the denominator in its ratio, SROI necessitates the identification of the dollar amount of "investments" in a social enterprise. A financial investment is typically defined as the "process of exchanging income for an asset that is expected to produce earnings at a later time." Investors buy assets (e.g., stocks, bonds, and money market instruments) with the intent purpose of gaining income or interest from their appreciation or sale. Here, REDF consciously chose to employ market language to describe the entirely different type of the economic support provided to a social enterprise by itself and by other potential actors (distinct from the company's acquisition of revenue through the sales of goods and services). Recall that REDF's support to its portfolio of social enterprises in actuality took the form only of philanthropic donations to the managing nonprofit of the social enterprise (REDF 2000). It did not financially invest in any of the social enterprises in its portfolio. In fact, investments were not even possible, by REDF or by others, since all the social enterprises it funded were privately owned by charities that are legally forbidden by the US federal government from receiving investments.

However, the use of the term of investment was only intended as a metaphor, one REDF staff believed could be legitimately used to capture actors' non-market (i.e., foundations' philanthropic or government's public) provision of resources to social enterprises (or the nonprofits that owned them). As noted earlier, their faith in the legitimacy of the transposition of the term investment to describe charitable activities was based in their view that many of these funders, including George Roberts, venture philanthropists, and some charitable foundations, already employed the language of investment to describe their philanthropic support to recipients (see, e.g., Emerson et al. 1998).

SROI & the calculation of social enterprise value

Once the decision was made to represent the value of social enterprises through the transposition of the tool of Return on Investment, another decision to be made was how to capture the "social" value of social enterprises. What aspects of the social project would be included as the "return" on a philanthropic investment on a social enterprise?

Foremost, REDF staff wanted to ensure the inclusion of all types of value – economic and social – that were produced by social enterprise in the measuring device. This desire was motivated by both the social project of social enterprise (where financial viability was one central key to its purported appeal) and the communicative goal of justifying social enterprises to key stakeholders. First, the inclusion of the organization's economic profit, alongside that of its social value, was required in order to demonstrate the viability of REDF's portfolio of social enterprises. As one initial proponent of SROI explained, "we had to demonstrate to others that our social enterprises could stand on their own feet and make a go of it from the business side of things. At the time, there was an idea that social enterprises were nice in theory but weren't viable business models."

But, in addition – as noted earlier – REDF staff were cognizant of the mindset of the resource provider who sought as big a return as possible on their philanthropic investment. "If you're going to ask somebody to take either a subsidy or a below-market return on their capital," explained an early leader of REDF, "how do you think about the way to monetize the economic value of the social impacts so that you can talk about what the total performance was, not what the business is doing, or what the social enterprise was doing, but what the two together were creating, relative to value."

In order to calculate the total, "blended" benefit produced by social enterprises as the numerator in the SROI ratio, REDF employed the metric of money to capture both a social enterprise's economic profit and one specific measure of its social impact. Here, the total success of social enterprise was defined as the sum of its "economic value" and its "socio-economic value," as shown in

TABLE 3.2 *Types of value in SROI*

Type of value created	Metric	Definition
Economic	Enterprise value	Present value of excess cash generated by enterprise's business operations (excluding social operating expenses and subsidies)
Socio-economic	Social purpose value	Present value of projected social savings and new tax revenue generated by employees of social purpose enterprises less social operating expenses
Socio-economic	Blended value	Enterprise value + social purpose value − long-term debt
Social	-	-

Source: REDF (2000)

Table 3.2. In this case, the economic value of the social enterprise was defined as the "present value of excess cash generated by [the] enterprise's business operations" (REDF 2000). REDF extended great time and effort in collecting social enterprises' data on their economic performance.

This economic data was then added to the social performance of social enterprises. Here, REDF needed to convey the societal benefits that followed from the work of social enterprises in providing job training and employment opportunities to clients. They had a number of existing metrics available to them in the philanthropic world of nonprofits, including the count of a social enterprise's outputs (how many clients they had assisted) or the count of their outcomes (changes in clients' lives that could be attributed to the social enterprise). But, REDF staff saw themselves as constrained by their desire to assign a monetary value to the social benefits of social enterprises (in order to approximate the metric of Return on Investment) and by their desire to demonstrate the worth of social enterprises to government actors as potential funders of social enterprise. Ultimately, in REDF's worldview, it was government who was responsible for financing and addressing the problem of homelessness and so it was critical to demonstrate the value of social enterprises for it. For REDF, "the term 'society' [in the calculation of the social benefits of SROI] refers specifically to those governmental entities upon which the social 'cost' of poverty falls. Creating social and socio-economic value clearly is of benefit to individual program participants and communities and we also recognize that the immediate burden of poverty falls upon families and communities. However, the actual dollar expense of social and other programs accrues to the public sector which is supported by tax-payer dollars and, thus, society at large" (Emerson et al. 2000:141).

In result, REDF staff chose to measure the social impact of a social enterprise by reference to its "socio-economic value." Socio-economic value referred to the societal or collective benefits produced by a social enterprise. REDF's mission was to fund social enterprises that assisted members of the local homeless community in finding employment. To determine its "socio-economic value" or "social purpose value," a social enterprise would begin by collecting outcome data on its clients – tracking their salient attributes affected by participation in the program (e.g., labor force participation, wages, use of government programs, etc.) for two years following their exiting of the social enterprise's workforce development program. As one staff member recounted: "We asked [social enterprises' clients] the same series of questions across seven different outcome areas, including things like job stability – are they still in a job – income level, housing stability, their self-esteem, social support system, and their usage of various social services, like public services, such as emergency rooms, health clinics, food stamps, uh, at the time, what was called ASDC or TANF, which was, like, welfare dollars, disability – so we tried to track every six months, up to two years, for every single person hired into every enterprise in our portfolio across these seven different outcome areas."

Then, and unlike the tool of outcome measurement in the nonprofit sector, the calculation of SROI then required the monetization of those outcomes in terms of their benefits for the community as a whole as operationalized by the indicator of government savings.[23] A monetary value would be assigned to clients' outcomes in terms of either generating government income in the form of tax revenue (under the assumption that a client who was a paid member of the workforce would therefore pay income tax) and/or by generating government cost savings (under the assumption that a client who was a paid member of the workforce would no longer require public assistance or social service programs) (Emerson and Twersky 1996; Gair 2002).[24]

However, one consequence of using government savings as the measure of social enterprises' social value was the omission of the benefits of those organizations for individual clients. REDF staff called this third type of value produced by social enterprises, alongside economic value and socio-economic value, that of "social value."

Social Value is created when resources, inputs, processes or policies are combined to generate improvements in the lives of individuals or society as a whole. It is in this arena that most nonprofits justify their existence, and unfortunately it is at this level that one has the most difficulty measuring the true value created. Examples of Social Value creation may include such "products" as cultural arts performances, the pleasure of enjoying a hike in the woods or the benefit of living in a more just society ... Social Value can be found in anti-racism efforts, some aspects of community organizing, animal rights advocacy and folk art. It has intrinsic value, but can be difficult to agree upon or quantify (REDF 2000:12).

Despite recognizing its ontological existence as a type of social value, REDF omitted the measure of "social value" – changes to clients' lives – from the calculation of the total "return" of SROI. Managers omitted this data for methodological reasons. If the goal of SROI was to construct a measuring device that paralleled the rigor of the data (what one respondent called "real data, real credible data") produced for financial analysis in the stock market, then the problem with "social value" was that REDF staff did not see how it could be easily assigned a monetary value and so therefore aggregated with economic value and socio-economic value as another source of a social enterprise's total, "blended value." As one senior manager at REDF noted, "We were trying to be conservative and only using quantifiable, monetizable data, we inevitably ended up with an analysis that focused on savings to society as being the prime value [...] so if something could not be monetized, it really didn't get counted into that number." Another recalled the belief that "if we just capture the usage of public benefits, that would be easier to monetize and project out into the future."

SROI & money

Finally, as we have seen, SROI entails the monetization of the economic and the social worth of social enterprises. And the use of money as a measure of value has been understood by many social scientists as one indicator of the dominance of a market logic for organizations. In this view, as also noted in Chapter 1, the assignment of a dollar value to a good represents its perceived utility for individual consumers, typically as mediated by supply and demand for a specific product. And the use of money to capture other forms of personal or moral value is meant to result in the standardizing and abstracting of social relations. In this perspective, the employment of money subjects goods to economic rationalization, since money becomes the only standard for judging the worth of an object and other orders of worth are eliminated as a source of value. The presence of monetization, in other words, is seen as the ultimate signal that the logic of the private sector has come to dominate over other orientations of action (Titmuss 1971; Radin 2001).

Yet, this theoretical claim about money departs notably from why REDF chose to construct SROI so that it counted a social enterprise's social impact in dollar terms. REDF explicitly viewed the use of monetization in SROI as the optimal form by which to capture the social value of social enterprises in the eyes of potential resource providers. In this point, I draw from a broader discussion of the variable meaning of money in the moral market approach. As the work of Viviana Zelizer (1997, 2009) has shown, the use of money can serve many different forms and functions. Her research has demonstrated how individuals assign precise meanings to money, based on its source and/or intended use, in ways that limit its commensurability. Money's varying connotations are dependent upon careful consideration and construction by actors in specific and bounded social settings (Carruthers and Babb 1996; Fourcade 2011).

Similar processes were at work in REDF's development of SROI. First, as already noted, REDF leaders had constructed SROI as a way to convey the societal benefit of social enterprises to other actors, reflecting the communicative need that drove REDF's construction of SROI. They used money as the unit of measure in SROI (as opposed to other available measures from the nonprofit sector such as foundations' reliance on outputs or evaluation experts' employment of outcomes) for various reasons. Staff sought rigor in their count of social enterprises' value and viewed money as the most objective measure, paralleling given its status as the most prevalent and most easily understood unit of worth in contemporary society. Money was deemed the best medium to clearly and easily convey the positive outcomes of social enterprises, especially when compared to the qualitative and anecdotal data often used by foundations (see, e.g., Gair 2009). And, as one initial staff member of REDF recalled, "the use of monetization was premised on a belief that the value of these social mission activities was being discounted if all that we were getting was sort of the story side of things ... if you could show that there was value being created for, and or cost savings being realized by doing something, wouldn't that be appealing to a wider swath of the community?" In addition, REDF staff reckoned that the use of money to represent social benefits was not new in the public and nonprofit sectors. CBA – a legitimating justification for REDF's employment of a ratio of return on investment – had its start in the public sector, as a means for government actors to evaluate competing policy options. And CBA was premised on the count of the monetized benefits of a social program's desired impact. In other words, in the eyes of SROI's proponents, the use of money to count social good did not violate the premises of the nonprofit sector. As one consultant to REDF at the time recounted, money as a currency was how "government agencies already think about and measure the impact of its policies, going all the way back to how the federal government made decisions about Great Society programs. Money just made sense in a lot of ways."

In all, despite the existence of constrained creativity in the absence of social value in SROI, the case of this measuring device demonstrates the ways in which actors are capable of transposing market metrics and measures to pursue social ends. Just as the social project of the field highlighted the use of market methods to achieve social ends, so too did these value entrepreneurs draw from their varied and extensive valuation repertoire in order to creatively employ indicators of a market logic in order to convey the social benefits of social enterprises for society.

Notes

1. The actual title of the panel has been changed.
2. Admittedly, a range of other measuring devices exist for social enterprises, as the field has not coalesced completely around the use of SROI as in the case of the nonprofit sector and outcome measurement. Other valuation tools for social enterprises present in the United States include the Balanced Scorecard, the Acumen Fund's BACO Ratio, and the Robin Hood Foundation's cost-benefit ratio. Yet, consistently,

throughout my interviews, and as evident in a review of scholarly literature and advisory texts and in my field research, SROI was most commonly and consistently discussed as the prevalent valuation tool available to members of this field.

3. More technically, SROI consists of the calculation (over a ten-year period) of the ratio of the dollars invested in a social enterprise to the socio-economic value (governmental dollar value of savings and tax revenues produced by the social enterprise) produced added to the estimated economic value of the social enterprise (revenue excluding operating costs and subsidiaries), with future benefits discounted to their present value. To obtain that data, REDF calculated the economic value of a social enterprise by gathering extensive "change data" (including employment status, housing situation, criminal history, and income sources) on employees for at least twenty-four months and then calculating the economic development value created for public agencies' expenditures and revenue by using government documents (REDF 2000).

4. This chapter draws from interviews with REDF staff, interns, and consultants that I conducted alone and with Matthew Hall and Yuval Millo, as part of a stand-alone research project that compared the formation of SROI in the United States and the United Kingdom (Hall, Millo, and Barman 2015).

5. The term of "social enterprise" has been subject to a variety of multiple and competing definitions (Galaskiewicz and Barringer 2012). For some, the term of "social enterprise" is used to describe organizations that employ "transformational methods and innovative leadership" to address social and/or environmental problems across the nonprofit and private sectors (Dees and Anderson 2003). In Europe, the concept of social enterprise instead refers to private social cooperatives or associations in the voluntary sector (often recognized as a legal form) emerging to meet social and economic problems. Typically, social enterprises in Europe involve members' employment or participation in the organization and the distribution of any economic benefits to those members (Kerlin 2009).

6. In this form, social enterprises also are known by a variety of other terms, including for-profit social ventures, social purpose enterprises, mission-based businesses, or social businesses, among others.

7. And, while social enterprises may employ the Fair Trade model in terms of obtaining supplies, it may not be their only focus in terms of social good. Correspondingly, Fair Trade products may be sold by mainstream businesses, without making them social enterprises.

8. As other scholars have shown, many social enterprises are not reliant solely on market revenue, particularly when they are first formed. Instead, they have relied on philanthropic support from foundations (Child 2015).

9. Because social enterprises are reliant on market revenue, proponents also sought to distinguish them from traditional corporations. Businesses historically have exercised their social responsibility through corporate philanthropy (the donation of a percentage of profits for charitable purposes). By the 1990s, as discussed in Chapter 5, some companies also began to consider the social and/or environmental implications of their production processes for stakeholders (what is often called Corporate Social Responsibility). In contrast, a social enterprise was understood to produce social value through the organization of its business model, with no or little concern for the larger implications of how that product was produced and its

effect on stakeholders. As one proponent of social enterprise outlined: "Social enterprises *directly* confront social needs through their products and services rather than *indirectly* through socially responsible business practices such as corporate philanthropy, equitable wages and environmentally friendly operations" (Institute for Social Entrepreneurs 2008).

10. While some nonprofits that rely on market-based revenue classify themselves as social enterprises, some key exceptions are hospitals and universities, which overwhelmingly rely on fee-for-service income but are rarely classified as social enterprises.

11. Social enterprises are distinct in their organizational identity from other hybrid organizations that merge market and mission, such as B Corps (Cooney 2012). While social enterprises are characterized by their provision of equitable access to the market for disadvantaged groups as their solution to social inequality, B Corps are companies that are publicly owned and that legally allowed by some state governments to recognize their duty to shareholders and stakeholders – they pursue profit via the firm's adoption of adequate policies concerning accountability, employees, consumers, community, and environment.

12. Most histories of social enterprise trace their earliest history back to workers' cooperatives that were formed in the heyday of the Industrial Revolution (Kerlin 2009).

13. Historically, a number of nonprofits have always relied on commercial revenue alongside philanthropic support and government funding (Hall 1992), such as universities and hospitals, but social enterprises are also distinguished by their use of market exchange as a means to social betterment for their beneficiaries.

14. Not all members of the nonprofit sector have encouraged the use of market methods to achieve social goods. Some funders and observers note nonprofits' lack of adequate business training and the high rate of failure (Eikenberry and Kluver 2004).

15. More broadly, the use of CBA, central to SROI has been picked up by other philanthropic funders. Beginning in 2004, the Robin Hood Foundation, another early venture philanthropy foundation, began to base funding on the estimation of a ratio of the monetized benefits to costs in order to make funding decisions in four portfolios: Jobs & Economic Security, Education, Early Childhood and Youth, and Survival (Tuan 2008). From 1998 to 2005, the Rockefeller Foundation engaged in the Provenex Fund (the Program Venture Experiment Fund) – an early effort to make for-profit investment in early stage double bottom line organizations. It sought to measure its impact by using a cost-benefit tool to assess its impact (Boston Consulting Group 2002).

16. Similarly, in 2002, the Calvert Foundation developed an online "SROI calculator" for potential investors in its Community Investment Note portfolio organizations (Olsen and Galimidi 2008). And, through the 2000s, the Global Social Venture Competition, a global MBA student plan competition for social enterprises, required participants to employ SROI to demonstrate their submission's proposed impact.

17. Somewhat surprisingly, the diffusion of SROI across both the nonprofit and social enterprise fields has occurred despite the fact that its initial proponent – REDF itself –ceased using SROI to evaluate its portfolio of social enterprises after only one year of use. The organization professed to do so for a multiple reasons, including criticisms based on SROI's omission of non-monetizable forms of social value, the amount of resources required to conduct SROI, and the inability to ascertain the

attribution of social enterprises in achieving social change, among other problems (Javitz 2008). In fact, REDF then started to employ outcome data on social enterprises' clients as its main measure of social value (Gair 2009). However, given the growing popularity of SROI in the fields of nonprofits and social enterprises both in the US and elsewhere, REDF is now considering the re-implementation of SROI in a modified form.

18. As predicted by literature that has emphasized moral resistance to the use of money, the monetization of social welfare was particularly troublesome for some members of this field. Several respondents noted that assigning a monetary value to some attribute of a social enterprise's clients was to them ethically question-able – that it created, in the one words of a senior staff at a charitable foundation, an "irreducible discomfort." In a history of social impact assessment, one con-sulting firm that works with nonprofits and social enterprises – similarly con-cluded in an internal document (provided to me by a study participant) that "while a number of organizations adopt SROI analysis, others express concern about reducing dynamic and complex human experience to a financial measure."

19. REDF later became incorporated as a stand-alone nonprofit.

20. Other venture philanthropy entities followed in quick succession, with the majority founded after 1998 (Moody 2008).

21. In publications and in interviews, REDF identified several problems with how foundations assessed the success of their funding of nonprofits. Foundations relied on the qualitative and anecdotal measurement of funded charities' outputs (of the number of services provided or clients served), they engaged in the retrospective assessment of impact after funding was concluded, they were directed by funders' needs rather than by nonprofit managers' use of ongoing learning, and they unduly focused on a single program's results rather than the nonprofit's entire performance (Emerson and Twersky 1996). In one conversation, a senior staff person at the time recalled how disparagingly REDF staff viewed foundations at the time. Foundations would select a nonprofit to fund solely "because it pulls on their heartstrings." In the eyes of another REDF employee, foundations were not making their "decisions based on data." In short, REDF rejected foundations' historical mode of valuation as a viable technique by which to measure the success of its own efforts with social enterprises.

22. "In fact, neither HEW analysts nor any others have made much effort to refine estimates of the present value of income increases attributable to health and education programs" (Rivlin 1971:56).

23. REDF's emphasis on government saving is curious in that a reliance on government savings as a measure of "benefit" is not inherent to the method of CBA – another more dominant version of CBA entails the calculation of shadow prices for those individuals affected by a policy or program (Karoly 2008).

24. Socio-economic value occurs when an entity "makes use of resources, inputs, or processes; increasing the value of these inputs, and by then generating cost savings for the public system or environment of which the entity is a part. These cost savings are potentially realized in decreased public dollar expenditures and partially in increased revenues to the public sector, in the form of additional taxes" (Emerson et al. 1998:138).

PART II

MARKET MONITORS

4

Morals and finance

Socially Responsible Investing

In 1971, two employees of the United Methodist Church involved in the anti-Vietnam War movement decided that investors should have the opportunity to enact their values in their financial decisions. They created Pax World Fund, one of the first mutual funds in the United States to engage in "Socially Responsible Investing (SRI)" through its employment of both social and financial criteria to select securities. Pax World Fund possessed an anti-war mission – it screened out companies producing weapons from consideration of investment. By 1980, Pax World Fund also had banned investment in newer "instruments of war," such as electronics, computers, aircraft manufacturers, and nuclear power, as well as the "sin stocks" of liquor, tobacco, and gambling. Today, Pax World Investments continues its commitment to SRI with over $3.2 billion in assets under management.[1]

In the 1980s, the carpet industry in India came under intense scrutiny for its extensive use of child labor. In response, the South Asian Coalition of Child Servitude, a local NGO, decided to pursue a new strategy to produce industry wide change. The organization worked with local government, industry leaders and international NGOs, including UNICEF and the Indo-German Export Promotion Program, to form the Rugmark Initiative in 1994. As a case of Corporate Social Responsibility (CSR), Rugmark would provide a label to any carpet produced in a factory that did not use child labor, as monitored and certified by the NGO. The goal was to provide consumers with the means to select carpets made in a socially responsible manner and to boycott other products. Since then, GoodWeave (as Rugmark is now known) has provided its label to over 11 million carpets (Seidman 2007).

In each of these cases, an assortment of private individuals and organizations came together in the belief that businesses' pursuit of shareholder return alone was not acceptable. SRI and CSR each brought a concern for social welfare into the market by pointing out the consequences of firms' activity, including their products and how those products were produced, for society. Rather than turn to government to regulate firms in this regard, these actors – investors, nonprofits, employees, customers, and others – attempted to privately change the behavior of big business. Emerging out of the new social movements of the 1960s and 1970s, these two fields employed a range of market-based methods to pressure firms to behave in more socially and environmentally responsible ways.

In contrast to Chapter 2 and 3, which focused on organizations in or at the edge of the nonprofit sector, the book's focus now turns to a consideration of social value in the market. It examines these two moments when mainstream corporations became targeted for their lack of ability to deliver social value. Drawing from archival research, document analysis, and interviews with key participants, these two chapters provide a historical overview of SRI and CSR, as two "market monitors" who worked to mitigate corporations' harmful social and environmental effects and to promote socially beneficial products and production processes. In each field, social activists have held large US corporations, such as Eastman Kodak, GM, Levi-Strauss, and Wal-Mart, to account for their impact on society.

But, how did proponents of SRI and CSR seek to alter firms' conduct so that the pursuit of social welfare was to become as equally important as the pursuit of profit? Given the dominance of a market logic in the private sector, where the quest for financial profit was prized above all else, how did these actors attempt to demonstrate the worth of the social dimension of firms' performance? The measurement of companies' social value in and of itself – without reference to its monetary value – was central to each of these social projects. While these market monitors differed in their social project's diagnosis and denunciation of businesses' wrongs, they each employed the valuation instrument of the rating in order to gauge corporations' social performance. And proponents of SRI and CSR both publicly deployed those assessments as a form of private regulation in order to pressure companies to change their behavior.[2]

In this chapter, I first locate the turn to private regulation in the growth of the field of SRI. By the 1960s and 1970s, there was a growing awareness in the United States of the power and scale of corporations in society coupled with an emerging belief that companies had become unmoored from external controls such as government regulation. As a market-based social movement, SRI was an organized effort to respond to those challenges, driven by actors' beliefs that social problems could be addressed by financial activity and an insistence that economic and social value were not antithetical. Drawing from their expertise in finance, these value entrepreneurs constructed ratings that combined firms' financial and social performance to facilitate socially oriented investment and to influence corporations' behavior.

In contrast, as I show in Chapter 5, the field of CSR emerged in the 1990s as an outcome of broader concern about the impact of globalization on workers in developing nations. Again, the ratings of multinational corporations' social performance was central to the construction of this project, but what was to be gauged as social value and for what purpose diverged markedly from the case of SRI. Here, as part of the broader anti-sweatshop movement, proponents held apparel and footwear companies and their brands accountable for the labor conditions present in the firms in their supply chain. To achieve that end, members of multi-stakeholder coalitions drew from competing valuation repertoires in order to demonstrate corporations' conformity with contested expectations of good corporate governance, distinct from the financial implications of their social performance.

A HISTORY OF THE SOCIAL RESPONSIBILITY OF BUSINESS

To fully understand the goals of these two market monitors requires placing their efforts within the historical context of firms' social responsibility in the United States. For much of this time, expectations of business veered between two poles, with firms viewed either as solely profit producers or as social citizens. With the growth of public corporations in the late nineteenth century and the emergence of a large scale industrial economy, the corporation was first framed as a profit-producing vehicle for shareholders, based on a legal view of the firm as a "nexus of contracts." Such a view of business dominated the late nineteenth century. "Finance capitalism" during the Gilded Age consisted of the formation of monopolies and the rise of corporate barons like Andrew Carnegie, JP Morgan, and William F. Rockefeller, with little government regulation of the economy or protection of workers' rights (Davis 2009; Mizruchi 2013).

Beginning in the late nineteenth century, the idea of corporate philanthropy emerged – the obligation of companies to distribute a portion of its profits, products, or employees' volunteer time for charitable purposes. In the late 1800s, some managers sought to respond to the threat of unionization, the specter of socialism and concern over the scale of corporations in American life during the Gilded Age. Firms strove to prevent the organization of labor, increase public trust, and fend off government oversight by voluntarily investing in workers and the communities in which production took place. Motivated also by a desire to increase production rates, corporations engaged in "welfare capitalism" in order to improve the living conditions of their workers via the provision of health, housing, and education (Hall 1992; Davis 2009). The company town of Pullman, Illinois, is one highly cited example of welfare capitalism. George Pullman, the founder and president of the Pullman Palace Car Company, built the factory town in the 1880s as a community of residence for his workers. The company not only designed and constructed the municipality – its buildings and infrastructure – but also set rules of appropriate behavior, including banning alcohol and determining the appropriate moral bounds of public entertainment (Buder 1967).

Yet, by the 1920s, corporations took on a new role in American society. With the growing autonomy of managers, a new ethos emerged, whereby corporate leaders "believed that it was in their long-term interest to have a well-functioning society" (Mizruchi 2013:8). Lasting through the 1960s, managerial capitalism was contingent upon the growth of the American economy. Managers recognized their firm's reliance on American workers as consumers for corporate well-being and supported the government's Keynesian provision of a social safety net, as well its economic and social regulation of the economy. They voluntarily paid their taxes and proved health insurance and pension plans to employees (Davis 2009; Mizruchi 2013). In 1922, Edward A. Filene (223–224), the owner of a department store in Boston, wrote that "real service in business consists in making and selling merchandise of reliable quality for the lowest practically possible price, providing the merchandise is made and sold under just conditions."

Corporate philanthropy expanded under managerial capitalism. It first occurred on a broad scale in the local community with the formation of the Community Chest in the early twentieth century. With support and funding from corporations via donations and their employees through payroll deduction, the Community Chest (the predecessor of today's United Way) operated at the level of a town or city; it fundraised and coordinated local nonprofits' provision of service (Barman 2006). Regulatory changes then further institutionalized and incentivized corporate philanthropy. In 1935, the federal government allowed firms to deduct charitable gifts of up to five percent of their taxable income, with the goal of encouraging corporate philanthropy. In the 1950s, a series of legal decisions and regulatory decisions at the state level further broadened the acceptable scope of firms' charitable deeds.[3] In result, companies began to engage in corporate philanthropy not just in support of their local United Way but also by creating their own foundations and giving offices (Hall 1992).

MARKET MONITORS: THE TURN TO PRIVATE REGULATION

Yet, broader changes in society during the 1960s and early 1970s put the dominance of managerial capitalism in question. The social movements of the time, including the civil rights movement, the women's movement, and the environmental movement, reflected a growing skepticism of the establishment, coupled with anger over government and business support for the Vietnam War (Carson 1962; Nader and Green 1973). Beginning in the late 1960s, a range of private actors whom I call "market monitors" – including nonprofits, investors, consumers, and multilateral organizations – sought to intervene in the economy by addressing firms' effects on society and the environment. Firms were held to account for these negative consequences and they were encouraged by critics to develop socially and environmentally beneficial products and production processes. These market monitors rejected the premises of managerial capitalism – that the interests of firms were the same as the interests of their consumers, employees, and the community.

Yet, for market monitors to hold firms to account in these regards was not new. From the nineteenth century and on, social activists have been concerned about the effects of capitalism on society and the environment. They have long engaged in what scholars have called market-based social movements, where contentious activism has been aimed at affecting change in the economy (Bartley 2007b; Seidman 2007; Soule 2009). Historically, the target of these market-based social movements has been the government, which has been deemed responsible for implementing laws to limit firms' negative exter nalities for workers, consumers, and society, including unsafe working condi tions, dangerous products, and pollution. Central to the Progressive Era, for instance, was a push by social activists for government regulation of products to ensure consumer safety. In the 1970s, pressure from the consumer activist movement led to the federal government's creation of the Environmental Protection Agency, the Equal Employment Opportunity Commission, and the Occupational Safety and Health Administration (Glickman 2009; King and Pearce 2010).

Theoretically, this move of non-state actors to intervene in the free market constitutes a case of Polanyi's (2001 [1944]) concept of the "double movement." As noted in Chapter 1, Polanyi's goal was to understand the historical conditions of the formation of a capitalist economy in the West. On the one hand, he noted that the central and key defining characteristics of the market, including an emphasis on self-interest and the use of money as a medium of exchange had come to govern social relations in non-market spaces. The economy had moved into society more broadly. On the other hand, the historical establishment of a free market – including the construction of land, labor, and money as "fictitious commodities" – required the simultaneous or double move of government, as a separate societal actor, into the economy. For the economy to function, the state needed to construct appropriate laws to produce and govern appropriate behavior by actors in the private sector. In other words, the market is not capable of its own "self-regulation" but instead requires public regulation in order to function (Block 2003).

However, the rise of various modes of non-governmental efforts to sanction corporations in the economy since the late 1960s constitutes a new form of a double movement, what other scholars have called "private regulation" or "private governance" (Bartley 2007b; Büthe 2010). Rather than turn to the government to impose new laws that ensure corporations' protection of consumers, society, and the environment, these new market-based movements now target businesses themselves and attempt to pressure firms to voluntarily adopt their guidelines of socially and environmentally appropriate behavior. Two recent efforts to impose these new private standards on firms in the contemporary economy have been SRI and Corporate Social Responsibility, alongside consumer boycotts, ethical consumption, and popular protests often oriented around specific products or production processes (King and Pearce 2010).[4] These market monitors sought to influence business' social conduct not via appeals to the state to intervene in the economy, but through non-governmental, voluntary, and market-based interventions both in the United States and abroad. The "private regulation" of business relies on the construction of market incentives to hold companies to a standard of good behavior (Bartley 2007b). In both cases of SRI and CSR, these market monitors sought to direct firms' behavior towards the production of social good without recourse to public regulation. So how precisely did they achieve their goals? How did they seek to hold business accountable for their social responsibility through private regulation?

RATINGS AS A MEASURING DEVICE

For these market monitors, the measurement of firms' social value, in and of itself and distinct from its shareholder value, was central to their political efforts. As I have shown, value entrepreneurs in each field rated firms' social performance according to their own specific criterion of value. These market monitors evaluated companies in terms of whether their products, policies, and/or practices met the desired expectations of good social conduct. They then publicly rated or ranked firms according to whether or how well they had met those external expectations.

As a measuring device, a rating entails the assignment of an entity to a position or value on a specific scale. Ratings can take various forms: the allocation of a letter grade, a percentage out of one hundred or, more simply, the designation of pass or fail. And ratings can take a number of different names and forms, including certification, standards, and rankings, among others. The ability to engage in the act of rating is contingent upon several prior steps. It relies on the work of a third party to engage in the task of the valuation of other entities. The construction of a rating system entails the creation of a category of similar objects that are deemed equivalent, it entails the reduction of a variety of disparate qualities about those objects to a single salient criterion, and it necessitates the construction of an objective scale by which the object can be assessed. In result, the act of rating necessarily involves the construction of commensurability – all relevant entities can be compared according to a single scale or standard (Espeland and Stevens 1998; Karpik 2010; Bartley 2011).

In social science literature, the purpose of the rating (or ranking) as a tool of valuation is debated. On the one hand, economists typically have seen ratings as facilitating the work of markets. In a market for a specific commodity, the monetary value of that good is expected to be generated out of price comparisons between buyers and sellers. However, some markets contain goods characterized by "singularity," in that they are difficult to evaluate and compare given that they are valued for their quality (rather than simply by their price or technical attributes) – a criteria notoriously difficult to assess. Examples of singular goods include wine, movies, education, and healthcare, among others. In markets with singular goods, third party arbiters (often experts with detailed knowledge of the market) step in between buyers and sellers to generate "judgment devices" – tools, measures, and practices that provide independent evaluation of the quality of the goods in question (Karpik 2010). One example of a judgment device is a rating system, which is then employed by consumers to compare the quality of the range of available products in the market. Notable cases of ratings based on singular goods include TripAdvisor's ranking of hotels and *US News and World Report's* ranking of law schools (Espeland and Sauder 2007; Jeacle and Carter 2011).

In contrast, other sociologists have been more sanguine about the purpose of ratings, often based on the study of fields and spaces outside the market. These scholars have instead viewed ratings as one instance among many of the use of numbers in the establishment and perpetuation of relationships of power. Ratings can be implemented towards the control of others (Foucault 1979, 1994; Power 1994). As suggested in Chapter 2, one mode of authority can be not by the direct exercise of force but instead based on "governing by numbers" (Miller 2001). Rankings and ratings serve as a "technology of governance" by creating a normative classification system which assigns a score or value to each entity and then ranks them as to their worth compared to a standard of performance and/or to others. The result is reactivity – those actors who are being evaluated know that they are being rated and, equally critically, that others will use such ratings in their decision-making. Those under evaluation will then voluntarily act in ways to improve their performance and so conform to the norms of the ratings system (Foucault 1979, 1994; Espeland and Sauder 2007). And, while this technology of governance via numbers was historically formulated by government as a mode of discipline over citizens and then over agencies in the public and nonprofit sectors (as outlined in Chapter 2), the use of ratings as an intentional strategy to exert control as mode of governance has been taken up in other fields as well, such as the market (Townley 1993), academia (Gendron 2013), and education (Hallett 2010).

SRI

To be able to explain the employment of ratings by these two sets of market monitors requires attention to the nature of the social projects offered by proponents of each field. The first move by market monitors to insert social concerns into the private sector occurred with the growth of SRI in the late 1960s – a field that continues on today, albeit in a modified form. SRI, also known as social, ethical, moral, or integrated investing, concerns a range of investment activities that mix "money and morality" (Diltz 1995). To begin,

SRI is often framed in contrast to mainstream investing, where investors purchase equity (typically ownership in the form of stocks) in a company with the intent of acquiring future financial return on that investment. In conventional investing, investors rely on the criteria of risk and return in order to generate optimal economic gain. Estimations of economic return and risk are based on the evaluation of a stock's financial characteristics. Investors are assumed to pursue the highest level of economic return on an investment based on a particular level of risk. They do so, following the tenets of economic theory, by investing in a diversified portfolio of stocks in order to distribute risk and increase the possibility of return.

In contrast, SRI is commonly defined as financial investment that incorporates both economic and social considerations for the pursuit of both shareholder and social return. Like conventional investing, SRI involves the purchase of equity in stocks with the goal of future financial gain, often as part of a portfolio of investments. However, SRI also involves conscious and deliberate decision on the part of individuals and institutions to approach their investment practices based on social criteria as well. It relies on a view of investment as a private, non-governmental means to effect social change through the market (Vogel 1978; Domini and Kinder 1984).

To achieve these double bottom-line goals of shareholder and social return, SRI is composed of three central market-based methods: community investing, shareholder activism, and social screening. Community investment originates from concern for the "low-income, at-risk communities who have difficulty accessing [the market] through traditional channels" (Schueth 2003:191).[5] It is intended to provide a market-based supplement to the work of government, including the Community Reinvestment Act of 1977, a US federal law that requires banks to eliminate the practice of discriminatory lending (also called "redlining") and to make investments in disadvantaged communities. Community investing consists of direct investment in locally based community development financial vehicles, including community development banks, community development credit unions, community development loan funds and community development venture capital funds. These organizations then engage in the financing of low-income housing, small business development, and/or loans and guarantees to individuals and institutions in disadvantaged communities that have historically been denied resources from traditional financial entities (Schueth 2003).

Secondly, SRI in the form of shareholder activism consists of actors using their equity stake in a firm to engage with management in order to alter corporations' policies. Shareholder activism can take a variety of forms including proxy voting, the creation of shareholder proposals, divestment, dialogue with management, and/or publicity campaigns. Beginning in 1970, qualified shareholders became able to submit proposals on the company's proxy statements for vote by all shareholders at the company's annual meeting (Profitt and Spicer 2006). One of the first historical uses of the shareholder proposal was

Ralph Nader's placement of a shareholder resolution on the GM proxy ballot to include consumer advocates on the corporation's board of directors (Hutton, D'Antonio and Johnsen 1998). From 2008 through 2010, more than two hundred institutions – including public funds, labor funds, religious investors, foundations, and endowments – and investment management firms filed or co-filed proposals concerning specific social or environmental issues (Social Investment Forum 2010).

Finally, the most prevalent form of SRI (in terms of total dollars invested) is social screening (Social Investment Forum 2010). This form of SRI alters the traditional means by which the screening of investments takes place in mainstream investing. Typically, investors evaluate the appeal of stocks based on just economic criteria – the assessment of a stock's risk and return dependent on investors' financial objectives. With SRI, social screening instead includes not only economic considerations but also the assessment of stocks based on investors' ethical preferences. Initially with SRI, social screening meant negative or exclusionary screening – the elimination of corporations from investment based on the social and environmental consequences of a product. In 1928, for example, the Pioneer Group created the first "sin" screen by excluding companies that produced alcohol or tobacco from consideration of investment (Domini and Kinder 1984).

THE HISTORY OF SRI

The origins of SRI are traced back to the earlier financial practices of religious communities, including Methodists and Quakers, who attached moral conditions or restrictions to their financial activities. Friends Fiduciary, for example, was founded in 1898 to provide financial assistance to organizations in the Quaker community based on the principles of peace, simplicity, integrity, and justice. SRI then appeared as a strategy to pursue social justice in multiple social movements of the 1960s and 1970s. It emerged as a result of not only political changes but also alterations in the structure of the stock market.

For one, community investment and shareholder activism were key components of various social movements. The Civil Rights movement provided one of the very first instances of shareholder action took place in 1967. A coalition of local community activists led by Saul Alinsky purchased shares in Eastman Kodak in order to protect the company's minority hiring practices in the Rochester, New York area (Domini and Kinder 1984; Schueth 2003). The resurgence of consumer activism in the 1960s was also central to the growth of shareholder activism. As noted earlier in this chapter, this long-time social movement was directed towards ensuring the quality, safety, and cost of consumer goods through both appeals for public regulation and private, market-based strategies (Glickman 2009). The Project on Corporate Responsibility, with support of Ralph Nader, used a proxy proposal to address the lack of diversity on General Motors' board and to create a Committee for Corporate Responsibility, which included membership from the project, the United Auto Workers, and the board (Alperson, Marlin, Schorsch, and Will 1991; Hutton et al. 1998). Protests against the Vietnam War also motivated the use of shareholder activism. From 1942 to 1970, the Securities and Exchange Commission had permitted proxy proposals by shareholders but had forbidden proposals concerned with social issues. It was not until 1968 when the Medical Committee for Human Rights sought to challenge Dow Chemical's production of napalm for use in Vietnam through the use of a proxy proposal. While initially forbidden by the SEC, the group successfully sued in federal court, opening the way for shareholder activism (Profitt and Spicer 2006).

Political activists' use of shareholder activism with corporations then drew the attention of institutional investors who held a growing power in the stock market. Institutional investors are actors who manage and invest pooled investment assets, such as banks, insurance companies, public and private pension funds, labor unions, and religious organizations. As one type of institutional investor, the assets of all private and public pension funds grew exponentially in the 1970s, from $21.4 billion in 1950 to $619.1 billion by 1979 (Barth and Cordes 1981). In result, the proportion of the average firm's equity controlled by institutional investors, as opposed to individual investors, increased substantially during this time, from 15.8 percent in 1965 to 42.7 percent in 1986 (Useem 1993).

Many religious groups, ranging from local churches to national denominations, sought to enact their moral beliefs through their financial practices. In 1967, the Unitarian Universalist Association adopted an Investment Policy that required the organization to "exercise the power represented by the Association's ownership of common stock as an effective instrument for promoting social justice" (Unitarian Universalist Association 2014). In 1970, the United Church of Christ recommended that a portion of its unrestricted program funds be directed towards socially responsible investments (Bruyn 1991). As noted earlier, the first SRI-themed mutual fund was the Pax World Fund, which was motivated by the desire of some members of the United Methodist church not to invest in companies profiting from the Vietnam War. The Interfaith Center on Corporate Responsibility, a research and advocacy center organized by and for religious institutional investors, was formed in 1970. Its mission has been to use the "lens of faith" to build a "more just and sustainable world by integrating social values into corporate and investor actions" (Interfaith Center for Corporate Responsibility 2014). As late as 1995, religious investors were still a significant force in the field, providing 30 percent of all socially responsible investment funds (Social Investment Forum 1995).

Similarly foundations and universities began to view their investments in a political light (Powers 1971; Longstreth and Rosenbloom 1973; Alperson et al. 1991). In 1967, the Ford Foundation enacted a new policy by which it would use a small percentage of its capital (what is often called a "Program Related Investment") to invest in economic development vehicles in disadvantaged neighborhoods (Bruyn 1991). In addition, many large universities including Yale, Harvard, and MIT among others, began considering or moving forward with socially oriented investment. Harvard University, for instance, developed an Advisory Committee on Shareholder Responsibility in 1972 (Harvard University 1971; Simon, Powers, and Gunnemann 1972). To facilitate their investment decisions, an assortment of large foundations and prominent universities then formed the Investor Responsibility Research Center in 1972 as a research center that could provide guidance on investment (Alperson et al. 1991).

Separately, some institutional investors began to apply social constraints to their investments, as part of a broader shift away from managerial capitalism and towards shareholder oversight of firms (Davis 2009). Historically, most pension funds had been managed by employers, including corporations and governments, or by financial institutions in the name of the funds' employee contributors. Investors also had abided by the "Wall Street Rule," the belief that investors should abide by managers' decisions. If investors disagreed, they would sell their shares – what was known as the "Wall Street Walk" (Bruyn 1991). In contrast, union activism and federal legislation in the 1970s led to employees' growing control over the direction of their investments (Barth and Cordes 1981). Given a realization of the growing power of pension funds in the economy, the AFL-CIO began to review existing investment policies with an eye to their alignment with pro-union principles. It adopted a series of policies, beginning in the late 1960s, which encouraged the investment of union-negotiated pension funds into union friendly projects (Barth and Cordes 1981; Bruyn 1991). At the federal level, legal changes also encouraged the growing participation of pension fund managers in the investment process. The Employee Retirement Income Security Act of 1974 required that pension musts be operated "solely in the interest of plan participants and beneficiaries" (Gray 1983:1).

As a different type of investor, individual investors were also expressing an interest in SRI. Their number had grown exponentially beyond the wealthy with the emergence of portable defined contribution pension plans (such as 401ks and IRAs) and the resulting growth of mutual funds and retail investors in the 1980s (Davis 2009). These new investors were those who had come of age during the Civil Rights and anti-war movements, who continued to be personally engaged in politics, and who now possessed the necessary financial capital to invest in the stock market (Schlesinger 1984; Kinder, Lydenberg, and Domini 1994). The impression at the time was that these socially responsible investors were those "people who grew up as activists in the 1960s are emerging as adults with capital for investment in the 1980s. Many of these people, some of whom never envisioned themselves to be providers of capital for the industrial complex, are anxious to ensure that their new participation in finance does not violate their hard-fought political principles" (Rosentiel 1983).

Finally, the case of South Africa sparked further engagement with SRI and was widely perceived as a triumph of divestment as a political tactic. SRI in the form of shareholder activism formed part of the broader use of the boycott as a means to pressure the South African government to end its policy of apartheid. In 1973, the Episcopal Church first called on General Motors to exert pressure for the end of apartheid in South Africa. Continued outrage over apartheid led many institutional investors, including universities, churches, and public pension funds, to voluntarily divest from companies involved in South Africa. A number of local and state pension funds were legally prevented from investing in companies doing business in South Africa by local and state laws (Kristol 1985). The success of the divestment movement in leading to the end of apartheid in 1993 was widely understood to catalyze the field of SRI and led to a growth in SRI-themed investments (Brill and Reder 1993; Social Investment Forum 1995).

In all, the growing embrace of SRI among individual and institutional investors led to the construction of a market infrastructure that facilitated the institutionalization of SRI. Finance professionals formed a number of SRI investment vehicles, including investment advising firms, mutual and money market funds, and portfolio management companies. New, non-religiously oriented SRI mutual funds were formed during this time, including Dreyfus Third Century (1972), Franklin Research & Development Corporation (1982), Parnassus Fund (1984), and KLD (1988), as were money market funds, including Calvert Social Investment Fund (1982) and Working Assets Fund (1983). An advisory infrastructure soon developed for the field, including the formation of the Council on Economic Priorities in 1969, the Investor Responsibility Research Center in 1972, the Social Investment Forum in 1981, and the Council for Institutional Investors in 1985. Given the rapid growth of resources directed to SRI, a wider and more traditional array of finance institutions also began to offer SRI-oriented financial vehicles for investors, including TIAA-CREF and Vanguard (Guay, Doh, and Sinclair 2004).

The growth of SRI-focused institutional and individual investors also led some conventional investment firms who managed the resources of these investors based strictly on financial considerations to also engage in SRI. Franklin Management, a conventional financial management firm, began offering ethical investment at the request of institutional investors at the University of California Berkeley, which then contributed to the formation of a SRI-oriented affiliate, Franklin Research & Development (Rosenstiel 1983). Similarly, Alice Teppler Marlin, the founder of the Council on Economic Priorities, initially had worked as a securities analyst and portfolio manager at a conventional investment firm. Asked by a local synagogue to select a "peace portfolio" for them, she then convinced her managers to advertise the firm's work with socially oriented investing, ultimately to great success (Alperson et al. 1991). By 1985, $55 million invested in total in the United States according to social principles (Bronstein 1985). By 2000, funds invested according to the principles of SRI had grown to over $2 trillion dollars and today, most accounts estimate investments with SRI criteria to constitute about between ten and twenty percent of all investments in the Global North (Capelle-Blancard and Monjon 2012).

THE SOCIAL PROJECT OF SRI

Located in the private sector but based on a critique of the market, the field of SRI was premised on a distinct social project with a particular definition of social value. At its core, the social project of SRI relied on the use of a market logic in a number of ways. First, it focused on corporations as a potential type of social purpose organization that were capable of delivery of social value through their sale of products, geographical location, and/or as a result of its corporate conduct, although SRI was based on a subjective definition of social value as to which types of products, places, and/or policies were salient. In this conceptualization, market activity, in the form of investment, would lead to corporate change and so the generation of social value via three different but complimentary routes. In result, the social project at the heart of SRI was contingent upon a view of the market as composed of a plurality of values, all centered on a faith in firms as potential vehicles of social good.

Corporations as social purpose organizations

As a means to social change, proponents of SRI highlighted companies as producers of social good. Thus, in contrast to the nonprofit and social enterprise fields, actors in the market were perceived as the vehicles by which greater societal welfare could be achieved, alongside the work of government and nonprofits. In this view, companies could produce social value through three distinct means: their products, place, and policies. First, and perhaps most famously, SRI entailed attention to the implications of a firm's products for the well-being of both consumers and the broader society. SRI's concern for the harm caused to society by companies' products has its origins in religious organizations' avoidance of sin stocks, including alcohol, tobacco, and gambling. But, attention to these types of products extended in the 1960s and on to other goods deemed socially pressing by investors, including weapons, nuclear power, and unsafe products (Bruyn 1991; Social Investment Forum 1995).

The place or geographical location of a firm's business activities might also matter for socially responsible investors, given that companies' trade with local economic actors also provided support to the region's political regime by granting political legitimacy to and generating economic resources in the form of wages and tax dollars to the government (Rockness and Williams 1988). The first instance of SRI based on a company's location was the successful economic boycott of South Africa, but more recent cases include the call for divestment from Sudan (Soederberg 2009). Finally, advocates of SRI viewed firms' policies as a source of social value, typically extending beyond the existing government regulation of firms to focus on companies' just and equitable treatment of employees. Issues here in the early history of SRI included the presence of women and minorities on a corporation's board of directors and the existence of corporate codes of conduct ensuring respect for workers' human rights (Kinder et al. 1994; Bruyn 1991; Social Investment Forum 1995). In the early 1980s, for instance, the Calvert Group screened investments based on companies' history of employee involvement in decision-making, fair negotiation with workers, and the provision of equal opportunities in the workplace (Gray 1983).

The subjective meaning of social value

Yet, beyond a concern for the effects of a company's products, place, and/or policies on society, the meaning of social value for SRI was decidedly *subjective* and so infinitely varied and divergent in nature, as with the case of charities in the nonprofit sector. That is, precisely which types of goods, which geographical locales, and which types of managerial or operational conduct were deemed to be of social concern varied across participants in the field. Marked differences were understood to exist across members of the arena as to how to define the "social." And, while the meaning of social value is constrained in the nonprofit sector by legal regulation in the form of the 501(c)(3), as discussed in Chapter 2, the boundaries of the field of SRI were driven solely by proponents' normative ideals of the social good, as mediated by investment intermediaries.

This emphasis on the personal nature of the social in SRI is at the core of the field's self-understanding, as evidenced in media publications on SRI, advisory texts, and in how initial advocates of SRI defined the social project of this field. An early guide to SRI for individual investors asserted, "SRI is not about satisfying someone else's political or social agenda. Although most socially responsible investors would agree generally about a broad range of issues, the emphasis on SRI is on your individual ethical stance" (Brill and Reder 1993). Another publication on the state of the field concluded that "SRI means different things to different people depending on the social concerns or objectives they want to achieve" (Shapiro 1992:11). Finally, in one interview I conducted, I asked a long-standing participant in the field of SRI to define the meaning of "social" in SRI. She replied by saying that "we see the economy – in the sense of making money through profit, economic return, etcetera – as a means to an end, not as an end in itself. But the question is who gets to decide those ends? There's no agreement on that. And that's part of the appeal of this view of investing."

Market-based action for social good

In Chapter 3 on social enterprises, we saw how the social project in that field relied on the use of market solutions to social problems. The social value generated by market-based action – including both a reliance on market revenue and the inclusion of disadvantaged populations in the market – was central to the identity of social enterprises. Similarly, at the core of the social project of SRI was a similar belief that economic activity – this time in the form of investment in corporations – constituted a means to social value. Proponents of SRI rejected what sociologists have called a "hostile worlds" perspective where the market consists only of the pursuit of rational self-interest and economic gain (Zelizer 2009). Instead, the premise and promise of the social project of SRI lay in the intentional dismissal of a view of morals as located only outside of the private sector and in the domestic, political, or nonprofit spheres of society. For actors in the field of SRI, the economy was a societal sector possessing both economic value and personal values. The CEO of Pax World Management summarized the "hostile worlds" perspective as he saw it enacted in mainstream investing: "You make your money over here and then you go and you spend it wisely over there. You do some nonprofit work or you get involved in politics."[6] In this rejected view, financial activity is considered value-neutral; it only becomes moral in nature when any ensuing profit or return is used for social ends in other spheres, such as making a charitable donation to a nonprofit. In contrast, the point of SRI for proponents was to bring morals to the marketplace. One respondent – the current president of a high-profile SRI fund, emailed me in response to my query to interview him. Instead of participating in a phone interview, he instead wrote me with his thoughts on SRI, pleading little free time to talk. For him, the core belief "at the heart of ethical investing [what he called SRI]," is that "to invest in the market is to invest in society."

Yet, despite this consensus, proponents of the field of SRI offered two different rationales as to how SRI as a form of market-based action could produce social value: investing served as an expression of individuals' values as an end in itself and as a means of control over corporations' behavior. In the first view, reflecting the religious origins of SRI, social value is created when an actor's investment decisions reflects their personal beliefs, regardless of its societal consequences or lack thereof (Hutton et al. 1998). Social value here is produced when actors are able to act according to their values in the market. In their articulation of the philosophy of SRI, Amy Domini and Peter Kinder, two early proponents of the field, asserted that the premise of this first view of the social project of SRI is "less to draw attention to something than to refuse to profit by it" (Domini and Kinder 1984:3). As one investor in the nascent SRI industry similarly proclaimed, "If I put my money into something that made bullets and I was driving a Mercedes because of that investment, I couldn't enjoy it … . I'd rather gain slowly and feel good about it" (as quoted in Schlesinger 1984).

In sociological terms, this first motivation of SRI is an example of what the classical sociologist Max Weber (1922/1978) called "value-rationality," in that action is guided by the pursuit of value or morally oriented action, irrespective of its outcome or without concern for achieving a goal in the most efficient manner possible (Kalberg 1980). Value rationality is a "conscious belief in the value for its own sake of some ethical, religious, or other forms of behavior" (Weber 1922/1978:25). The distinctive point of this conception of the social project of SRI is that it allows actors to extend value-rational action beyond the nonprofit and public sectors, where political activity had typically occurred, and to the private sector as well. Similarly, when I asked one early participant in the field of SRI to describe why he had gotten involved in this type of market-based social activism, his reply emphasized his commitment to the merit of realizing his morals in the financial sphere. Nelson told me:

It's hard to explain but when I'm asked this question, I always think about John Wesley's [one of the founders of Methodist church in the late 18th century] sermon on the 'Use of Money.'[7] When I admitted that I hadn't heard of this sermon, he expanded on his claim for me. "Basically, in a nutshell, Wesley said that we can't think of our money and how we use it – how we invest it, save it, earn it, or spend it – as being somehow distinct from our values. An ethical life includes our investments, if we're lucky to have that kind of money, and of course Wesley wasn't really talking about investing in the stock market. [laughs]. But everyone can make a choice about what products they buy and who they buy them from so that their economic choices are an expression of their values. It's hard work but we *can* work for that. So that to me pretty much sums up the ethos that I have always tried to live by and that motivates my work with SRI, both back then and now.

In contrast, a second group of proponents of SRI articulated the ability of actors to pursue social value in the market in another, more results-oriented way. Here, financial investment in traditional corporations was understood to constitute a new means by which actual societal change could be achieved by altering the behavior of corporations. The goal of this view of SRI, as early advocates summarized in one publication, was to "make money work for social good" (Alperson et al. 1991:2). How then could this kind of economic action affect social change? In this second version of SRI, the success of SRI depended on which form of SRI was in question. Community investment was seen as a straightforward use of financial capital to promote economic development in disadvantaged communities otherwise excluded from traditional market actors' – such as banks – distribution of loans and investments. Shareholder activism was meant to achieve social change by bringing critical issues up for managers' consideration and to raise publicity about those concerns with other investors, employees, consumers, and the general public in an effort to induce a change in a firm's behavior. The use of screening as a strategy of SRI was perhaps the least obviously apparent in terms of how financial investment could achieve social value. Yet, proponents offered a justification for this type of SRI. As present in both publications at the time and in interviews with early proponents, the act of SRI was posited to provide market incentives to engender corporate change through two distinct mechanisms. First, the scale of SRI mattered in creating an economic penalty for firms. Proponents claimed that the growth of socially responsible shareholders would put pressure on business' managers to act more responsibly out of fear of losing that share of current investors and losing future investors. In one early advisory text for individual investors, the authors wrote, "money withdrawn from companies and government agencies that behave unethically *'punishes that behavior'* and makes it less likely to occur in the future. Money invested in companies and government activities that are socially beneficial *'reinforces* that behavior' and makes it more likely to occur in the future" (Brill and Reder 1993:4). Here, as advocates were careful to note, the growth of the SRI market was necessary for this threat of investor exit of negatively sanctioned corporations and the promise of shareholder purchase of positively sanctioned firms to actually be effective in driving corporate change (Kinder et al. 1994).

Secondly, similar to the motivating premise underlying the use of shareholder activism, screening would induce firms' production of social value through the presence of ratings. In this view, ratings of firms' performance in terms of their products, place, and policies, as created by SRI research firms, investment advisors, and mutual and money market funds, would be disseminated and publicized beyond members of the field itself (Kinder et al. 1994). The public naming and shaming of corporations based on the screening process would result in public attention to those issues and force firms to engage in self-regulation. In 1986, one investment analyst for US Trust, a Boston-based bank that offered socially oriented accounts, articulated the goal of SRI for his institution. "We believe that social investment is a symbol and is a mechanism to influence corporate behavior – that's important to us and to our clients."[8] One early SRI advisory handbook for individual investors provided a similar rationale for how the act of socially responsible investment could produce social value:

> If avoidance investors' decisions to sell stocks or not to buy them in the first place were secret, those decisions probably would have virtually no effect at all. Markets in these issues are so broad and so efficient that even if an avoidance investor's action temporarily depressed the price of a stock by some fraction of a point, other investors, unconstrained by considerations of social responsibility, probably would step into the breach quickly in order to take advantage of the selloff as a bargain buying opportunity and the stock would be right back up where it was before very long. The fact is, however, that once these decisions are made, they generally are not kept secret, at least not by institutional investors, but are disclosed in ways intended to create maximum adverse publicity for the affected company or companies (Miller 1991:35).

SOCIAL VALUE AND SHAREHOLDER VALUE

If market activity through investment could produce social value, what was the presumed relationship between SRI and shareholder value? Here again, proponents saw the social project of SRI as entailing the intertwining of social and economic value. In contradiction to the premises of "market fundamentalism," whereby the economy is governed by the rational pursuit of self-interest and in contrast to a "hostile worlds" thesis in the social sciences, this view of SRI assumed that social value for society and financial value for the investor were co-produced at once through the act of socially responsible investment (Kinder et al. 1994; Schatz 1985; Brill and Reder 1993). Proponents did not believe they need to "sacrifice profit to effect social change," to quote from one respondent in the field.[9] The pursuit of double bottom line return was framed by multiple members of this field in their interviews as "doing well while doing good."[10] We can see evidence of this intertwining of social value and shareholder value in various ways. One of the co-creators of Pax World Fund, one of the first SRI mutual funds, noted that, "people are realizing that they can make money and still make a social statement. They want a good, solid investment, but they don't want to hurt anybody" (Trausch 1981). Similarly, in one interview that I conducted, a long-time proponent of SRI told me that his catch phrase, whenever he presents on the idea of SRI to members of the conventional investing community, is "profit is not a dirty word."

In the insistence that investors can "earn interest on their principals" (Schatz 1985), advocates of SRI departed from two conventional understandings of how to obtain financial return on investment. In the view of mainstream investment, SRI violated the premises of Modern Portfolio Theory, which argues that an efficient market rewards investors who have sufficiently diversified their stocks (Markowitz 1952; Langbein and Posner 1980). By limiting stocks to only those that are positively screened based on moral criteria, critics argued that SRI prevented an adequate amount of diversification in an investor's portfolio of stocks and so increases the rate of risk in investment.[11] The chairperson of a large money manager in the early 1980s described the problems with SRI in precisely those terms. He noted that SRI "increases the difficulty of obtaining superior returns. By shrinking the universe of stocks, you make it more complex for the money manager, at least of an actively managed portfolio. You lose both diversification and flexibility" (Kristol 1985). A second argument against the ability of socially responsible investments to produce a parallel rate of return to conventional investing lay in the issue of cost. Firms' engagement with socially responsible behavior in terms of their products, place, and policies was argued to involve economic outflows that rival firms were not incurring based purely on the use of financial considerations. In result, the expenditures of socially responsible firms would be higher than their peers, thus lowering the rate of return for shareholders (Friedman 1970; Waddock and Graves 1997).

The result of these theoretically driven critiques of SRI was that various observers of the field, including the media and scholars, sought to confirm the predictions of portfolio theory by determining the effect of socially responsible investments on financial outcomes. Newspaper and magazine reports typically used case studies of specific mutual funds as compared to the performance of the stock market or to similar mainstream mutual funds, highlighting both the negative and positive returns of socially responsible investment (Bronstein 1985; Kristol 1985; Martin 1986). In contrast, scholars engaged in empirically-based research in order to test this hypothesis as to the presumed negative effect of SRI on the generation of shareholder return by comparing mutual funds or investment portfolios (Capelle-Blancard and Monjon 2012). Between 1971 and 2001, for instance, over one hundred studies were published on this question (Margolis and Walsh 2003). Interestingly, the results of this research have not supported economists' critiques of SRI. With some exceptions (Vance 1975; Wright and Ferris 1997), the vast majority of studies have found either no difference between the different strategies of investment (Bruyn 1991; Hamilton, Jo, and Statman 1993) or identified a positive effect of SRI on the rate of financial return (Shane and Spicer 1983; Orlitzky, Schmidt, and Rynes 2003). As I will show in Chapters 6 and 7, this growing conclusion that socially oriented investment produced either equivalent or greater shareholder value than conventional investing led to a substantive re-framing of how to gauge the social worth of corporations away from the criteria of social value, however subjectively defined, and towards that of shareholder value, particularly after the market crashes of 2001 and 2008. More broadly, the cumulative findings of this research played a key role in the justification then offered by proponents of caring capitalism as a new type of social project.

In addition to the work of reporters and academics, proponents of SRI were quick to try and address these critiques of their growing field. Some mutual fund managers offered up the track record of their funds as proof that socially responsible investment need not impinge on financial return (Shapiro 1983; Martin 1986). Other actors devised more explicit measures of the capacity of SRI to produce both financial and social return. In 1990, Peter Kinder, Amy Domini, and Steve Lydenberg created the KLD Domini 400 Social Index, which was an SRI-oriented index intended to benchmark the Standard & Poor's 500 Index (a list of 500 large publicly owned corporations), as one traditional stock market index. The KLD Domini 400 Social Index was made up of 400 primarily large-cap US corporations, selected based on both negative and positive screening of SRI eleven criteria.[12] Towards their goal of constructing a SRI mutual fund, the goal was to show that the financial performance of the KLD Domini 400 Social Index (which then became the Domini Social Equity Fund) either would be parallel to or superior to that of the S&P 500 as a proxy for conventional investing (Kurtz, Lydenberg, and Kinder 1992).

THE ROLE OF RATINGS IN SRI

As a growing field, SRI was premised upon and motivated by a combination of these three distinct rationales for how the act of financial investment could produce social value. SRI was viewed as an ethical act in and of itself, it was viewed as a means to sanction firms through the threat of investors' exit or the promise of investors' entry, and it was viewed as a strategy to influence companies through public naming and shaming. In each of these cases, the ratings of firms' social performance were necessary for the act of SRI to take place and for the field of SRI to grow. For one, investors needed to know if corporations' social performance aligned with their personal understandings of desired behavior in order to be able to engage in SRI. Initially, investors were encouraged to evaluate companies and make such decisions for themselves based on their own values. Advisory texts were published that led investors through the process of SRI (Domini and Kinder 1984; Brill and Reder 1993). But, as the field became institutionalized, third-party actors soon developed SRI ratings systems of corporations as a type of "judgment device," as discussed earlier (Karpik 2010). Given the complexity of evaluating corporations' social performance, ratings served as a means to facilitate investors' selection of stocks. In this capacity, ratings also served another instrumental function for proponents of the field. Ratings were developed by SRI advocates not just to assist individual investors' exercise of their values but also as motivated by the ultimate goal of growing the total size of the market of SRI in order to increase investors' influence on firms (Miller 1991). In one conversation I had with the founder of an early mutual fund, I asked Saul about why he had settled upon a mutual fund as a vehicle for socially responsible investment. His reply was informative – "I needed to make a living, but I also was morally committed to SRI as a solution to some societal problems and the more people who invested with their morals, the more powerful it would be."

Finally, the construction of SRI ratings of firms was considered necessary to place public pressure on low-rated companies by signaling the preferences of the SRI community, irrespective of whether individual investors actually acted on those evaluations or not (Council on Economic Priorities 1970a). Here, confirming another prediction of social science literature, as already outlined in this chapter, ratings served as a form of third-party control by external actors over corporations (DeJean et al. 2004; Espeland and Stevens 2008). While SRI raters did not possess the authority to sanction firms who failed their ratings, they did seek to assess corporations in terms of their products, place, and/or policies as a means to public sanction and so businesses' self-discipline. It was hoped that corporations would alter their products, places of production, and policies in order to avoid or mitigate the threat of media attention, consumer boycotts, and/or sanctions from investors that hopefully would follow from a low SRI rating.

It is important to note that in this desire to communicate the social performance of firms to investors, the motivation of some raters to produce SRI assessments were not purely communicative in nature in terms of aiding investors, growing the market, and/or addressing corporations. Early proponents of SRI, like the Council on Economic Priorities and the Investor Responsibility Research Center, did disseminate SRI ratings of corporations for free through newsletters and other publications. However, some later actors, as Saul noted earlier, began to see a chance for their own economic livelihood in the growing market of SRI, in that they could sell SRI ratings as a commodity for profit, similar to research analysts who performed stock research and rated firms based on their financial worth in mainstream investing. This set of SRI rating analysts could either sell their information to investment advisors or to institutional investors (for example, KLD Research & Analytics, which had developed the KLD Domini Social Index 400, also was a stand-alone ratings firm) or a SRI ratings analyst could be employed on the buy-side to provide in-house ratings for a money management firm, such as a SRI pension fund (e.g., CalPERS – the California Public Employees' Retirement System – was an early adopter of SRI criteria) or a SRI mutual fund (e.g., Dreyfus Third Century).

Rating stocks for SRI

If the specific goal of SRI was to limit investment to those stocks that were both ethically sound and financially rewarding, how did investors select stocks that aligned with their values? How were corporations to be assessed for their social value? In the case of social screening (the most popular form of SRI), financial intermediaries have served as value entrepreneurs in the field. These mutual and money market funds, investment analysts, and research firms were formed with the specific goal of providing individual and institutional investors with investment opportunities that fit their values and to pressure corporations to modify their policies. To do so, these value entrepreneurs needed to rate stocks as worthy of inclusion or exclusion of investment consideration based on both financial and social considerations.

To evaluate companies for consideration of investment, these value entrepreneurs drew from their expertise in finance in order to create ratings that fit with existing measurement devices in the investment industry (Markowitz, Cobb, and Hedley 2012). Proponents of SRI brought a background in both social activism and conventional investment to the formation of the field. As noted earlier, the growth of SRI historically can be traced to a pool of investors who sought both financial and social return. But, the success of SRI as an institutionalized field was contingent upon the work of finance professionals who provided investment expertise and who constructed the necessary vehicles and infrastructure so that socially responsible investment could occur. Many of these early proponents were individuals either with a professional background in social advocacy and business who viewed investment as an untapped method to achieve social change or they were individuals in the finance industry who identified unmet demand for socially responsible investment in ways that aligned with their personal politics (Waddock 2008b). For one, Jerome Dodson created both the Working Assets Fund (the first money market SRI fund) and the Parnassus Fund (an early SRI mutual fund) in the early 1980s. His work with investment vehicles based on social screening followed his work with the alternative SRI strategy of community investment. Dodson had received an

MBA from Harvard in 1971, worked for an economic development corporation in the Bay Area, and then devised a new financing mechanism for solar energy while working at a local savings and loan bank (O'Connor 1989). Similarly, Joan Bavaria, who founded Franklin Research and Development Corporation as an affiliate of the conventional financial advisory firm Franklin Management Corporation and then led the formation of the Social Investment Forum, had been an investment officer at Bank of Boston in the 1970s assigned, in her own words, to work with wealthy investors who wanted to ally their political values with their financial decisions but who lacked the appropriate vehicle to do so (Waddock 2008b). Her goal was to "market traditional expertise in vehicles compatible with the interest of investors" (Trausch 1981). Finally, the Council on Economic Priorities, formed in 1969, was one of the first organizations to generate data on corporations' social and economic performance on a company-by-company basis. Alice Teppler Marlin, the founder of CEP, had worked as a securities analyst and portfolio manager for a mainstream bank while working in her own time in the anti-war movement. Once aware of the extent of client demand for SRI options, Teppler then realized the capacity of the tool of financial investing as a means to produce greater social good and so formed CEP to that end (Alperson et al. 1991).

How did these value entrepreneurs transpose their knowledge of financial investment to the case of SRI? With conventional investment, the role of financial analysts is to evaluate stocks for consideration of others' investment. These analysts – both at that time and today – typically have relied solely on financial considerations, drawing either from data that concerned the firm's characteristics (what is called "fundamental stock analysis") or that focused on the dynamics of the broader stock market (what is called "technical analysis"). With fundamental stock analysis, which served as the model for SRI, financial analysts (also often called ratings analysts) draw from a range of institutionalized yardsticks to determine the actual or "intrinsic" value of a company and potential for future growth relative to its current stock price. Firms that are underpriced will produce greater future shareholder value than a firm that is priced accurately or that is overpriced relative to future performance. To make this judgment, analysts typically evaluate a firm's financial statements and look at a number of the firm's financial characteristics, including total assets, revenues, and earnings, past performance or stock price, and/or price to earnings ratio, among others, often combined with the study of the firm's broader context within an industry or other macroeconomic factors, as well as a more in-depth, qualitative analysis of the corporation. They then employ this data in order to determine if a stock is underpriced or overpriced relative to its value and to provide a corresponding rating of the stock for investors, often by using the rating scale of buy, hold, and sell (Graham 2006).

Given the background of many advocates of SRI in conventional investing, these proponents realized that socially responsible investors would require similar ratings of corporations in terms of their financial *and* social performance. Many of them, including Alice Teppler Marlin and Amy Domini, were capable of generating those ratings based on their prior professional expertise in analyzing stocks. As the field of SRI emerged and became institutionalized, three different types of organizations began to offer ratings. First, a number of early advocates of the field of SRI published assessments of companies, intended for use by investors, in regard to firm performance on a specific social issue of concern of relevance to the rater in question. Typically, these guides would identify those firms most culpable of a particular offense, implicitly recommending the exclusion of companies with a particularly egregious record from consideration of the audience's investment. Beginning in 1970, for example, the Council on Economic Priorities published the "Economic Priorities Report," with each volume based on a specific social or environmental issue (the first several issues focused respectively on manufacturers of antipersonnel weapons, companies in the petroleum industry, and corporations involved in the airline industry) and incorporated their own concern for companies' record of minority employment, environmental issues, defense production, and foreign investment. Each publication outlined the social and/or environmental nature of the issue, listed the worst corporate offenders in that area, as well as giving updates on related instances of shareholder activism (Council on Economic Priorities 1970a, 1970b, 1970c). The Investor Responsibility Research Center's "News for Investors," first published in 1974, also provided SRI updates for members of the field. The newsletter reported on shareholder activism, gave detailed updates on issues relevant to the SRI community, such as South Africa, and occasionally listed firms involved in a sanctioned area (Domini and Kinder 1984; Investor Responsibility Research Center 1987).[13] A similar publication was the work of Franklin Research & Development, an early investment advisory firm. Beginning in 1987, it issued "Insight," a newsletter for investors that ranked companies from excellent (1) to poor (5) based on an index of multiple criteria, including a selection of firms' products and their corporate conduct (Schlegelmich 1997).

Secondly, both mainstream and SRI investment advisors began to provide buy-side ratings of corporations for investors on a tailored, case-by-case basis. Here, the selection of criteria for the social screening of firms was driven by the investor's stated preferences (Shapiro 1983; Schatz 1985). Starting in 1981, the Prudential Insurance Co. responded to demand from union pension-fund clients to invest in all-unionized construction projects by selecting firms that aligned with that preference (Schlesinger 1984). Another example was The Alliance Capital Management Corporation, a money manager that managed more than $15 billion in total assets using traditional financial screens. Of that total, over $300 million came from private and public pension funds, which required screening for South-African related investments (Kristol 1985).

A third group of raters was composed of analysts for mutual funds, money market funds, and research firms. They sought to address critiques of socially responsible investment based in the claim that that the SRI market was not based on the use of systematic data (which was claimed to characterize conventional investing) where ratings created commensurability across the entire universe of firms in an industry. Recall from earlier that the earliest raters, including the Council on Economic Priorities and the Investor Responsibility Research Center, had sporadically evaluated corporations on an issue-by-issue basis. What this last set of raters sought to develop was a single and consistent rating of companies using a methodology and presented in a form comparable to the use of ratings in mainstream investing. Perhaps the most famous example here was the formation of KLD Research and Analytics, a stand-alone SRI research firm, formed in 1988 by the same value entrepreneurs who also created the KLD Domini Social Index 400. As one of the three founders of KLD explained, the research firm's "stated mission was to reduce the barriers to social investing and its strategy to do that was to develop products that were systematic and could serve the mainstream financial community" (Waddock 2008b:95).

THE METHODOLOGY OF SRI RATINGS

To engage in the ratings of firms, value entrepreneurs faced two critical decisions. First, these actors had to negotiate the subjective nature of social value in the field. It was widely recognized that the essence of SRI consisted of investors acting on their own idiosyncratic and so varying moral values. Nonetheless, raters needed to evaluate stocks according to a finite list of criteria. How did they resolve this challenge? Secondly, raters sought to evaluate stocks according to both social and economic criteria, given that SRI was premised on a belief that investors need not exchange financial return for social gain. How did they address this difficulty?

To rate firms for their social orientation, analysts proceeded in four steps. Employing both financial and social data, an investment professional needed to select the social and financial criteria of relevance, gather necessary financial and social information on a company, and then determine how to rate a firm as worthy of inclusion of consideration of investment based on both financial and social considerations (Waddock and Graves 1997; Hutton et al. 1998; Rockness and Williams 1988).[14] First, given the subjective nature of the social in SRI, the first step in rating corporations was to determine the criteria to be used in the screening stocks. Raters varied in their selection of salient issues across different products, places, and policies. As discussed earlier, early research firms and trade associations, like Franklin Research & Development and the Council on Economic Priorities, drew on their own set of social and environmental criteria, while investment analysts relied on investors' preferences. In contrast, mutual and money market funds often sought to respond to market demands from socially responsible investors for new double bottom-line investment vehicles (Kurtz, Lydenberg, and Kinder 1992). The Dreyfus

Third Century Fund made the decision to screen investments via the benchmarks of equal employment, occupational safety and health, and protection and improvement of the environment, and product quality and safety, based on the founders of the fund's perception of and experience with public demand by investors (Gray 1983). Likewise, I spoke with one of the creators of an early mutual fund who said "in order to do it, we had to create in our mind the average investor – what would they want and what would they care about? We knew there was a lot of variation in terms of what different people considered to be ethical investment, but we also knew from our combined experience that there were a shared number of issues that were quite common."

This envisioning of the preferred goals of the average socially oriented investor resulted in a striking consensus around a core set of social criteria emphasized by these financial intermediaries in this early history of the field. Take the SRI strategy of exclusionary social screening. In 1995, the earliest year for which systematic data is available on the use of SRI by US money managers, the vast majority (86%) avoided tobacco stocks, almost three-quarters avoided alcohol stocks, and nearly two-third avoided weapons stocks (Social Investment Forum 1995).[15] Similarly, a survey of all mutual funds in existence in the US in the mid-1980s found agreement on the issues of equal employment opportunity, treatment of employees, environmental protection, and business with repressive regimes notably South Africa, product quality and innovation, and defense contracting (Rockness and Williams 1988).

Once a SRI ratings analyst decided on the criteria of worth for social value, the next decision was to gather necessary data about the performance of firms. Raters needed to select a population of possible companies in an industry, often relying on stock market indices or industry reports. They then collected information on their financial and social performance. To begin, these analysts would evaluate a company for its future financial performance based on the same considerations that were used in mainstream investing. They sought to determine if a company was currently undervalued, leading to the likely generation of long-term return for shareholders. Drawing from that pool, they then evaluated those companies for their social performance (Rockness and Williams 1988; Kurtz, Lydenberg, and Kinder 1992).[16] To engage in social screening, raters looked at a wide variety of data sources, including firms' publicly filed documents (including annual reports and disclosure reports), evaluations by other members of the SRI community, government data (including OSHA reports), industry and trade reports, media reports, and surveys sent out by the rater to companies (Domini and Kinder 1984; Brill and Reder 1993). A portfolio manager at the Third Century Dreyfus Fund explained that social screening of investments "is very expensive and difficult research to do. You have to go through government records, check for product recalls and have extensive interviews with people at the company. You also have to keep updating your files. Some companies are eager to cooperate and others won't talk to us" (Trausch 1981).

Finally, these raters needed to determine the methodology by which this data was to be used to categorize firms as excluded or included from consideration of investment based on social considerations. They varied in their methodology, in part based on their definition of social responsibility (Rockness and Williams 1988). Those actors that focused solely on corporations' products could exclude firms based on a specified cut-off of the maximum percentage of revenue that could originate from the undesirable product. The KLD Domini Social Index 400 allowed no more than four percent of a firm's revenue to come from common sin products while the Calvert Global Equity Fund cuts off firms at a maximum of ten percent of revenue from sanctioned goods (Brill and Reder 1993). Another strategy was to select the top ranked firms in each industry according to the relevant social criteria. The Dreyfus Third Century Fund screened investments based on the qualities of equal employment, occupational safety and health, and protection and improvement of the environment, and product quality and safety. Then, companies were ranked according to their social performance in the industry. Finally, the board of directors established a "cutoff point to divide eligible from ineligible investments" (Gray 1983:100).

Problems often arose when a rater employed an index (consisting of measures of multiple social criteria) and firms varied widely in their performance across the different dimensions. One early *New York Times* financial advice column, intended to assist readers already interested in SRI, described this problem in the following way. "It's pretty near impossible nowadays to find an established commercial enterprise that hasn't fallen from grace at least once along the way. And the promising candidates sporting genuine social positives are no different. Take a good, close look and chances are that you'll uncover at least one troubling social negative – enough to make investing in the company something less than a perfect ethical experience" (*New York Times* 1982). Similarly, a vice president at the United States Trust Co. of Boston admitted: "there may be no such thing as a 'clean' company meeting all the requirements of an ethical investment fund" (Martin 1986). In these cases, the rating agency might exclude a firm from inclusion based on very poor performance in one area (Rockness and Williams 1988). Ultimately, the consensus was that "the final choice of companies comes down to a judgment call" (Alperson et al. 1991:18).[17]

In all, a striking congruence existed between the social project of the field of SRI and the measuring devices that came to be used to assess corporations for their social performance. The goal of SRI was to ensure that corporations could not produce societal harm for customers, local communities, and/or employees through their products, place, or policies, while investors still received a sound financial return. The proposed solution to this problem was the strategic use of investing to generate both corporate change and shareholder value. The ranking of corporations' social performance (conditional upon their generation of return of investment) as a measuring device was critical to this project – it served the purpose of external control by not only facilitating investors' decision making so as to grow the market of SRI but also by drawing public attention to firms as a form of governing by numbers. While the task of rating companies based on their social performance was methodologically challenging given the expectations of mainstream investing, value entrepreneurs succeeded in generating a range of ratings based on investors' varied definitions of social value. This multipurpose nature of rankings was possible based on value entrepreneurs' expertise in conventional investing, thus providing them with the necessary valuation repertoire to achieve their goals.

Notes

1. Data on Pax World Fund was based on the content of an interview with a senior executive and from secondary research (Hylton 1992; Gittell, Magnusson, and Merenda 2012; Pax World Investments 2014).
2. For a summary of scholarship examining the efficacy of private regulation in the form of SRI, see later. For a discussion of the efficacy of CSR as a strategy of social change, see O'Rourke (2003), and Gourevitch, Lake, and Stein (2012).
3. In 1953, for example, the Supreme Court settled the case of *Smith* v. *Barlow* in which shareholders challenged the decision by A.P. Smith – a manufacturing firm – to make a donation of $1,500 to Princeton University. The Supreme Court concluded that firms had a responsibility for general social welfare in the communities in which they operate. Corporate philanthropy was further encouraged by changes to the tax system – foundations responded by increasing their rates of giving for a broader array of recipients, including educational, health, and scientific purposes (Hall 1992).
4. Prior instances of private regulation exist. During the late nineteenth century, for example, labor activists employed "unfair lists" to facilitate the secondary boycott of those firms that refused to allow their workers to unionize, until such practices were ruled unconstitutional in 1908 (Glickman 2009; Soule 2009).
5. In other words, the community investing strategy of SRI provides a portion of the resources employed by the social enterprises that own and operate community development financial institutions, as discussed in Chapter 3.
6. Joseph Keefe, President and CEO of Pax World Funds, as quoted in *Forbes Magazine* (Waghorn 2014).
7. He was referring here to John Wesley's 1760 sermon on the "Use of Money."
8. As quoted in Podger (1986).
9. Within the history of SRI, there have been some exceptions to this commitment to double bottom line investment but typically through direct investment, rather than stock market investment (Bruyn 1991). The Cooperative Assistance Fund was formed in the late 1960s by a consortium of large American foundations, which invested its pooled assets in community investment in low-income neighborhoods with the agreement that the investments would be high-risk and low return (Liou and Stroh 1998).
10. Here, the proponents of SRI were invoking the notion of "fiduciary duty." Under US law, a fiduciary is any actor who is delegated (usually in the role of a trustee or a money manager) to manage resources for another – they are legally obligated to manage those goods in the others' best financial interests via the exercise of due

care and prudence (Langbein and Posner 1980). However, in making the case for SRI, these advocates emphasized that social and shareholder value were mutually constituted, although they did not use the specific terminology of fiduciary duty (Domini and Kinder 1984; Schatz 1985; Brill and Reder 1993). Its absence is in market opposition to the centrality of the term in the justifications offered by proponents of Responsible Investment in the 2000s, as discussed in Chapter 6.

11. In addition, managers' engagement in social responsibility violated the premises of agency theory. Here, managers are agents who are charged with the shareholders' preferences. Shareholders are assumed to desire the optimal financial return on their investment. When managers expend resources on social responsibility, the costs of those expenditures are at the sacrifice of profit for shareholders. Thus, engaging in investing based on the criteria of social responsibility should deflate the rate of return relative to conventional investing (Friedman 1970).

12. It was only one year later that they then founded the Domini Social Equity Fund – a socially responsible investment mutual fund that tracks that same index.

13. In addition, the Interfaith Center on Corporate Responsibility's "Corporate Examiner," first published in 1971, was a "publication examining actions and policies of major US corporations in the areas of consumerism, environment, foreign investment, government, labor and minorities, military production, and corporate responsibility" but it focused only on shareholder activism and offered no ratings for investors (1975). In contrast, "Good Money" was a newsletter begun in the early 1980s by the Center for Economic Revitalization that offered evaluations of firms for individual investors.

14. See Entine (2003) for a critique of the methods used by SRI investment firms and ratings agencies to select socially responsible companies.

15. It was only later in the institutionalization of the SRI field that notable variation developed in terms of the criteria used by financial intermediaries to screen stocks. As the market for socially responsible investment grew, a number of targeted mutual funds were formed. These include the Amana Mutual Funds Trust, an Islamic fund that bars investing in banks, and the Ave Maria Mutual Funds, which is marketed at Catholic investors and precludes the purchase of stock in corporations that support abortion or are deemed to be "anti-family" (Amana Mutual Funds Trust 2012; Ava Maria Mutual Funds 2014).

16. Yet, the financial screening of stocks did not always occur prior to social screening – mutual funds, for example, varied in terms of whether financial screening happened first, simultaneously with social screening, or took place after firms were selected based on social screening (Rockness and Williams 1988).

17. Raters then engaged in the periodic monitoring of those firms that have passed their financial and social screens. The timeline of review ranges from annual re-assessment to re-evaluation every three to five years to reviews being triggered by news of changes in the corporation's behavior, such as a merger or a product recall (Rockness and Williams 1988).

5

Business and society

Corporate Social Responsibility

"Once all human differences and considerations have been wiped out and we are all integrated into the global economy – where we are expected under management's 'scientific methods' to produce the same the world over – then the corporate agenda literally tilts the entire playing field of production and trade to the lowest point in terms of wages, benefits and conditions. For the corporations, the lowest point becomes the common denominator".

(Kernaghan 1996)

As a market-based social movement, Socially Responsible Investing (SRI) reflected the specific structure and sentiment of American society at one particular historical moment. During the 1960s and 1970s, the nation's domestic economy was dominated by large corporations who employed workers to produce goods in their local factories, paid a living wage and offered employment benefits, and were held to government laws in the treatment of their employees. Proponents of SRI sought to go beyond the US government's social regulation of firms by ensuring that American corporations did not sell harmful products, damage local communities in which they conducted business, or engage in inequitable governance or management practices.

Yet, as I will discuss in this chapter, the growth of a global economy in the 1980s and 1990s led to a fundamental re-framing of the social and environmental harms produced by firms, leading to the growth of a new type of market monitor. Corporate Social Responsibility (CSR for short) focused on the new conditions of employment for workers in the US and abroad that resulted from the outsourcing of production by multinational corporations. Proponents of CSR offered a new vision of a market-based social project, whereby globalization created a new type of problem – one of low wages, human rights violations, and unsafe working conditions for workers, many of whom were located in the global south. Proponents of CSR sought to have firms voluntarily accord all of the stakeholders in their global value chain – including employees, customers, local communities, and local suppliers – the same protections they historically had provided to those same stakeholders in the global North.

To do so, CSR value entrepreneurs employed ratings as a form of private regulation of firms, here using the threat of consumer boycotts as a form of market incentive. Ratings took the form of the certification of firms' social performance by independent actors. But, in this case, the inclusion of corporations in a multi-stakeholder coalition of value entrepreneurs led to the construction of a compromise between the contrasting communicative purposes of this tool for market monitors versus firms' representatives, as they each sought to extend tools, techniques, and technologies from their own valuation repertoires to convey their conception of the worth of companies to key audiences. The result was a disjuncture between the field's initial social project and the resulting meaning of companies' social value, as recognized in the use of certification in the field of CSR.

CSR

While the field of SRI focuses on investors' ethical concerns about a company's products, place, and/or policies for society, another group of market monitors emerged in the 1990s to target the social and environmental consequences of a company's production processes in a global economy. "CSR", also called "corporate citizenship" (Davis 1973), focuses on the responsibilities of firms to multiple constituents in society and to the environment. While it is widely recognized that no single and shared meaning of CSR exists, the European Union (2001) provided one highly cited definition of CSR as "the continuing commitment by business to behave fairly and responsibly and contribute to economic development while improving the quality of life of the work force and their families as well as of the local community and society at large."

As with the field of SRI, the field of CSR historically constituted a case of civil society actors seeking to redress the effects of business on society and the environment. Unlike SRI, attention was given not to the social desirability of the good or service itself but to the social consequences of how that good or service was produced. Corporations could generate social value based on their production processes, in terms of their treatment of workers, customers, and the local community. And in a global economy where multinational corporations contracted with a number of suppliers in developing nations in order to produce a good, they were to be held accountable both for their own operations and for those of the companies in their supply chain. By emphasizing the social ramifications of the processes by which a good was made and omitting consideration of the good's impact on customers and the community, proponents of CSR offered a different social project than found in the field of SRI. For this new group of market monitors, the social problem to be solved was the quality of the relationship between a firm and its stakeholders. I interviewed an early proponent of SRI who had then later become a champion of CSR. When asked to distinguish the two approaches, he replied:

> With CSR – or you can call it corporate citizenship, or corporate accountability, or whatever – it wasn't about products anymore, and by that I mean what companies were selling. When I got started with [our organization], we were worried about the negative effects of cigarettes or guns and so forth for everyday people – the customers – and then more widely, through a ripple effect, for society. Who was using the product and did that product make their life better or worse. But CSR is instead about looking at the consequences of how the product was made, typically for workers elsewhere – it's global now. Was it made in a way that respected the rights of workers, for example? In a way, it has made the scope of corporate accountability much broader because now any type of product for sale here in the US or anywhere – no matter how benign or even how useful that product might be for its customers – can be scrutinized in this way, along with the company that made it.

Despite these differing definitions of social value, these market monitors shared a conviction with proponents of SRI that social problems were caused, and could be solved, by the work of corporations. And, unlike the efforts of actors in the public and nonprofit sectors, it was through market-based action – by seeking to minimize the impact of corporations' production processes on stakeholders – that members of this new field believed that social value could be produced. At their core, as with other market-based movements, both fields posed a challenge to the assumption of a free market ideology that the economy was the site of economic value and the public and nonprofit sectors were the sites of public or social value.

As was the case with SRI, proponents of CSR saw market-based activity as the solution to this problem. However, members of this new field did not draw from the strategy of socially oriented investing as a means to put pressure on firms to alter their behavior. We might expect that advocates of CSR would simply ask investors to transfer their activism from the concerns of SRI to the concerns of their new social project. Instead, as I will delineate later, the social project of CSR called for an entirely different market-based strategy to curtail corporations. CSR relied on market monitors employing the threat of consumer boycott and negative publicity as the means by which to assert external control over firms and to pressure them to alter their operations and resulting treatment of stakeholders. In result, CSR advocates did not offer both a social and a financial justification for this market-based activity, with implications for how and why ratings were constructed in this field.

THE ORIGINS OF CSR

The question of the societal obligations of firms, beyond the provision of products to consumers, jobs to employers, and taxes to government, is a long-standing question in the United States, as noted in Chapter 4. It began as a theoretical issue on the part of those academics who first voiced a concern for this matter. But it was not until market monitors took up the question in globalization of production in the 1980s that the field of CSR took on its current scale and contemporary meaning.

The origin of CSR is often tracked back to the 1950s, with the 1953 publication of Howard Bowen's book, *Social Responsibility of the Businessman*. As part of the broader embrace of the corporation as a "soulful" social institution in the broader society (Davis 2009), scholars encouraged managers to incorporate a concern of the "objectives and values" of society into their selection of their firm's policies (Bowen 1953:6). Bowen's work opened the door to a consideration of the obligations of corporations to society, beyond their economic activities (Berle 1959; Heald 1977). Broadly speaking, this literature sought to bring a normative emphasis to firm's social responsibility, with an understanding that those obligations could be enacted primarily through corporate philanthropy (Carroll 1999). Fortuitously, this emphasis on the social obligations of firms coincided with the legal ruling in 1953 that permitted corporations to donate a percentage of their profits to charity (Hall 1992).

A concern for firms' responsibility to society emerged again in the 1960s. As discussed in Chapter 4, public sentiment at the time was concerned over the growing concentration of political power in the hands of the economic elite (Galbraith 1967). This broad critique of the private sector was coupled with a perceived lack of adequate government regulation of business, as evidenced in the rise of the consumer movement, led by Ralph Nader, and the environmental movement (Carson 1962; Nader and Green 1973). These activists targeted the state, premised on their belief that it held the primary obligation and the regulatory capacity to rein in the power of corporations. The federal government responded to this political activism by passing a variety of laws, including the National Traffic and Motor Vehicle Safety Act in 1966, Wholesome Meat Act (1967), the Natural Gas Pipeline Safety Act (1968), the Wholesale Poultry Act (1968), the Radiation Control for Health and Safety Act (1969), the Occupational Safety and Health Act of 1970, and the Consumer Product Safety Act of 1972 (Bradley, Schipani, Sudnaram, and Walsh 2000).

Academics took up these regulatory changes by calling for firms' attention to their ethical obligations to society through self-regulation of their stakeholder relationships, as motivated by economic concerns.[1] First, while earlier efforts had emphasized the broader societal responsibility of firms (typically through corporate philanthropy), now corporations were asked to consider their impact on specific stakeholder groups. Stakeholders were defined as those groups impacted by the processes of production – the procurement of supplies, the production of goods, and the sale of products – and so included a firm's suppliers, customers, employees, and the local community in which production takes place.[2] The task of executives was to manage and shape the relations among these various stakeholders in ways that created value for all constituents, and not just for shareholders (Freeman 1984).

Secondly, the emphasis on corporations' social responsibility was no longer framed as a normative issue but increasingly presented as one of enlightened economic self-interest (Baumol 1970; Davis 1973). In this view, a firm needed not simply to produce shareholder return, as articulated by Milton Friedman in 1970 and other proponents of a neo-classical free market, but also was required to meet legal, ethical, and discretionary demands simply in order to survive. Companies would benefit in the short-term from CSR because it improved their public image and employee relationships and it had long-term rewards in that a better community and society would ultimately lower a corporation's costs of production (Carroll 1999). As Peter Drucker (1984:62), a management guru and early detractor of CSR, later concluded: "the proper 'social responsibility' of business is to tame the dragon, that is to turn a social problem into economic opportunity and economic benefit, into productive capacity, into human competence, into well-paid jobs, and into wealth."

In contrast, critics of CSR emphasized, as with similar critiques of SRI, that managers' attention to a firm's CSR entailed additional economic costs and so would reduce the rate of shareholder return. Further, the negative externalities produced by corporations on employees, the community, and/or environment should optimally be borne by government, rather than by companies themselves (Friedman 1970). This tension led to a body of research examining the effect of CSR on firms' financial performance, with an increasing consensus that the implementation of CSR leads to superior economic return (Margolis and Walsh 2003; Barnett and Salomon 2012). As I will discuss in Chapter 6, the growing recognition that a firm's CSR performance is positively related to its financial value has led to a more recent and ongoing re-configuration of the meaning and import of social value for corporations.

Globalization and CSR

While scholars articulated both normative and economic rationales for CSR, they also noted that the particular meaning of the "social" in CSR was not set but was contextually or societally dependent (Carroll 1999). In the 1990s, a concern for firms' engagement with society intensified greatly as a result of organized efforts by a multitude of actors to respond to economic and social changes occurring due to globalization. The result of these initiatives was that CSR shifted away from being solely an academic concept and took on its contemporary scale and focus. CSR became characterized by an attention to the rights of workers and the well-being of local communities entangled in multinational corporations' global supply chains.

First, the acceleration of economic globalization in the 1980s fundamentally changed the structure of firms' manufacturing. Firms headquartered in developed nations no longer located their production in their own factories in their home country, employing unionized workers subject to the local government's regulatory oversight. Instead, these companies maintained their design, development, and marketing functions in the global North while outsourcing the production of their goods through subcontracts and licensing agreements to a series of fragmented and loosely governed independent manufacturing firms in developing countries in order to take advantage of lower land and labor costs, the absence of costly environmental and safety standards, and tax reductions in those locations. These goods were manufactured and assembled abroad and then returned for sale in the developed world (Gereffi and Korzeniewicz 1994).

This shift in the organization of production has been exacerbated by the spread of neoliberal policy in the global economy. Originating in the United States and United Kingdom (and quickly taken up by other Northern governments) in the early 1980s, neoliberalism was next taken up at the global scale in the 1980s and 1990s through the efforts of developed nations, multinational corporations, and multilateral organizations. As guided by the World Bank and the International Monetary Fund as well as being codified in regional, bilateral, and multilateral agreements, the Washington Consensus entailed a commitment to privatization, liberalization, and fiscal austerity. Loans to developing nations were contingent upon the implementation of structural adjustment – whereby local governments replaced a long-standing commitment to industrial policy (regulations oriented towards the growth of the local economy via tariffs, local content restrictions, and export controls) with policies that encouraged a free market (including limiting social regulation) and unfettered foreign direct investment (Harvey 2005; Prasad 2006). And many local governments aggressively sought foreign direct investment from multinational corporations through lowering taxes, removing labor regulations, weakening workers' rights to organize, cutting customs duties, and establishing export-processing zones (Sassen 2007).

In the case of CSR, the restructuring of production in this new global economy generated conditions rife for the mistreatment of workers in the factories in MNC's supply chains. In both the United States and in the developing world, manufacturing conditions were increasingly characterized by low wages, child labor, forced labor, and unsafe working conditions. These new conditions of production in MNC's supply chains violated existing labor laws in the nations of the global north and transnational labor conventions – regulations that had been established over the course of the twentieth century to protect workers' rights (DeWinter 2001).

While heralded by many, the globalization of the economy also was met with widespread protests, typically focused on the threat of large, unregulated multinational corporations to the promise of democracy, human rights, working conditions, and the environment. In 1999, for example, over 50,000 people protested the activities of the World Trade Organization in Seattle (Stiglitz 2002). As part of this resistance to the Washington Consensus, a number of international coalitions emerged to fight these new working conditions – often viewed as the return of the banished sweatshop of the late nineteenth century. These coalitions were composed of local NGOs, religious activists, government actors, shareholder activists, unions, workers, student groups, and consumers. Many early participants in these groups were long-time peace activists or had been involved in the anti-apartheid movement. These groups included the National Labor Committee – a human rights organization, the Union of Needletrades, Industrial and Textile Workers (UNITE), the Interfaith Center for Corporate Responsibility, the United Students against Sweatshops, and Global Exchange, among others (Varley 1998).

As recognized in the literature, anti-sweatshop coalitions constituted an example of a "transnational advocacy network" (Keck and Sikking 1998:2). A transnational advocacy network consists of those "actors working internationally on an issue, who are bound together by shared values, a common discourse, and dense exchanges of information and services." These networks constituted an important new type of actor in global politics – they employed and exchanged information in order to pressure other, more powerful actors, including governments, multilateral organizations, and multi-national corporations, towards their preferred policy outcomes.

THE CORPORATE ACCOUNTABILITY MOVEMENT

To address the rise of sweatshops, the initial target of these anti-globalization networks were governments in the global North. As had occurred before, critics of the market lobbied states to adopt social regulation as a means to limit the actions of firms, as had occurred through much of the late nineteenth and twentieth century. Historically, the state has been deemed responsible for the social regulation of firms in terms of their treatment of employees, the community, consumers, and the environment by stipulating relevant laws and enforcing rules. Drawing from this repertoire of protest, members of these anti-sweatshop coalitions did target public and multilateral actors to address the new conditions of production in a global economy. Many organizations worked to have new regulations adopted by the US government or to have social clauses included in international trade agreements, but these efforts failed. Instead, as we will see later, many Northern governments encouraged the private and voluntary regulation of the economy as a solution to the labor problems seemingly inherent to globalization (Nadvi and Wältring 2001; O'Rourke 2003).

Critics of the global economy then turned to international organizations as alternative sources of authority to influence multinational corporations. The workers' rights movement in the global North had long sought to protect international workers, either through their inclusion in regional trade agreements or through the work of multilateral organizations. Many of these international entities, such as the United Nations, the Organization for Economic Development and the International Labor Organization, had a long history of working towards the implementation of global standards for workers. These efforts were formalized in the 1970s, resulting from recognition of the growing power of multinational corporations counter to the authority of local government and due to criticisms of the role of multinational corporations in the overthrow of Allende's left-wing government in Chile in 1973. While the United Nations failed in its effort to implement a UN Code of Conduct on Transnational Corporations, the OECD adopted its Guidelines for Multinational Enterprises (1976) and the ILO adopted its Tripartite Declaration of Principles Concerning Multinational Enterprises (1977).

However, reflecting the commitment of many governments to a free market ideology, both the OECD and the ILO lacked any power to enforce its conventions with multinational corporations – their codes of conduct were strictly voluntary in nature. By the early 1990s, the consequence was a varied and selective adoption of the ILO's conventions by nations. And other multilateral entities involved in the spread of globalization in the 1980s and 1990s, such as the World Trade Organization, repeatedly rejected the call to protect workers' rights in developing nations in that it would lead to unfair protectionism, in the name of an open and free global market (Varley 1998; Harvey 2005).

As a result of their failed efforts to enact domestic regulation and/or to shape global trade agreements, this coalition of market monitors then sought to hold multinational corporations accountable – to directly pressure them to adopt socially responsible standards of production to protect the rights of workers in their supply chains. Specifically, these coalitions targeted high-profile firms where the visibility of their logos and their brand reputation with consumers, such as Nike and Reebok, could be easily tarnished by negative attention to the treatment of workers in their supply chains (Bartley 2007b; Seidman 2007; Soule 2009). As Charles Kernaghan, the director of the National Labor Committee noted about multi-national corporations: "their image is everything," he said. "They live or die by their image. That gives you a certain power over them" (Greenhouse 1996).

Members of this emerging corporate accountability movement pressured corporations to implement workers' rights through the use of market incentives, seeking to make the adoption of labor standards more economically rewarding for firms than otherwise. They did so through the threat of negative publicity and, ultimately, the threat of a consumer boycott. Members of the corporate accountability movement employed several strategies to that end. They gathered data on instances of the mistreatment of workers, information often hard to procure given that factory conditions were typically protected by managers/owners and by local governments. They then shared disseminated this information carefully in media and consumer-friendly ways. The goal was to "wage a campaign of embarrassment against corporate America" (Varley 1998:14). Finally, they worked to raise the awareness of consumers and to educate them about their buying power. Their efforts paid off in terms of growing consumer awareness and increasing disapproval of sweatshops in the 1990s (Greenhouse 1996; Holstein 1996). Growing consumer activism was accompanied by the adoption of anti-sweatshop practices by other actors and institutions in the United States: several local governments began to adopt "anti-sweatshop" ordinances in the 1990s, as did many colleges and universities (Varley 1998).

The corporate accountability movement used this growing consumer sentiment to pose the threat of consumers' boycott of companies or brands selling goods made under poor labor conditions. In the United States, the threat of a consumer boycott has been a long-standing vehicle by which private actors could effect market change without involving government. Boycotts were used by unions in late nineteenth-century United States as a means to support and extend the effects of a strike. More recent examples of large-scale consumer boycotts have included the boycotting of California grapes in the 1960s to facilitate migrant workers' unionization in the 1960s and the boycott of Nestle in the 1970s to protest the corporation's marketing of formula to mothers in the third-world (Seidman 2007; Glickman 2009).

The corporate accountability movement also used shareholder activism as a market-based incentive for corporate change. Shareholders filed resolutions requesting the implementation of suitable codes of conduct and firms' labor practices were incorporated into the process of social screening. Notably, many of the key proponents of SRI now extended their critiques of corporations beyond their products to include the social consequences of their production processes. They began to use shareholder activism as a means to hold corporations to account for labor conditions in their supply chains.[3] Take the case of the apparel industry. With the growth of the anti-sweatshop movement in the 1990s, the apparel industry was the first to come under this type of scrutiny. An assortment of unions, human rights NGOs, student groups, academics, and others, located both the in the US and in developing nations, came together to bring attention to the issue. Working with employees and local NGOs, this transnational advocacy network successfully gathered data on the conditions of production in the local plants and then drew media and consumer attention to a number of high-profile US corporations that relied on the production of their goods in unrelated factors in the developing world, including Nike, Wal-Mart, and others (O'Rourke 2003). In the case of Nike, for example, the company had moved the production of its apparel products from the US to an ever-moving series of low-wage countries in South East Asia, including China, Indonesia, and Vietnam in order to take advantage of much lower wages in those areas. Local NGOs worked with international organizations to draw global attention to the plight of low paid, often underage, employees working in unsafe conditions in those regions. They succeeded in drawing media attention to and producing consumer outrage over the conditions of production in these factories (Vogel 2006).

CORPORATIONS' CODES OF CONDUCT

Yet, these criticisms of multinational corporations initially did not result in the establishment of the ratings of firms as a means of private regulation. Instead, faced with media attention, NGO activism, and consumer complaints, many besieged companies, such as Nike, Guess, and Wal-Mart, initially resisted calls for accountability. They denied both knowledge of and responsibility for worker's treatment in factories in their supply chains (Varley 1998; 2011). In the case of Nike, the target of early and frequent criticisms by anti-sweatshop activists, the corporation also was called to account for its apathetic response to those charges. In one case, NGOs brought the case of sweatshop conditions in Indonesian factories to the attention of the Nike executive in charge of production in that region. His reply was that "I don't know that I need to know. It's not within our scope to investigate" (Barnet and Cavanagh 1994:11).

Nonetheless, a small but growing number of companies in the apparel industry did respond to this pressure, choosing to reply to critiques by adopting a new code of conduct. Codes of conduct are "written statements of principle or policy intended to serve as the expression of a commitment to particular enterprise conduct" (Diller 1999:102). Historically, the concept of a corporate code of conduct is a long-standing business practice intended to demonstrate compliance with external expectations of good governance – it is a way to achieve legitimacy. Modern codes of conduct originated in the early twentieth century, with model codes on advertising and marketing practices developed by the International Chamber of Commerce in the late 1930s. During the 1960s and 1970s, codes of conduct proliferated in response to the Watergate scandal and the Foreign Corrupt Practices Act. And, in the late 1970s, many US corporations doing business in South Africa voluntarily signed on to the Global Sullivan Principles, a code of conduct intended to ensure the protection of all workers' rights and to foster economic and social equality in South Africa (Harvey, Collingsworth, and Athreya 2000).

In the 1990s, the new codes of conduct consisted of guidelines for the social conditions of production in a global economy. Either developed by the multinational corporation itself or by a business group for adoption by relevant firms, the codes of conduct were intended not simply to guide the practice of the firm itself but, more importantly, to specify the working conditions and labor rights of employees of the independent contractors in the firm's supply chain. Levi Strauss was one of the first companies to implement a code of conduct for the production of its products in 1992 after media attention to the use of Chinese prison labor in its affiliated factories in Saipan. The company adopted the Global Sourcing Guidelines to govern contracts with suppliers (Swoboda 1992). The code covered not just the firm but also its over 600 contractors.

Nike, Reebok, J.C. Penney, Wal-Mart, and other firms in the apparel and footwear industry, also quickly followed with their own codes of conduct. By 1998, for instance, Nike had responded to persistent criticisms of its suppliers by agreeing to new rules of conduct for its suppliers, including an assurance of the hiring of no underage workers, improved health and safety standards, and the external verification of firms' conduct by independent nonprofits. Having first resisted any responsibility over its supply chains and then begrudgingly adopting a code of conduct, Nike CEO Phil Knight conceded in 1998 that "the Nike product has become synonymous with slave wages, forced overtime and arbitrary abuse. I truly believe that the American consumer does not want to buy products made in abusive conditions" (Vogel 2006).

The growth of corporate codes of conduct among large American apparel and footwear firms was commonly understood to constitute an effort by these multinational corporations to most favorably respond to external criticisms of labor conditions in their supply chains. First, the adoption of a code of conduct as created by the firm let the company itself, rather than others, set the terms of its operations, thereby side-stepping the need for government regulation and minimizing pressure from market monitors. One consultant on labor issues to companies in the textile issue advised the adoption of a corporate code of conduct. "Although following these steps will not guarantee that you will not be bitten by the watchdog, they should ensure that any bites you get will be 'nips' as opposed to gashes that require rabies shots" (quoted in Clean Clothes Campaign, 1999, as quoted in Jenkins 2001). Secondly, the implementation of a code of conduct conveyed the corporation's commitment to labor rights to consumers. The adoption of prescriptions for the treatment of workers then limited the "reputational risks" (O'Rourke 2003) of a brand with customers in the market (Nadvi and Wältring 2001). Finally, while the growth of corporate codes of conduct in the early 1990s is often understood as a case of "private regulation," it is important to note the critical role of the US government in this development. Most centrally, President Clinton had received criticisms of his decision to grant most favored nation status to China in 1994. Rather than pass new regulations governing trade with China in response, the federal government instead responded by recommending the adoption of a voluntary code of conduct by US firms doing business in China. This recommendation of firms' adoption of the administration's "Model Business Principles," was extended in 1995 to all US firms with foreign supply chains (Varley 1998).

By 1998, the International Labor Organization (IOL) identified more than 215 corporate codes of conduct in existence globally (Diller 1999). While each and every one of these codes of conduct was designed to demonstrate the MNC's respect for labor conditions in their supply chains, they varied in how they defined the social dimension of firms' operational conduct based on their date of formulation. Many of the companies that implemented the earliest corporate codes of conduct, such as by Levi Strauss and Reebok, explicitly reviewed the OECD and ILO conventions for guidance. The ILO standards, for example, were adopted in 1977 and reflected consensus about the long-standing rights of workers, including the guarantee of freedom of association and collective bargaining, the elimination of forced labor, the elimination of discrimination in the workplace, and the elimination of child labor (O'Rourke 2003). Thus, the two earliest and most influential codes of conduct by Levi-Strauss and Reebok both forbade factories in their supply chain to engage in forced labor, workplace discrimination, and child labor. Yet, while Levi Strauss did not acknowledge the right of its foreign workers to form trade unions or bargain collectively, Reebok's code of conduct did indeed recognize the right of employees to organize and bargain collectively (Compa and Hinchliffe-Darricarrère 1995; Varley 1998).

While the initial proponents of codes of conduct were influenced by the ILO and OECD conventions, a review of subsequent corporate codes of conduct by the ILO in 1998 found that a much narrower, more business friendly, range of commitments characterized these later codes of conduct. They included – presented from most to least common – occupational health and safety (75%), discrimination in hiring (66%), elimination of child labor (45%), wage levels (40%), refusal to allow forced labor (25%). Notably, a commitment to freedom of association and collective bargaining, while listed in the ILO conventions, was present in only fifteen percent of corporations' codes of conduct (Diller 1999). These codes also varied in their degree of transparency, the presence of formal auditing, and the existence of a procedure for enforcement. Most of these codes of conduct did not require the public listing of a MNC's contractors, the corporations were to rely on their own staff, rather than independent entities, to monitor suppliers in their value chain, and these guidelines did not specify any sanctions of contractors who failed to uphold the code of conduct (O'Rouke 2003; Chatterji and Levine 2006).

Nonetheless, the adoption of corporate codes of conduct was heralded by many, if not all, as a successful means to protect workers' rights in the new global economy (Ortega 1995). But MNCs' implementation of these guidelines had two unintended and unforeseen consequences. First, it overturned the long-standing insistence by some American corporations, including Nike, that they were not responsible for the conditions of production in its supplier factories. The diffusion of codes of conduct legitimated the broader charge by members of the corporate accountability movement that US brands and retailers indeed could be held accountable for the labor conditions of the factories in their supply chain (Vogel 2006). Secondly, continued scrutiny and criticism of retailers and brands revealed that the presence of a corporate code of conduct was not an efficacious means to secure workers' labor rights, either in the United States or abroad. Members of the corporate accountability movement continued to draw media attention to ongoing labor and environmental violations in the supply chains of US firms, both domestically and elsewhere. In 1996, perhaps most notoriously, the National Labor Committee revealed that TV celebrity's Kathie Lee Gifford's clothing line was manufactured in Honduras by young girls (Herbert 1997; Rosato 1997; Varley 1998).

CERTIFICATION AND COMPROMISE

The continuing existence of sweatshops, despite the adoption of corporate codes of conduct, had one other significant implication. The ongoing occurrence of labor problems confirmed the pre-existing perception by many in the corporate accountability movement that firms' own CSR codes of conduct were largely implemented for publicity purposes only. Companies were deemed incapable of monitoring and sanctioning the subcontractors in their global supply chain. The loss of firms' legitimacy to do so led to the formation of other vehicles by which companies could be forced to oversee the social conditions of production of their goods. In short, members of the anti-sweatshop movement claimed that only private regulation of production in a global economy in the form of external certification by independent value entrepreneurs and monitors would possess adequate credibility to address the scale of critiques leveled at multinational corporations. Their goal of generating ratings to assess the social responsibility of MNCs was challenged, however, by the inclusion of those very actors in the construction of many of these certification systems.

By 2002, two main recognized external CSR certification systems had been developed: the Fair Labor Association (FLA) and Social Accountability International (SAI), to be later joined by a number of other certifying agencies. These multi-stakeholder coalitions, acting as value entrepreneurs, developed certification systems as measuring devices in the field of CSR. A certification system was intended to include the formulation of a code of conduct that specified the necessary standards for the social conditions of production and a certification procedure whereby an auditing organization assessed the social performance of a firm by use of company documents, surveys, and direct observation of its factory's production processes. The auditing organization would seek to determine if the necessary policies and procedures were in place in order to protect and safeguard workers' rights in that company. If a company demonstrated compliance with expectations, it would be rated as such and so receive formal recognition of having done so.

FLA

In 1995, the US government began a series of initiatives to pressure US corporations to source their goods from responsibly produced suppliers. It adopted the "Model Business Principles" – a set of guidelines for voluntary adoption by MNCs in China and the Department of Labor began the "No Sweat" campaign, which encouraged manufacturers to monitor labor conditions of their supply chain in the domestic garment industry. The campaign incentivized firms to do so both by the creation of a Trendsetter list of companies that complied and by the threat of government sanction for those who did not (Bartley 2007b).

Yet, the continuing exposés of problems in the global supply chains of high-profile US companies, such as Nike and Wal-Mart, led the Clinton administration to form the "White House Apparel Industry Partnership" in 1996. This multi-stakeholder alliance, with membership from apparel and footwear firms (Nike, Reebok, and Liz Claiborne, among others), trade representatives, anti-sweatshop NGOs (the International Labor Rights Fund), universities, consumers rights groups (e.g., the National Consumers League) and union groups (e.g., UNITE), was formed to create an accreditation system that would produce a universal code of conduct and generate an independent monitoring and verification system at the international level (Varley 1998; Dickson, Loker, and Eckman 2009).

The FLA, as the initiative became known, focused on the apparel and footwear companies. Starting in 1999, it began an effort to certify an entire brand by providing a service mark or "label" on goods so that consumers could know if a company had met the standards of the FLA. The FLA was intended to provide a type of Good Housekeeping seal of approval for the labor conditions of a brand's global supply chain. The goal was to "develop options to inform consumers that the products they buy are not produced under exploitative conditions" (as quoted in Varley 1998:464). In settling upon the certification of a retailer's brand, the FLA drew from the existing valuation repertoires of its members, including the National Consumers League and the International Labor Rights Fund. Both organizations had familiarity with the use of the label as a "highly visible means of communication ... about the social conditions surrounding the production of a product or rendering of a service" (Diller 1999:103).

The use of the label as a strategy of consumer activism has a long history in the United States. In 1900, the White Label movement was central to anti-sweatshop efforts and was employed to identify companies that produced women's underwear in safe and hygienic conditions. During the Progressive Era, the nascent consumer safety movement worked for greater government regulation to ensure correct informational content of labels for food, drugs, and cosmetics to ensure consumer safety (Glickman 2009). Similarly, the National Consumers League, a nonprofit devoted to protecting the rights of consumers, had a long experience in the use of labels to ensure private regulation of the market, having participated in the "Made in the USA" movement in the 1990s. The International Labor Rights Fund, another member of the FLA, also had been central to the creation of the Rugmark Label to combat child labor in the rug industry in India, with input from the National Consumers League (Bobrowsky 1999).

Drawing from the success of the federal government's "No Sweat" campaign, the initial goal of the FLA was to create a "No Sweat" label to be placed in the clothes produced by approved brands (Bartley 2003). However, corporate members of the FLA protested that the complexities of accrediting the multiple companies entailed in a single company's vast and ever changing supply chain would make a label expensive and placed the burden of proof on those businesses. Instead, the FLA settled upon a decision to employ public audits of individual factories in a MNC's supply chain as the measure of social value. In this final iteration of the certification system, monitoring would take place via accredited external monitors, with firms selecting and paying for monitors, and with little public disclosure of their findings beyond a listing of the factory's accreditation by the FLA.[4]

Ultimately, the FLA initiative ended up with mixed success. Some corporations felt the FLA requirements were too onerous and costly and so left the partnership. In contrast, a number of unions and civil society actors, including UNITE, AFL-CIO and ICCR, felt the FLA code of conduct was too lenient and so also departed the coalition. Nonetheless, the funding and support of the US government, as well as the continued participation of other members of the business community, universities, and colleges, and the corporate accountability movement led to the continuing existence and growth of the FLA (Varley 1998; Dickson, Loker, and Eckman 2009; FLA 2014).

SAI

SAI is another market monitor that certifies organizations involved in the global production of goods for their performance on CSR. SAI – a human rights organization created by the Council on Economic Priorities (an early proponent of SRI) with funding from the federal government – was created in the late 1990s as a multi-stakeholder coalition (Bartley 2007b). Working with a handful of corporations (including Levi Strauss and Liz Claiborne), it created a certification system, called the SA8000 standard for decent work, in 1997. A company in any industry could apply for certification if it met SAI's list of international labor standards. SA8000 focuses on the process by which any type of good is made, with a specific focus on workers' human rights. It includes nine core standards, including child labor, forced labor, health and safety, freedom of association and right to collective bargaining, discrimination, discipline, working hours, compensation, and management systems. SAI trained auditors, both professional and NGO, in SA8000 standards and they then evaluated a firm for compliance with the standard and SAI provided firms with a certification of compliance through both scheduled and unscheduled inspections. SA8000 was to be used by retailers to communicate their CSR performance with consumers but also was intended to be used by manufacturing companies to demonstrate compliance with labor standards for consideration by purchasers in a global supply chain (Varley 1998; Bartley 2003).

SA8000 is commonly understood to have constituted a conscious effort of its proponents to generate a certification mechanism that both incorporated a concern for workers' rights but also accommodated firms' preferences as stakeholders. First, it represented a compromise between members of the corporate accountability movement, who sought to have monitoring conducted by independent and local NGOs, and corporations, who wanted to hire professional monitors of their own choosing, such as the professional accounting firm PWC with whom they typically had pre-existing business relationships. The result was SA8000's recognition of a wide variety of auditors that could engage in accrediting. Secondly, SAI drew from a pre-existing valuation repertoire by extending the use of quality standards to the evaluation of companies' treatment of workers. Quality assurance standards, a certification method to ensure that a product or production process meets a pre-specified requirement, emerged as a market-based response to the growth of outsourcing and subcontracting across a varying and changing set of firms with globalization. Purchasers struggled to determine if a supplier's goods were of adequate quality. ISO 9000, created in 1987 by the International Standards Organization, was the first global quality accreditation system for manufacturing and service industries. Firms were evaluated by independent accrediting organizations to see if they met the nine standards of ISO 9000 and suppliers could use the certification as a signal of quality. Similarly, the goal of SAI was to facilitate purchasers' review of suppliers for their just treatment of workers via the presence of SA8000 accreditation (Harvey 2000; Nadvi and Wältring 2001; SAI 2014).

By the early 2000s, FLA and SAI were joined by a growing number of other accreditors of firms' social performance. These included WRAP (Worldwide Responsible Apparel Production), an accrediting system set up by representatives of the US apparel industry, the Workers' Rights Consortium (WRC), an organization formed by the United Students Against Sweatshops to promote a code of conduct for use by firms in the global apparel industry to inform purchasing decisions by universities and colleges, and the Ethical Trading Initiative, a European coalition of trade unions, NGOs, and firms that has been committed to developing best practices in the specification of a code of conduct and development of an auditing system for its member organizations (Nadvi and Waltring 2001; O'Rourke 2003).

The multiple communicative purposes of CSR ratings

As we have seen, the value entrepreneurs that produced the FLA and the SAI, as two of the prevailing measuring devices in the field of CSR, were multi-stakeholder in nature in that they included the participation of a wide variety of government, nonprofit, and market actors. In result, as valuation instruments, these CSR certification systems held a two-fold communicative purpose for the value entrepreneurs involved. Ratings served as both a form of control by critics over companies' social performance and as a means for companies to demonstrate their legitimacy to others.

First, as with the broader goals of the corporate accountability movement, these accrediting organizations were intended to allow external actors to privately regulate the actions of corporations. Government and civil society actors sought to establish universal norms of socially responsible behavior and to elicit both compliance with those standards and to ensure the disclosure of corporate social behavior to key audience members, including consumers and the media. In this way, certification as a measuring device constituted a form of what Keck and Sikkink (1998) call "leverage politics" – one strategy by which trans national advocacy networks may influence the behavior of key targets, such as states, multinational corporations, or multilateral organizations. Leverage politics occurs when actors "mobilize information strategically to help create new issues and categories, and to persuade, pressurize, and gain leverage over much more powerful organizations and governments" (Keck and Sikkink 1998:89). Thus, the creation of CSR ratings, in the form of certification, constituted just one arm of the corporate accountability movement, alongside the earlier use of media attention, to "name and shame" companies that violated expectations. These civil society actors relied on the threat of consumer purchasing or boycott as a form of market incentive, as discussed earlier. These market monitors used the rating of companies' CSR performance as a market incentive to engender good behavior in firms.

In one interview with the founder of a nonprofit involved in the formation of an early rating system on workers' labor rights, I asked the respondent to describe how proponents of firms' CSR accreditation had considered the pluses and minuses of this approach. She replied:

> We wanted to act on this negative publicity of Nike, Wal-Mart and the other big TNCs and it increasingly seemed clear to everyone involved that these guys weren't going to be trusted to do the dirty work for themselves. So we needed to do something – it seemed like a moment where some American consumers... this was more prevalent in Europe, of course.... but it did seem like some American consumers – those who lived in big cities, who had gone to college, who read the New York Times, yada yada yada – they really did care about how their gym clothes were made and if child labor was involved. If we could just find a way to convey this information to those people, there seemed the promise that they might use that when they decided on where to get their next pair of running shorts. And, additionally, whether they would really do so or not, we could always take that to a firm and tell them there was the potential for customers to use that info to decide what to buy or what not to buy and so they should get rated by us just in case.

Similar to the field of SRI, the intent behind NGOs' development of CSR accreditation was to place pressure on firms by drawing attention to their social performance. As in the case of Rugmark, as detailed earlier, the claim was that a bad rating or the absence of accreditation might result in market repercussions, such as a consumer boycott, employee disapproval, and/or negative press (O'Rourke 2003; Seidman 2007; Soule 2009). There was a market "price" to non-compliance (Bartley 2011).[5] However, CSR value entrepreneurs did not attempt to quantify the financial value of CSR accreditation. They did not make a "business case" for firms' implementation of socially responsible practices (Vogel 2006). In result, despite the lingua franca of the market being the currency of money, the measure of CSR via the use of ratings, as shown earlier, remained limited to the analysis of a firm's policies and practices concerning their production processes and their hypothesized social repercussions.

In addition to influencing consumers' buying choices (or the threat of them doing so), the presence of a rankings system also could encourage firms' adoption of socially responsible policies and practices through the mechanism of competition. Members of the corporate accountability movement saw accreditation as a means for firms' to tout their social performance. Ratings opened up a new means by which a corporation could signal to consumers that they were socially responsible. As outlined by SustainAbility, a CSR consulting firm, "a common aspiration across these ratings is for such measurement and comparison – often public – to stir the competitive juices in companies to improve their sustainability performance and/or disclosure" (SustainAbility 2010:2). One nonprofit formulator of a rating system for corporations' CSR performance confirmed the centrality of competition as a type of market incentive in our conversation together. I had asked him where the idea for his rating system had come from. He replied in a slightly gleeful tone:

One thing I have always noticed is that you can get anyone to do anything if you make it a competition. There is no end to what a man will do if he knows he might lose to someone else. Men *cannot* stand losing. So, that's basically the philosophy underlying our work. We came up with the idea of giving companies stars for how well they do as corporate citizens. What's funny is that it really is *our* standard of corporate citizenship – it's essentially based on my own beliefs, based on my research and experience, about what corporations need to do to make the world a better place or maybe . . . not to make it a worse place . . . but what I believe is important could matter less to the companies – they just don't want to look bad.

Yet, the formation of accreditation systems also served several critical communicative purposes for multinational corporations as well. Several US companies had already sought to respond to external critiques not just by adopting a code of conduct but also working to create collective vehicles by which to address the problem of sweatshops. Formed in 1992, the Business for Social Responsibility consisted of a membership association of firms, such as Levi Strauss and Stride, which shared a commitment to CSR. Other American companies had worked with the federal government in earlier efforts to address the domestic challenge of sweatshops in the apparel and footwear industry (Varley 1998; Bartley 2009).

This handful of US companies, including Liz Claiborne, L.L. Bean, and Nike, joined early efforts to create accreditation standards for several reasons. First, they realized that the federal government was insisting on private modes of social regulation in a global economy and to fail to participate would be to risk the implementation of legislation or the insertion of social clauses into multilateral agreements instead. Secondly, external codes of conduct would address consumers' worries. If an independent, third-party accreditation system was created, it would allow firm to then use their certification to demonstrate compliance with those new norms to others, such as investors, consumers, buyers, and employees. As one apparel industry executive explained, the purpose of accreditation systems was so that "companies will be better able to protect their reputations" (as quoted in Ramey 1997). The construction of a rating system was deemed to make economic sense. In 1989, the chairman of Shell articulated this viewpoint on why corporations participate in the CSR movement. He concluded that "'by taking a constructive interest in social matters we are reinforcing our identification with society. If we can gain acceptance as a responsible, understanding and sympathetic neighbour, the size of the audiences prepared to give us a fair hearing in matters of public debate about our activities is increased. In other words, social responsibility is good business and good business is socially responsible" (Pike 1989).

The multiple meanings of social in CSR ratings

The presence of multiple value entrepreneurs in the construction of CSR ratings affected not only why these tools were created and for what purpose, but – not surprisingly – also determined their content. A comparison of the major CSR ratings systems by the end of the 1990s, including the FLA, SAI, WRAP, Workers' Rights Consortium, and the Ethical Trading Initiative, shows the consequences of competing stakeholders in these coalitions for how CSR ratings defined the meaning of social value (Douglas 2001; O'Rourke 2003). While the ratings shared some critical commonalities, a noted divergence existed between how initial proponents of CSR (those from the corporate accountability movement) envisioned firms' social obligations and the varying content of those five early and influential certification systems.

As a whole, these ratings conceived of the social as a "relatively finite set of criteria" – a concern for how firms' production processes affected workers (Fombrun 1998:338). All of the codes focused on the same ten issues: compliance with local labor legislation, occupational safety and health, freedom of association, harassment and abuse, collective bargaining, non-discrimination in employment, wages and benefits, forced labor, hours of work, and child labor (Douglas 2001). As was the case with earlier CSR corporate codes of conduct, these shared emphases reflected the common influence of earlier private regulatory efforts to protect international workers' rights, including the International Labor Organization's Declaration on Fundamental Principles and Rights at Work, the Universal Declaration of Human Rights, and the United Nations Convention Against Corruption (Business for Social Responsibility 2000).

Yet, critical differences remained across these standards as to what constituted adequate social performance on the part of firms. Key debates existed around issues such as freedom of association, the specification of required wages and benefits, and the scope of "nondiscrimination" clauses (Douglas 2001; O'Rourke 2003). For example, the more corporate interests dominated the process of its formation, the less likely a rating was to include protection of workers' rights to collective bargaining. Collective bargaining, for example, was an omitted issue in the WRAP code, which had been created only by representatives from the apparel industry. Perhaps the biggest difference existed around the issue of wages, in part because the definition of a living wage, unlike other workers' rights, was never clarified in either the ILO or OECD's conventions, and in part because of resistance from member corporations (Harvey 2000). While all of the codes required firms to pay at least the legal minimum wage prevailing in the country of production, market monitors contended that such legal requirements were too low and that expectations of a living wage from the Global North should be extended elsewhere. In result, some of the codes, including the SA8000, required a living wage for workers while others with greater corporate representation, including FLA and WRAP, allowed firms to pay the local legal wage (Douglas 2001).

Finally, differences existed across these codes in terms of their recognition of community involvement as a dimension of CSR. Community involvement is commonly understood to reference a company's treatment of the local communities in which they operate, the inclusion of disadvantaged groups as employees, and the extent of their corporate philanthropy. A concern for firms' community involvement was absent from the seminal ILO and OECD conventions (although are central to the scholarly formulation of CSR) (Carroll 1999). Not surprisingly, then, early efforts by human rights organizations to codify CSR in a rating omitted mention of community involvement while those codes developed with corporate representation were likely to emphasize its importance (Douglas 2001; O'Rourke 2003).

In all, the inclusion of those very same corporations that were targeted by market monitors in the construction of ratings resulted in competing understandings of the meaning of social value and the communicative purpose of a rating system. These disagreements resulted in a disjuncture between the social project that drove the formation of CSR and the content and form of the measuring devices that would come to evaluate it. Thus, the involvement of business interests in the construction of a certification system resulted in the alteration of the field's meaning of social value, as a case of the broader ability of corporations to strategically respond to market movements and to minimize or co-opt criticisms (Baron 2001; King and Pearce 2010).

THE GROWTH OF CSR

Beyond the academic origins of CSR and the ensuring emphasis placed by market monitors on the working conditions of production in a global economy, two later developments also are key to understanding the historical growth of CSR. First, the defining concerns of the sustainable development movement, as relevant for corporations (and often called "sustainability"), have been incorporated into the definition of CSR (and now CSR and sustainability are often used interchangeably to describe the extra-financial responsibilities of firms). Secondly, the use of CSR ratings to evaluate firms' performance has expanded beyond market monitors invested in protecting workers' rights in the global supply chain to an assortment of other actors in the private sector.

CSR and the sustainable development movement

In the history of the field of CSR, initial attention to the human and labor rights of employees in developing nations was supplemented by the concerns of the sustainable development movement.[6] The most famous definition of sustainable development comes from the United Nation's World Commission on Environment and Development's Brundtland Commission (World Commission on Environment and Development 1987:9) – "sustainable development" consists of meeting the "needs of the present without compromising the ability to meet the future generation to meet their own needs." Premised on environmentalism, the sustainable development movement requires that an actor's contemporary engagement with her material surroundings is conditional upon future economic, social, and ecological well-being (Lele 1991). The sustainable development movement has had a number of areas of focus including individuals' consumption habits, governmental policy-making, and corporations' conduct (Bartley 2007b).

The turn to corporate sustainability resulted from a larger shift in the sustainable development movement, away from simply a focus on the environment and towards the three "pillars" of economic, social, and environmental sustainability, as articulated in the 2002 World Summit on Sustainable Development (Kates, Parris, and Leiserowitz 2005). The pressure for firms to address their environment impact was intensified by the occurrence of the Exxon Valdez Alaskan oil leak in 1989 and the Bhopal gas leak disaster in India in 1994 and then by a growing concern over climate change, leading to a crisis in legitimacy of the capacity of corporations to voluntarily consider their effect on the environment. Initially, firms' engagement with sustainability was governed not only by their codes of conduct, but also a number of independent and external principles, codes of conduct, and ratings systems (Bartley 2007b). Ceres, for example, is a nonprofit founded in 1989, that created the Ceres Principles, a ten-point code of conduct for firms' environmental performance. The Marine Stewardship Council is a nonprofit that certifies for sustainable fishing practices (Pattberg 2007). Over time, the consideration of a firm's sustainability performance became incorporated into CSR ratings (Chatterji and Levine 2006; Waddock 2008a).

The proliferation of CSR rating and reporting

The presence of ratings in CSR expanded beyond its initial origins in contestation between market monitors and firms over the corporate accountability of MNCs for the labor conditions in their global supply chains. Other actors, including media outlets, stock market intermediaries, and consultants, began to offer ratings, rankings, and certifications of corporations in regard to their CSR performance. They developed generic, market-wide CSR ratings as well as extending their assessments beyond the apparel industry to other sectors, such as forest products, oil and gas, and mining, among others (O'Rourke 2003). By 2010, the field had expanded to include over one-hundred CSR ratings (SustainAbility 2010).

A variety of actors produced their own CSR ratings of corporations. Some media publications began to offer CSR assessments of firms. Beginning in the 1980s, *Fortune* Magazine annually published lists of the Most Admired Companies, the Global Most Admired Companies, and the Best Companies to Work for, relying on peers' subjective evaluation of corporations (Fombrun 1998; Waddock 2008a). In addition, the field of SRI moved to incorporate CSR issues. As noted in Chapter 4, SRI originally had involved community investing, shareholder activism, and the social screening of stocks based on investors' preferences about a company's products, place, or policies. Investment funds as well as research and ranking agencies, which had provided data on firms' SRI performance, now also began to generate data and conduct evaluations of firms' CSR or sustainability performance for investors (Kinder 2005). In result, the acronym of SRI now often is used not to summarize the concept of "SRI," as originally intended, but instead to represent the goal of "Sustainable and Responsible Investing," as noted by several interviewees. Further, as the field of CSR has become institutionalized, both for-profit and nonprofit consultants emerged that offered their own rating systems of firms and that provided guidance to firms on the implementation of CSR or advice to investors on CSR issues. As with SRI, the generation of CSR ratings has become an industry in and of itself, expanding beyond the political intentions of the field's early proponents. Examples of consulting firms that also rate corporations for their CSR performance include SustainAbility, Innovest Strategic Value Advisers, Verité, PWC, and HIP Investor Inc., among others (Waddock 2008a).

Alongside the growth of CSR ratings, some CSR proponents have championed corporations' self-reporting as the means to demonstrate their commitment to sustainable development. Despite its absence in the early history of CSR, the United Nations has become a key proponent of this latter effort. In 1999, Kofi Annan, then UN Secretary General, initiated the Global Compact. With feedback from MNCs, union groups, government representatives, and NGOs, the Global Compact identified nine principles of corporate citizenship (later extended to ten principles), which embodied an "enlightened global business" approach. Multinational corporations were encouraged to voluntarily sign on to the compact and to implement the principles in their global supply chains, albeit with no monitoring or sanctioning mechanisms built into the compact. Drawn from existing international standards, the ten principles include companies' respect for human rights in the regions in which it operated, protection of the labor rights of workers (including freedom of association and collective bargaining, forced labor, child labor, and workplace discrimination), respect for the environment, and an anti corruption policy. By 2013, as noted in Chapter 1, over 12,000 entities had signed onto the compact (Rasche and Kell 2010; United Nations Global Compact 2014).

More recently, the Global Reporting Initiative (GRI) has become widely recognized as providing the dominant format by which firms report their sustainability performance. Formed in 1997 by CERES with support from the United Nations Environment Program, GRI is modeled after the principles of financial reporting and is aimed at providing a framework for sustainability reporting that is equivalent in regard to "comparability, auditability and general acceptance" (Willis 2003:233). GRI delivers guidance to firms as to both the principles governing a firm's reporting of sustainability (with a focus on inclusiveness, sustainability context, and materiality) and the content of the self report. For each of the three dimensions of sustainability – economic (e.g., wages, community development); environmental (e.g., waste generation, energy consumption), and social (e.g., workplace issues, human rights), the GRI lists a number of recommended disclosures and accompanying performance indicators. GRI quickly became the accepted standard for sustainability/CSR reporting (Etzion and Ferraro 2010). By 2011, the GRI guidelines were employed by over three-quarters of the top 250 companies in the Fortune Global 500 in their self-reporting (KPMG 2013).

In all, the diffusion of CSR in the private sector in the form of an array of rankings and rankings represented a substantive shift from its origins in the efforts of civil society actors to monitor the activities of MNCs in a new global economy. As we will see in Chapter 6, the increasing institutionalization of CSR in the private sector, coupled with the growing acceptance of the financial return of socially informed investing (whether in the fields of SRI or CSR), led to a new configuration of social value – one where money and mission became seen as complimentary in the pursuit of shareholder return.

Notes

1. Another response to this emphasis on firm's social obligations was the articulation of a free market ideology, as discussed in Chapter 6 (Friedman 1970; Jensen and Meckling 1976).
2. A later version of CSR – called Responsible Investing, as will be outlined in Chapter 6, includes the environment as a key stakeholder and incorporates a consideration of a firm's governance practices.

3. The Investor Responsibility Research Center formed in 1972 to provide guidance on ethical investment to member universities and colleges, recognized in the 1990s the labor problems resulting from globalization (Varley 1998). Similarly, the Center on Economic Priorities, founded in 1969 to conduct research on corporations' social performance, then used its expertise to develop SAI, a CSR social standard for corporations. And Joan Bavaria, who had founded both an early SRI investment firm and the Social Investment Forum, also went on to co-found CERES in 1989, an early proponent of sustainability and a key leader of the Global Reporting Initiative (Varley 1998; Waddock 2008b).

4. Later, in response to criticisms, the FLA incorporated greater unannounced monitoring visits into their policy, removed firms' ability to select monitors or pay for monitors and increased public disclosure of findings (Chatterji and Levine 2006).

5. In contrast, as with SRI, the assumption of those in the corporate world was that firms' attention to CSR possessed negative repercussions for financial return (Margolis and Walsh 2003).

6. The sustainability movement changed the content of CSR for organizations in the market in at least three ways. First, the initial focus of CSR had been on firms' members as stakeholders. Sustainability required firms to also consider the intersection of the market and the environment. Secondly, sustainability explicitly altered the timeline by which firms should consider their extra-financial impacts. CSR was concerned with the immediate or near effects of a firm's production processes on stakeholders. In contrast, sustainability called attention to the long-term impact of firm's actions on the environment. Finally, the concept of sustainability changed the spatial scale of social responsibility. CSR had been fundamentally concerned with its effects on those people and places directly affected by its business activities – ranging from suppliers, local communities, employees, to consumers. In contrast, the sustainability movement sought to bring attention to the global environmental implications of a firm's spatially embedded activity.

PART III

MARKET ENTHUSIASTS

6

Just good business

Responsible Investment

> The debate on the capital market surrounding ESG is complex, and not always comprehensible, even to the experts. One thing, however, is clear: ESG is not ethical valuation but about understanding and measuring material risks impacted through ESG for companies in every industry
>
> (DVFA 200814)

Beginning around the start of the twenty-first century, caring capitalism, as a new and purportedly gentler model of the market, began to be promoted by key actors in the global economy. As a social project, caring capitalism heralds the capacity of compassionate companies to produce principal and principle at one and the same time. Firms can generate social and financial value through their business models, including how they source supplies, whom they employ and how they treat their workers, how they distribute their products, and/or what products they sell and to whom. Unlike the negative view of the market found in Chapters 4 and 5 of this book, advocates of caring capitalism champion the work of businesses as a solution to social problems. The third and last part of this book analyzes the implications of this rise of caring capitalism, which has taken a number of distinct fields, for the pursuit of social good. What happens to the meaning and measure of social value when caring capitalism is framed by market enthusiasts both as an answer to social inequities and as a new source of wealth creation?

As outlined in Chapter 1, scholarship in the social sciences offers us a number of competing expectations. One traditional prediction is that the movement of goods into the economy, where they will to be bought and sold as commodities, subjects them to the logic of the market. They will become evaluated solely in terms of their monetary worth for consumers and their capacity to generate economic gain for producers and investors. In this view, what gets to count as social value with caring capitalism should become determined not by actors' values (their ideals concerning a just and equitable society) but by the criteria of value (the pursuit of profit). In result, social value as an order of worth (or, alternatively, as an institutional logic or repertoire of evaluation) should become restricted to those business practices that not only generate social good but that also generate return for investors, given that shareholder value has "become the privileged metric for assessing corporate success" (Krippner 2011:7).

A second prediction is that actors are able to draw from and integrate different orders of worth even when located in the private sector (Boltanski and Thévenot 2006; Zelizer 2009). Rather than the "hostile worlds" outcome, goods deemed sacred or moral in some way can be bought and sold as commodities without losing their ethical intent, through the careful use of relational work. Actors create social relationships around the market exchange of those entities, bounding them of as distinct from the trade of other goods. In the case of caring capitalism, we should expect to see proponents enact a social project as a moral market by ensuring the use of money as a medium of exchange and as a mode of valuation for goods that are heralded as a market-based solutions to social problems in ways that protect the social value of those commodities and limit the impact of a market logic.

In contrast, in Chapters 7 and 8, I find a range of valuation instruments present across different fields within the broader movement of caring capitalism, with contrasting implications for what gets to count as social value. To explain these differing outcomes in terms of the measure and so meaning of social value across these varying fields of caring capitalism is the task of this next chapter and the next. As I will show in Chapter 7, in some versions of this newer, purportedly kinder global economy, companies are judged for their social worth in and of itself and distinct from their financial performance. In another version of caring capitalism, as discussed in this chapter, the emerging measuring devices assign a dollar figure to companies' societal contributions and gauge firms' efforts based on the generation of shareholder return, with critical consequences for the meaning of social value.

Drawing from literature in economic sociology on the formation of markets, I show that the construction of measuring devices in the case of Responsible Investment (RI) served to address the "problem of value" for potential investors, in order to justify this new form of investment to key audiences. And, even here, the "marketization" of compassionate companies' social worth by reference to their economic value has been neither automatic nor compulsory. Instead, facing resistance from the intended audience of mainstream investors who viewed social value and economic value as oppositional (and hence embodied social scientists' "hostile worlds" perspective), value entrepreneurs in the field have had to exert sustained effort to deploy market indicators in order to assess firms' social performance in ways deemed legitimate to those key stakeholders. Importantly, the consequence has been that of a marked disjuncture between what counts as social value in the envisioned social project at the core of RI and what counts in that field's prevailing measuring devices.

THE RISE OF CARING CAPITALISM

To understand the turn to compassionate companies as a new type of social purpose organization requires attention to broader changes in the global economy. To begin with, the occurrence of the financial crisis in 2007 through 2008 resulted in a systematic and sustained reconsideration – by not only long-standing critics (such as the proponents of SRI and CSR) but also by some champions of a neoliberal agenda – of the guiding principles of business' responsibility to shareholders and to society. Through the 1980s and 1990s, shareholder capitalism had dominated the global economy, replacing the logic of managerial capitalism that had guided business' social and economic activities in the US since the Second World War, as outlined in Chapter 4. Shareholder capitalism has been defined as a principle of corporate governance that privileges firms' pursuit of short-term financial return to shareholders, as part of the broader financialization of the global economy. Shareholder capitalism originated in the declining economic performance of American firms facing international competition in the 1970s (Davis 2009; Mizruchi 2013). It was further driven by the rise of the institutional investor and the creation of stock-based compensation for managers as a means to solve the principal-agency problem for shareholders, where stock price was employed as the measure of corporate performance (Jensen and Meckling 1976). Managers could drive up the market value of a stock's price by cutting labor costs and selling off physical assets. Business' adoption of the shareholder value ideology both contributed to and was reinforced by the discourse and practices of neoliberalism. The dominance of shareholder capitalism possessed critical implications for firms' understanding of their social responsibility. Proponents of shareholder capitalism have viewed the only responsibility of a firm as being profit maximization for its shareholders and corporations' societal obligations as ending with its economic, technical, and legal responsibilities (Davis 2009).[1] Corporations, in this view, should externalize the social and environmental costs of their activities to government and the larger society, often in the name of the benefits of shareholders and at the expense of stakeholders. The economist, Milton Friedman, famously articulated this perspective in a 1970 article in *Time* magazine, stating "the social responsibility of business is to increase its profits."

However, the market crash in 2001 and the global financial crisis of 2008, along with long-standing critiques of growing inequality in the global economy, led to a fundamental reexamination of the legitimacy of shareholder value as the orienting principle of the global economy (Davis 2009; Krippner 2011). Several institutional actors, including finance professionals, government agencies, multilateral organizations, and civil society actors, have offered up solutions to correct the perceived flaws of shareholder capitalism (Martin 2011; Stout 2012). These efforts to correct the premises of global capitalism have taken three main forms. First, there has been a call for and move to increased government regulation over the economy (Financial Crisis Inquiry Commission 2011). Others have sought to implement increased shareholder control over firms through attention to their governance practices (Gourevitch and Shinn 2005). Finally, a third group has offered up an assortment of new and improvized versions of the free market that allow actors, including investors and firms, to voluntarily work to correct for the errors implicit to a neoliberal, shareholder-centered configuration of the global economy.

I group this last assortment of strategies under the broad umbrella of caring capitalism, or what also has been called creative capitalism (Gates 2008), conscious capitalism (Mackey 2013), and inclusive capitalism (Hart 2005). Caring capitalism consists of the explicit and concerted efforts of a cluster of advocates, whom I call "market enthusiasts," to promote a new imagined vision of business in which the pursuit of mission and money are viewed as mutually constitutive so as to produce a more just and sustainable global economy. To do so, proponents have developed a range of vehicles by which principal and principle can be achieved in the private sector. Their goal has been to encourage investors and firms, including both multinational corporations and local companies, to implement one or more of these models as a means to resuscitate the global financial economy. Theoretically, caring capitalism constitutes another case of private regulation, as discussed in Chapters 4 and 5, whereby market actors voluntarily work to engage in market-based social change without the necessity of additional government oversight and intervention.

Caring capitalism perhaps has been most prominent in a new envisioning of the long-standing goal of poverty reduction in the project of international development. Poverty, in this view, is caused by individuals' lack of access to the free market. This new model of international development, often called "inclusive development," prioritizes the role of the private sector in poverty alleviation, based in part on companies' capacity for scale and self-sufficiency, and de-prioritizes the historically dominant efforts of the public and nonprofit sectors to address poverty and other social problems. In all, the shared assumption of caring capitalism is that firms will pursue the same set of social goods as government and NGOs, just in a more effective and efficient manner (Stiglitz 1989; World Bank 1991, 2001; Department for Industrial Development 2006; Commission on Growth and Development 2008).

Caring capitalism takes a variety of investment and business forms, each premised on a faith that market actors can do well at doing good, as discussed in Chapter 1. Multinational corporations, for example, can produce social and economic value at one and the same time in several ways. They can pursue a double bottom line through the optimal organization of their production processes (via their just treatment of stakeholders, including employees, local communities, and supply chains) (Hebb 2012). Other MNCs pursue principal and principle by selling socially beneficial products to low-income consumers (those at the "Bottom of the Pyramid") in new ways that still produce profit (Prahalad 2004). And, in the developing world, local companies, often called "small and medium enterprises" or SMEs, facilitate social welfare in their community by expanding individuals' access to the economy as employees, entrepreneurs, and suppliers (Ferranti and Ody 2007). Finally, microfinance is a much-heralded strategy for providing financial services to individuals who previously have been unable to acquire the capital necessary to start or grow a small business from traditional banking institutions (Yunus 1999). In all of these cases, for-profit actors and entities in the private sector are heralded as possessing new and optimal means to make money while also making the world a better place.

THE CASE OF RI

This chapter focuses on the field of RI – a new and emerging view of financial capital that sees firms' performance on environmental, social, and governance issues (what is often called "ESG") as one critical source of shareholder value. In its formulation of the social obligations of business, proponents ground RI in the tenets of Corporate Social Responsibility (CSR), but now seek to make the business case for CSR and to create a new financial market around it. To do so, proponents of RI, including the United Nations, governments, consultants, and large finance institutions, have worked to integrate the use of ESG data into mainstream investment (United Nations Global Compact 2004; World Economic Forum 2005; International Finance Corporation 2012). However, the challenge for proponents of growing RI as a market has been that it challenges the traditional premises of stock valuation in the stock market. Typically, only financial data is employed by stock analysts to assess the worth of a company and corporations' attention to society and the environment is perceived to violate a firm's financial duty to shareholders. In result, many members of the mainstream investing community have responded to the concept of RI with skepticism and resistance. How then have proponents of RI sought to make the business case – to demonstrate the positive bottom line of firms' non-financial ESG performance – for this new version of investing? How have they worked to create a market of RI? And what are the implications of RI for how social value is defined and assessed as a case of caring capitalism, compared to the pursuit of social value by social purpose organizations in other fields both in and out of the market?

Literature in economic sociology on the construction of markets provides one useful perspective for addressing these questions. An economic market is typically understood as a setting or field in which the repeated economic exchange of a commodity (a specific good or service) between buyers and sellers (either consumers or other businesses) takes place (Fligstein 2001). The traditional view, typically found in neo-classical economics, is that the formation of a market is the natural and inevitable result of individuals' desire to trade a particular good. Markets are self-regulating entities that arise spontaneously out of individuals' rational pursuit of self-interest as buyers or sellers. As most famously espoused by Adam Smith (1776), the market is governed by a mechanism that ensures that the price of a good reflects the balance of demand and supply.

In contrast, economic sociologists emphasize that markets are socially constructed and require sustained effort by multiple actors, including suppliers, competitors, customers, government, and civil society actors, in order to emerge and to operate (Fligstein 2001; White 2002). For a market's participant, it must make sense to buy and sell those objects rather than exchange them in other settings (such as the domestic sphere, the government, or the nonprofit sector) using an alternative basis of exchange, such as reciprocity or redistribution (Polanyi 1957). A successful market must be constructed "cognitively, structurally, and legally" (Levin 2008:119) in order for the successful exchange of goods to occur (Abolafia 1996; Carruthers and Stinchcombe 1999). In this framework, a market is viable only when the objects to be exchanged are legitimately viewed as commodities, in that they can be assigned a price and that they are understood to produce profit for the company and value for the consumer. Actors in a market must be able to determine the economic value of competing commodities in order to make a judgment of worth, compare alternatives, and make a purchase or investment with an expectation of economic gain or competitive advantage (Callon 1998; Espeland and Stevens 1998). Among issues of coordination, this "value problem" (Beckert 2009) in a market can be resolved not only by the subjective estimations of market members, but also by the construction of institutions, conventions, and devices that can calculate the worth of goods for the market as a whole and its members (Callon 1998; Callon and Muniesa 2005; Karpik 2010). [2]

The implication of this latter view is that the construction of a market around a good or service is not automatic. Further, the conversion of an object into a commodity is relatively straightforward in some cases but in other cases is more complicated and even unfeasible in yet others. Often goods that are considered "sacred" or "intimate" in society (items such as blood, eggs, cadavers, and organs) face the greatest challenge in being classified as a commodities that should be bought and sold for money (Anteby 2010; Almeling 2011; Chan 2012). The move of a good from other societal spheres to the market is often fraught and requires thoughtful and concerned effort on the part of that new market's proponents. How, for example, have advocates of the new global market of gestational surrogacy attempted to frame the sale of women's reproductive capacities in ways that limit ethical concerns? (Spar 2013) In such industries with "contested" goods (Radin 2001), proponents struggle to create legitimacy and the necessary infrastructure for the market exchange of that good, sometimes meeting with mixed success (Levin 2008; Turco 2012).

How can this literature on the social construction of markets help us to understand how advocates of Responsible Investment sought to construct this new field? As we will see, the success of this new market, while still unfolding, has been dependent on the sustained efforts by proponents of the social project of RI to convince others that it is a legitimate form of financial investment. Here, contrary to the predictions of the "hostile worlds" perspective, resistance to the formation of this market came not from those actors committed to the moral value of firms' treatment of stakeholders, but instead from mainstream investors committed to the traditional criteria and methods of stock valuation as a means to make money. To build a market of RI, value entrepreneurs worked to develop the appropriate measuring devices necessary to solve the "value problem" as an analytical case of justification as a communicative purpose, as outlined in Chapter 3. They sought to demonstrate the capacity of a firm's ESG performance to generate shareholder value through the monetization of that array of a corporation's non-financial characteristics. To construct suitable tools, proponents of RI drew from their expertise in traditional capital markets in order to extend and modify mainstream investing's existing measurement devices to this new market. But, the consequence has been that what counts as social value has become restricted by the conventions and devices present in the broader quest for shareholder value in a finance economy.

DEFINING RI

Emerging in the early 2000s, RI, also called Sustainable Investment (World Economic Forum 2011), is a view of investing that incorporates a concern for firms' ESG performance, alongside their financial performance, into the estimation of a stock's value. ESG is an acronym for "Environmental Social Governance" and draws attention to how corporations negotiate their environmental impact, how they manage their social relationships with employees, suppliers, customers, and local communities, and the policies in place by which they are governed (United Nations Global Compact 2004; World Economic Forum 2005; Eccles and Vivier 2011).[3] Like SRI and CSR, RI consists of a set of expectations of good corporate behavior that extends beyond the traditional measure of financial performance to include additional policies and practices, including a concern for firms' production of social value.

However, RI is distinct from CSR in two ways. First, RI draws attention to a different cluster of firm characteristics than CSR. While drawing from CSR's long-standing concern for a firm's environmental and social negative impacts, the concept of ESG also incorporates the concept of "corporate governance" (Paine et al. 2005). Corporate governance concerns the procedures and processes according to which an organization is directed and controlled. It typically is focused on ensuring appropriate guidelines are in place to govern the behavior of a company's board of directors, including its prescribed activities,

composition, and compensation. This focused concern for corporate governance in the global economy emerged in the 1990s. It is traced to the growth of
shareholder control of corporations, the rise of agency theory (which assumes a
disjuncture between the interests of firms' shareholders and managers), as well
as an effort to implement corporate accountability following the notorious
collapses of Enron and Worldcom (O'Sullivan 2001; Gourevitch and Shinn
2005).[4]

Secondly, RI's attention to ESG represents a departure from CSR in that it
is based on mainstream investors' expectations of economic return, rather
than on the normative concerns of market monitors as was the case with
CSR, as outlined in the last chapter. With RI, proponents have offered a new
justification for attention to a firm's performance on ESG factors. As shown
in Figure 6.1, ESG criteria are salient for financial, rather than moral, reasons
(Kinder 2005; Hebb 2012). RI is about "value not values," to quote from
one senior executive that I spoke with at a mainstream investing firm who
worked in its RI office. In RI, this attention to ESG issues is justified in the
belief that firms that incorporate a concern for those non-financial matters
will not only produce social value but also will have better, long-term
financial results than their peers whom they outperform on these dimensions
(United Nations Global Compact 2004; World Economic Forum 2005). As
the United Nations, an early proponent of RI, asserted: "From asset managers, pension trustees and stock exchanges to project leaders and insurers,

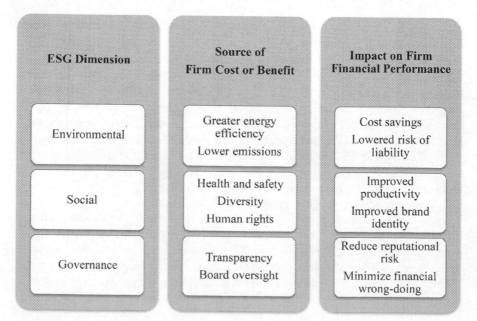

FIGURE 6.1 Social and financial value in Responsible Investing

the investment community increasingly connects – ESG – performance to long-term viability and financial performance" (UN Global Compact Office 2007:12). One proponent of RI explained that firms' ESG performance is "about risk management, not morality. Thus what 'ought to be' is not considered relevant."[5]

This economic rationale for attention to ESG performance draws from the fundamental assumptions of finance theory but alters it in key ways. One central premise of finance theory is that the valuation of a firm's stock is based on its future price, in order for an investor to acquire profit by a stock's price movement. Profit is earned by buying firms priced at less than their actual value and losses are avoided by selling stocks that are over-priced relative to their actual value. As I discussed in Chapter 4, to estimate the intrinsic value of a stock, analysts engage in "fundamental analysis" by examining a firm's characteristics to determine its total discounted cash flows in the future. Historically, this estimation of a stock's intrinsic value has been based on financial considerations, employing economic information about a company presented in various firm publications, including financial statements and annual reports. Typically, investors and analysts examine key characteristics including revenue, expenses, liabilities, and assets, among others, which they insert into well-established financial equations (such as a price to earnings ratio) to determine a stock's intrinsic value. This quantitative data on a firm is then synthesized with further research on the industry, as well as a more in-depth analysis of the corporation itself. Research analysts draw from this mix of information in order to determine a stock's intrinsic value and, in result, if the stock is underpriced or overpriced relative to its current value in the stock market (Graham 2006).

Extending this perspective, proponents of RI argue that the incorporation of data on a firm's ESG performance alongside financial data provides a more accurate picture of a stock's intrinsic value and thus its potential for long-term financial return (Bassen and Kovacs 2008). In contrast to the assumption of the efficient market hypothesis (that the price of a stock reflects all relevant information), the supposition of this valuation method is that analysts' inclusion of ESG data in the valuation of a firm will create a better understanding of its future risk-adjusted return. In result, ESG performance, along with other "intangible assets," is argued to be financially material. The integration of ESG data into the procedure of fundamental analysis should occur because it is understood to present financial risks and/or opportunities for a company in a complex, changing, and global economy. Risks consist of the costs incurred by a firm from an ESG issue, such as carbon emissions or the threat of a lawsuit, and opportunities include the creation of new markets, cost savings for firms, and brand enhancement with consumers and employees. Attention to a company's ESG performance also matters because it is often perceived as a proxy for its quality of management. A firm that addresses its social and environmental impact, as well as possesses good governance practices, will also be more likely to produce shareholder value through its production and/ or sale of its products. As one United Nations' report (United Nations Environmental Programme Finance Initiative Asset Management Working Group 2006:8) concluded, "Well-managed companies generally do not abuse the planet, or unfairly exploit their workers, their suppliers, or their communities." Finally, RI alters the premises of finance theory by changing the temporal orientation of shareholder return. Typically, financial analysis is attuned to a stock's production of short-term value. It is expected that shareholders seek to acquire an immediate return on their investment. In contrast, the incorporation of ESG data into the estimation of a stock's intrinsic value is understood only to create long-term future profit for the investor, given the nature of the risks and opportunities represented by a firm's ESG performance (United Nations Global Compact 2004; Hebb 2012).

THE ORIGINS OF RI

The origins of RI can be traced to concerted efforts by an assortment of proponents, each with a distinct motivation for encouraging the growth of the field. The first set of RI advocates consisted of multilateral organizations that sought to respond to the global financial crashes of 2001 and again in 2007–2008 (World Economic Forum 2005). As discussed earlier, multiple solutions were proposed to prevent a recurrence of the financial crisis, including increased government intervention and regulation, greater shareholder control over firms' governance practices, and caring capitalism as an effort to construct a more just and sustainable global economy.

As one strand of caring capitalism, RI attributes the financial crisis to mistakes in mainstream investing, particularly an over-emphasis on short-term financial return and the misspecification of stocks' fundamental value. An assortment of actors, including multilateral organizations, governments, and civil society actors, have called for a reconfiguration of the finance market towards long-term shareholder value, and the integration of corporations' social and environmental impacts into stock analysis, either through private efforts or government regulation, along with a greater emphasis on governance issues (Aspen Institute 2009; Stout 2012).[6] RI has been promoted as a means to a more durable and justifiable capital market. RI constitutes a private, nongovernmental effort by market enthusiasts to institutionalize a new form of investment that recognizes and rewards corporations that produce goods in a socially and environmentally responsible manner while generating long-term economic return.

The embrace of RI by these actors also has been supported by other changes in the global economy. The growth of knowledge-based industries has increased the perceived importance of "intangible assets" such as intellectual capital, alongside the traditional emphasis on "tangible assets" such as physical and financial assets (Bassen and Kovacs 2008; International Integrated

Reporting Committee 2011). In addition, as was the case with the earlier sustainability movement, the growing awareness of corporations' impact on the environment, and their economic repercussions for the firms' bottom line, has been critical to the growth of RI. Globally, companies were increasingly forced to consider the effect of their carbon emissions given consumer pressure and recent regulatory requirements in the United States and elsewhere (UNEP FI 2004; United States Securities and Exchange Commission 2012).[7]

In response, several global actors have sought to grow the market for RI, motivated by both political and economic interests. Most importantly, the United Nations, drawing from its earlier sustainability initiatives, became a proponent of this new strategy of investment as a means of private regulation of the capital market. Investors would serve as the vehicle of corporate governance (Ho 2010). In 2005, ex-UN president Kofi Annan, launched the United Nations Principles for Responsible Investment (now called the "Principles for Responsible Investment" or PRI). The PRI is an investor-led collaboration, in partnership with the UN Environment Programme Finance Initiative (UNEPFI) and the UN Global Compact, to encourage institutional investors to incorporate ESG principles into their investment analysis and decision-making and to encourage the growth of the field (PRI 2014).[8]

To facilitate the formation of a market of RI, the UNEP FI, along with other advocates, sought to demonstrate the economic viability of RI. First, advocates published a series of papers that demonstrated either a neutral or positive relationship between firms' ESG performance and their rate of shareholder return (United Nations Environmental Programme Finance Initiative Asset Management Working Group 2004, 2006; Sustainability Asset Management 2008). This effort to demonstrate the financial, rather than solely the normative, value of ESG was also based on a line of academic research demonstrating the positive effects of SRI and CSR performance for firms' financial performance, as discussed in the last two chapters (Waddock and Graves 1997; Margolis and Walsh 2003; Capelle-Blancard and Monjon 2012).

Secondly, the UNEPFI co-sponsored an influential publication on the implications of RI for the enactment of fiduciary duty (UNEPFI and Freshfields Bruckhaus Deringer 2005). Under US law, a fiduciary is any actor who is delegated (usually in the role of a trustee or a money manager) to manage resources for another – they are legally obligated to manage those goods in the others' best financial interests via the exercise of due care and prudence. Many critics had long expressed concern that investments based on non-financial considerations (such as Socially Responsible Investing and CSR) would violate the fiduciary duty of institutional investors by having a negative effect on the generation of financial return (see, e.g., Langbein and Posner 1980). Yet, based on a review of academic and practitioner research showing the positive financial benefit of firm's ESG performance, the UN's commissioned report asserted that fiduciaries' duty necessitated inclusion of ESG issues in their management decisions.

In addition, a small but growing number of investors and financial intermediaries were engaging in RI – using ESG data and financial data together in their evaluations of firms and estimates of a stock's value (Tullis 2011). Some of these actors, like Pax World Investments, were motivated not only by economic interest but also by an ongoing political concern for corporations' non-financial performance. They have extended their original involvement in the fields of SRI and then CSR to now espouse RI for both normative and material reasons (Wood and Hoff 2007; Social Investment Forum 2010). As first noted in Chapter 4, leaders of the United Methodist Church formed Pax World in 1971 as a mutual fund with an anti-war mission. Today, however, Pax World Investments offers a notably distinct, albeit related, set of financial services to investors by "fully integrating ESG factors into investment analysis and decision making" (Pax World Investments 2014).

Other long-term participants in the move to include non-financial criteria in the capital market were institutional investors with an extended engagement with socially responsible investment. CalPERS (the California Public Employees' Retirement System) – one of the nation's largest and earliest socially responsible institutional investors – decided in 2008 to alter its investment strategy, shifting from the guidelines of Socially Responsible Investment to employing ESG criteria (Eccles and Sesia 2009). Yet other advocates of RI were members of the mainstream investment industry who now were taking up the criteria of ESG, seeing this form of investment as a potentially new source of revenue through the offering of new products to new customers (Cui 2007). Several large investment firms, including Goldman Sachs, UBS, Merrill Lynch, and Credit Suisse, have created divisions that focus on RI (Tullis 2011). Their work has been facilitated by the growing provision of ESG data to investors and investment advisors by large data providers and research firms, including Thomson Reuters, Sustain Analytics, Bloomberg, and MSCI. To do so, these research and ratings agencies often bought out ESG-only analysts, such as MSCI's purchase of KLD (an organization that began with the production of SRI and then CSR ratings, as detailed in Chapter 4) (Bendel 2011). Similarly, to tap into this new market, stock market indices that use ESG criteria have appeared, including the Thomson Reuters Corporate Responsibility Indices, FTSE4GOOD, and the Dow Jones Sustainability Index (FTSE 2011; Sustainable Asset Management 2012; Thomson Reuters 2014). By 2013, over 1200 organizations, including asset owners, investment managers, and professional service partners, had signed on to the United Nation's Principles for Responsible Investment, which asks investors to pledge to integrate ESG criteria into their stock market decisions (PRI 2013).[9]

VALUING THE SOCIAL IN RI

Despite this embrace of RI by multilateral organizations and some actors in the capital market, many mainstream institutional investors and asset managers, particularly in the United States, have not readily taken to the inclusion of ESG as a new principle to guide financial investment. Notably, of the twenty-one American asset owners who have signed the United Nations' Principles for Responsible Investment, the vast majority consists of pension funds and non-profit organizations (which invest their endowments according to the PRI guidelines), with the one exception being the International Finance Corporation, a quasi-governmental organization affiliated with the World Bank (PRI 2013). Similarly, despite the growth of actors embracing RI, it was estimated that only seven percent of all assets under management involved ESG criteria in 2010 (PRI 2011).[10] And a 2012 study found that only a quarter of top investment consulting firms (advising more than 95% of the assets held by all institutional investors) incorporated a concern for ESG into their analysis and recommendations (Ceres 2012).

In one interview that I conducted, a senior executive at a relatively new institutional equity manager that employs ESG data recounted his experience in trying to find clients. He explained:

I initially approached institutional investors who were signatories of the Principles for Responsible Investment, basically saying to them that you need me because I'm going to provide you with an opportunity to do what you say you want to do. No success with that, absolutely none. So, now instead I use our track record – the fact that we have had a higher return rate than traditional comparison benchmarks. They listen to that; it's the oldest saying in the world but it's true – money talks. ESG has to be a means to make money for [this market] to take off.

Thus, despite a growing proclamation of interest in RI, many mainstream financial intermediaries and investors were not convinced of the merits of this new market. Drawing from interviews with respondents in this field and reports by proponents of the field, advocates attributed this skepticism to multiple causes. Many remained committed to the premises of the efficient market hypothesis, where the price of a stock reflects its fair value, and so they argued that if ESG factors were indeed material, they would already be integrated into the price of a stock. Others saw a company's concern for ESG issues as generating additional costs not born by industry competitors, hence limiting their economic performance. Another group understood the financial merit of the consideration of these "intangibles" but was not sure how to integrate ESG data into their decision-making. Finally, some analysts did not trust the quality of ESG data currently made available by firms, claiming it lacked rigor and commensurability compared to data on financial characteristics (World Economic Forum 2011; Commonfund Institute 2013).

To promote the growth of RI, advocates of this new financial market sought to address these sources of resistance by creating new valuation instruments. These valuation entrepreneurs consist of two distinct groups: those actors who work to promote RI's use by others in the field and those actors who sell financial products based on ESG integration. The first group consisted of the

PRI (initially sponsored by the United Nations), the World Business Council for Sustainable Development (a coalition of multinational corporations interested in CSR issues), and Business for Social Responsibility (a membership-based business association for socially responsible businesses), among others. The latter group consists of a small but growing assortment of financial information providers – either "sell-side" members of the finance industry (those who create and advise on the sale of stock products to those who advise or buy investment services) or in-house analysts for buy-side actors, such as asset managers, who seek to promote the use of ESG data (World Economic Forum 2011). Many were early adopters of Responsible Investment, including the ESG/RI offices of mainstream investment firms (including Goldman Sachs, UBS, Merrill Lynch, and Credit Suisse), established data providers and research firms that expanded to include RI services (including Thomson Reuters Asset4, MSCI ESG Research, and Bloomberg), accounting professionals (such as the AICPA's Enhanced Business Reporting Consortium), and new sustainability stock market indices (such as the Dow Jones Sustainability Index).

The task of these advocates of RI has been to facilitate the incorporation of ESG data into mainstream investing. The ultimate goal has been to encourage those analysts and investors who currently employ only financial data to determine a stock's value to also employ ESG data. In this project of promoting RI, the task of valuation is critical and is two-fold (Enhanced Analytics Initiative 2008; Ho 2010). First, proponents have sought to make the business case for this type of investing. Showing that the use of ESG data is "just good business" (to quote from one respondent) involves the pragmatic challenge of creating measurement devices that could determine and demonstrate the shareholder value of companies' ESG performance to date, at the firm level or the industry level. As one major organizational proponent of RI, Business for Social Responsibility (2008:3), observed in a report on the state of mainstream investing, "investors are waiting for vetted proof of long-term materiality before fully incorporating the criteria."

Secondly, these advocates of RI have worked to have ESG data included in the task of fundamental analysis itself (what is called "integrated analysis"). Recall from Chapter 4 that stock valuation has traditionally relied on only financial information about a company to estimate the intrinsic value of a stock. The goal now is to render firms' ESG performance "calculable for profit" – to be able to assign a monetary worth to those salient policies and practices in terms of a stock's intrinsic value (Amaeshi 2010). The problem of RI, as communicated to me by one long-time proponent, is that investors and analysts "often feel and tell us that 'we don't know how to use sustainability information because it doesn't fit into our models.'" Value entrepreneurs have worked to create the measurement devices needed for participants to be able to estimate the value of an individual stock using both financial and non-financial criteria. As with any other market, as outlined above, the challenge of RI was to solve the value problem, thus allowing for *commensurability* – the ability of market members to determine the value of different products using ESG data and to compare them for the purpose of investment. To do so, as outlined later, they have transposed conventions and devices taken from their valuation repertoire, as made possible by their professional backgrounds in the finance industry, based on an explicit belief that mainstream investors would be most likely to adopt this new method of stock valuation if they could use familiar and accepted conventions and devices to do so.

MEASURING THE SOCIAL IN ESG

These value entrepreneurs have worked to address these two challenges of valuation for the market of RI through three distinct strategies: the use of ESG ratings, the development of "integrated reporting," and the monetization of ESG data via fundamental financial analysis, with consequences for the meaning of social value. Most importantly, the ensuing definition of the "social" in the field's measuring devices looks markedly narrower than that espoused in the field's social project, as driven by the mimicry of the conventions of the finance industry and as structured by the assignment of monetary value and the employment of the criteria of shareholder return to the gauge of firms' social performance.

ESG ratings and materiality

When proponents of RI sought to establish and grow the field, one of their first tasks was to generate the ratings of stocks that incorporated ESG data. In the case of RI, ESG ratings were produced by a number of value entrepreneurs in this field, including the RI/ESG offices of mainstream investment firms (including Goldman Sachs, UBS, Merrill Lynch, and Credit Suisse), established data providers and research firms that include ESG services (including EIRIS, Thomson Reuters Asset4, MSCI ESG Research, and Bloomberg), and the key sustainability/ESG stock market indices (FTSE4GOOD and the Dow Jones Sustainability Index).[11] For these value entrepreneurs, firms' ESG ratings served two purposes: they facilitated investors' use of ESG data in their selection of stocks and ratings could demonstrate the positive financial impact of firms' ESG performance for the generation of shareholder return.

As detailed in Chapter 4, the use of stock ratings to evaluate firm's non-financial performance certainly was not new. In the case of Socially Responsible Investing, value entrepreneurs' generation of ratings was a central tactic to the growth of the field. Firms were rated based on their financial performance and on a negative screening in terms of their products, place, and policies, as contingent upon a subjective understanding of social good. With the growth of CSR in the 1990s, both SRI activists and mainstream investment actors also began to offer ratings of firms based on their sustainability performance for interested investors. These actors, such as KLD and Innovest, gathered data via surveys or by examining company reports in order to assess a firm's CSR performance. A firm's commitment to each dimension of CSR was counted by the presence of a specific policy (e.g., whether a corporation has a policy guaranteeing employees the freedom of association) and/or by a count of a firm's outputs (e.g., a tally of a company's average annual employee training hours) (Bendel 2011).[12] These analysts either rated companies based on an aggregate CSR score or ranked them as "best-in-class" in their industry. As with the case of Socially Responsible Investing, CSR ratings included an initial screen based on a firms' financial performance. The goal for these information intermediaries was for morally oriented investors to use the CSR rating to make their investment decisions (Eccles and Vivier 2011).

With the growth of RI, however, the worth of firms' ratings became re-framed by actors in the finance industry around the financial goals of mainstream investors whose primary focus was on the production of economic return (albeit only for those investors with a long-term value orientation). In consequence, the content and methods of the ESG ratings produced by financial information providers then departed from those prior SRI and CSR ratings. Not only was an attention to CSR criteria replaced by a concern for ESG criteria, but and perhaps more importantly, the selection of the relevant ESG factors for inclusion in firms' ratings was based on a financial, rather than a normative, criterion.

Historically, fields with social purpose organizations – including nonprofits, social enterprises, SRI, and CSR – have based the institutionalized definition of social value on actors' own beliefs about the nature of social value. What counts, at least as articulated as the guiding premise of each field, is determined by what proponents (as articulated in the field's social project) believe is normatively required to address social inequities. In the case of SRI, for example, proponents emphasized the extra-regulatory obligations of US corporations regarding their products, their place of production, and their policies. The field of CSR was premised on the private regulation of multinational corporations in terms of the social and environmental implications of the production processes of their supply chains in developing nations. In contrast, with RI, the determination of what counted as the "social" for a company in the generation of ESG ratings looked quite different. Here, claims about the normative nature of social good were indeed made by ESG advocates, largely as extended from the field of CSR. But, they were then filtered through the additional criterion of their financial value – a consideration of their "materiality" (Eccles et al. 2011). Taken from the concept of financial materiality in accounting, materiality technically refers to the "magnitude of an omission or misstatement of accounting information that, in the light of surrounding circumstances, makes it probable that the judgment of a reasonable person relying on the information would have been changed or influenced by the omission or misstatement" (Financial Accounting Standards Board 1980:132). In mainstream investing, the analysis of a corporation's financial performance requires the reporting of only those issues that would be deemed salient or "material" for a mainstream investor, who is concerned only with the pursuit of shareholder return, to make an informed decision about a firm.

When applied to the estimation of a firm's ESG performance, financial materiality required the evaluation of ESG issues in terms of their relevance for a firm's creation of long-term business value for shareholders (Kinder 2005). For instance, Business for Social Responsibility (2010:1), a membership association and consulting firm for socially responsible businesses, defines materiality as "rather than trying to address every sustainability risk and potential opportunity, leading companies focus their reports on areas that deliver the greatest value to their business and to their most important stakeholders." The "materiality test" included such issues as financial impact/risks, legal/regulatory/policy drivers, peer-based norms, stakeholder concerns and societal trends, and opportunity for innovation (Lydenburg, Rogers, and Wood 2010).

In this procedure, a financial intermediary who engages in the evaluation of a firm's ESG performance, including actors like MSCI, GS Sustain, Robeco and SAM, would begin by identifying the universe of potential ESG issues. In regard to the meaning of the Social in ESG, the list of possible indicators was markedly similar to conception of the social found in CSR's normatively guided emphasis on the impact of a firm's production processes on stakeholders. With some exceptions, the social here incorporated corporations' treatment of employees (the issues of fair compensation, health and safety, diversity, and human rights), the composition of their supply chain (extending the rights of employees to those of their suppliers), and engagement with the local community (community investment and business ethics).[13] This marked overlap of the definition of social value for RI and CSR resulted from the historical trajectory of the ESG industry – its emergence out of CSR and the codification of CSR's notion of firms' social responsibility in the UN's Global Compact and the Global Reporting Initiative – and the continued role of many of the same investment analysts and ratings agencies involved in both arenas, including KLD and Innovest. Yet, while the field of RI shared with CSR a definition of social good based on how goods are produced, its concern for financial materiality ultimately determined which social criteria (and, similarly, which environmental and governance criteria) actually got to be included in a firm's ESG rating.

Most commonly, value entrepreneurs made decisions about the materiality of ESG issues based on the economic sector in which a company was located (United Nations Global Compact 2004; Eccles, Krzus, Rogers, and Serafeim 2012). The industry of the company mattered because it presented a distinct set of long-term challenges for those member corporations – a set of risks and opportunities that required attention to the relevant ESG indicators as signals of a company's capacity to manage those sector-specific difficulties. The result was that the indicators used to measure a firm's performance on each dimension varied by industry, as did the balance given to each of the three dimensions of ESG.[14] In short, the determination of the "social" in ESG has become dependent in RI on which labor-related factors will increase shareholder value through limiting risks and increasing opportunities on a sector-by-sector basis.

In one instance, I spoke with the head of ESG investment for an international investment firm. I asked her how her company (and their analysts) decides on what counted as the "Social" in ESG. She replied in a way that emphasized the criteria of materiality as central to the process.

The S is sector specific and depends on the type of work being done in that industry. Take the case of how employers treat their employees. In service industries, we're interested in what benefits a company offers to workers because then they can attract the best and the brightest, which we see as increasing a firm's profit over the long run. In contrast, in sectors like manufacturing, we are interested in whether or not the company monitors the human rights of workers in their supply chain. And in the case of mining, we consider the rate of workplace accidents, which could lead to higher employee replacement costs and perhaps also more regulatory scrutiny by the local government or maybe even international NGOs. So in each case, or rather sector, it differs but it's always all about whether or not the S provides either a risk or an opportunity for firms.

Similarly, take the case of GS Sustain, the long-term investment strategy of Goldman Sachs' Global Investment Research division. First conducted in 2007, GS Sustain generates a focus list of companies by industry that are expected to provide superior, long-term economic return for shareholders, based on an integration of their financial performance, industry positioning, and ESG performance (what GS Sustain views as a proxy for management quality). Drawing from companies' public reports, GS Sustain collects a large number of verified data points on each firm, which are combined into twenty to twenty-five ESG indicators, and companies are assigned a score for their performance on each indicator. While about two-thirds of indicators are universal, the remainder of the key indicators is selected based on the company's industry location. In the pharmaceuticals industry, for example, the social performance of a firm counts for 58% of its total score, while it counts for just 48% in the food and beverages industry. And industries also vary in terms of which indicators of the social matter. In the case of sector of Global Energy, GS Sustain selects the social indicators of fatality rate, lost time injuries, total recordable injuries, and business ethics and human rights as relevant for that industry, from a longer list of possible social indicators (taken from the UN Global Compact) which also includes gender diversity, employee training and health management, and employee compensation, among others (GS Sustain 2009).

As these two examples show, the introduction of materiality into the valuation of firms' ESG performance results in the inclusion of those ESG factors that have a theorized causal impact on a firm's investment value, rather than selection based only on normative concerns about firms' social responsibilities to society (Kinder 2005).[15] For example, the World Intellectual Capital Initiative (2010:3), a public-private sector collaboration intended to generate a

standard reporting framework for a firms non-financial performance, concluded that their proposed indicators of ESG "have different attributes from
those indicators required by civil society to achieve its own objectives and
purposes." The implication of a concern for materiality in the field of ESG
was that the meaning of the social was not driven by moral concerns or shared
norms about corporations' effects on society. Instead, the selection of salient
social factors was selected from the broader list, as historically originating in
moral concerns, but as dependent on the specific economic issues faced by a
firm's industry as they generated financial value for shareholders.

Integrated reporting and parsimony

A second strategy used by advocates of RI to grow this financial market has
been to press for firms' employment of "integrated reporting" – the incorporation of systematic ESG data into their traditional reporting of only financial
data (Eccles and Krzus 2010; Lydenberg, Rogers and Wood 2010; International Integrated Reporting Committee 2011).[16] Integrated reporting consists of a "more-comprehensive model that encompasses significant elements of
traditional financial reporting and ESG reporting within a single presentation"
(Deloitte 2011:3). It was meant to replace corporations' use of stand-alone ESG
or sustainability reports that exist alongside and distinct from their financial
reporting.[17] The purpose of integrated reporting was to make firms' non-
financial behavior as transparent as financial data but also to show the "interdependencies," to quote from one respondent, between a firm's ESG data and
its financial performance for investors and analysts.

Integrated reporting entails a firm's selection of which ESG issues are most
germane to the creation of long-term shareholder value, the measurement of a
firm's performance on each issue, and – at least ideally – the demonstration of
the financial value of the company's performance on each ESG dimension.[18] In
2012, as one example, Deutsche Bank published a report on the state of
Responsible Investment. The authors concluded that corporations' growing
use of integrated reporting was facilitating the growth of the field. They
described an integrated report as one in which "financial information is combined with non-financial information in such a way that shows their quantified
impact on each other using established guidelines, standards and key performance indicators (KPI)" (Fulton, Kahn, and Sharples 2012:26).

A range of accounting bodies, ESG standard bearers, academics, and consultants have worked both to demonstrate the value of integrated reporting and
to establish guidelines for integrated reporting as a suggested measuring device
for investors. These include the International Integrated Reporting Council
(formed in 2010 by the Global Reporting Initiative and Accounting for
Sustainability), One Report, the Sustainability Accounting Standards Board
(SASB), and the joint effort by the European Federation of Financial Analysts
Societies and the Germany's Society of Investment Professionals (DVFA 2008;

Eccles and Krzuz 2010; Lydenberg, Rogers, and Wood 2010; International Integrated Reporting Committee 2011; Warren and Thomsen 2012). Integrated reporting also has been promoted by a number of mainstream financial and accounting professionals including Deloitte, KPMG, PWC, and UBS (Deloitte 2011; Hudson, Jeaneau, and Zlotnicka 2012; PWC 2013).

The rationale for developing integrating reporting was premised on a belief in investors' growing interest in non-financial data (Eccles, Serafeim, and Krzus 2011). Integrated reporting matters because it serves as a type of measuring device – it facilitates investors' use of ESG data in their financial analysis by making both non-financial and financial data transparent, commensurable, and connected both within a firm and across firms. As one proponent has argued: "Companies, investors and governments are beginning to recognize that long-term sustainable performance relies on an understanding of the interdependency between financial, social and environmental factors. However, this recognition is far from main stream and action is needed to drive change such that sustainability becomes embedded in organizations' strategy, operations and reporting" (Accountability for Sustainability 2013).

How does the growth of integrated reporting affect the meaning and measure of social value? Most importantly, the inclusion of non-financial data in integrated reporting must be governed by the principle of materiality and must be presented in a form comparable to how the equivalent financial data was presented in the report, often through the use of KPI. As with any effort to quantify the social world (Espeland and Stevens 1998), the result has been a move to *parsimony* – a narrowing of the meaning of the "social" in ESG to only those dimensions that fit with the conventions of mainstream finance in both content and form, thus rendering invisible other dimensions.[19] First, as with ESG ratings, integrated reporting results in a constriction of social value based on the principle of materiality. As before, materiality necessitates the inclusion of only those ESG issues in an integrated report that are critical for a firm's production of shareholder value – they are deemed germane for an investment decision. As detailed in Chapter 6, the Global Reporting Initiative began in 1997 as a means to ensure comparability of corporate reporting on sustainability issues in the field of CSR. It has since become oriented around ESG issues and framed around the criteria of materiality, moving towards the endorsement of integrated reporting (Etzion and Ferraro 2010). In one recent report, the organization concluded that: "The emphasis on what is material encourages organizations to provide only information that is critical to their business and stakeholders. This means organizations and report users can concentrate on the sustainability impacts that matter, resulting in reports that are more strategic, more focused, more credible, and easier for stakeholders to navigate" (Global Reporting Initiative 2013).

Who decides what dimensions or indicators of the social count as material in integrated reporting? For some proponents of integrated reporting, a company must make its own decisions as to which ESG issues are financially material

(International Integrated Reporting Committee 2011). For others who seek to generate universal standards, including the Global Reporting Initiative and the Sustainability Accounting Standards Board (2013), materiality typically was contingent upon the specification of a universal list of considerations as mediated by a firm's industry, as was the case with many ESG ratings. In the case of the SASB, for instance, materiality was driven by: "(a) Financial disclosure (issues that may have a financial impact or may pose a risk to the industry in the short-, medium-, or long-term; (b) Legal drivers (Issues that are being shaped by emerging or evolving government policy and regulation; (c) Industry norms (Issues that companies in specific industries tend to report on and recognize as important drivers in their line of business); (d) Stakeholder concerns (Issues that are of high importance to stakeholders, including communities, NGOs and the general public, or reflect social and consumer trends, and which rise to the level of interest to investors when they have economic implications); and (e) Innovation opportunity (Competitive advantage created from potential innovative solutions that benefit the environment, customers, and other stakeholders)" (SASB 2013:15).

For proponents of integrated reporting, secondly, the inclusion of non-financial performance should be driven not only by the selection of materially pressing ESG issues but also by the standards of typical financial reporting. The goal of these advocates was to develop integrated reporting guidelines that would deliver ESG data to investment professionals in a familiar form, one that helps them to identify a stock's fundamental value – to do so "data is quantified, comparable, and benchmarkable" (DVFA 2008:6). Here, some advocates of integrated reporting have proposed the use of KPIs, a long-standing component of financial reporting (Lydenberg, Rogers, and Wood 2010; Eccles et al. 2012). In 2008, for example, the United States Securities and Exchange Commission published a report encouraging the development of a standardized list of KPIs for companies' non-financial characteristics, so that investors could have a full understanding of corporate performance.

As a measuring device, KPI have been common in firms' traditional reporting of financial performance. They consist of the identification of a short list of salient measures of a company's status. Each resulting KPI is a numerical measure of how well a firm is performing relevant to a goal deemed critical for its success (Parmenter 2011). In mainstream investing, KPIs provide companies and its shareholders with a set of clear, quantified, and quickly understandable metrics of performance that are considered indicators of economic success and so producers of shareholder value. Similarly, for advocates of integrated reporting, the goal has been to select KPIs that capture the critical material dimensions of ESG performance for each sector. Corporations are then expected to report their performance on these KPIs, to facilitate investors' employment of this data in integrated analysis. "Unlike qualitative information, performance indicators, especially if reduced to key figures, have the advantage that given their numeric character they offer a fast, condensed overview of a business's actual performance on extra-financial matters" (Bassen and Kovacs 2008:186).

For some RI proponents, KPIs are encouraged for use by firms, and they should be tailored to each company's situation (International Integrated Reporting Committee 2013). Take the case of an international communications services corporation that is considered to be at the forefront of integrated reporting in this field. At one conference on corporate sustainability that I attended, a senior CSR executive at the firm outlined the company's reporting practices in the United States. The company had identified twelve KPIs as the core dimensions of its "non-financial" ESG performance. In an example of how the corporation was moving towards integrated reporting, a Powerpoint slide was posted overhead. For each ESG KPI listed on the slide, a quantified measure of the firm's performance in that regard was listed alongside, followed by the source and dollar amount of each ESG KPI's financial value, either in the form of costs or revenue for the corporation. For example, the company's engagement to keeping employers healthy was measured as "number of sick days" and assigned a monetary value based on the company's "sick pay costs." As the speaker put up the slide, he provided a background on the company's use of ESG KPIs in their annual report. He noted, "We use KPIs because we think they will help us to become a truly sustainable business – they tell us where we are and where we need to go. But I have to tell you that many investors don't get it. And, as you all know, they are hard to convince. But it's the best we can do." At this point, there is general laughter (what strikes me as nervous laughter) from the other presenters on the panel and from the audience, all of who were proponents of RI. This anecdote makes clear that the use of KPIs to calculate the economic value of a firm's ESG performance is sometimes only a precarious extension of corporations' traditional use of financial data to convey this purported new source of shareholder value.

Alternatively, other proponents of integrated reporting have drawn from their valuation repertoire to generate standardized KPIs that vary not by firm but by sector (DVFA 2008; Global Reporting Initiative 2013; SASB 2013). It is here that the criterion of parsimony is particularly notable – an effort to identify KPIs based on the criterion of brevity. Take the case of the SASB, a nonprofit that seeks to hold a parallel function to the Financial Accounting Standards Board. It is working towards providing sector guidelines on materiality by sector, along with accompanying standardized performance metrics, which can then be used by corporations. In one recent report, the organization clearly specifies the basis for its selection of KPIs. "In developing such metrics, SASB will default to the minimum information that is still decision-useful (i.e., it presents a relative view of performance by which peers can be compared), rather than a complete accounting that may be necessary for public policy – or government target-settings" (SASB 2013:11). Similarly, the German Society of Investment Professionals' (DVFA) and the European Federation of Financial Analysts Societies together produced a highly cited list of general and industry-specific KPIs. Their goal was to formulate a comprehensive list of "useable" ESG KPIs based on the criteria that they "should be manageable in dimension ('Key'), e.g. small set of 30 KPIs max" (DVFA 2008:6). The result is that companies are required to disclose only 10 specified KPIs to capture ESG performance, contingent upon subsector (Garz, Schnella and Frank 2010).

In short, value entrepreneurs' design and diffusion of integrated reporting has had critical implications for the meaning of social value in the field of Responsible Investment. For these proponents, integrated reporting was premised on a belief that the linking of firm's non-financial and financial behavior in a single report would facilitate financial professionals' use of integrated analysis. The result has been that what counts as social value (as one component of a firm's ESG performance) is delimited not only by the criteria of financial materiality but then again narrowed down by the need to present that data in a format similar to the conveyance of financial data, using a parsimonious list of quantified performance indicators. The inclusion of KPIs in integrated reporting has a dual effect. It increases the likelihood that a mainstream investor will consider a firm's social performance in the valuation of a stock. At the same time, the use of KPIs curtails the number of dimensions of social value that can be incorporated in that measuring device, in the estimation of a firm's performance, and in terms of what counts as social value in the field of Responsible Investment.

Assigning financial value to firms' ESG performance

Finally, the construction of a market for RI has entailed the construction of new types of measurement devices that assign a monetary value to firms' ESG performance in relationship to its generation of shareholder return. Initially in this field, firms' ratings held a dual purpose – they not only served as a judgment device for investors' but proponents also employed them to demonstrate the long-term, financial value of firms' ESG performance. A company's ESG rating was intended to measure, alongside the traditional measure of their financial performance, one critical dimension of a company's intangible performance for the purpose of investors. These "intangibles" include management's ability to negotiate risks (e.g., carbon emissions cost or the threat of lawsuits) and/or to generate opportunities (brand enhancement, employee appeal) present in their environment. A better ESG performance was postulated to have beneficial consequences for the stock's generation of long-term financial return through cost savings or improved revenue. Proponents of Responsible Investment supported these claims either by reference to relevant research findings that linked initial ESG ratings to a later rate of shareholder return or by showing the historical outperformance of a selection of top-ESG rated corporations compared to industry peers (UNEPFI 2007; Fulton, Kahn, and Sharples 2012).

The use of ratings as a means to demonstrate the long-term financial value of firms' ESG performance, however, had its critics. The difficulty was that ESG ratings, as either a measure of firms' ESG performance or as a signal of that behavior's generation of long-term shareholder value, kept distinct the gauges of a stock's non-financial and financial performance. Practically speaking, as with the case of GS Sustain previously, different groups of research analysts engage in the two assessments, employing two distinct sets of criteria. The financial and non-financial performance of a firm was then aggregated to produce a best-in-class ESG ranking of corporations by industry. In result, these ratings did not calculate the financial value of a firm's ESG performance. For proponents of Responsible Investing, the use of ESG ratings to convey shareholder value then departed from the traditional estimation of a stock's current value in mainstream investing, where all data is presented using the metric of money and as a measure of financial value.

This disjuncture between how value should be represented and how value was present in early ESG ratings was felt by some in the field to have impeded the incorporation of ESG data into stock analysis (PRI 2013a, 2013b). In result, some value entrepreneurs worked (and are still working) to create new measuring devices that incorporate a firm's ESG performance into the process of fundamental equity valuation itself. The goal is to put a "price" on ESG activity. As outlined in Chapter 4, fundamental equity valuation examines the characteristics of a company, besides its trading history, that are considered germane to a determination of its stock's intrinsic value. In the case of a firm's equity valuation, analysts seek to determine the economic well-being of the firm by review of its financial statements. They employ a number of established financial formulas, including the discounted cash flow rate or the dividend discount model, which incorporate a firm's income (calculated as the balance of revenue and expenses) to identify its future financial performance and to determine a stock's intrinsic value.

Recall that the premise of RI is that a company with a strong ESG performance will provide a superior long-time financial return for a shareholder than a peer with a weaker ESG performance. The goal of these new and emerging measurement devices, part of what is sometimes called "integrated analysis" or "enhanced analysis," is to identify the monetary value of a firm's ESG performance following the lines of traditional fundamental analysis and to integrate that value into the calculation of one of those formulas that typically have governed the fundamental equity valuation of a firm (World Economic Forum 2011). At its most basic, integrated analysis requires ESG data to be monetized either as a source of revenue or as an expense to be incorporated into fundamental valuation. In one instance, I spoke with Sarah, a representative from a recently formed investment firm that touts its use of Responsible Investing. When I asked about how the company incorporates ESG into its estimation of a stock's value, she responded:

First, our analysts determine what E, S, and G factors are relevant by sector. Then, they would look at an individual company and – relying both on data provided by the company to us and using other existing data out there as well – they try and determine the financial and non-financial performance of the company. To estimate the value of ESG performance, they also then ask the company to provide the monetary value of an indicator, which usually get estimated as cost savings or revenue generation.

One well-cited and relatively long-standing example of this incorporation of ESG data into fundamental equity valuation is RobecoSAM's Equity Valuation Model. Formed in 1995, RobecoSAM is an asset management firm, located in Switzerland, that focuses exclusively on Responsible Investment. It was one of the first companies to generate ratings to assess firms' sustainability perform-ance, which then have become employed in the Dow Jones Sustainability Index. In its capacity as an asset manager, the company uses ESG data on firms to calculate the "fair value" of a company, based on its discounted cash flow – a long-standing formula in mainstream investing to estimate the value of a company or stock by estimating the current value of future cash flow projec-tions. To do so, SAM employs ESG data to adjust the value on two critical inputs into the formulation of a company's fair value: the cost of capital and return on invested capital. For SAM, companies that perform well on industry-specific ESG factors possess two advantages: first, they are deemed to be better able to manage risks and thus benefit from a lower "weighted average cost of capital" and, secondly, their ESG performance generates competitive advan-tages that lead to greater operational efficiency, leading to a positive impact on the company's "return on invested capital" (RobecoSAM 2012, as cited in PRI 2013b). The result is the assignment of a SAM Fair Value score to each company, allowing for investment decisions based on exploitation of discrep-ancies between a stock's fair value (which was now argued to be more accur-ately estimated due to the inclusion of ESG data) and its market value.

Another example is the work of Bloomberg, a company that historically has provided comprehensive, real-time market financial data to subscribers in the finance industry. Bloomberg added data on firms' ESG performance to its service in 2009, providing data on a set of ESG indicators. And, in 2011, Bloomberg announced the launch of the ESG Earnings Valuation Tool, which provides an estimation of the future revenue and costs generated out of a company's ESG performance in order to identify its financial impact on a company's share price. The tool converts the value of a firm's ESG indicators into monetized profits or losses by applying standardized pricing procedures, such as measures of carbon and oil prices, waste treatment costs, and paper costs. For example, Bloomberg identifies "accident severity rate" as one key social issue in a company's ESG performance. Based on firm-level data gathered on that indicator, Bloomberg then prices the amount of lost labor time – as an additional company cost – that is generated by a firm's performance by refer-ence to the standardized measure of "employee salary." By aggregating the economic impact of thirteen different ESG indicators, the company claims the tool is able to more accurately calculate a company's future earnings before interest and tax as a ratio to its share price (Elders and Evans 2011; International Federation of Accountants 2012).

As apparent in these examples, the question of social value in RI in integrated analysis is fundamentally driven by these value entrepreneurs' efforts to refashion the measuring devices used in mainstream finance in order to solve the value problem in this new market for traditional investors. Despite its origins in the morally oriented frame of CSR, the rationale for investors' use of ESG to assess stock value has meant that social value is now framed within the imperative of shareholder return. First, what counts as the "social" of ESG is determined by the criteria of materiality. Notwithstanding its shared concern with CSR for the effect of big businesses' production processes on stakeholders, including employees, suppliers, community, and customers, value entrepreneurs in the field of RI only count those dimensions of a firm's social behavior that are germane to reducing risk and increasing return within the firm's industry. Secondly, the need to have ESG data equivalent in form and amount to that of financial data in mainstream investment analysis has resulted in a reduction of the number of aspects of a firm's social behavior that are counted in public reports and so deemed relevant. Finally, a new measure of a firm's ESG performance calculates its dollar worth in the estimation of a stock's fundamental value, yet further delimiting what counts as social value by valorizing only those ESG measures that can be assigned a dollar value. In all, the consequence of Responsible Investing for social value is that the evaluation of firms' social performance will be driven less by actors' moral understanding of a "good society" and more by the pursuit of economic gain.

Notes

1. In this approach to the market, companies are considered unfit to intentionally pursue social betterment via their business practices, outside of their provision of goods and offering of employment opportunities. First, the fiduciary responsibility of firms to shareholders both legally impinges on their ability to provide social goods and negatively affects their capacity to do so (Friedman 1970). Adam Smith (1776:478) emphasized that the market was not the best method by which to achieve social betterment: "I have never known much good done by those who affected to trade for the public good." More recently, George Soros (2000:118) – the famous hedge fund manager and philanthropist – contended, "social justice is outside the competence of the market economy." In this view, oversight and responsibility for the well-being of society is best assigned to actors in other sectors, including government agencies in the public sector and charities in the nonprofit sector.

2. Institutionalized conventions and tools can provide actors with the ability to act when the "complexity of the situation and the informational constraints do not allow them to assign probabilities to the possible consequences of choices" (Beckert 1999:779).

3. Relatedly, the terms of Socially Responsible Investing, Corporate Social Responsibility, Sustainability, and Responsible Investing are increasingly becoming interchangeable, largely in reference to ESG criteria (Robeco and Booz and Co. 2005). In 2011, for example, the World Economic Forum defined "sustainable investing" as an "investment approach that integrates long-term ESG criteria into investment and ownership decision-making with the objective of generating superior risk-adjusted financial returns."

4. As also noted in Chapter 2, agency theory is an academic perspective that views the firm as characterized by the relationship between two groups: shareholders as principals and a firm's managers (its executives and board of directors) as agents – those actors hired to run the firm. Ownership and control are separated. In result, principals must develop procedures to control and monitor the work of agencies – what then became the task of corporate governance (Jensen and Meckling 1976).

5. As quoted in Bendell (2011:14).

6. In 2006, the United Kingdom adopted a new *Companies Act*, which codifies the "enlightened shareholder value" approach, where a company's directors are expected to incorporate a concern for not only shareholders but also for the long-term value of the company through attention to stakeholders' interests (U.K. Parliament 2006).

7. These regulatory changes included the pricing of greenhouse gas emissions following the European Union's adoption of the Emissions Trading Scheme and, in the US, the Securities and Exchange Commission' recommendation in 2010 that corporations make disclosures concerning climate change.

8. Interestingly, the PRI's six principles do not specify the actual content of the three key criteria of ESG issues, but instead commit the signatories to incorporate ESG principles into their investment-making activities (PRI 2014)

9. In addition, a number of multinational corporations voluntarily have implemented ESG into their public communications via the use of integrated reporting, including Novo Nordisk, Pfizer, and Philips Electronics (Eccles and Krzus 2010).

10. In contrast, the percentage of all assets under management in the United States that incorporate some kind of socially responsible orientation (including ESG, SRI or CSR) is estimated at eleven percent (US Social Investment Forum 2012).

11. To identify the range of social issues included in the construction of ESG ratings, I examined the methodology employed by the largest members of the industry, including the ESG offices of mainstream investment firms (including Goldman Sachs, UBS, Merrill Lynch, and Credit Suisse), established data providers and research firms that include ESG services (including EIRIS, Thomson Reuters Asset4, MSCI ESG Research, and Bloomberg), and the key sustainability/ESG stock market indices (FTSE4GOOD and the Dow Jones Sustainability Index).

12. Observers have noted that little concern exists for measuring whether and how a firm's policies and practices actually affects key stakeholders, such as employees, the local community, or the environment (United Nations Trade and Development 2011).

13. Less universal dimensions of the social in ESG include a concern for customers' rights and wellbeing (e.g., Thomson Reuters Asset4 and MSCI ESG), the dimension of "talent attraction and retention" (SAM's attention to the presence of performance appraisal processes and compensation), and a consideration of the treatment of the local population (e.g., MSCI ESG).

14. Several key intermediaries have sought to create sector-specific standards of materiality for firms' reporting of ESG performance (Lydenburg, Rogers, and Wood 2010; Eccles et al. 2012; SASB 2013; Deloitte 2013). The goal is to produce a standard of materiality of non-financial issues that is as transparent and established as those used by the US Generally Accepted Accounting Principles (US GAAP) or International Financial Reporting Standards (IFRS) (Eccles et al. 2012).

15. As Kinder (2005) points out, the evaluation of ESG issues via the criteria of materiality privileges ESG factors omits those where establishing a causal impact is problematic.

16. Currently, corporations' use of integrated reporting in the United States is strictly voluntary; in contrast, South Africa requires integrated reporting.

17. Currently, the dominant standard for the separate reporting of ESG data is that of the Global Reporting Initiative.

18. In this section, I draw from document analysis conducted on texts produced by the main proponents of integrated reporting, including the International Integrated Reporting Committee, the SASB, the Global Reporting Initiative, and DVFA.

19. Similarly, in their overview of commensuration, Espeland and Stevens (1998:317) note that the comparative evaluation of goods "can render some aspects of life invisible or irrelevant."

7

Market solutions to poverty

Inclusive Business and Impact Investing

"Aid alone will not deliver development. A vibrant business sector – one that is innovative, acts responsibly and works in collaboration with other actors – is also required to apply new models for development solutions, scale up existing development initiatives and build new markets"

(International Business Leaders Forum 2005).

The last chapter focused on Responsible Investment (RI) as one field within the broader embrace of caring capitalism by actors in the global economy. In its emphasis on firms' ESG (an acronym for Environment, Social, and Governance) performance as a source of social value and shareholder value, RI constitutes just one type of caring capitalism. Proponents of other visions of caring capitalism also bring together different orders of worth by claiming that firms' generation of social return can produce shareholder return – love and lucre are not opposed. This chapter focuses on the question of social value for two other fields where market enthusiasts have articulated alternative conceptions of the social project of caring capitalism. Inclusive Businesses are a new variant of multinational corporations that benefit low-income individuals and communities in the developing world through the encompassing organization of their business model. Impact Investing is a form of financial investing that focuses on achieving both economic and social return for shareholders based on the work of local microfinance vehicles and small and medium enterprises (SMEs) in addressing social inequities through market participation. The social projects of both fields are centered on the goal of poverty reduction through compassionate companies' provision of market access to the economically disadvantaged.

Unlike the case of RI, however, the prevailing measuring devices for each of these two fields do not employ the market indicators of money and shareholder value. Instead, they gauge a firm's social value by a count of a company's provision of economic development and/or broader development benefits to local individuals and communities. As cases of caring capitalism, these two fields provide surprising exceptions both to the theoretical expectation that a market logic should predominate over other logics in the private sector, as seen in Chapter 6 on RI, and to the scholarly belief that actors will create a market wherein money constitutes an acceptable medium by which to evaluate the moral worth of traded goods and services, as outlined in Chapter 1.

The question pursued in this chapter is that of *why:* *w*hat explains the disjunctures between the content of the social projects at the heart of Inclusive Business and Impacting Investing and the measuring devices used to evaluate worth in these fields? Why did these measuring devices not reflect and so enact the intertwining of economic and social value that was promoted by market enthusiasts as characteristic of each field? These discrepancies might be explained by the "hostile worlds" perspective, whereby value entrepreneurs morally resist the application of a market logic to the pursuit of social good. Instead, accounting for these two anomalies requires attention to the expertise and communicative purpose of the value entrepreneurs commissioned to create these tools. In the case of Inclusive Business, valuation instruments were constructed to convince skeptical local stakeholders of the ability of Inclusive Businesses to produce social value in the form of economic development benefits for local communities. Yet, the ability of value entrepreneurs to generate a measuring device that could capture and so convey the social project of the field was limited by their professional expertise. These actors lacked the adequate repertoire of tools, technologies, and techniques to align the measuring device with its social project.

In contrast, in the case of Impact Investing, value entrepreneurs sought to construct a device intended to solve the value problem in this new financial market that prioritized both social and shareholder value, as had happened in the case of RI. Yet, they faced multiple audiences who held differing understandings of the intended purpose of Impact Investing, differing in their definition of social value and their understanding of the relative priority of an investment's social versus financial purpose. To address this value complexity, value entrepreneurs created measuring devices that could provide customized commensurability for all potential investors in part by keeping the measures of shareholder value and social value distinct.

INCLUSIVE BUSINESS: MARKET-BASED SOLUTIONS TO POVERTY

If RI constitutes one version of caring capitalism, a second is that of "Inclusive Business" (United Nations Development Programme (UNDP) 2008; World Business Council for Sustainable Development/SNV 2008). Inclusive Businesses seek to address the problem of poverty, typically in developing countries, through the intentional design of their business models or "core business activities" to *include* the poor and to grow the local economy. Inclusive Businesses strive to alleviate economic disadvantage via their engagement with the poor as suppliers, employees, distributors, and/or consumers. This approach is premised on the neoliberal assumption that poverty results from individuals' exclusion from the market, rather from the quality or nature of their participation in the global economy (World Bank 2001; Cooney and Shanks 2010). To address the problem of market exclusion, firms can "deploy market-based innovations – radical and incremental changes to products and processes – designed to help overcome some of the barriers hindering the poor from more actively participating in markets" (Mendoza and Thelen 2008:428).

In this social project, Inclusive Businesses generate social value by their intentional inclusion of the poor in their value chain as suppliers, employees, distributors, and consumers.[1] First, Inclusive Businesses can be multinational corporations that organize their supply and distribution chains by contracting with locally owned companies, often called SMEs, as a way to facilitate local economic development SMEs are small businesses, typically defined by the size of their personnel and by their revenue (Halberg 2000; Ferranti and Ody 2007). In the development literature, SMEs are framed as a necessary supplement to the microfinance industry's micro-level provision of economic assistance to individuals (ideally resulting in the formation of micro-enterprises) and the macro-level work of large firms and multinational corporations. SMEs economically and socially benefit a region by residents' empowerment as owners and employers (Beck, Demirguc-Kunt, and Levine 2005; Ramirez 2011).

Inclusive businesses, in the form of MNCs or SMEs, also may address poverty by engaging in "job creation." By hiring local individuals who are otherwise excluded from the market (with a focus on women and other marginalized groups), Inclusive Businesses produce two different types of social good: they not only provide income and benefits to employees but also deliver job training, and so "develop the skills and employability of local people," thus developing their human capital and facilitating their further economic advancement (Nelson and Prescott 2008:10). Finally, both international and local firms may engage in an Inclusive Business model by selling goods to consumers at the "bottom of the pyramid" (Prahalad 2004). This group of consumers is defined as the largest but the economically poorest sector of the global population – those over 4 million people living on less than $8 a day (UNDP 2008). As articulated by BOP proponents, this segment of the population previously has been omitted from the market due to their inability to afford goods; in result, they lack critical commodities, including communication, transportation, health, and food, that would improve their life opportunities (Prahalad 2004).[2] Firms can deliver goods to this population through various innovations, including lowering prices and employing new methods of payment, while still achieving a profit (Mendoza and Thelen 2008).[3]

THE ORIGINS OF INCLUSIVE BUSINESS

The emergence of the concept of Inclusive Business emerges from a number of historical developments, both inside and outside of the market. First, a new model of international development emerged in the 1990s in response to the widely understood failure of a free-market ideology, as embodied in the Washington Consensus, to facilitate economic growth to those in the global South. Here, the focus of international development, as led both by critics of structural adjustment and by an ever-pragmatic World Bank, changed from the status of a nation's over-all economy (measured by its GDP) to a concern for economic growth without excessive income inequality, as emphasized in the United Nations' Millennium Development goals in 2000 (UNDP 1990; World Bank 1990; Sen 1999).[4] The focus was on the problem of extreme poverty. The United Nation's Millennium Declaration signed in 2000 by 189 countries declared: "We will spare no effort to free our fellow men, women, and children from the abject and dehumanizing conditions of extreme poverty, to which more than a billion of them are subjected."[5] The project of international development also was re-conceptualized in terms of its solution to the problem of extreme poverty. Drawing from the lessons of economic growth and failure in the 1990s, the World Bank, among others, recognized the inability the program of structural adjustment, premised on trade liberalization, deregulation, and privatization, to deliver "inclusive," "sustained," or "pro-poor" growth (Commission on Growth and Development 2008; Ianchovichina and Lundstrom 2009). At the micro-level, poverty resulted in part from inadequate human and social capital on part of the unemployed and in part from the insufficient supply of market opportunities as entrepreneurs, workers, and consumers in the domestic economy. The solution to poverty, according to this view, was not the government's provision of cash transfers but rather "making markets work for the poor," to quote from the UK government agency responsible for delivering overseas aid (Department for International Development 2000). To address these problems, local governments would provide basic social services to the poor and they would engage in private sector development by putting in place the infrastructure and regulatory policies and institutions needed for economic growth by the poor (Stiglitz 1989; World Bank 1991, 2001; Department for Industrial Development 2006). Here, in contrast to the premise of structural adjustment, the local government should not withdraw completely from the economy but rather would work, along with civil society and private actors, to eliminate market failures that excluded the poor from participation in the market. In the eyes of an executive at the UNDP, "The private sector is where much of our focus is going to have to be to meet the overarching challenge of poverty reduction and human development. Growth, jobs and opportunity belong there not in the gift of government."[6] In this view, the efforts of Inclusive Businesses to include the poor in their business model constitutes an additional strategy by which private sector development can occur, alongside parallel efforts by governmental and civil society actors.

A belief in the capacity of market actors to facilitate inclusive growth further was encouraged by the early success of microfinance, which many observers, funders, and policy makers viewed as justifying the further use of market methods as a solution to poverty. As popularized by the Grameen Bank in Bangladesh, microfinance extends access to financial services – loans, credit, insurance, and savings – to disadvantaged populations who have been unable to access traditional banking opportunities as a means out of poverty (Yunus 1999; Roy 2010).

In addition, the idea of Inclusive Business has been motivated by the changing structure of the global economy. As it had occurred in the field of RI, as detailed in Chapter 6, the financial crises of the 2001 and 2008 led to the search for novel sources of economic growth and for new orientations to the finance economy. As multinational corporations became aware of the growing saturation of their traditional economies in the global North, they sought out novel sources of profit. The emerging field of Inclusive Business constituted one component of these firms' growing view of developing countries as new and emerging markets (Hart 2005). In an early publication by the World Business Council for Sustainable Development (2005:4) that promoted the concept of Inclusive Business, the authors proclaimed: "Most of the world's population is left out of the markets and remains trapped in poverty. By 2050, 85% of the world's population of some nine billion people will be in developing countries. If these people are not by then engaged in the marketplace, our companies cannot prosper and the benefits of a global market will not exist. Clearly it is in our mutual interest to help societies shift to a more sustainable path."

Given these changes to the logics of international development and the finance economy, a multitude of Northern governments and multilateral organizations, such as the World Bank, the United Nations, and the World Business Council for Sustainable Development, began to articulate and disseminate the new social project of Inclusive Business, one where market-based strategies by multinational corporations constituted one critical solution to poverty in the developing world. In 2003, for instance, the United Nations Development Program sponsored the Commission on the Private Sector and Development, whose goal was to identify the obstacles blocking the expansion of local economies (UNDP 2003) and in 2006, it launched the "Growing Inclusive Markets Initiative" (UNDP 2008), while the International Finance Corporation embarked on its "The Next Four Billion" campaign in 2007 (International Finance Corporation 2007). The idea of Inclusive Business has been taken up by some business associations, including Business Call to Action (BCtA) (a collaboration of the United Nations and the bilateral donor agencies of the United States, United Kingdom, Australia, and the Netherlands) and the World Business Council for Sustainable Development, and by government multilateral organizations such as the G20, which in 2010 declared support for the role of private sector actors in the development project (World Business Council for Sustainable Development 2005; G20 2010; BCtA 2013).[7]

INCLUSIVE BUSINESS: SOCIAL VALUE AND THE LOGIC OF THE MARKET

As with many of the other fields of social purpose organization addressed in this book, such as social enterprises, Socially Responsible Investing, and RI, proponents of Inclusive Businesses see firms' social value and economic value as not hostile or opposed but rather as fundamentally interconnected. However, as shown in Figure 7.1, the social project of Inclusive Business is based on a new and distinctive articulation of this relationship, one that reflects the origins of the concept at a particular historical moment in the global economy, as outlined earlier. Inclusive Businesses integrate social value and economic value in two different ways. Social value is produced through firms' economic activity through their intentional inclusion of the poor in their core business activities. In addition, companies' production of this precise type of social value is viewed as a source of shareholder value.

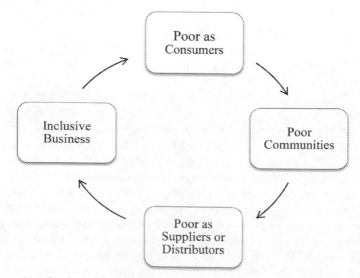

FIGURE 7.1 Social value of Inclusive Businesses

First, as with the case of social enterprises, social value results from the economic development value gained by targeted actors. Inclusive businesses produce this version of social value by their incorporation of previously economically excluded actors into the market.[8] Companies' inclusion of the poor in their value chain is largely understood to have the economic development benefits of generating entrepreneurial opportunities for local businesses, improving employees' wages and developing their skills, and providing customers with access to goods, thus improving the lives of individuals and the local community. As the president of the World Business Council for Sustainable Business stated in 2008: "Businesses cannot succeed in societies that fail. Likewise, where and whenever business is stifled, societies fail to thrive."[9] Access to the market produces societal benefits beyond simply providing individuals and communities with economic resources. Many proponents of inclusive business also emphasize how private sector participation can affect more traditional measures of social well-being (also framed as "capabilities" in the human development perspective), such as increased access to education and health, as well as additional tax revenue for local government (Mendoza and Thelen 2008; World Business Council for Sustainable Development/SNV 2008). Others note that inclusive business also may bring social value in the form of social capital – the store of trust and reciprocity that accrues for participants and local communities, especially via microfinance and SMEs (London 2009).

Strikingly, and in marked contrast to the cases of Corporate Social Responsibility (CSR) and RI, proponents of the social project of Inclusive Business do not incorporate a concern for the quality of firms' relationships with stakeholders, such as suppliers, employees, distributors, and consumers, as a source of social value. As outlined in Chapter 5, the history of CSR originated in market monitors' efforts to extend workers' rights, as codified in the global standards of the Organization for Economic Development and the International Labor Organization, to those in the developing world. Specifically, they worked to improve the harmful working conditions characteristic of multinational corporations' global supply chains. Similarly, RI, as noted in the last chapter, is premised on a faith that firms' improved treatment of stakeholders will result in increased economic opportunities and decreased risk for companies, thus improving their performance and the rate of shareholder return. In contrast, despite a shared concern for the conduct of multinational corporations in the developing world as a source of social value for suppliers, employees, distributors, and customers, the concept of Inclusive Business emphasizes the economic and social benefits that arise from the poor's access to the market as an end in itself (Hahn 2012).[10] A discourse of workers' rights (focusing on companies' provision of labor standards and human rights to their employees), as characteristic of the fields of CSR and RI, is absent from the seminal publications that have outlined the social project of Inclusive Business (World Bank 2001, 2004b; World Business Council for Sustainable Development/SNV 2008; International Finance Corporation 2007; UNDP 2008).[11]

In part, this difference between the premises of CSR, RI, and Inclusive Business results from their respective definitions of economic disadvantage. Historically, CSR emerged out of a concern with workers in developing nations employed by local factories which contract with MNCs and who receive low wages with no job stability or benefits. The result is that the field of CSR (and the subsequent field of RI) has been bounded by a concern for how firms affect stakeholders through their policies and practices, and so omits attention to those not employed by the company (Boyle and Boguslaw 2007). In reference to CSR, one scholar has noted that, "almost by definition, the poor are those who do not have a stake" (Jenkins 2005:540). In contrast, proponents of Inclusive Business view poverty as driven by exclusion from the market (rather than by the growth of low-paying jobs in global commodity chains) and seek to supply employment opportunities to the poor, irrespective of the quality of the resulting firm-stakeholder relationship. As an illustration of this point, I interviewed a staff member at an international NGO committed to ending global poverty. The organization recently had developed a program that focused on promoting the concept of Inclusive Business among multinational corporations headquartered in the United States. Once Celeste had outlined the case for Inclusive Business as a strategy to alleviate poverty, I asked her about the importance of ensuring workers' rights in that project, implicitly drawing in my mind from the logic of CSR. She hesitated and was silent for a moment before replying in what I took to be a defensive tone, "Well, of course jobs should be safe and workers should be happy, but right now, we're just working to get more poor people access to an income in any way, shape, or form. That's the primary goal right now." As evidenced in this quote, the premise of Inclusive Business is that global poverty is a key challenge of contemporary society and the solution is for firms to facilitate individuals' entry into the market.

Secondly, the economic viability of Inclusive Businesses is another source of social value. In their reliance on "market mechanisms and private sector incentives," as with social enterprises, Inclusive Businesses are posited to be a superior replacement to the work of government agencies or NGOs in the project of international development in that they are not dependent on the unpredictable nature of tax revenue or charitable donations (World Bank 2004b). In the words of one employee of a key proponent of Inclusive Business that I interviewed, the "profit motive is really key to this idea because it ensures that firm-based solutions to poverty are both scalable and replicable." Similarly, Malik Fal, a proponent of inclusive business in Africa at the Omidyar Foundation, concluded: "When communities receive trucks of United Nation aid – food programs – it only goes so far for so long. It's when you have a local business that's thriving, that's employing people, that's enabling employees to send their kids to school, to change their habitat, to get the health benefits and so on: this is what really transforms communities" (Poverty Cure 2014).

Finally, the idea of Inclusive Business represents a case of caring capitalism: the more recent perspective on companies that sees the market and mission as being mutually complimentary. Like RI, the idea of enlightened shareholder value structures the consideration of how Inclusive Business is proposed to generate firm profit (UNDP 2008; World Business Council for Sustainable Development/SNV 2008). In an early interview with Samantha, a consultant who had been a long-standing proponent of Inclusive Business, I asked her to define what she saw to be the difference between a multinational corporation and an Inclusive Business, as much as to improve my early and so somewhat tentative understanding of the field as to generate a data point for the book. But her reply was telling in both regards:

> It's not just about helping the poor. It's also about making money. If a company can't make a profit by helping the poor through their incorporation in some way in its core business, then it doesn't count as an Inclusive Business. I guess we could say instead that it's either a failing TNC [transnational corporation] or a charity that doesn't quite know it yet.

Similarly, the World Business Council for Sustainable Development (2005:14), an early proponent of this model of business, noted in a publication: "Inclusive business – also termed bottom of the pyramid (BOP), pro-poor, or sustainable livelihoods business – refers to doing business with the poor in ways that simultaneously benefit low-income communities and also benefit the company engaged in this initiative. These innovative business models focus on fostering economic development and helping low-income families build more secure livelihoods, while creating new markets for companies. It is about 'doing well by doing good.'" In this view, the inclusion of the poor as suppliers, employees, distributors, or customers, as well as investing in the local economy, can generate shareholder return by minimizing a corporation's risk and/or by producing new business opportunities. As with the case of RI, as outlined in Chapter 6, the field of Inclusive Business reflects a growing emphasis on how corporations should create long-term shareholder value.

In proponents' articulation of the concept of inclusive business, three financial advantages are highlighted to follow from the inclusion of the poor in firms' value chains. First, the practice of inclusive business creates a "sound business environment" in that companies will benefit from access to market-ready employees and consumers and from a functioning, well-regulated, and non-corrupt local market. Inclusive Business also produces the economic benefit of lowering firms' "direct costs and risks" by decreasing the costs of operation and improving productivity while minimizing environmental and regulatory challenges and increasing companies' legitimacy and brand appeal with consumers and employees in the global north. Finally, corporation's inclusion of the poor results in "new business opportunities" – the emergence of markets for new products, services and technologies (UNDP 2008; World Business Council for Sustainable Development 2008a, 2013).

VALUING THE SOCIAL FOR INCLUSIVE BUSINESSES

As the field of Inclusive Business has emerged, multiple measuring devices have been created by evaluators which to gauge Inclusive Business' distinctive value. Some of the most prominent of these include BCtA's Results Reporting Framework, Oxfam's Poverty Footprint, and the World Business Council for Sustainable Development's Measuring Impact Framework, among others (World Business Council for Sustainable Development 2008a, 2008b, 2013; Oxfam International 2009; BCtA 2010).[12] These measuring devices have been used by several multinational corporations that identify as Inclusive Businesses to report the social and economic developmental impact of their work in a geographical region, including Coca-Cola in Zambia and El Salvador, Unilever in Indonesia, and Nestlé in Peru (Clay 2005; Coca Cola/SAB Miller 2011; Nestlé Peru and the WBCSD-SNV Alliance for Inclusive Business 2011). Yet, while these multiple measuring devices are present and often considered synonymous with the field, none as of yet have become the prevailing tool for use by Inclusive Businesses, in part due to how recently this new field has emerged (Wach 2012; Boechat, Faria, Pimenta, and Ferreira 2014).

As a whole, these tools seek to value the worth of MNCs according to some, but not all, of the constituent aspects of the social project of the field of Inclusive Business. All the three measuring devices require a firm, working in conjunction with stakeholders, to provide a quantitative count of the impact of a firm's (or a firm's business initiative) inclusive organization of their value chain (including suppliers, employees, and customers) on poverty and development in the area of operation. All three tools require firms to quantify their involvement with local firms in their value chains as a measure of their contribution to the growth of local SMEs. All three tools necessitate Inclusive Businesses to demonstrate that they created local jobs, either via a total count of direct and indirect jobs or also by estimating the average increase in wages for local employees that resulted from its efforts. And, relatedly, all three tools also entail corporations' count of their offering of training (as a measure of human capital) to those in their value chain, including suppliers and employees. Finally, Inclusive Businesses are required in each case to demonstrate that local customers benefit economically (in terms of a lower price) and/or socially from their products.[13]

Yet, these measuring devices also vary, diverging in their content not only from each other, but also from the social project of Inclusive Business, extending beyond the meaning of social value as characteristic of the field and also omitting certain dimensions of the field's defining characteristics.[14] For one, variation exists in the extent to which the tools necessitate the assignment of a monetary value to the benefits of an inclusive business practice. Most of these tools simply require a count of the number of market actors (individuals and/or firms) that benefit from the corporation's inclusive value chain. For example, in all three cases, Inclusive Businesses should list the number of small businesses aided or created by the firm's inclusive procurement practices. But, they rarely require, with the exception of the BCtA tool, that a MNC estimate the monetary benefit of such an impact, with the exception of employment creation (where firms are asked to estimate the average improvement in salary for their employees as opposed to other employers). Even here, the suggested indicators are quite crude, especially when compared to the complexity of data required by the tools used in the fields of social enterprise and Responsible Investing to assign a monetary figure to a firm's social value.

For another, these tools differ in the scope of the development benefits that are recognized as produced by an Inclusive Business, in ways that extend beyond the social project of the field. While all three tools require firms to estimate the effect of their business practices on local economic development for suppliers, employees, and consumers, two of three measuring devices also estimate the effect of those inclusive business practices for a more standard and extensive range of development outcomes. When it conducts a Poverty Footprint of a firm, for example, Oxfam (2009) promises to specify the impact of a company's core business practices for "five critical factors that are important for poverty alleviation: standard of living; health and well-being; diversity and gender equality; empowerment; and stability and security." Similarly, the World Business Council for Sustainable Development (2013b) asks companies to hypothesize the causal link by which their inclusive business practices will not only have a "socio-economic impact" but also affect key development issues in the local community, as identified by stakeholders, including such possible issues as education, public health, and capacity building.

Perhaps more curiously, beyond capturing the development benefits produced by a MNC for a local community, these tools also require firms to demonstrate different types of social value than those at the heart of the field's social project. Drawing from the already existing social projects of CSR and Responsible Investing, all three measuring devices include a gauge of a company's environmental impact on local communities and the WBCSD's Measuring Impact even extends to a consideration of an Inclusive Business' performance on governance issues (including sanctions for non-compliance, transparency and disclosure, and codes of conduct), as emphasized in the field of Responsible Investing's attention to ESG issues. Finally, both the WBCSD's Measuring Impact Framework and Oxfam's Poverty Footprint include a concern for not only the economic development benefits produced by an Inclusive Business' provision of employment but also the quality of that employment, including the insurance of diversity and the provision of a living wage, benefits, and the protection of workers' human rights, as transposed from the social project of CSR. In essence, firms that claim the identity of Inclusive Business are evaluated according to a wider range of social responsibilities than is entailed by the distinguishing characteristics of the field's social project.

Yet while these measuring devices capture notions of social value taken from both the field of Inclusive Business and elsewhere, these tools do not capture all of the dimensions of value central to the social project of Inclusive Business. As with the broader turn to caring capitalism in the global economy, the definition of Inclusive Business includes not only a concern for the social value of a multinational corporation but also for the shareholder value that is produced by a firm's business model. In a range of publications and in interviews, as outlined earlier, both proponents of the field and key value entrepreneurs asserted the economic worth of inclusive business practices. The profit generated by inclusive value chains was both socially valuable (in that it facilitated firms' scale and sustainability) and it was financially valuable (in that it served as a source of shareholder return). Take the case of the World Business Council for Sustainable Development (WBCSD/SNV 2008:2): one of its publication introducing the concept of Inclusive Business asserted that "Inclusive Business leads to: Increased profitability for a company as a result of lower supply costs, market expansion through the inclusion of low-income sectors, and greater sustainability of the business activity." In Oxfam's introductory overview of the Poverty Footprint, the authors likewise claim: "There is a well-acknowledged circular relationship between the societal impacts of business and business performance" (Oxfam 2009:7).[15]

Curiously, however, despite the field's shared emphasis on mission and money with the field of Responsible Investing, the prevailing measuring devices for Inclusive Business look markedly different from those found in the case of RI. Recall that the emerging valuation instruments in the field of RI seek to capture the monetary worth of a firm's ESG performance in terms of their generation of shareholder value through attention to the resulting risks and opportunities. For example, in the case of a corporation's treatment of workers (in terms of the provision of safe working conditions), a dollar amount of the ensuing cost savings for the firm is calculated and incorporated into a traditional estimation of the financial value of the firm.

Yet, in contrast, the measuring devices that prevail for Inclusive Businesses focus exclusively on capturing corporations' social value as an end in itself, without incorporating a gauge of the financial value of those practices in terms of generating additional economic profit and/or shareholder return. Even on the one occasion when measures of a firm's economic performance are included, as in the case of the BCtA's Results Reporting Framework, they are framed by the value entrepreneurs as indicators of a business' ability to generate resources for their stakeholders as a source of economic development value. The BCtA's

Results Reporting Framework requires a firm to report a count of the cost savings and profits in dollars that resulted from each business initiative, but only as a gauge of the firm's ability to use business operations for development as an "economic multiplier" (Nelson 2003). In other words, these tools do not seek to demonstrate either that Inclusive Businesses are financially viable (as a source of social value) and/or that they generate additional long-term economic profit by minimizing risks and maximizing opportunities (as a source of shareholder value). To make sense of this divergence between what is of value in the field's social project and what and how it is valued by the field's measuring devices argue requires empirical investigation.

The communicative goal of value entrepreneurs

To understand the precise nature of the measuring devices used in this field requires attention to these objects' history or biography – who created these tools and to what purpose/s. Here, value entrepreneurs included the BCtA, a membership organization composed of a number of developed nations' development agencies, as well as several United Nations offices. In 2008, these actors decided to form the BCtA in order to encourage corporations to work towards the Millennium Development Goals. The BctA challenged "companies to develop Inclusive Business models that offer the potential for both commercial success and development impact" (BCtA 2013). In 2010, the BCtA commissioned the creation of a measuring device, the Results Reporting Requirement, which it required member companies to implement and to share their results with the association.

Similarly, the World Business Council for Sustainable Development is a membership-based business association that was created in 1995 to serve the needs of corporations with a self-identified commitment to socially and environmentally responsible behavior. In 2005, the WBCSD developed the term of "Inclusive Business" in order to convey and promote the idea of corporations that could profit from and address poverty through their business models. Three years later, the WBCSD (2008a, 2008b) formulated a measuring device, the Measuring Impact Framework, for use by its member organizations that identified as Inclusive Businesses.

Oxfam, the international relief and development organization, created the third measuring device, the "Poverty Footprint." First developed in 2004 in a case study of Unilever's work in Indonesia, and then formalized in 2009, the "Poverty Footprint" is a tool to be employed by Oxfam at a firm's request in order to estimate the effect of the company's business operations on economic and social development for the local community (Clay 2005; Oxfam 2009). The Poverty Footprint was part of Oxfam's broader recognition of the capacity of compassionate companies to address poverty, as outlined in one Poverty Footprint report in 2011. "We have often viewed and exposed multinational companies as a threat to poor communities and, historically, our relationships with the private sector have focused more on campaigning than collaboration," wrote the president of Oxfam America (Coca Cola/SAB Miller 2011:10), but now "we recognize they can also drive innovation, job creation and economic growth in the developing world."

These proponents developed measuring devices for Inclusive Businesses with a particular communicative purpose in mind – that of legitimacy. As noted in Chapter 2, a tool of valuation is constructed to generate legitimacy when it is intended to convey the "generalized perception or assumption that the actions of an entity are desirable, proper, or appropriate within some socially constructed system of norms, values, beliefs, and definitions" (Suchman 1995:574). In the case of legitimacy, a measuring device serves as a "political solution to a political problem" (Porter 1995:x). The pursuit of legitimacy is contextually specific and its meaning for focal actors depends on the expectations of powerful others in a particular setting at a precise historical moment. For instance, Chapter 2 showed that public and nonprofit resource providers of nonprofits in the 1990s developed outcome measurement in order to assert their legitimacy by meeting their own funders' expectation that they should oversee recipients via the use of performance measurement techniques.

In this nascent field, Inclusive Businesses faced a particular challenge to their legitimacy, one that reflected the experience of developing nations in the global economy over the prior decades. By definition, Inclusive Businesses are large multinational corporations that locate at least some of their value chain in a developing country. To obtain access to a local economy, these companies must obtain "license to operate" from powerful local stakeholders. These constituencies include government agencies (who engage in public regulation over the economy) and civil society actors, such as NGOs and community representatives (who seek to exercise private regulation over market actors), who together provide the formal and social license for MNCs to operate in that region's economy. It has been to these local stakeholders that all MNCs – and so all Inclusive Businesses – had to demonstrate their legitimacy in order to obtain public and private permission to operate in a region.

Yet, obtaining license to operate was difficult; corporations faced an environment that was highly critical of the consequences of foreign direct investment for developing nations. First, over the last two decades or so, multinational corporations have faced growing public regulation regarding performance requirements, which firms must meet in order to gain access to the desired industrial sector of the local economy. These performance requirements are specific laws or regulations on foreign direct investment which mandate that a certain percentage of component parts or other inputs used in the production process be sourced from domestic manufacturers and that a certain percentage of citizens from the host country be hired and trained by the corporation. Despite being technically forbidden by the World Trade Organization, these formal regulations are on the rise, particularly in the infrastructure industries of oil, gas, and mining, as a way to maximize national value creation for developing countries by generating local benefits via the composition of the supply chain and employment (Hufbauer and Scott 2013). One example is the case of Nigeria, where the national government in 2010 adopted a law privileging local companies and favoring foreign companies that considered employment and local procurement in any contracts granted in their oil and gas industry (Government of Nigeria 2010).

In addition, actors in civil society, such as NGOs and community groups, have protested the consequences of globalization for the developing world, in part by instituting private regulation of corporations. As discussed in Chapter 5, a range of transnational networks has pushed back against the neoliberal policy of structural adjustment and the presence of multinational corporations in the global South. For many, globalization has possessed largely negative ramification for developing nations, including forced urbanization and dispossession, increased economic inequality, and environmental degradation. While some protests were oriented against multilateral organizations like the International Monetary Fund, the World Bank, and the World Trade Organization (as in the 1999 Seattle anti-WTO protests), others have been directed at a specific MNC (such as the indigenous community's protests in the 1990s against Shell's operations in the Niger Delta in Nigeria).

The existence of such a skeptical environment and the presence of both public and private regulation over the operations of multinational corporations in the global South helps both to explain the turn to Inclusive Business (as a discursive move to highlight the positive effects of MNCs for their regions of operation) and the creation of measuring devices (given their ability to generate data to demonstrate compassionate companies' social and economic benefits for their region of operation). As required by public regulation, MNCs required evidence that they met the requirements of local employment and sourcing in order to obtain formal license to operate. And these firms also would benefit from the voluntary provision of evidence of their positive impact in order to obtain social license to operate from key actors in civil society, as evident in the earlier case of CSR.

In both cases, we can understand the rise of measuring devices here as yet another instance of the broader realization by multinational corporations of the necessity of meeting external expectations of legitimacy, beyond purely market-based considerations. As scholars have demonstrated, MNCs came to see that any "hazards or harms" they engender through their business operations, even if not illegal, would be subject to "public censure, government action, and legal liability." In result, companies voluntarily have sought to go beyond local regulatory requirements and to obtain a "social license to operate" from key stakeholders (Gunningham, Kagan, and Thornton 2004).[16]

Evidence of this desire to assert compliance with both formal and informal expectations of legitimacy on the part of value entrepreneurs in the field of Inclusive Business is found throughout their publications and in interviews with members of the field. In the case of the WBCSD's Measuring Impact

Framework, the organization proclaimed that the tool "can help companies show communities, government authorities, and other stakeholders, like donors and civil society groups, that their activities create net benefits for the economies and societies in which they operate – and mitigate the risk of negative publicity, protest, and declining government support for current and future operations" (World Business Council for Sustainable Development 2013b:8). Somewhat predictably, one of WBCSD's first case studies with the framework was with Saipem, an Italian multinational that engages in oil and gas extraction in Indonesia, precisely the type of industry subject to state oversight of foreign direct investment and to scrutiny from civil society members (World Business Council for Sustainable Development 2013a). One of the earliest efforts to measure the social value of inclusive businesses in order to obtain social license to operate was conducted by Oxfam GB for Unilever's operations in Indonesia (Clay 2005). In the preface to the report, the group chief executive for Unilever wrote, "at times it has been hard for our managers to find their values and behaviours subjected to such sceptical scrutiny, and to see their achievements, when operating in a complex business context, so lightly passed over" (Clay 2005:10). The BCtA's Results Reporting Requirement was constructed with the goal of the BCtA using the aggregated data to demonstrate the benefits of Inclusive Business to key audiences and to "inspire additional action by the private sector in this area" (BCtA 2010:2). And, in the words of a senior staff member of one major advocate of Inclusive Businesses, "social impact measurement is needed because of the risk management side of things – meaning the need for multinationals to get license to operate in order just to get access to some places. It can show local governments how companies manage their business and how they avoid dodgy practices in the community."

Understanding the communicative purpose of these measuring devices for Inclusive Businesses helps to account for which aspects of the field's social project were included, and which were excluded, from these measuring devices. These tools specifically were created in order to disseminate the necessary data on Inclusive Businesses' social performance in order to demonstrate legitimacy by conformity with expectations of formal and informal providers of MNC's license to operate, thus explaining their focus on the social value of Inclusive Businesses and their omission of a concern for the financial value of these companies.

The role of the valuation repertoire

Yet, explaining the disjuncture between the social project of Inclusive Businesses and the types of value gauged in the prevailing measuring devices in this field also requires consideration of the capacity of value entrepreneurs to construct an appropriate instrument. Charged with the precise communicative purpose of demonstrating the legitimacy of MNCs to stakeholders in the global

South, valuation entrepreneurs (either the staff of organizational advocates of Inclusive Business or one-time consultants hired for this purpose) drew from their professional expertise to construct a suitable measuring device for the task at hand. As noted in Chapter 1, the formation of a new measuring device constitutes a concerted effort on the part of an actor/s to devise a tool to gauge entities by reference to a specific criterion. As we have seen in other chapters, value entrepreneurs do so by relying on the range of models available to them in their valuation repertoire. However, the implications of the concept of a valuation repertoire for understanding value entrepreneurs' action are not straightforward. On the one hand, as we have seen in past chapters, the possession of a valuation repertoire composed of multiple tools, techniques, and technologies means that those entrepreneurs have a number of options available to them when they seek to construct a measuring device. These actors then can draw from an existing valuation tool/s that can be suitably re-fashioned in order to negotiate a specific challenge or pursue a particular goal. In the case of social enterprises, as detailed in Chapter 3, proponents of this new type of social purpose organization relied on their expertise in both the nonprofit sector and the finance industry to construct the new measuring device of Social Return on Investment (SROI), one which successfully monetized the societal value of social enterprises to demonstrate their worth to targeted audiences. On the other hand, the limited and finite nature of a repertoire means that, on occasion, actors will lack access to a practice or method in their toolkit that would allow them to pursue their goals or interests. In an early seminal articulation of the concept of the repertoire (using instead the metaphor of the toolkit), Swidler (1986), for example, showed that actors can be disadvantaged by a disjuncture between their intentions and the absence of items in their toolkit necessary to achieve that line of action. In these cases, individuals or groups must make do with the tools they have present in their repertoire or they can search for new techniques more suitable for their intended task, contingent upon the possession of adequate resources to do so (Schneiberg and Clemens 2006).

Attention to the valuation repertoire at the disposal of value entrepreneurs here can help to account for the construction of measuring devices that focused solely on an inclusive business's social impact and omitted a gauge of an inclusive business model's financial value. These actors drew from their professional backgrounds in a variety of fields. In the case of the World Business Council for Sustainable Development, the professional association employed the sustainability consulting firm, Environment Resource Management, to develop a measuring tool and drew from the valuation work of the International Finance Corporation (an arm of the World Bank devoted to promoting private investment in emerging markets to facilitate development) (World Business Council for Sustainable Development 2008a). Oxfam's Poverty Footprint was initially constructed by an executive at the World Wildlife Federation with a background in indigenous rights, fair trade, and seafood sustainability

(Clay 2001; Clay 2005).[17] And BCtA relied on the efforts of several staff with professional experience in sustainable development, finance, CSR, and international development (BCtA 2010).

Given their professional background, these value entrepreneurs employed and re-fashioned existing measurement tools with which they were already familiar in the arenas of sustainable development and international development for use in the new field of Inclusive Business.[18] The emergence of sustainable development in the 1980s and 1990s, as outlined in Chapter 5, placed expectations on businesses to produce a measure of their usage of environmental resources. One tool created for corporations was that of the ecological "footprint:" a company can quantitatively estimate its carbon, ecological, or water "footprints" in order to capture the amount of resources it uses or the level of demand it makes on the environment as compared to what is deemed to be sustainable, with the intentional omission of the financial impact of such a ratio (Wackernagel and Rees 1996; Wright, Kemp and Williams 2011). Given the popularity of the tool of the footprint in sustainable development, one value entrepreneur in the field of Inclusive Business drew from that measuring device to generate a similar method to gauge the consequences of a company's business model for a local community. Specifically, when Oxfam worked to develop a social valuation tool in collaboration with Unilever in 2005, the author of this new methodology, with an educational background and professional expertise in indigenous rights, fair trade, and seafood sustainability, intentionally transposed the metaphor of the "footprint" to capture the firm's success in including the poor into the market as a source of economic and developmental value (Clay 2005). As one officer at Oxfam United States later recounted about the genealogy of the Poverty Footprint: "The environmental community has done a tremendous job in being able to properly demonstrate the value in measuring environmental impact. The challenge is trying to do the same around social impact" (Sand 2010).

While some in the field extended a measuring device originally designed to demonstrate a firm's environment to gauge a firm's development value, other value entrepreneurs drew from their expertise in international development to develop tools for the field of Inclusive Business. Reflecting their professional knowledge, these actors took valuation instruments created originally to assess the work of bilateral, multilateral, and NGO efforts in the developing world, but modified them for use by Inclusive Businesses (BCtA 2010, 2011; World Business Council for Sustainable Development 2008a, 2008b). Beginning in the post-War II period, when the project of international development took off, the field witnessed the growth of various valuation tools and technologies, as developed and employed by an industry of government actors, consultants, and academics (Krause 2014). As a whole, as with the related project of evaluation in the domestic public and nonprofit sectors (as outlined in Chapter 2), funders in international development seek to assess the success of an intervention (a program, policy, organization, or collaboration) in achieving its intended social change. Several variants of evaluation were developed during this period to gauge the success of an international development project. The first, "Impact Evaluation" relies on either use of the LogFrame model (which requires the collection of data on the program's goals, results, and activities to demonstrate its success) or the use of randomized control trials (RCTs) comparing a treatment and control group in order to establish causal attribution after the completion of the project (Banerjee 2007; Krause 2014). Development projects may also be assessed through the use of Monitoring & Evaluation (M&E), which is conducted in order to ascertain the effectiveness of a program against intended targets by the gathering of key indicators on an ongoing basis, which are typically intended for the purpose of external reporting and organizational learning (World Bank 2004a; Wach 2012). In both cases, the effectiveness of a development project typically is not monetized in these approaches but rather counted in terms of the amount of the intended change achieved in the targeted community, dependent on the specific goal of the development intervention.

Drawing on their experience with these conventions and devices, some value entrepreneurs in the field of Inclusive Business extended them in new ways to capture the social and economic impact produced by this new type of compassionate company (BCtA 2011). They kept an emphasis on conceptualizing social value via reference to the collection of indicators of development impact, thus delimiting social value to non-monetized changes in clients and populations. Tellingly, when I asked a consultant hired to develop a measuring device for one advocate of Inclusive Business, she replied: "a lot of the starting point was the development sector approach, you know, M and E, where you try to monitor and evaluate and you think of the logic chain behind a development intervention or program. What was taken out of it when we developed this for the client was the complexity of the terminology to try to simplify it for business and to be more manageable. And then the goals too, the goals of M and E are always project specific, so in our case we filled in the blanks with our client's preferences – their attention to what a business is going to be assessed for, specific to the task of ending poverty through their core business activities."

In 2008, similarly, the World Business Council for Sustainable Development (2008a, 2008b) – an early proponent of the concept of inclusive business – developed the Measuring Impact Framework, intended to measure the effect of a firm's business activity on economic development in its region of operation. These value entrepreneurs intentionally transposed the valuation tools of International Development into its framework. In its publication disseminating the framework, for instance, the authors noted: "There are some similarities between the terminology used in this Framework and the logical framework used by many development agencies/multilaterals such as OECD and IFC" (World Business Council for Sustainable Development 2008b:73). The Measuring Results Framework requires an Inclusive Business first to specify the societal "impact" (both direct and indirect) of its value chain via attention to its assets (including infrastructure, products, and services), people (jobs, skills, and training), financial flows (procurement and taxes), and governance and sustainability (corporate governance and environmental management). Secondly, with feedback from local stakeholders, the firm then would identify the potential "value" of these impacts for local economic development (including not only the creation of jobs, but other potential issues of human rights, education and health (as taken from the UN Global Compact) in order to posit the hypothetic effect of firms' activities on those development issues. However, a company is not required to gather data to prove the posited causal relationship, beyond collecting feedback from stakeholders about its perceived validity (World Business Council for Sustainable Development 2008b).

By drawing from their professional expertise, value entrepreneurs were able to construct measuring devices to demonstrate the development benefits of Inclusive Businesses, as required by these tools' communicative purpose of acquiring legitimacy with skeptical stakeholders in the global South. They transposed and re-fashioned items from their valuation repertoire to the new case of Inclusive Business in order to successfully capture those social dimensions of value. Yet, the limited nature of their valuation repertoire also can help to explain the exclusion of the measure of the financial value of those inclusive business practices from these same measuring devices. Unlike value entrepreneurs in the case of Responsible Investing, these actors did not possess a background or knowledge of finance. In several interviews, respondents involved in the creation or dissemination of these tools suggested that they were aware of the benefits of conveying the financial value of inclusive businesses' business models to external audiences but that they lacked the capacity to do so. Here, the conceptualization of culture as a repertoire (or toolkit) emphasizes that it can possess a constraining effect on actors (Swidler 1986). In one interview, I asked a respondent who had worked on the development of one of these measuring instruments to recount how the staff had arrived at their final product. In part, Tamara outlined how they had settled on the list of indicators to demonstrate a MNC's social impact in its region of operation. When she came to the topic of a corporation's provision of employment opportunities in a local community, she noted: "We ended up with a count of job creation – if you look at our methodology recommendations, a company is meant to tally up how many jobs they provided to locals. But we really wanted to be able to also get that company to estimate the income produced by those new jobs over a prolonged period of time – which would have been a large number and so pretty impressive. That would have been pretty easy for a firm to estimate and more indicative as well of the value of their impact on the local economy. But, the problem was that then there would be non-comparable units across the different indicators of a firm's social impact because we didn't know how to calculate a dollar value for those other indicators, particularly when it came to the company's value chain – you know, how do you calculate the monetary worth of including more locally owned companies as suppliers or how do you estimate the dollar worth of selling sewage pumps to poor people? That we didn't know how to do and we didn't think our member companies would know how to estimate either, much less the question of did they keep that kind of data? So we ended up just using number of jobs created to keep things simple and to keep the numbers comparable."

Similarly, at the end of another conversation with a staff person charged with the administration and dissemination of a measuring device for Inclusive Businesses for an international business coalition, I asked Barbara about whether she or other staff had ever considered trying to calculate the value produced by inclusive business practices in relation to financial value. Such a question was relevant given that she had just told me about the superiority of Inclusive Businesses to traditional forms of international development aid based on these firms' economic viability (as compared to philanthropic aid or government redistribution). In response, Barbara told me: "We'd love to. We talk about this as one of our goals – how does supporting local SMEs or creating local employment cut expenses or grow a market for the corporation? But right now we don't have the means or really the know-how to do so. It would be very tough. We are thinking about it and looking around for examples of this to guide us." Clearly, Barbara knew the business case offered for Inclusive Business and knew that it would increase the appeal of this new type of company to a variety of audiences, but neither she nor other staff members possessed the tools in their valuation repertoire to enact that justification of the field in a measuring device. Caught up in our conversation, I told her about the case of RI where value entrepreneurs are developing methodologies to estimate the economic impact of a firm's ESG practices on its long-term generation of shareholder return, as a possible model for something similar in the case of Inclusive Business. I asked if she'd heard of any of this. She was quick to reply. "No, I haven't, but it sounds really useful for us. Could you send me any information you have on it? We'd love to see it."

Clearly, as this exchange illustrates, the assignment of monetary value and shareholder value to evaluate the worth of these compassionate companies is not straightforward. The construction of a formal tool by which to value firms according to this financial criterion and via the metric of money requires adequate capacity and knowledge to do so. However, value entrepreneurs in this field were constrained in this effort by their professional expertise and their accompanying possession of a limited repertoire of valuation tools and methods.

IMPACT INVESTING: FINANCE FOR DOUBLE BOTTOM LINE RETURN

A third variant of caring capitalism is the case of Impact Investing. As another new field that intersects economic and social value, Impact Investing, sometimes called "Social Finance" (Antadze and Westley 2012), consists of institutional and individual investors' direction of private equity funds (either loans or investments), with the assistance of intermediaries, to investment funds and/or firms for the intended generation of both financial and social return. It is focused specifically on investment in SMEs and microfinance vehicles in developed and developing countries that are "double bottom line" in nature. These locally-owned and operated firms produce financial value for investors and generate social value in their community of operation through entrepreneurship opportunities and/or through their sale of socially beneficial goods and services (Bugg-Levine and Emerson 2011; Simon and Barmeier 2011). In 2012, over $9 billion was invested as impact investments and some observers have projected the market to grow to $1 trillion by 2018 (Monitor Institute 2009; J.P. Morgan 2013).

As with other economic markets, one challenge recognized by proponents of this new field was to generate a resolution to the "value problem." As discussed in Chapter 6, the value problem exists in a market because members must be able to calculate the worth of goods and compare alternative options to in order to select their preference (Callon 1998; Beckert 2009). In the case of Impact Investing, advocates recognized that the growth of this financial market was contingent upon members being able to gauge and compare the value of different investment opportunities on both their economic and/or social dimensions. How then was the "value problem" to be solved in Impact Investing? As had occurred in the field of Inclusive Business, the valuation instruments constructed to facilitate the growth of Impact Investing demonstrated a marked difference between proponents' envision of the field's social project and the types of value actually gauged by its formal valuation tools. The measuring devices that were created in the case of Impact Investing focused only on an investment's social return, and they did not assign a monetary value to an investment's economic development value for local individuals and communities or calculate how social value produced economic profit and so shareholder return, as we saw in Chapter 6. Accounting for this puzzle constitutes the task of the remainder of this chapter.

Social value in Impact Investing

At face value, Impact Investing seems similar to other fields in the broader turn to caring capitalism. A number of other markets have arisen, including Inclusive Business and Responsible Investment, where market enthusiasts have argued that investors may obtain both financial and social return. Similarly, Impact Investing disrupts the assumption that money in the market can only be oriented around economic gain. The traditional expectation, asserted one leading proponent of the field, is that "financial assets are used to fulfill two very distinct purposes: the bulk of assets are invested to maximize profit, and a very small portion is dedicated to charity. Impact investing challenges this way of thinking and enables investors to seek positive social and environmental impact with much more capital than is possible with charity alone" (UBS 2011).

Proponents of Impact Investing have offered a vision of the social project of the field where social value results from the employment of market methods to address a range of social problems. And, similar to other instances of caring capitalism, these advocates attribute the superiority of companies to achieve social value versus the capacity of NGOs and government agencies to firms' sustainability and scale (Monitor Institute 2009; J.P. Morgan 2011; Bugg-Levine and Emerson 2011). However, proponents of Impact Investing highlight the benefits of a new type of social purpose organizations by which market engagement can produce social good. For the first time, the focus is not on large corporations headquartered in the global North and operating in developing countries (as characterizes other types of caring capitalism), but rather on directing loans and equity investment to small, locally owned companies (often called SMEs, as discussed earlier) whose business model is premised on solving a social problem. The goal of impact investment is "local in nature," to quote from a respondent, where investors should direct "capital directly into companies and projects," rather than invest in multinational corporations that operate in socially or environmentally beneficial sectors (e.g., clean energy), that practice CSR, or that operate in the global South (Bugg-Levine and Emerson 2011).

One instance of this definitional distinction occurred at an impact investing conference that I attended. One panel member was a partner in a small boutique investment firm that focused on emerging markets. He had been invited to present on his company's decision to invest in a green start-up in Mexico as a case of impact investment. But, in the Q&A session, he argued that all of his firm's investments in emerging markets should qualify as "impact investments" given that they served to grow the economy of developing nations, with corollary societal benefits. The other panel members and the audience were quick to reject his claim, with many loudly noting that the specific purpose of Impact Investing is to place investment and loans with locally owned firms whose business models constitute a solution to a social problem. As one panelist exclaimed vehemently: "Money alone is not the answer!"

In the social project of Impact Investing, investments to SMEs must be oriented towards economic development benefits as a source of social value (through investment in micro-finance vehicles and community development institutions) or towards facilitating the growth of firms that sell goods or services that solve social and/or environmental problems or that are targeted to those at the Bottom of the Pyramid. Examples here include companies involved in sustainable agriculture, affordable housing, affordable and accessible healthcare, clean technology, and financial services for the poor, among others (Monitor Institute 2009).[19] One example is Selco, an Indian company that provides access to affordable solar energy to those living below the poverty line (Milligan and Schøning 2011). Advocates of the field recognize that, in the process of producing these types of goods and services, local companies may also generate social value by sourcing, hiring, and distributing locally. However, the incorporation of the poor into the market is viewed as only one source of social value in the field of Impact Investing, as opposed to the premises of the field of Inclusive Business (J.P. Morgan 2010).

The origins of Impact Investing

The origins of Impact Investing can be traced back to the concerted effort of a small group of nonprofit funders and government agencies, led by the Rockefeller Foundation. They sought to formalize and scale an existing interest by philanthropists to provide investment support to small firms in developing countries as a new, optimal solution to social problems through the construction of a new organizational field. These advocates, historical shift from funding nonprofits to companies as vehicles of social welfare reflected broader changes occurring both inside and outside the field of philanthropy in the United States over the last several decades. First, the Rockefeller Foundation, as was occurring both in the nonprofit sector and in the field of international development, had embraced market-based solutions to societal problems (Rockefeller Philanthropy Advisors 2006). As discussed in Chapter 3, not only had many traditional foundations like the Rockefeller Foundation taken up this market-based approach to social problems, but they were joined by a new group of institutional donors – many of whom self-identified as "venture philanthropists" – who specifically funded market-based efforts to end poverty, including the Roberts Enterprise Development Fund (REDF), New Profit Inc., the Acumen Fund, Investors' Circle, and the Calvert Group/Calvert Special Equities (Moody 2008). But, these advocates of Impact Investing also believed that not only were social inequities to be solved through ensuring market access to the disadvantaged, but also that the scale of assistance available through private, marked-based means was far larger than through philanthropic funding of NGOs. In the words of the president of the Rockefeller Foundation, one of the key proponents of impact investing, "we recognized, if you put a price tag on all the social and environmental needs around the world, it is in the trillions. All of the philanthropy in the world is only $590 billion. So, the needs far exceed the resources. The one place where there is hundreds of trillions of dollars is in the private capital markets. So we, and others, began to wonder are there ways to crowd in private funding to some of these incredible needs" (Kozlowski 2012).

Secondly, the Rockefeller Foundation's interest in Impact Investing resulted from many foundations' embrace of Mission-Related Investing, a new rationale for how charitable foundations should direct their assets. Foundations in the US legally are required to direct five percent of their assets annually to nonprofits in pursuit of their charitable mission and the remaining ninety-five percent of their assets typically is invested to generate financial return. Historically, that latter pool of capital has been invested according to the legally defined fiduciary duty of being a "prudent investor" through traditional investment strategies that privilege a high rate of financial return, regardless of the social nature of the investments. In contrast, Mission-Related Investing occurs when foundations invest a portion of their capital assets in ways conducive to the pursuit of their charitable mission but also seeking a market-rate of return (Reis 2003; Cooch and Kramer 2007; Godeke and Bauer 2008).[20] In a sense, Mission-Related Investing constitutes a form of Socially Responsible Investing in that the definition of social value that guides investing is tailored to the foundation's mission. Pioneered by a small number of foundations in the 1990s (including the Jesse Smith Noyes Foundation) and catalyzed by media criticism of the Gates Foundation's investment of its capital in 2007 (Piller, Sanders, and Dixon 2007), Mission-Related Investing is an increasingly common strategy on the part of large foundations to direct some of their capital assets for both financial and social return. Starting in 1998, for example, the Rockefeller Foundation had experimented with MRI, where it invested its capital in for-profit endeavors through its Program Venture Experiment (World Economic Forum 2005).

Finally, proponents of Impact Investing drew from the broader embrace of double bottom line businesses and socially oriented investing outside the nonprofit sector. As with the case of Inclusive Business, the economic viability and success of microfinance in improving the lives of the poor and producing profit for investors legitimated the concept of Impact Investing (Silby 2011). Advocates also highlighted the scale of resources invested in community development initiatives as proof of the viability of Impact Investing (Bugg-Levine and Goldstein 2009). And the growth of Socially Responsible Investing, CSR, and RI among not only market monitors – motivated by political activism – but also among mainstream investors interested in market-rate return was seen as evidence that a market of Impact Investing could be constructed whereby market monitors could join with philanthropic funders and traditional investors seeking a market-rate of return (Monitor Institute 2009; Hope Consulting 2010; J.P. Morgan 2013).

CONSTRUCTING THE MARKET OF IMPACT INVESTING

The goal of the proponents of this field, including philanthropic foundations, government agencies, and multilateral organizations, was to construct a new organizational field – to build a new type of capital market, similar to that of RI, which was based on financial and social return.[21] They sought to bring together an assortment of previously distinct and autonomous types of financing strategies and social purpose organizations, including investors with a social interest (i.e., participants in the fields of SRI, CSR, and RI) and local companies in developing areas with a double bottom line (including community development actors, microfinance vehicles, SMEs, and firms selling BOP products), into a single financial market. The term of "impact investing" served as a "broad, rhetorical umbrella under which a wide range of investors could huddle" (Monitor Institute 2009; Bugg-Levine and Emerson 2011:8).[22]

In 2007, the Rockefeller Foundation convened many of resource providers in a meeting to try and determine the scope and challenges of using investing as a financing mechanism for for-profit solutions to social problems. And, in 2008, the Rockefeller Foundation committed itself to the formation of a market for impact investing by earmarking $38 million for an Impact Investing Initiative, drawing from grants, program-related investments, and non-grant activities. In 2009, the Global Impact Investing Network (GIIN) was formed by proponents of the field as a stand-alone organization in order to facilitate the development of the market of impact investing; it was dedicated to creating the necessary "infrastructure, conventions, and networks" needed to grow the industry (Bugg-Levine and Emerson 2011). To that end, several research reports were commissioned by these proponents to specify the challenges faced by proponents in growing a market and to propose solutions to address these problems (Bugg-Levine 2009; Monitor Institute 2009; Rockefeller Philanthropy Advisors 2010; J.P. Morgan 2011).

Intentionally using traditional capital markets as the model of a successful investment market and drawing from interviews with impact investors, three key challenges were specified as critical for the growth of impact investing. A market of impact investing had to address the lack of intermediation to facilitate investment (i.e., the presence of vehicles that facilitated investors' identification of investment options). Proponents would have to resolve the lack of transparent, absorptive investment capacity (i.e., the availability of scalable double-bottom line funds and firms that could integrate large amounts of capital). Finally, proponents of this new market would need to correct for what social scientists have called the "value problem" in a market. For a market to succeed, members must be able to determine the value of the goods that are to be exchanged. Discourses and devices must be constructed that provide the necessary information about the worth of goods so that the act of calculability and commensurability by market actors is possible (Callon 1998; Beckert 2009; Karpik 2010). Similarly, these reports on the future of impact investing as a finance market emphasized the existing absence of an enabling infrastructure, which included the lack of "reliable social metrics" (Monitor Institute 2009; J.P. Morgan 2011). "In the absence of concrete data, current explanations of sector performance inevitably rely on cheery anecdotes and case studies to outline social impacts" (Simon and Barmeier 2011:27). As a senior executive at the Rockefeller Foundation proclaimed, "the success of impact investing may well hinge on our ability to meaningfully and credibly capture, track, report, and measure social and environmental impact" (Brandenburg 2010:47).

Here, the resolution of the value problem was deemed necessary by proponents for the market to succeed for two reasons. First, a measure of social impact was critical to defending the emerging market against charges that it was actually oriented only around the pursuit of profit, a criticism also lodged against the field of Inclusive Business. In the words of one academic advisor to the field that I interviewed, "what GIIN is worried about is that impact investing is seen by others as a way to greenwash mainstream investment in a world that's increasingly critical of globalization." The term of "greenwash" here refers to critiques aimed at corporations that claim to be environmentally responsible but who do not implement any substantive policies or practices to that end (Laufer 2003). Similarly, a consulting firm's recommendations for the growth of Impact Investing concluded that the formation of a measuring device to demonstrate firms' social value would "help protect the credibility and reputation of the field from conventional investments being promoted as impact investments" (Monitor Institute 2009:47). As evident in earlier chapters, the construction of a measuring device served to demonstrate "mechanical objectivity" (Porter 1995) on the part of actors.

More importantly in their mind, according to interviews and document analysis, market enthusiasts claimed that a resolution to the value problem was needed so that participants in Impact Investing could engage in the necessary assessment of worth. Firms would benefit from the ability to communicate their value to resource providers, double bottom line investment funds would require the capacity to screen potential investment opportunities based on both financial and social/environmental impact without undue expenditures of cost and time, and investors and investment managers would need to engage in commensurability. To quote from one senior staffer of an organization that was an early proponent of impact investing, "we realized really soon that we needed a way for investors to figure out how much social impact they could have so that they could compare different investment possibilities. Without that, impact investing would never get to scale."

Just as the market of impact investing was modeled after the mainstream financial market more broadly, so too did the quest to establishment the metrics of social value also seek to emulate how valuation occurred through established accounting practices in traditional capital markets (J.P. Morgan 2011; Antadze and Westley 2012). Mainstream investing assesses investing opportunities using the common and standardized scale of money and by employing institutionalized performance criteria of a company's economic performance and so its intrinsic value, as discussed in other chapters. For advocates of impact investing, the establishment of a single metric of worth, to be generated by a universal measuring device, was deemed necessary for estimating and comparing the social value of firms in this new double bottom line market. One proponent of the field argued that: "Arguably the biggest obstacle to the creation of social capital markets is the lack of a common measure of how much good has been done: there is no agreed unit of social impact that mirrors profit in the traditional capital markets" (Bishop 2009).

In sum, advocates recognized that one key challenge for the market of impact investing was the generation of a single measure of social value across the entire market that could be used by investors to engage in commensurability as to the social return of their investments. These advocates presumed that, with the presence of a suitable valuation instrument to facilitate such calculation for market members, investors would be more willing to invest in the field, based on both the premises of behavioral economics and the history of traditional, profit-oriented markets (Monitor Institute 2009; Rockefeller Philanthropy Advisors 2010; Bouri 2011). The current level of impact investments, according to two proponents of the field, "could be much greater if there were a way to more clearly measure the good that came from these investments. With such a measure, more capital would flow to that activity" (Hagerman and Ratcliffe 2009:44).

Challenges to solving the value problem

In its establishment of a market of Impact Investing, the resulting goal for GIIN was to create a single measuring device for the gauging of an investment's value. For this organization, however, creating one shared valuation instrument for this new market required addressing two challenges inherent to Impact Investing's pursuit of both financial and social return. First, GIIN had to resolve how to generate a single measuring device for the entire industry when investors' desired balance of financial and social return varied across members, making difficult the assignment of economic value to an investment's social impact. Secondly, GIIN had to solve the problem of the varied and subjective meaning of social value in the market's pursuit of social return, making difficult the establishment of commensurability across investment opportunities. These two challenges to a resolution to the value problem resulted from the impact investing's aggregation of an array of existing fields, each characterized by its own social project, including its definition of social value and its expected relationship to economic value.

Social versus financial return

The first problem for GIIN in addressing the value problem arose from staff's recognition that impact investors differed in their desired balance of social and financial return. Through its sponsored research, the Rockefeller Foundation quickly realized that investors held contrasting goals or "investment theses" for their impact investments (Monitor Institute 2009; Bouri 2011; J.P. Morgan 2011). Four main types of investors were identified in an early report on the state of the industry: "financial first investors" who sought market-rate return with some social and/or environment benefit, "impact first investors" who privileged social and/or environmental return with a minimal financial benefit or even below-market return, others who sought both a high rate of financial and social return, and those who were comfortable with some financial return and some social and/or environmental benefit (Monitor Institute 2009).[23] Another early report on the field concluded that: "Some investors expect financial returns from their impact investments that would outperform traditional investments in the same category, while others expect to trade off financial return for social impact" (J.P. Morgan 2011).

This variation in investors' preferred balance of financial and social return reflected the range of different actors and fields that advocates of Impact Investing strove to bring together into a single market, including not only responsible investors committed to ESG practices as a means to long-term financial gain, but also participants in Socially Responsible Investing, who viewed financial investing as a way to express their moral values through market-based action while not sacrificing economic return, and charitable foundations with a long history of making mission-related investment and/or community investments with an expectation of below-market return. In all, there was a realization that no single and over-arching criteria existed by which investors evaluated the worth of their investments: the balance of social versus financial return varied (Rockefeller Philanthropic Advisors 2010).

For GIIN, one consequence of "impact first investors" was that, despite its effort to model the valuation of social impact on the conventions of mainstream investing, the metric of money could not be used as the universal and single measure of social impact. Money certainly was a viable and established measure of an investment's social return. As detailed in Chapter 3, the federal government has used cost-benefit analysis to assess the relative merit of its social policies since the 1930s and many governments, NGOs, and multilateral organizations now employ the concept of the "value of a statistical life," which estimates how much people are willing to pay to reduce their mortality risk (Viscusi and Aldy 2003). Likewise, the methodology of SROI, as promoted by REDF and as outlined in Chapter 3, estimates the monetary value of social financing in terms of government savings (REDF 2000). More broadly, as evidenced in the growing employment of valuation techniques for items such as natural resources, the environment, and cultural heritage (Champ et al. 2003), increasingly "money is a good enough metric for the 'utility' we get from commodities" (Fourcade 2011:1721).

Similarly, as with the case of Inclusive Businesses, it is technically possible to monetize many of the social benefits of double bottom line businesses, in terms of their economic development impact. As key observers point out, "many of the benefits of [Proactive Social Investments] are monetary or can be readily valued at market rates. Social investments often produce jobs, increase productivity, and generate higher wages to employees or profits to the owner. The business's products or services may save customers time or money that can also be valued. Other economic impacts may be external to the business, such as increased taxes paid to the government, or increased purchasing from other businesses in the region. All these dimensions can be quantified in monetary terms" (Kramer and Cooch 2006:40-41).

However, the use of money as a currency to gauge social value did not occur in the emerging market of impact investing. According to participants in the field, the lack of monetization of an investment's social value was due to the expectations of one core group of resource providers. Compared to other participants, impact first investors wanted a "clear separation between financial returns and impact" (Rockefeller Philanthropy Advisors 2010:12). Money, in other words, was viewed by these investors as an indicator of economic return and so was not considered a legitimate measure of social impact for that type of investor. Drawing from a value rational version of Socially Responsible Investing, as detailed in Chapter 4, impact-first investors pursued social value first and economic return second (if at all), some even accepting below-market rates of return. Tellingly, a senior staff member at GIIN explained to me the problem with monetizing social impact in the field of Impact Investing. "There is one kind of person we are dealing with who thinks about their investments as a kind of way to change the world – so quite different from what a traditional investor wants to do, just get more money. And so trying to give a dollar value to what is going on would be anathema to them. Uh, [uncomfortable laughter] and, for me, just thinking about trying to assign a dollar value to a child's life saved by a malaria net; that, for instance, makes me incredibly uncomfortable. How could you do that? That would just be so wrong."

For that reason, rather than due to the perceived difficulty of monetizing social impact (as had occurred in the field of Inclusive Business), the use of money to capture social impact was not deemed feasible in the market of impact investing given the preferences of one type of investor. To monetize social value, as had happened in the fields of social enterprise or RI, would be to potentially antagonize that set of investors.

Further, GIIN staff believed that other potential investors worried more about receiving a market rate of return had access to traditional measures of financial return on their investment. To woo those investors as participants in Impact Investing, as outlined by the CEO of GIIN in 2011, GIIN was committed to employing financial data on investment opportunities to demonstrate that the industry of Impact Investing "spans a wide spectrum of risk and return profiles" (Kanani 2011). GIIN's goal then became to create a measuring device of an investment's social value that still mimicked mainstream investing in the use of a single metric and measuring device but without employing the common measure of money to estimate social return.

The varied meaning of social value

A second challenge for the construction of a measuring device in this new market was the varied meaning of social value across the field's members. While social good is often discussed as a universal and fixed concept, this field in fact encompassed a number of different contents and meanings, dependent on the perspective of the actor in question, as also found in the nonprofit sector (as outlined in Chapter 2). In this way, the field of Impact Investing constitutes an example of what Stark (2011) calls "heterarchy" – the presence of multiple and competing orders of worth. Here, the lack of fixity as to the definition of social value in this nascent field followed again from the origins of impact investing in a number of different fields, each and all premised on a belief in the ability of market methods to achieve social value. Yet, despite that shared premise, proponents of Impact Investing also recognized that these fields had substantively different social projects – they were characterized by contrasting understandings of how local companies can produce social welfare by market means (Monitor Institute 2009; Harji and Jackson 2012). Impact Investing, to quote from one report, is "a market in which the beneficial outcomes from products and services are subjectively interpreted" (Bouri 2011:147).

Broadly speaking, the field of impact investing incorporates two competing conceptions of social value. Firms can address social inequities via two different strategies: the implementation of socially beneficial production processes (e.g., the inclusive organization of its value chain and/or the provision of human rights and decent working conditions to workers) or the sale of socially beneficial products (e.g., water, housing, or education) (J.P. Morgan 2011). The first strand of Impact Investing emphasized how firms could generate social goods by their production processes: companies improve the state of society (or avoid inflicting harm on society) via their profit-producing business models – in terms of from whom companies source, whom they hire, and how they treat actors in their value chain. The second strand of Impact Investing emphasizes the social value that follows from firms' sale of goods that address social inequities (in that either these goods had not previously been available on the market or they were to be sold to those at the Bottom of the Pyramid). In result, proponents of Impact Investing recognized that individual actors defined socially beneficial goods according to their own values and/or worldview. As I was told by one employee of an organization that promotes investment in SMEs, "Overall, Impact Investing is about the quest for "public goods" through private means. But what that social value looks like is firm specific. The sources or criteria vary. For example, one company might provide rural electricity in Africa while another might engage in water sanitation to a village in India. Others might produce social value through direct or indirect employment."

The varied meaning of the concept of corporations' social value along these two axes of products versus production processes posed a critical challenge to the intended function of a measuring device in the field of impact investing (Monitor Institute 2009). Ideally, as outlined earlier, the problem of value in a market is solved when a consensus is reached about the criterion of worth for the goods in question (as recognized and made real by a measuring device), thus creating the ability for market members to compare commodities in the same way. Yet, when value is varied in nature, different actors bring distinct meanings of the concept to the project of commensurability. For the case of Impact Investing, the resulting concern was that a measuring device that carried within it a single quality of social value would be rendered useless, as each actor sought commensurability only for investment possibilities that met her own definition of social value. As one recent report on impact investing concluded, "Since various actors have diverse views on what matters, it is challenging to achieve agreement on a single metric or approach" (Harji and Jackson 2012:47).

Similarly, in an overview of the state of Impact Investing, Mark Kramer, a long-time scholar of performance measurement for social purpose organizations concluded, "social returns are not fungible like financial returns. An investor might be neutral between two investments with the same financial returns, but that doesn't mean he would be indifferent to the choice between an impact investment that created USD 1 million in reduced carbon emissions, compared to one that produced USD 1 million in additional income to impoverished farmers in Africa. One cannot compare two completely different impact initiatives" (Credit Suisse 2012:11).

In result, GIIN modified its efforts to solve the "value problem" in the market of impact investing. It sought to develop the capacity for calculation that did not impose a single meaning of social impact on all market members but rather provided the capacity for commensurability and ranking in a tailored way, contingent upon the investors' values. One early report on the future of the field concluded: "We need to find a metric that preserves each investor's flexibility at driving toward their individual impact investment objectives" (Monitor Institute 2009).

DEVELOPING A VALUATION INFRASTRUCTURE
FOR IMPACT INVESTING

The consequence of these two challenges was that – contrary to the predictions of economic sociology and contrary to GIIN staff members' hope that it could model the market after mainstream investing – money could not be used as the metric of social value and, moreover, no single criteria of social value, as embodied in a single measuring device, could be employed by all market members. Instead, GIIN sought to develop a solution to the value problem that mimicked mainstream investing in another way – by creating the same institutions and tools as financial investing, but with the goal of allowing "customized commensurability" based on each investor's definition of social and/or financial return could occur. As discussed in Chapter 2, customized commensurability consists of the ability of any actor in a field to engage in valuation based on his or her own subjective and idiosyncratic definition of value, but through the use of a single measuring device or set of measuring

TABLE 7.1 *Measuring devices in Impact Investing*

Type of Impact Investor	Meaning of Social Value	
	Products	*Production processes*
Financial first investors	ImpactBase: financial measures + Impact Base: floor of social impact based on Investor's values	GIIRS: financial measures and floor of ESG performance
Impact first investors	ImpactBase: social impact based on investor's values	GIIRS: ranking based on ESG performance

devices. To that end, as shown in Table 7.1, the GIIN, along with a number of other actors in the field, created three distinct measurement tools: IRIS, GIIRS, and ImpactBase.

Impact Reporting and Investment Standards (IRIS)

Developed in 2008 by the GIIN along with the Rockefeller Foundation, the Acumen Fund, and B Lab, the IRIS consisted of a standardized reporting system to be used by local companies to report on their performance. IRIS consisted of a "universal language" of impact investing, based on over four hundred metrics covering firms' financial, social, and environmental performance. Each metric includes a precise definition of the term and a prescribed indicator. This taxonomy of firm performance included an organization description, a product description, financial performance, operational impact (i.e., information on a firm's CSR to stakeholders), and social impact (GIIN 2014). Take the case of "school enrollment," which IRIS defines as "number of students enrolled as of the end of reporting period, both full-time and part-time, where each discrete student is counted regardless of number of courses."

Offered for free as a "public good" by GIIN, the creation of IRIS was intended by value entrepreneurs to address the problem that common terms were being used in impact investing to describe a firm's goals, but they were being defined and measured differently, making commensurability difficult for market actors (Harji and Jackson 2012). As a standardized reporting system, IRIS was designed by its creators to play the same role in impact investing that the Generally Accepted Accounting Principles (GAAP) or International Financial Reporting Standards (IFRS) played in mainstream investing (Bouri 2011).

In the words of the salient value entrepreneurs: "IRIS is designed to address a major barrier to the growth of the impact investing industry – the lack of transparency, credibility, and consistency in how organizations and investors define, measure, and track their performance" (IRIS 2013).

To construct IRIS, and reflecting the goal of GIIN to incorporate existing double bottom line vehicles and fields into a single market of impact investing, value entrepreneurs incorporated the dominant reporting standards that already existed for the fields that together composed Impact Investing, including microfinance vehicles and SMEs. "A crucial element of creating these standards is convening leaders within the prominent subsectors of impact investment (e.g., community development, international development, environmental investing, etc.). These leaders can build from existing practice to develop consensus for standards tailored to the specific investing issues in each area" (Bugg-Levine and Goldstein 2009:35). For example, in the case of microfinance, IRIS drew from the existing work of the Microfinance Information Exchange in generating measures of social impact and in sharing data. In industries with no reporting standards, IRIS staff worked with evaluation experts in the field to devise comparable indicators (Bouri 2011; Kanani 2011).

Using IRIS, local firms in the field of impact investing were expected to report annually on their performance and submit the data to GIIN. GIIN would then collect the resulting reports and aggregate the data in order to generate information on the performance of the market as a whole and for the purposes of commensurability by industrial sector (such as access to financial services, agricultural products, or clean, alternative energy) or by geographical region (IRIS 2011). "IRIS will also aggregate social performance data and release benchmarking reports that enable impact investors to compare investments against their peers – a capacity that proved central in the growth of mainstream venture capital and private equity" (Rockefeller Philanthropy Advisors 2010:122).

IRIS was critical to how proponents of Impact Investing sought to address the value problem in this new market. By incorporating a range of different dimensions of financial, social, and environmental impact in its taxonomy, IRIS then allowed for the presence of a varied conception of "investment return," both in terms of the relationship of social value to financial value and in terms of the multiple meanings of social good present in the field. IRIS facilitated firms' reporting on many of the existing conceptions of social value by specifying the needed metrics of a firm's inclusive organization of its value chain, its just and equitable treatment of stakeholders, and its sale of socially beneficial products. By incorporating metrics of these different regimes of value, IRIS allowed for a wide range of investors with different impact objectives to employ this data in order to make comparisons across investment options. In an article on the construction of IRIS, a senior executive at GIIN explained: "Impact investments are a result of investors' management of their investments toward the creation of specific social or environmental benefits along with financial returns. Managing these multiple factors requires a credible, consistent, and rigorous set of metrics that includes social, environmental, and financial performance indicators" (Bouri 2011:148). Similarly, the online guide to using IRIS emphasizes that: "There is no single combination of metrics that is right for everybody; that's why IRIS is designed as a catalog that you can browse to find the most appropriate metrics for your work ... IRIS is a useful resource for impact investors working around the world, in different sectors, and with a variety of social and environmental impact objectives" (IRIS 2015).

Yet, as publications on IRIS admit, this tool is limited to the generation of comparable data based on investors' preferences. As a measuring device, IRIS does not engage in the act of commensurability (Espeland and Sauder 2007) – it does not evaluate and rank investment opportunities according to a particular criterion of worth (IRIS 2015). Investors "need to know not only that everyone calculates metrics like carbon tonnage or defines terms such as "low income" the same way, but also how those reported metrics stack up against those from comparable companies and against a generally accepted set of benchmarks for low, medium and high impact investments" (Krogh 2009:17). To facilitate investors' comparison of investment opportunities, proponents of Impact Investing then constructed multiple measuring devices to perform such a task, with each tool recognizing distinct understandings of the meaning of social value in this field.

Global Impact Investing Report System (GIIRS)

Begun in 2009 by the B Lab (an independent nonprofit) in conjunction with the GIIN, GIIRS is an independent, third party ranking system of the social and/or environmental impact (but not financial performance) of either a double bottom line company or investment fund. GIIRS' ratings were intended to be analogous to Morningstar's investment rankings or S&P credit risk ratings. Using data provided by respondents in response to a B Lab survey of 50 to 120 questions concerning companies' production processes (employing IRIS definitions and indicators), GIIRS provides a total rating (out of a possible total of 200 points) of the company or investment fund based on an aggregation of their provision of a several dimensions of positive social and environmental value, as weighted by a company or fund's geography, size, and sector. These scores could then be comparatively employed by companies and funds seeking investment and by potential investors hoping to identify those opportunities that provide the most social/environmental return (Bouri 2011; B Lab 2012).

The conception of social good inherent to this ranking system reflected the effort by GIIRS' value entrepreneurs to incorporate a wide range of existing conceptions of social value present in this field. On the one hand, GIIRS positively scored a company according their possession of a specified list of appropriate practices taken from the fields of CSR and RI, concerning firms' treatment of stakeholders, including governance, workers, community, and the environment. For example, in the area of workers, GIIRS (2012) awards points for the presence of desirable practices concerning "compensation and wages, worker benefits, training and education, worker ownership, job flexibility/ corporate culture (developed markets only), human rights & labor policy (developing markets only), management and worker communication, and occupational health & safety."

However, GIIRS also awarded points to a firm or fund for the presence of what it calls "intentional business models," including the sale of socially or environmentally beneficial products and the presence of value chains that facilitated ownership models designed to increase wealth and decision-making power of historically underserved stakeholders (e.g., SMEs). Rather than valuing firms for their performance in this regard, GIIRS instead converted the presence of these inclusive production processes and products into the appropriate category of a firm or fund's treatment of stakeholders: governance, workers, community, or the environment. So, a firm that focused on workforce development would receive points in the relevant impact area of the community, as one instance of the practice of equitable compensation, benefits, and training. In sum, as a measure of social value, GIIRS subsumed attention to the market inclusion of the poor (as suppliers, employees, and customers) (as central to Impact Investing) into the stakeholder-centered criteria of social value, as found in the fields of CSR and RI (GIIRS 2011, 2012). The result was a rating system that evaluated firms according to a single quality of worth.

ImpactBase

Begun in 2009 by Imprint Capital Advisors and RSF Social Finance and then taken up by GIIN in 2010, ImpactBase is a searchable online platform that allows impact investors to evaluate investment opportunities according to criteria of their choice. Service providers, including funds and firms, provide to GIIN an annual report, which includes an overview (including fund manager track record, fundraising status, location, and current investors), a financial section (including detailed information on a fund's financial strategy including target returns, asset class, and investment size) and an impact section (including a fund's impact strategy, including impact goals and the measurement of social and environmental metrics) (GIIN 2015c).

Investors then could employ ImpactBase to compare data on potential investment vehicles based on their own specific search criteria, including both financial performance (including asset class, fundraising status, and assets under management) and/or social or environmental issues (including a list of pre-specified "impact themes" and geographic targets) (GIIN 2015a). For example, an investor interested in service providers focused on clean energy in Africa would choose only investment opportunities with that mission and location. Upon selection of their search criteria, investors were then provided with a summary of financial, operational, and social impact data for all qualifying firms or funds.

As with IRIS and GIIRS, ImpactBase was framed as akin to similar devices in mainstream investing; in this case, it provided the same type of data for impact investors as is produced for a traditional investor by investment research firms (as outlined in the case of Socially Responsible Investing in Chapter 4) (UBS 2011). As one presenter explained to a crowded audience at a conference on impact investing, "ImpactBase basically does for an impact investor what J.P. Morgan or Deutsche Bank has done to date for a regular investor – it gives them the information they need to make an informed decision."

While GIIRS provided a rating system for a notion of social value based only on firms' treatment of its stakeholders in its production process, ImpactBase was devised to allow for the estimation of social value based on any criteria of worth, recognizing the varied and subjective nature of social value for many members of this field. It was specifically designed by its value entrepreneurs to address the challenge of commensurability in this market, given investors' varied balance of financial and social return and multiple meanings of social value. To do so, the website solicited from investors their definition of the type of social return they hoped to achieve from a wide list of pre-arranged list of options, as guided by IRIS' taxonomy, and so included the options of a firm's products, inclusive business models, and/or treatment of stakeholders. Having specified their preference, the investor then was provided by the website with data on the social performance of all investment opportunities that aligned with her specific definition of social value (GIIN 2015a).

For example, an impact investor interested in facilitating women's participation in the workforce would choose that impact theme and then be able to compare the performance of those funds, drawing from data based on the salient IRIS standardized measures of social impact for those organizations. Another impact investor who wanted to support firms that provided children with access to low-cost health services would similarly specify that goal in his ImpactBase search, and he would then be provided with comparable information on relevant funds and companies.

However, while ImpactBase provided the germane data on all impact investing opportunities for an investor, it was up to each actor to engage in the ranking of those options based on their own weighting of social versus financial issues. In an interview, one senior Rockefeller Foundation staff outlined precisely such a use of ImpactBase, giving the scenario of a fund manager who wants to invest in local farming cooperatives in developing countries. By using ImpactBase, the respondent outlined, the "manager is able to easily access a range of investment vehicles that address this concern. They can then employ the impact reports provided by Impact Base in order evaluate their investment opportunities. They can choose to evaluate these options based on total amount of social impact that their investment would produce or they might assess their options based on a ratio of investment cost to return. Or possibly some other consideration might be relevant. It's up to them."

In all, proponents of Impact Investing faced a particular challenge. They sought to create a market that was based on a social project centered on a belief in the capacity of investment to generate both financial and social return. In their initial articulation of the market, advocates sought to mimic the structure of mainstream finance in order to increase the potential pool of investors. To address the value problem, they envisioned a single, standardized meaning and metric of social value across all investments, as supported by the formation of a suitable measuring device. Yet, the varied contrasting preferences of investors altered the communicative goal of value entrepreneurs. These actors ended up solving the "problem of value" in this market in ways that recognized the varying goals of investors, both in terms of their weighting of financial versus social return and in terms of their varied definition of social value. Drawing on their knowledge of mainstream investing, these value entrepreneurs transposed the devices and vehicles of valuation from the traditional capital market to this new setting, modifying them to align with the presence of those multiple registers of value. The construction of the three component parts of the valuation infrastructure of this market, consisting of IRIS, GIIRS, and ImpactBase, would provide any and all investors with standardized, comparative data that then allowed them to engage in the relative evaluation of investment options no matter what their own criteria of worth.

More broadly, for the purposes of a theory of social value, the case of impact investing allows us to see how a commitment to a kinder, gentler vision of capitalism need not necessitate a particular type of measuring device that employs the currency of money or prioritizes shareholder value over all else. Here, despite the dual commitment to both economic and social return present in proponents' articulation of the field's social project, the resulting valuation instruments were intended to address a range of investors who held contrasting understandings of the purpose of market activity and the meaning of social good.

Notes

1. Inclusive Businesses also generate economic and social good in local communities by their investment in local infrastructure and their generation of tax revenue for local governments.
2. Yet, while BOP has been advocated by many proponents of Inclusive Business, others have expressed concern about the ethics of profiting at the expense of the poor and sought to clarify that not all products sold to the poor generate social benefits (Karnani 2007).
3. A small but growing body of scholarship examines the challenges involved in the implementation of Inclusive Business, finding mixed success in the effort to reduce poverty (Halme, Lindeman, and Linna 2012; Ramani and Mukherjee 2014).

4. The United Nations' Millennium Development goals were to eradicate extreme hunger and poverty, achieve universal primary education; promote gender equality and empower women; reduce child mortality; improve maternal health; combat HIV/AIDS, malaria, and other diseases; ensure environmental sustainability; and develop a global partnership for development.

5. A concern for poverty was not new on the part of the World Bank. In the 1970s, for example, the "New Directions" era of development also was concerned with the goal of poverty reduction, but the efforts of key actors, such as the World Bank, were centered on ensuring local governments' provision of social welfare programs to facilitate economic development, along with an emphasis on community participation (Goldman 2005).

6. Mark Malloch Brown, Administrator, UNDP (OECD 2004).

7. In these proponents' formulations, companies can participate in the project of global development in a number of ways – not only through an inclusive business model, but also via a commitment to sustainability, the exercise of corporate philanthropy, and engagement with public advocacy and dialogue (United Nations Global Compact 2010; UNDP 2010).

8. For proponents of Inclusive Business, the target population to be assisted is the poor in the developing world, as motivated by the broader project of international development. In contrast, the initial and motivating purpose of social enterprises, as covered in Chapter 3, was to facilitate market access for a variety of disadvantaged communities in the United States, as a new vehicle to pursue the goals of the domestic nonprofit sector. A new iteration of the literature on social enterprise emphasizes its role in alleviating poverty in developing countries (e.g., Seelos and Mair 2005).

9. Bjorn Stigson, as quoted in World Business Council for Sustainable Development/ SNV (2008).

10. This absence reflects the focus of the United Nation's Millennium Development Goals. Some critics of the MDGs have noted that the emphasis on halving poverty as a goal of global development overrides a concern for a broader array of human rights. "There is a clear shift in the perspective in favour of a narrower frame focusing essentially on absolute aspects of some key measurable facets of poverty and deprivation, and away from a broader, more essentialist rights-based approach" (Saith 2006:1170).

11. The one exception is the early publications on Inclusive Businesses by the United Nations, which sought to bring the principles of its 1999 Global Compact (with a concern for human rights, labor standards, and the environment) to its unfolding effort to encourage companies and business coalitions to play a role in the achievement of the Millennium Development Goals. But they limited those expectations to multinational corporations, rather than extending them to the corporate governance practices of local SMEs as well (UNDP 2003, 2004). And a concern for CSR's focus on human rights, labor standards, and the environment is notably absent from later publications on Inclusive Business (UNDP 2008).

12. For additional measuring devices for Inclusive Businesses, see WBCSD (2013).

13. Interestingly, of the three tools, only Oxfam's Poverty Footprint (2009:6) entails a concern for the consequences of a firms' practices for the local community's regulatory environment and civil society, including consideration of the "effects of lobbying, direct investment, and procurement and distribution practices in relation to the development of institutions (such as producer organisations, unions,

cross-sectoral learning labs, social networks, women's groups) and policies that focus on trade, finance, education, and health."

14. These measuring devices also depart in their methodological requirements – for example, the BCtA's Results Reporting Framework includes universal indicators while the WBCSD and Oxfam's reporting requirements suggest company-specific measures, as dependent on feedback from local stakeholders.

15. While Oxfam's report (2009:7) continues: "An important part of every Poverty Footprint Study is analysing the 'business effects' and using this analysis to identify risks and opportunities, as well as to make recommendations that are based on a sound business case," neither the methodology of the Poverty Footprint nor a highly-publicized example of a Poverty Footprint (Oxfam's 2011 study of the Coca-Cola/SAB Miller value chain impacts in Zambia and El Salvador) actually incorporated measures of or data on these factors.

16. Social license is defined as the "demands and expectations for a business enterprise from neighborhoods, environmental groups, community members, and other elements of the surrounding civil society" (Gunningham, Kagan and Thornton 2004:308).

17. The decision by the Oxfam/Unilever coalition to employ a World Wildlife Fund executive to devise a social impact tool arose from Unilever's earlier partnership with the World Wildlife Fund in 1997 to promote sustainable fisheries, resulting in the formation of the Marine Stewardship Council.

18. Sources for this section include the formal publication of these organizations' measuring devices and their accompanying documentation as well as other organizational reports and media publications. See, for example, Clay (2005), Oxfam (2009), World Business Council for Sustainable Development (2008a, 2008b, 2013b), BCtA (2010, 2011), and Coca Cola/SAB Miller (2011).

19. In its articulation by proponents, Impact Investing differentiates itself from Socially Responsible Investing through its focus on "positive" social or environmental benefit, as opposed to SRI's focus on negative screening (J.P. Morgan 2010).

20. Similar to the strategies of Socially Responsible Investing, Mission-Related Investing can take various forms, including not only investing a portion of endowment assets – typically quite small – in double-bottom line return but also shareholder advocacy and the positive or negative screening of loans (Cooch and Kramer 2007).

21. The efforts of the Rockefeller Foundation to construct the field of Impact Investing constitutes a case of the wider capacity of charitable foundations to "champion a particular model of social order and attempt to build new arenas of social life – that is, new organizational fields – to institutionalize that model" (DiMaggio 1991; Bartley 2007a:231).

22. Proponents of Impact Investing also have identified environmentally oriented investors as part of the field. See, for example, Bugg-Levine and Emerson (2011).

23. An example of an impact-first investor is Calvert Investments (an early SRI mutual fund), which has historically kept one percent of its assets for making socially desirable investments that produce below market returns (Silby 2011).

8

Conclusion

This book has examined the effect of caring capitalism on the meaning and measure of social value. It has asked how the embrace of market actors and market-based methods to solve social problems, in the form of new types of compassionate corporations and new forms of socially oriented investing, has shaped the valuation of social good. It tested competing theoretical expectations about the capacity of caring capitalism to monetize social value and so to subject it to the logic of the market. To do so, the meaning and measure of social value in the fields of caring capitalism were compared to those present in the nonprofit sector and to those evident in earlier efforts in the private sector to critique firms for their lack of social responsibility.

We have seen, on the one hand, that the social projects that characterize the fields of caring capitalism do indeed demonstrate a new and distinct commitment to a market logic. Proponents of caring capitalism believe that companies provide the best solution to social inequities. In this view, the simultaneous pursuit of mission and money allows firms to obtain the required scale required to achieve the desired social change and to generate economic gain for firms and shareholders. Yet, on the other hand, we also have seen a marked disjuncture between the content of a social project and the type of social value recognized, and so rewarded, in the field's prevailing measuring device/s. Despite the embrace of market solutions to social problems as a means to social and shareholder value, few of these tools assign a monetary worth to the efforts of social purpose organizations. And, while the monetization of social value does end up limiting what gets to count as social value in these cases, in only one field of caring capitalism does a measuring device exist that assigns financial value to companies' social performance. In short, understanding the conception of social value in caring capitalism does not help us to understand the act of valuation in terms of what counts and how it gets counted.

To explain this disjuncture between value and valuation, I turned to existing literature in economic sociology. Scholarship on the role of the market in society offers two opposing predictions: either the logic of the market will lead to the privileging of economic gain over social welfare or actors can negotiate the use of market-based exchange and media in ways that further the quest for social good. Yet, an analysis of measuring devices shows that neither of these expectations can account for the particular meanings and measures of social value that have come to prevail across the fields of study. Neither the logic of the market nor actors' moral understandings alone determined the content of these tools, techniques, and technologies of social value. Instead, by comparing fields that differ by their sectoral location and in their normative orientation to market exchange as a solution to social inequities, we can see the relative autonomy of measuring devices. Specifically, the presence of a conjuncture or disjuncture between a field's social project and its valuation instrument/s can be explained by not viewing measuring devices as straightforward reflections of a particular social project (that is, of a particular definition of social value), as is often claimed by social scientists. Instead, they should be understood as material objects that require sustained effort and adequate capacity on the part of value entrepreneurs – those actors charged with the construction and dissemination of measuring devices. In order to understand the presence of conjunctures and disjunctures between the social project of a field and the prevailing measuring device, we must analyze the communicative purpose of the valuation instrument and the professional expertise of valuation entrepreneurs in that field.

First, a valuation instrument is created in a specific relational context. It is intended to serve a specific function vis-à-vis an intended audience: it may demonstrate the legitimacy of member actors in a field, it may be used to influence the behavior of others, or it may justify a new field by demonstrating its relative merit or by solving the value problem. Secondly, with that communicative intent in mind, valuation entrepreneurs then seek to construct a suitable measuring device. However, they are limited in their ability to do so by their professional expertise, particularly in terms of the content of their valuation repertoire. These actors draw from their stock of knowledge of existing valuation tools, technologies, and tactics that they seek to extend and refashion to suit the task at hand. At times, they are able to devise a measuring device that fits both its intended communicative purpose and the social project of the field, but at other times, value entrepreneurs simply satisfice (Simon 1956) by constructing a measuring device that fails to capture the type/s of social and/or shareholder value present in the field's social project but that nonetheless is adequate for the task at hand.

In this last chapter, I will take a step back to consider the broader implications of my findings for a conceptualization of social value as a quality of worth, for scholarship on value and valuation more broadly, and for the analysis of the role of the market in society.

CONCEPTUALIZING SOCIAL VALUE

Scholarship on the question of value has emphasized the existence of a multiplicity of institutionalized understandings of value available to actors, with scholars variously employing the concepts of "orders of worth" or "institutional logics" to describe this aspect of social life. Broadly speaking, these concepts describe an organizing principle that is institutionalized in society and so can be called upon by actors as a guide for action, in that it specifies what value, quality or goal matters and how a judgment of worth can be made. Examples of dominant orders of worth include that of the market, the family, and government, among others (Friedland and Alford 1991; Boltanski and Thévenot 2006).

Yet, while the list of these recognized orders of worth been expanded to recognize ever more qualities (Lafaye and Thévenot 1993; Thornton, Lounsbury and Ocasio 2012), markedly little attention has been given to the study of social value as an order of worth, defined as a commitment to the private and voluntary pursuit of social good. In the case of the United States, such an oversight is surprising given that the work of private, non-governmental actors has been deemed central to the vitality and well-being of American society (Tocqueville 1835/1966; Putnam 2000). Further, the United States is commonly understood as a liberal welfare state, premised on the central role of the nonprofit sector in the provision of social welfare (Esping-Andersen 1990). Finally, as we have seen in this book, the combined effects of a policy of neoliberalism and the rise of New Public Management have resulted in a hollowing out of the government and an embrace of the nonprofit delivery of services (Smith and Lipsky 1993; Prasad 2006).

Despite all this, social scientists have yet to advance a theory of social value as a distinct order of worth. While a debate about the meaning of the common or public good – as the responsibility of government – is longstanding (Mills 1861/2007; Rawls 1971; Sen 1979), we know much less about how the concept of social value is defined, enacted, and assessed in practice. Further, the study of social value is complicated by the shifting landscape of social purpose organizations and, in particular, the growth of market-based providers of social goods. In result, the task of this book was to delineate exactly how this assortment of private, nongovernment actors understand, pursue, and gauge social value as a shared orientation of action and how the rise of caring capitalism has affected the meaning and measure of this distinct order of worth.

Drawing from the literature on the commodification of intimate or sacred goods (Healy 2006; Almeling 2011; Chan 2012) and scholarship that examines how objects take on new regimes of value as they move through different societal arenas (Appadurai 1998; Kopytoff 1998), I began this book with a particular expectation in mind as to the consequences of caring capitalism for social value. What I thought I would find was companies taking up the distribution of those socially beneficial goods and services that had once been the sole purview of nonprofits. Efforts to create markets around these objects would be accompanied by debate and contestation over businesses' sale of those commodities for economic profit. Further, once these goods were established as commodities, including the assignment of price as a measure of their value, their social value would be subsumed to or made conditional upon the firm's production of economic profit and shareholder return.

Yet, I found something quite different to these expectations. As traced out in the preceding chapters, the meaning of social value as an order of worth is not understood, practiced, or assessed in a singular, shared way across these sites. Thus, the rise of caring capitalism has not entailed firms taking up the same social project as nonprofits. Instead, the turn to caring capitalism has meant the creation of entirely new ways of conceiving of social value as an order of worth. This suggests that social value is not a "fixed entity" (Abbott 2001). Social value as a criterion of value is "multivocal" in nature: it is understood differently by actors across different settings (Padgett and Ansell 1993). As an order of worth or institutional logic, social value is espoused by many but its proponents hold competing and contradictory conceptions of the meaning of that quality, how it can be achieved, and how judgment can be made. It is polymorphous in practice and perception; multivocal in meaning and measure.

This multivocality can be seen when we look at social value along two distinct dimensions: what types of goods generate social value and how a market logic intersects with the pursuit of social good. First, some actors view social good as occurring via the provision of products (e.g., goods or services) that they themselves deem to generate social benefit for customers and clients. Here, as we saw in the cases of the nonprofits, Socially Responsible Investing, and Impact Investing, the definition of social good is inherently subjective and so endlessly variable. For a second group, social value consists of firms' inclusion of the otherwise economically disadvantaged into the market, by facilitating their inclusion in a value chain as suppliers, employers, and/or customers, as evident in the fields of Social Enterprise, Inclusive Business, and Impact Investing. Finally, others propose a view of social value that results from a company's equitable and just treatment of its stakeholders (including suppliers, employees, the community of operation, and customers), including Corporate Social Responsibility and Responsible Investment.

Further, these conceptions of social value draw from the logic of the market in a variety of ways. For one, these fields differ in how proponents conceive of the best type of organizational vehicle to address their identified social problem. While some champion nonprofits, others embrace businesses as the best purveyors of social good and yet others seek to correct for the tendency of firms to impose harm on society. Another source of divergence is on whether social value is limited to the growth of economic development value for individuals and the local community or whether it encompasses a wider array of benefits, such as civic, political, and otherwise. And these understandings of social value also differ in terms of their reliance on economic profit and shareholder return as a means to and motivation for social good.

To recognize the multivocality of social value as an order of worth possesses broader pragmatic and theoretical implications. To date, the multiplicity of meanings for social value as an institutional logic holds unexpectedly mixed consequences for social purpose organizations. On the one hand, as we might suppose, there is a growing expectation that compassionate companies should employ each and all of these manifold conceptions of social value in their business practices. Multinational corporations, in particular, increasingly are held accountable by global proponents of caring capitalism for the inclusion of the poor in their value chain, for the sale of socially beneficial products, for the just and equitable treatment of their stakeholders, and for their ongoing engagement with corporate philanthropy to fund nonprofits (United Nations Global Compact 2010). And, as we have seen, if each of these notions of social value entails its own test (in the use of a specific measuring device that requires the employment of a particular kind of proof), then the demonstration of social value on the part of compassionate companies becomes ever-more time-consuming, laborious, and expensive.[1]

On the other hand, given the varied range of understandings of social value present for social purpose organizations that constitute caring capitalism, we might ask about their potential implications for nonprofits as well. As companies have become accountable for the economically inclusive organization of their value chain and the equitable treatment of stakeholders, have nonprofits also become subject to these same multiple criteria of social value? For example, the Global Reporting Initiative – the international body charged with developing a uniform reporting system for corporations' sustainability – was intended by advocates to be used not just by corporations but also by nonprofits.[2] Further, a substantive body of literature has established that charities historically have been subject to the logic of the market, as discussed in Chapter 2, suggesting that these expectations from the business world should filter into the nonprofit sector (Eikenberry and Kluver 2004).

Interestingly, however, nonprofits have not – as of yet – been held accountable for these market-derived definitions of social value. As one example, nonprofits have been resistant to the implementation of the Global Reporting Initiative (GRI). Of the nearly 10,000 reports in GRI's database by 2012, only 261 were published by non-governmental organizations (GRI 2012b).[3] More broadly, nonprofits are not held accountable by regulatory agencies or by ratings organizations for the inclusive organization of their value chain or their just treatment of stakeholders. Nor are they moving to the voluntary self-report or the mandated report of their sustainability performance (Graddy-Reed et al. 2012; CharityNavigator 2014; Internal Revenue Service 2014a).[4]

Theoretically, the question becomes how to reconcile the existence of a multiplicity of meanings of social value across societal sectors with scholarly literature on the question of value. As a whole, this scholarship has emphasized the plurality of orders of worth, institutional logics, and repertoires of evaluation available to actors in a situation or setting (Boltanski and Thévenot 2006). In so doing, these authors fruitfully have moved the study of culture away from a sectorally-specific notion of culture and also away from a values-based understanding of culture. The resulting task for those scholars has been to understand and account for how and why actors select from, negotiate between, and integrate these alternative notions of value in and through their lines of action in a particular context. Yet, while emphasizing the plurality of orders of worth, these scholars nonetheless assume that any order of worth, logic, or repertoire of evaluation itself is necessarily singular; it is "structured, coherent, and encompassing" (Weber, Patel, and Heinze 2013:351). In other words, while culture is seen to be fragmented and multiple, an order of worth is not. In contrast, one recent strand of literature has sought to question this tendency to view orders of worth as uniform and internally consistent in nature. These studies have emphasized the "plurality of worths" present within an order of worth, as in the case of the multiple and competing views of ecology found within an environmental logic (Blok 2013) or the category of modern architecture, where organic and functional definitions of this field companionably co-exist (Jones, Maoret, Massa, and Svejenova 2012). In a similar vein, this book conceptualizes social value as an order of worth that encompasses a multiplicity of meanings yet still retains a bounded quality and that actors nonetheless draw from as a criterion of worth and as orientation of action.

THEORIZING THE MARKET IN SOCIETY

This book is a study of how actors make sense of the move of a specific type of activity – the pursuit of social value – into the market. It examines the changing connotation of social value when it intersects with economic discourse, actors, and modes of exchange. This book has analyzed when, how, and why the meaning and measure of social value becomes subject to the logic of the market in the project of caring capitalism. Thus, the book provides us with a new way to think through the import of the economy in contemporary society.

Similarly, scholarship in economy sociology has honed in on the question of how actors make sense of the proper role of the market in the organization of society. Largely in response to an assumption that economic practices have diffused to all corners of society or that economic practices impede the pursuit of value-rational action, these authors have sought to illuminate how actors employ market forms of exchange, modes of payment, and sources of valuation to create relational lives, where economic practices can be employed towards moral, meaningful ends. People create spaces, networks, and practices that draw from a market logic but they do so in a way that allows them to realize their values, often within and as bounded by institutional constraints (Fourcade 2011; Chan 2012; Reich 2014). Yet, one recent strand of this approach has begun to investigate cases where the construction of a market is varied or uneven. To explain these divergent outcomes, these scholars have emphasized that the creation of a moral-market nexus is, at its heart, an entrepreneurial project. Its construction requires intensive cultural effort to demonstrate the social benefits of a new market and so to achieve its legitimate status within the economy. Actors engage in extensive discursive work to frame economic activity around a particular good or service as morally oriented and so acceptable (Healy 2006; Zelizer 2009; Anteby 2010).

In the case of the use of money as a medium of exchange (as a form of payment, mode of valuation, and so forth), the critical work that occurs has been understood to be largely moral or cultural in nature, often around the question of whether money can be legitimately employed. By and large, the question has concerned how money is earmarked and made specific to a particular kind of activity and/or relationship (Quinn 2008; Fourcade 2011). One oft-cited example is that of "pin money," where wives' income is acceptable only when it is seen as intended only for their own discretionary purchases, rather than for general use by the family (Zelizer 1997, 2009).

In this book, I have sought to contribute to this burgeoning literature on the construction of markets. I have shown the tremendous amount of cultural work and material labor that goes into the construction of each of the markets that together constitute caring capitalism. However, the book also demonstrates that such efforts are often uneven and incomplete. Most centrally, it upsets the assumption that the use of money is not only a cultural project in the construction of a moral market. Instead, entrepreneurs must not only strive to claim a new field as a moral market but they also must engage in another, related type of entrepreneurial labor for the successful completion of their endeavor. They must have the knowledge and resources to develop the conventions and devices needed for members of the field to assign monetary worth to the objects that circulate in these moral spaces in ways that accord with and so reproduce their discursive claims.[5]

In other words, it is not enough for entrepreneurial actors to successfully frame a new relationship as a morally legitimate site of market exchange and to demarcate that space as distinct from others. In addition, actors' formation of the socio-material infrastructure for actors to circulate goods via the use of money also is always necessary. Further study that recognizes and accounts for the varied and uneven nature of this otherwise overlooked facet of moral markets would strengthen our theoretical understanding of the role of the market in society.

THEORIZING VALUE

A growing body of literature in the social sciences is concerned with the question of how and why value gets produced and assigned in contemporary society (Lamont 2012). The study of value (and the act of valuation) is analyzed in order to show the social construction of market processes (Callon 1998; Beckert and Aspers 2011), to comprehend the outcomes of micro and meso-level interactions, to explain institutional change (Friedland and Alford 1991; Boltanski and Thévenot 2006), and to parse the distribution of power and status in a specific field (Bourdieu 1993; Lamont 2012). While substantive disagreements in this scholarship exist, this literature nonetheless coalesces around three key claims. First, as discussed above, this emerging work on value finds that value is not singular, but rather that actors in a setting have access to multiple orders of worth, regardless of their societal location. Secondly, the selection of a salient quality of value in a situation is driven not by actors' preferences or values but instead is socially contingent, driven by contextual factors ranging from political-institutional configurations to interpersonal interactions (Boltanski and Thévenot 2006; Fourcade 2011). Third, the act of valuation, via material devices, not only reflects the selected order of worth in a setting but also has a reactive effect. These tools, techniques, and technologies bring into being – through the process of performativity – the specific order of worth upon which they are predicated (Callon 1998; MacKenzie and Millo 2003; Espeland and Sauder 2007).

This book has drawn from this literature on value and valuation in order to study social value. It asked how social value as a distinct quality, logic, or order of worth has been defined and assessed in and across a range of societal settings. It has focused on the act of valuation – through the study of measuring devices – as a way to think through how social value gets enacted through specific tools, techniques, and technologies in ways that are shaped by actors' understandings of the meaning of social value, given varying societal locations and contrasting imaginings of a social project (Smith 2007; Fourcade 2011; Lamont 2012).

The book's findings make two interventions into this literature. First, it complicates our understanding of the role of measuring devices in the act of valuation. As outlined above, measuring devices are a formal means by which actors can gauge the value of an entity or actor in a situation. They perform the act of calculation by assigning a value to a good. Measuring devices are presumed to do so through the generation of commensurability. Commensurability entails the "translation of different qualities into a single metric" so that comparison can occur (Porter 1995; Espeland and Stevens 1998). By settling on a specific quality of worth, a measuring device determines what counts and how to count it. As these scholars have shown, the use of a measuring device reduces a plurality of available orders of worth to a single type of value (Callon and Muniesa 2005; Boltanski and Thévenot 2006). And, in terms of the entities in question that are to be evaluated, the use of a measuring device creates commensurability through the removal of multiple characteristics from those objects given the selection of a single characteristic deemed relevant for assessment (Espeland and Stevens 1998).[6]

When the meaning of value is ambiguous or complex in a setting, several alternatives exist to address to this challenge. A measuring device may be constructed by powerful actors that imposes a single criterion of worth onto a situation, regardless of the subjective and contested nature of meaning among participants (Boltanski and Thévenot 2006). In the field of Socially Responsible Investing, for instance, investing intermediaries initially devised rating systems for firms that included only those issues they saw as most salient for investors, necessarily then omitting the concerns of other investors. Alternatively, in markets characterized by singularity (where goods are multidimensional, incommensurable, and difficult to evaluate), different actors may design competing measuring devices for goods that are each embody a distinct understanding of worth (Karpik 2010). These can be formal, as in the case of the different ratings systems published for wine (e.g., *Wine Advocate*, *Wine Enthusiast*, and *Wine Spectator*). Or, it may be that actors instead resort to their own subjective estimations of worth and omit the use of a formal measuring device. In her study of the peer review process, Lamont (2009) shows how academics determine the worth of scholarship on a case-by-case basis in ways both individual and collective in nature.

I have argued here that another solution is possible when the meaning of value is ambiguous or incommensurable. As evident in the fields of nonprofits and Impact Investing where understandings of social value are inherently subjective and so endlessly variable, value entrepreneurs have created tools that produce what I have called customized commensurability. These measuring devices do not instantiate a particular quality of worth but are instead empty of judgment. In result, their ability to gauge the merit of an entity and to allow for comparison across entities (i.e., to do the work that measuring devices are tasked with doing) is conditional upon actors' specification of a salient criterion. In other words, these measuring devices' capacity for commensurability is limited or tailored to each user's own idiosyncratic definition of value. Clearly, the theorization of value should extend to recognize both that measuring devices may perform commensurability or customized commensurability and to include a consideration of how, and under what conditions, measuring devices are constructed to create customized commensurability.

The book's second, and more central, contribution to the theorization of value is to highlight the socially constructed nature of measuring devices as way to further our understanding of value and valuation. With some exceptions (Heuts and Mol 2013), scholarship to date has focused largely on actors' determination of value – how they select from among, negotiate, and integrate multiple orders of worth available to them in a situation. The act of valuation itself has received less attention, often because it is assumed that the tools, techniques and technologies used to gauge the worth of entities reflect a prior understanding of value; they "support and enable" pre-existing evaluation criteria (Lamont 2012:208).

But we have seen that measuring devices do not necessarily instantiate a specific quality of worth – that disjunctures can exist between the meaning and metric of value present in a specific tool and the criterion of value it is intended to represent. To make sense of these disjunctures, analytical attention must be given to the work of those actors – whom I have called value entrepreneurs – whose efforts serve to intervene or mediate between an espoused quality of worth and the test, tool, or technique used to gauge entities according to that criterion. Here we see the salience of actors' communicative goals and their professional expertise for explaining what types of devices are possible. More broadly, this book contributes to a more careful and more comprehensive understanding of value by extending our attention beyond the question of how decisions are made about value to include consideration of how value is assigned to goods through the act of valuation as a result of actors' construction of specific tools and technologies.

Notes

1. More speculatively, the multiplicity of meanings of social value also seems likely to increase the likelihood of "goodwashing" – firms' exercise of only ritualistic, ceremonial compliance with these multi-faceted expectations of good social behavior.
2. GRI developed a sector supplement in 2010 specifically for NGOs, to guide them in reporting their sustainability performance in terms of their environmental, social, and governance policies (GRI 2012a).
3. One exception is that of diversity, where nonprofits are often held to account for not only ensuring diversity in their funding patterns but also in terms of the gender and racial/ethnic diversity of their staff and board of directors (Capek and Mead 2007).
4. Of course, as noted in Chapter 3, nonprofits may hold a social mission specifically oriented around the just inclusion of the economically disadvantaged in the market and the provision of needed goods to customers excluded from the market.
5. A similar critique might be offered of institutional literature that assumes that an institutional logic, understood as the dominant set of norms as to good practice in a field, can easily be adopted by organizations in order to display ceremonial conformity with those expectations and to achieve legitimacy in the eyes of key stakeholders (DiMaggio and Powell 1983; Thornton, Ocasio, and Lounsbury 2012). Instead, organizations must possess adequate capacity (sufficient resources and expertise) in order to adopt a new tactic or form (Barman and MacIndoe 2012).
6. The commensurable capacity of measuring devices has a political dimension in that renders some aspects of the social world visible and of note, while reducing the import of other aspects of the social world (Espeland and Stevens 1998; Lamont 2012).

Appendix: Methods

To examine the effect of caring capitalism on the measure and meaning of social value, I conducted a cumulative four-year research project that employed mixed methods, including interviews with key actors, field research at professional conferences, archival research, advisory texts, professional reports, media publications, and secondary research. Assuming a constructionist approach to valuation, my task was to identify and account for the dominant measuring device or devices present in and across a range of salient fields, with the goal of outlining the history or biography of the tool as a material object constructed by actors with particular interests, out of all possible meanings and measures of social value (Appadurai 1998; Kopytoff 1998; Desrosières 2001; Espeland and Stevens 2008).[1] I then employed the historical-comparative method in order to develop an explanatory framework in order to account for the effect of caring capitalism on both the articulation of a social project and the measuring devices correspondingly used to gauge the worth of social purpose organizations.

First, employing purposive, sequential sampling, I conducted semi-structured interviews with 67 professional experts involved in the fields of study.[2] I began by speaking first with representatives from the largest and most influential members in the field (based on a review of media publications and secondary research) in order to gain an understanding of the history and goals of the field and also to identify the prevailing measuring device/s in the field. As another strategy to specify the dominant measuring device/s in a field, I also relied on my field research at conferences and I conducted a search of media publications, advisory texts, academic publications, and websites in each field in regard to any discussion of the challenge of valuation and the presence of a measuring device/s in the field. I triangulated my findings from these multiple sources in order to identify the most popular tools and techniques used to gauge social value in each field.

I then sought to interview staff at those organizations involved in the creation and/or dissemination of those measuring devices.[3] To contact each organization when a prior respondent did not refer me on to a specific staff member, I contacted respondents by either emailing the organization's general email address or by sending emails to staff members with job duties relevant to my project (e.g., those with job titles referring to performance measurement, evaluation, social impact assessment, community affairs, or social responsibility), including a brief description of my project. If and when they replied, the respondent would either consent to an interview or would direct me to the staff member who they deemed most relevant to my research purpose. Interviews were conducted over the phone and lasted from thirty minutes to two hours. I relied on a semi-structured interview schedule.[4] All interviews involved questions concerning how the organization defined their goals, how they described the history and social project of the field, whether and how they sought to measure their performance in that regard (by what criteria and which tool/s), and what challenges or difficulties they faced in the practice of valuation. For staff at those organizations involved in the construction of a measuring device, I also asked them to provide an account of how the organization historically had decided to construct that tool and to provide me a history of its intended purpose as well as to recount the process of creating the instrument, including listing any challenges faced by the organization in doing so and modifications made to the device in response. These interviews often expanded to include other topics of interest that respondents deemed relevant to this list of questions.

In addition, I engaged in field research at practitioner-oriented conferences held by trade or member associations in each field. A growing body of scholarship views professional conferences as a space where actors make claims, contest over, and/or come to consensus concerning the field's identity through presentations and face-to-face interactions (Garud 2008). At each conference, I attended as many sessions as possible, with a particular focus on sessions focused on the topic of social value and valuation, including the use of terms such as "performance measurement," "social impact," and/or "metrics."[5] At each session I attended, I took detailed notes on the title and description of each session and the content of each presentation and the biography of each presenter, as well as giving attention to the themes present in the question and answer period. While this data is certainly not representative of all conferences taking place in that field, this ethnographic observation provides a unique perspective on questions concerning social value by focusing not on the formal claims made by key actors to external audiences but by examining conversations and interactions occurring among professionals in that arena. Attending these conferences, for example, gave me the chance to observe and note the questions, doubts, and concerns voiced by participants in each field about the meaning of social value, how it was being measured, and how it should best be measured.

Third, I engaged in textual analysis of a range of publications and media sources. I reviewed all available documents, reports, and websites produced by each respondent's affiliated organization and by other organizations central to the history of the field and/or to the formation of a measuring device. I also conducted document analysis of popular advisory texts in each of the fields, the largest trade publications in each field, and mainstream media sources. For each source, I sought to identify how the author/s discussed the history of the field, the social project of the field, and the measuring devices used by actors in the field, including any accounts of the genealogy of that tool. To supplement this assortment of primary data, I drew from secondary research on each field in order to address parallel questions. The data from these multiple sources was analyzed using the central tenets of grounded theory (Glaser and Strauss 1967; Miles and Huberman 1994).

To assess the effects of caring capitalism on the measure and meaning of social value, I employed the comparative case study method to select my cases and to establish my causal claims (Mill 1950). The comparative case study method consists of the purposeful selection of cases so that differences in the outcome of interest can be explained by reference to differences in the configuration of the fields under study, employing both a deductive approach to test existing expectations and the inductive method to note emerging causal patterns. I then engaged in the triangulation of my multiple sources in order to specify the precise historical causal mechanisms at work, to outline the interdependencies existing between fields, and to identify the broader, socio-economic factors at work across these fields (Lieberson 1991; Sewell 1996).

In regard to sampling, the relevant population was all fields in which the pursuit of social value was central to the field's stated identity, based on knowledge gained from my past scholarship and from a preliminary review of media publications and secondary research. As shown in Table 1.1, I selected seven organizational fields as cases for analysis: nonprofit organizations, social enterprises, Socially Responsible Investing (SRI), Corporate Social Responsibility (CSR), Responsible Investment (RI), Inclusive Businesses, and Impact Investing. These seven cases were selected based on the intersection of two different causes that have been hypothesized by scholars to be relevant for understanding the meaning and measure of social value. First, I selected cases based on their sectoral location, ensuring that I was studying fields that were located in the nonprofit and in the private sector. Secondly, I selected cases based on their normative orientation to the market, specifically whether or not the field's envisioning of its social project included the embrace of market methods as the solution to social problems. Finally, based on my emerging findings, I then decided to oversample cases that represented instances of caring capitalism, in order to be able to demonstrate the causal effect of the communicative purpose of the tool and value entrepreneurs' own characteristics on the construction of those measuring devices.

My research project is perforce limited along several dimensions. First, I do not examine all measuring devices that are present in each field. Rather, my study focuses on those specific valuation instruments that, based on the triangulation of multiple data sources, are considered prevailing in the field and that are considered to have reactivity effects for constituents of the field. However, I do not focus, or collect empirical research, on the question of how organizations in the field employ these measuring devices, either in terms of their rates or patterns of use or in terms of whether and how their use of the tool causes "reactivity" for them or the field more broadly.

Secondly, in terms of the population of relevant cases for inclusion in this study, I intentionally omitted several other fields, due to issues of access to key actors in the field, the prior existence of research on the question of valuation in that arena, or the straightforward constraint of space.[6] The book, for example, overlooks other cases of caring capitalism, including B-Corporations (Cooney 2012), microfinance (Roy 2010), and markets oriented around the ethical consumption of products (O'Rourke 2005). I also chose not to include fields that focused on environmental issues, although certainly it is often hard to empirically disentangle concerns for the social and the environmental, as in the case of the sustainability movement.

I also omitted the analysis of measuring devices that did not focus on the topic of social value. For example, in the case of international development, I sidestepped the study of tools devoted to the measure of health, given that the impact of health-based interventions on individuals and communities can be more easily measured than those concerned with the more amorphous and broader goal of social welfare. In the field of nonprofit organizations, I further limited the analysis to the study of measuring devices intended for social purpose organizations that offer direct services to clients and omitted those oriented to the provision of other type of social goods, including advocacy, arts, technical assistance, and research, except to discuss when and how they are affected by larger trends in how to measure social value.

Finally, the collection and analysis of data was limited to the case of the United States. Similar concerns about performance measurement and related valuation methodologies as present in the US are found in other nations, such as the United Kingdom, Australia, Canada, and many European countries; however, differences in nations' cultures, histories, and regulatory demands have led to a variety of distinct outcomes regarding how social value is defined and measured – both in the nonprofit sector and in the market. The result is that what is occurring in the United States is not necessarily occurring elsewhere and nor it is not occurring in a similar fashion (Wright 2001; Gjølberg 2009; Kerlin 2009).

Notes

1. For empirical examples of this approach to valuation, see Heimer (1985) and Goede (2005).
2. Some respondents had been involved in the construction of multiple fields (particularly in the cases of SRI, CSR, Responsible Investing), and I interviewed them in regard to each field's history of valuation efforts.

3. In Chapter 3, I also drew from interviews conducted with Matthew Hall and Yuval Millo for a related project on Social Return on Investment that was cross-national in its focus (Hall, Millo and Barman 2015).

4. Telephone interviews do not provide the non-verbal cues and contextual data of a face-to-face interview, but nonetheless are considered an acceptable means to generate oral histories from respondents (Sturges and Hanrahan 2004).

5. Here, I drew from knowledge gathered from an overview of media publications and secondary research in order to be able to identify the salient terminology concerning my research topic for that conference.

6. See, for example, Gourevitch (2011).

References

Abbott, Andrew. 2001. *Chaos of Disciplines*. Chicago: University of Chicago Press.
——— 1988. *The System of Professions: An Essay on the Division of Expert Labor*. Chicago: University of Chicago Press.
Abolafia, Mitchell. 1996. *Making Markets: Opportunism and Restraint on Wall Street*. Cambridge, MA: Harvard University Press.
Abramson, Alan J., Lester M. Salamon, and C. Eugene Steuerle. 1999. "The Nonprofit Sector and the Federal Budget: Recent History and Future Directions," Pp. 99–139 in *Nonprofits and Government*, edited by Elizabeth Boris and C. Eugene Steuerle. Washington, DC: Urban Institute.
Accountability For Sustainability. 2013. "About Us." www.accountingforsustainability.org/about-us. Retrieved September 15, 2013.
Alford, Robert R. 1994. "Paradigms of Relations between State and Society." Pp. 63–76 in *The State: Critical Concepts*, edited by John A. Hall. London: Taylor & Francis.
Almeling, Rene. 2011. *Sex Cells: The Medical Market for Eggs and Sperm*. Berkeley: University of California Press.
Alperson, Myra, Alice Tepper Marlin, Jonathan Schorsch, and Rosalyn Will. 1991. *The Better World Investment Guide*. New York: Prentice Hall Press.
Amaeshi, Kenneth. 2010. "Different Markets for Different Folks: Exploring the Challenges of Mainstreaming Responsible Investment Practices." *Journal of Business Ethics* 92:41–56.
Amana Mutual Funds Trust. 2012. "Islamic Investing." www.amanafunds.com/islamic_investing.shtml. Retrieved August 28, 2014.
Anderson, Beth and J. Gregory Dees. 2006. "Rhetoric, Reality and Research: Building a Solid Foundation for the Practice of Social Entrepreneurship." Pp. 144–180 in *Social Entrepreneurship: New Models of Sustainable Change*, edited by Alex Nicholls. New York: Oxford University Press.
Ansari, Shahid and K. J. Euske. 1987. "Rational, Rationalizing, and Reifying Uses of Accounting Data in Organizations." *Accounting, Organizations and Society* 12(6):549–570.

Antadze, Nino and Frances R. Westley. 2012. "Impact Metrics for Social Innovation: Barriers or Bridges to Radical Change?" *Journal of Social Entrepreneurship* 3(2):133–150.

Anteby, Michel. 2010. "Markets, Morals, and Practices of Trade: Jurisdictional Disputes in the US Commerce in Cadavers." *Administrative Science Quarterly* 55(4):606–638.

Appadurai, Arjun. 1998. *The Social Life of Things: Commodities in Cultural Perspective*. Cambridge: Cambridge University Press.

Aspen Institute. 2009. "Overcoming Short-Termism: A Call for a More Responsible Approach to Investment and Business Management." www.aspeninstitute.org/sites/Default/files/content/docs/business%20and%20society%20program/overcome_short_state0909.pdf. Retrieved August 2, 2014.

Auerswald, Philip. 2009. "Creating Social Value." *Stanford Social Innovation Review* Spring 51–55.

Ava Maria Mutual Funds. 2014. "About Us." http://avemariafunds.com/aboutUs.php. Retrieved August 28, 2014.

B Lab. 2012. "B Corp Legislation." www.bcorporation.net/publicpolicy. Retrieved June 2, 2013.

Bandelj, Nina. 2012. "Relational Work and Economic Sociology." *Politics & Society* 40(2):175–201.

Banerjee, A. V. 2007. *Making Aid Work*. Cambridge, MA: MIT Press.

Barman, Emily. 2006. *Contesting Communities: The Transformation of Workplace Charity*. Palo Alto: Stanford University Press.

Barman, Emily and Heather MacIndoe. 2012. "Institutional Pressures and Organizational Capacity: The Case of Outcome Measurement." *Sociological Forum* 27(1):70–93.

Barnet, Richard J. and John Cavanagh. 1994. *Global Dreams: Imperial Corporations and the New World Order*. New York: Simon & Schuster.

Barnett, Michael L. and Robert M. Salomon. 2012. "Does It Pay to Be Really Good? Addressing the Shape of the Relationship between Social and Financial Performance." *Strategic Management Journal* 33(11):1304–1320.

Baron, David P. 2001. "Private Politics, Corporate Social Responsibility, and Integrated Strategy." *Journal of Economic Management Strategy* 10:7–45

Barth, James R. and Joseph J. Cordes. 1981. "Nontraditional Criteria for Investing Pension Assets: An Economic Appraisal." *Journal of Labor Research* 2(2):219–247.

Bartley, Tim. 2011. "Certification as a Mode of Social Regulation." Pp. 441–452 in *Handbook on the Politics of Regulation*, edited by David Levi-Faur. New York: Edward Elgar Publishing.

2009. "Standards for Sweatshops: The Power and Limits of the Club Theory Approach to Voluntary Labor Standards." Pp.107–132 in *Voluntary Programs: A Club Theory Approach*, edited by Aseem Prakash and Matthew Potoski. Cambridge, MA: MIT Press.

2007a. "How Foundations Shape Social Movements: The Construction of an Organizational Field and the Rise of Forest Certification." *Social Problems* 54(3):229–255.

2007b. "Institutional Emergence in an Era of Globalization: The Rise of Transnational Private Regulation of Labor and Environmental Conditions." *American Journal of Sociology* 113(2):297–351.

2003. "Certifying Forests and Factories: States, Social Movements, and the Rise of Private Regulation in the Apparel and Forest Products Fields." *Political Sociology* 31:433–464.

Bassen, Alexander and Ana Maria Kovács. 2008. "Environmental, Social and Governance Key Performance Indicators from a Capital Market Perspective."*Zeitschrift Für Wirtschafts-und Unternehmensethik* 9(2):182–192.

Battilana, Julie. 2006. "Agency and Institution: The Enabling Role of Individuals' Social Position." *Organization* 13:653–676.

Battilana, Julie and Silvia Dorado. 2010. "Building Sustainable Hybrid Organizations: The Case of Commercial Microfinance Organizations." *Academy of Management Journal* 6:1419–1440.

Battiliana, Julie, Matthew Lee, John Walker, and Cheryl Dorsey. 2012. "In Search of the Hybrid Ideal." *Stanford Social Innovation Review* 10(3):50–55.

Baumol, William J. 1970. *A New Rationale for Corporate Social Policy.* New York: Committee for Economic Development.

Beck, T., A. Demirguc-Kunt, and R. Levine. 2005. "SMEs, Growth and Poverty: Cross Country Evidence." *Journal of Economic Growth* 10(3):199–229.

Beckert, Jens. 2009. "The Social Order of Markets." *Theory and Society* 38:245–269.

1999. "Agency, Entrepreneurs, and Institutional Change: The Role of Strategic Choice and Institutionalized Practices in Organizations." *Organization Studies* 20(5):777–799.

1996. "What is Sociological about Economic Sociology? Uncertainty and the Embeddedness of Economic Action." *Theory and Society* 25(6):803–840.

Beckert, Jens and Patrick Aspers. 2011. *The Worth of Goods: Valuation and Pricing in the Economy.* New York: Oxford University Press.

Bendel, Jem. 2011. "ESG Analysis in Deep Water." *The Journal of Corporate Citizenship* 40:6–25.

Benjamin, Lehn M. 2012. "Nonprofit Organizations and Outcome Measurement from Tracking Program Activities to Focusing on Frontline Work." *American Journal of Evaluation* 33(3):431–447.

Berle, Adolf. 1959. *Power without Property: A New Development in American Political Economy.* New York: Harcourt, Brace & World.

Berman, Elizabeth Popp. 2012. *Creating the Market University: How Academic Science Became an Economic Engine.* Princeton, NJ: Princeton University Press.

Bernstein, Nina. 1996. "Giant Companies Entering Race to Run State Welfare Programs." *The New York Times* September 15(1):1.

Binder, Amy. 2007. "For Love and Money: Organizations Creative Responses to Multiple Environmental Logics." *Theory & Society* 36:547–571.

Bishop, Matthew. 2009. "Capital Markets with a Conscience." *The Economist* September 1.

Blalock, Ann Bonar. 1999. "Evaluation Research and the Performance Management Movement from Estrangement to Useful Integration?" *Evaluation* 5(2):117–149.

Blau, Peter Michael. 1955. *The Dynamics of Bureaucracy: A Study of Interpersonal Relations in Two Government Agencies.* Chicago: Chicago University Press.

Block, Fred. 2003. "Karl Polanyi and the Writing of the Great Transformation." *Theory and Society* 32(3):275–306.

Blok, Anders. 2013. "Pragmatic Sociology as Political Ecology: On the Many Worths of Nature (s)." *European Journal of Social Theory* 16(4):492–510.

Blowfield, Michael and Catherine S. Dolan. 2014. "Business as a Development Agent: Evidence of Possibility and Improbability." *Third World Quarterly* 35(1):22–42.

Bobrowsky, David. 1999. "Creating a Global Public Policy Network in the Apparel Industry: The Apparel Industry Partnership." *UN Vision Project on Global Public Policy Networks.*

Boechat, Cláudio Bruzzi, Junia Faria, Mariana Pimenta, and Marilia Carneiro Ferreira. 2014. "Measuring Businesses Inclusiveness-New Drivers from Inclusive Market Approach." *Socially Responsive Organizations and the Challenge of Poverty*, edited by Milenko Gudi, Al Rosenbloom, and Carole Parkes. Sheffield: Greenleaf Publishing.

Boltanski, Luc and Laurent Thévenot. 2006. *On Justification: Economies of Worth.* Princeton: Princeton University Press.

Boston Consulting Group. 2002. "Assessing ProVenEx Performance and Identifying Directions for the Future." http://cw.redemmas.org/content/assessing-provenex-performance-and-identifying-directions-future. Retrieved August 11, 2012.

Botner, Stanley B. 1970. "Four Years of PPBS: An Appraisal." *Public Administration Review* 30(4): 423–431.

Bourdieu, Pierre. 1993. "Some Properties of Fields." Pp. 72–772 in *Sociology in Question*, translated by Richard Nice. London: Sage.

Bouri, Amit. 2011. "How Standards Emerge: The Role of Investor Leadership in Realizing the Potential of IRIS." *Innovations Journal* September: 145–159.

Bowen, Howard R. 1953. *Social Responsibilities of the Businessman.* New York: Harper.

Boxenbaum, Eva, and Julie Battilana. 2005. "Importation as Innovation: Transposing Managerial Practices across Fields." *Strategic Organization* 3(4):355–383.

Boyle, Mary Ellen and Janet Boguslaw. 2007. "Business, Poverty and Corporate Citizenship: Naming the Issues and Framing Solutions." *Journal of Corporate Citizenship* 26(Summer).

Bradley, Bill, Paul Jansen, and Les Silverman. 2003. "The Nonprofit Sector's $100 Billion Opportunity." *Harvard Business Review* 81(5):94–103.

Bradley, Michael, Cindy A. Schipani, Anant K. Sundaram, and James P. Walsh. 2000. "The Purposes and Accountability of the Corporation in Contemporary Society: Corporate Governance at a Crossroads." *Law and Contemporary Problems* 62(3):9–86.

Brandenburg, Margot. 2010. "Making the Case for Social Metrics and Impact Investing." *Development Investment Review* 6(1):47–49.

Bratton, William J. 1998. "Crime is Down in New York City: Blame the Police." Pp. 29–42 in *Zero Tolerance: Policing a Free Society*, second edition, edited by Norman Dennis. London: IEA.

Brill, Jack A. and Alan Reder. 1993. *Investing From the Heart: The Guide to Socially Responsible Investments and Money Management.* New York: Crown Publishers.

Bronstein, Scott. 1985. "Developing an 'Ethical' Portfolio." *New York Times* November 17:FP20.

Bruyn, Severyn T. 1991. *The Field of Social Investment.* Cambridge: Cambridge University Press.

Buder, Stanley. 1967. *Pullman: An Experiment in Industrial Order and Community Planning, 1880–1930.* New York: Oxford University Press.

Bugg-Levine, Anthony. 2009. "Impact Investing: Bold Models to Drive Development at Scale." *Beyond Profit* June: 17–21.

Bugg-Levine, Anthony and Jed Emerson. 2011. *Impact Investing: Transforming How We Make Money While Making a Difference*. San Francisco: Jossey-Bass.

Bugg-Levine, Antony and John Goldstein. 2009. "Impact Investing: Harnessing Capital Markets to Solve Problems at Scale." *Community Development Investment Review* 6(1):30–41.

Business Call to Action. 2013. "About Us." www.businesscalltoaction.org/about/about-us/. Retrieved November 26, 2013.

2011. "Barriers to Progress: A Review of Challenges and Solutions to Inclusive Business Growth." www.businesscalltoaction.org/wp-content/uploads/2010/11/Barriers-to-Inclusive-Business-Final-11.12.2010-LR.pdf. Retrieved August 4, 2014.

2010. "Measuring Value of Business Call to Action Initiatives: A Results Reporting Framework." www.businesscalltoaction.org/wp-content/uploads/2010/07/BCtA-Reporting-Results-FINAL.pdf. Retrieved March 26, 2013.

Business for Social Responsibility. 2010. "Corporate Responsibility Reporting: A View for the Next Cycle." www.bsr.org/reports/BSR_Corporate_Responsibility_Reporting.pdf. Retrieved March 5, 2014.

2009. "Corporate Responsibility Reporting: A View to the Next Cycle." www.bsr.org/reports/BSR_Corporate_Responsibility_Reporting.pdf. Retrieved March 3, 2014.

2008. "Environmental, Social and Governance: Moving to Mainstream Investing?" http://uksif.org/wp content/uploads/2012/12/BSR-2008.-Environmental-Social-and-Governance-Moving-to-Mainstream-Investing.pdf. Retrieved March 3, 2014.

2000. *Comparison of Selected Corporate Social Responsibility-Related Standards*. San Francisco: Business for Social Responsibility.

Buthe, Tim. 2010. "Private Regulation in the Global Economy: A (P)Review." *Business and Politics* 12(3):1–38.

Buxbaum, Carl B. 1981. "Cost-Benefit Analysis: The Mystique versus the Reality." *The Social service Review* 55(3):453–471.

Cairns, Ben, Margaret Harris, Romayne Hutchison and Mike Tricker. 2005. "Improving Performance? The Adoption and Implementation of Quality Systems in UK Nonprofits." *Nonprofit Management and Leadership* 16(2):135–151.

Calhoun, Craig. 1998. "The Public Good as a Social and Cultural Project." Pp. 20–35 in *Private Action and Public Good*, edited by Walter W. Powell and Elisabeth Clemens. New Haven: Yale University Press.

Callon, Michel. 2007. "What Does It Mean to Say that Economics is Performative?" Pp. 311–357 in *Do Economists Make Markets? On the Performativity of Economics*, edited by Donald D. MacKenzie, Fabian Muniesa and Lucia Siu. Princeton: Princeton University Press.

ed. 1998. *The Laws of the Markets*. Oxford: Blackwell.

Callon, Michel and Fabian Muniesa. 2005. "Economic Markets as Calculative Collective Devices." *Organization Studies* 26:1229–1250.

Campbell, David. 2002. "Beyond Charitable Choice." *Nonprofit and Voluntary Sector Quarterly* 31:207–230.

Campbell, Donald T. and Julian C. Stanley. 1963. "Experimental and Quasi-experimental Designs for Research on teaching." Pp. 171–246 in *Handbook of Research on Teaching*, edited by N. L. Gage. Chicago: Rand McNally.

Capek, Mary Ellen S. and Molly Mead. 2007. *Effective Philanthropy: Organizational Success through Deep Diversity and Gender Equality.* Cambridge, MA: MIT Press.

Capelle-Blancard, Gunther and Stéphanie Monjon. 2012. "Trends in the Literature on Socially Responsible Investment: Looking for the Keys under the Lamppost." *Business Ethics: A European Review* 21.3: 239–250.

Carman, Joanne G. and Kathleen A. Fredericks. 2008. "Nonprofits and Evaluation: Empirical Evidence from the Field." *Nonprofits and Evaluation: New Directions for Evaluation* 119:51–71.

Carroll, Archie B. 1999. "Corporate Social Responsibility Evolution of a Definitional Construct." *Business & Society* 38(3):268–295.

Carruthers, Bruce G. and Arthur L. Stinchcombe. 1999. "The Social Structure of Liquidity: Flexibility, Markets, and States." *Theory and Society* 28(3):353–382.

Carruthers, Bruce G. and Sarah Babb. 1996. "The Color of Money and the Nature of Value: Greenbacks and Gold in Postbellum America." *American Journal of Sociology* 101(6):1556–1591.

Carruthers, Bruce G. and Wendy Nelson Espeland. 1998. "Money, Meaning, and morality." *American Behavioral Scientist* 41(10):1384–1408.

Carson, Rachel. 1962. *The Silent Spring.* New York: Houghton-Mifflin.

Cavanaugh, James J. and Stuart Haggard. 1998. "Performance Measurement and Performance-Based Management: An Interview with Joseph S. Wholey." www.orau.gov/pbm/links/wholey.pdf. Retrieved February 6, 2014.

Ceres. 2012. "Incorporating Environmental, Social and Governance into Investing: A Survey of Investment Consultant Practices." http://www.ceres.org/resources/reports/incorporating-environmental-social-and-governance-factors-into-investing-a-survey-of-investment-consultant-practices/view. Retrieved September 4, 2013.

Champ, P. A., K. J. Boyle, and T. C. Brown. 2003. *A Primer on Nonmarket Valuation.* Dordrecht: Kluwer Academic Publishers.

Chan, Cheris Shun-Ching. 2012. *Marketing Death: Culture and the Making of a Life Insurance Market in China.* London: Oxford University Press.

Chandler, Jr., Alfred D. 1977. *The Visible Hand.* Cambridge, MA: Harvard University Press.

Charity Navigator. 2014. "How Do We Rate Charities?" www.charitynavigator.org/index.cfm?bay=content.view&cpid=1284#.VBhPXEtGihO. Retrieved September 2, 2014.

Chatterji, Aaron K. and David Levine. 2006. "Breaking Down the Wall of Codes: Evaluating Non-Financial Performance Measurement." *California Management Review* 48(2):29–51.

Child, Curtis. 2015. "Tip of the Iceberg: The Nonprofit Underpinnings of For-Profit Social Enterprise." Nonprofit and Voluntary Sector Quarterly http://nvs.sagepub.com/content/early/2015/03/04/0899764015572901.abstract.

Christensen, Jon. 2003. "Exploring New Ideas for Making Finances Clearer and Scandals Rarer." *New York Times* November 17.

Clapp, Raymond. 1926. *Study of Volume and Cost of Social Work 1924.* Cleveland: Welfare Federation of Cleveland.

Clay, Jason. 2005. *Exploring the Links between International Business and Poverty Reduction: A Case Study of Unilever in Indonesia.* London: Oxfam GB, Novib, Unilever and Unilever Indonesia.

2001. "Aquaculture's Environmental Footprint Some Findings Research on Shrimp Aquaculture." A paper presented to the Conference, How to Farm the Seas II: The Science, Economics and Politics of Aquaculture on the West Coast.

Clemens, Elisabeth S. 1993. "Organizational Repertoires and Institutional Change: Women's Groups and the Transformation of US Politics, 1890–1920." *American Journal of Sociology* 98(4):755–798.

Coca Cola India. 2014. "Innovation." www.coca-colaindia.com/sustainability/innov ation.html. Retrieved December 3, 2014.

Coca Cola/SAB Miller. 2011. "Exploring The Links between International Business and Poverty Reduction." www.oxfamamerica.org/files/exploring-the-links-between-international-business and-poverty-reduction.pdf. Retrieved November 11, 2013.

Coleman, James. 1990. *Foundations of Social Theory*. Cambridge, MA: Harvard University Press.

Commission on Growth and Development. 2008. *"Growth Report: Strategies for Sustained Growth and Inclusive Development."* Washington, DC: The World Bank.

Commonfund Institute. 2013. "From SRI to ESG: The Changing World of Responsible Investing." www.commonfund.org/InvestorResources/Publications/White%20Papers/ Whitepaper_SRI%20to%20ESG%202013%200901.pdf. Retrieved August 3, 2014.

Compa, Lance and Tashia Hinchiiffe-Daricarrere. 1995. "Enforcing International Labor Rights through Corporate Codes of Conduct." *Columbia Journal of International Law* 33:663–689.

Cooch, Sara and Mark Kramer. 2007. *Compounding Impact: Mission Investing by U.S. Foundations*. Boston: FSG Social Impact Advisors.

Cooney, Kate. 2012. "Mission Control: Examining the Institutionalization of New Legal Forms of Social Enterprise in Different Strategic Action Fields." Pp. 198–221 in *Social Enterprises: An Organizational Perspective*, edited by Benjamin Gidron and Yeheskel Hasenfeld. New York: Palgrave-Macmillan.

2011. "An Exploratory Study of Social Purpose Business Models in the United States." *Nonprofit and Voluntary Sector Quarterly* 40(1):185–196.

Cooney, Kate and Trina R. Williams Shanks. 2010. "New Approaches to Old Problems: Market-Based Strategies for Poverty Alleviation." *Social Service Review* 84(1):29–55.

Corry, Olaf. 2010. "Defining and Theorizing the Third Sector." Pp. 11–20 in *Third Sector Research*, edited by Rupert Taylor. New York: Springer.

Council on Economic Priorities. 1970a. *Economic Priorities Report* 1(1).

1970b. *Economic Priorities Report* 1(2).

1970c. *Economic Priorities Report* 1(3).

Credit Suisse. 2012. *"Investing For Impact: How Social Enterprise Is Redefining the Meaning of Return."* Cologne: Credit Suisse and Schwab Foundation.

Cui, C. 2007. "How Social Conscience Hooks Hedge Funds." *Wall Street Journal*, November 27.

Cutlip, Scott. 1965. *Fund Raising in the United States*. New Brunswick, NJ: Rutgers University Press.

David, Robert J., Wesley D. Sine, and Heather A. Haveman. 2013. "Seizing Opportunity in Emerging Fields: How Institutional Entrepreneurs Legitimated the Professional Form of Management Consulting." *Organization Science* 24(2): 356–377.

Davis, Gerald. 2009. *Managed by the Markets: How Finance Re-Shaped America.* New York: Oxford University Press.

Davis, Keith. 1973. "The Case for and Against Business Assumption of Social Responsibilities." *Academy of Management Journal* 16:312–322.

Dees, J. G. 1998. "Enterprising Nonprofits." *Harvard Business Review* 76:54–69.

Dees, J. G. and B. B. Anderson. 2003. "For-Profit Social Ventures." Pp. 1–26 in *Social Entrepreneurship*, edited by M. L. Kourilsky and W. B. Walstad. Dublin: Senate Hall Academic Publishing.

Dejean, Frédérique, Jean Gond, and Bernard Leca. 2004. "Measuring the Unmeasured: An Institutional Entrepreneur Strategy in an Emerging Industry." *Human Relations* 57(6):741–764.

Deloitte. 2013. "Disclosure of Long-Term Business Value: What Matters?" www.corp gov.deloitte.com/binary/com.epicentric.contentmanagement.servlet.ContentDelivery Servlet/USEng/Documents/Board%20Governance/Short-%20and%20Long-termism/ Long%20term%20Business%20value_September2013.pdf. March 14, 2015.

2011. "What Is Integrated Reporting?" www.deloitte.com/assets/Dcom-MiddleEast/ Local%20Assets/Documents/Services/ERS/me_ers_integrated_reporting_sept11.pdf. Retrieved October 12, 2013.

Department for International Development. 2006. "Private Sector Development Strategy – Prosperity for All: Making Markets Work." www.icco.org/sites/www.round tablecocoa.org/documents/DFID%202009_Private%20Sector%20Development% 20Strategy.pdf. Retrieved August 27, 2014.

2000. "Making Markets Work Better for the World." www.valuechains.org/ dyn/bds/docs/684/OPM%202000_MMW%20Framework%20Paper.pdf. Retrieved October 31, 2014.

Desrosieres, Alain. 2001. "How 'Real' Are Statistics? Four Possible Attitudes." *Social Research* 68: 339–355.

Devine, Edward Thomas. 1911. *The Spirit of Social Work: Addresses.* New York: Charities publication Committee.

Dewey, John. 1939. *Theory of Valuation.* Chicago: University of Chicago Press.

DeWinter, R. 2001. "The Anti-Sweatshop Movement: Constructing Corporate Moral Agency in the Global Apparel Industry." *Ethics & International Affairs* 15(2):99–115.

Dickson, Martha A., Suzanne Loker and Molly Eckman. 2009. *Social Responsibility in the Global Apparel Industry.* New York: Fairchild Books.

Diller, Janelle. 1999. "A Social Conscience in the Global marketplace? Labour Dimensions of Codes of Conduct, Social Labelling, and Investor Initiatives." *International Labour Review* 138(2):99–130.

Diltz, David J. 1995. "The Private Cost of Socially Responsible Investing." *Applied Financial Economics* 5(2):69–77.

DiMaggio, Paul J. 1988. "Interest and Agency in Institutional Theory." Pp. 3–22 in *Institutional Patterns and Organizations*, edited by Lynne Zucker. Cambridge, MA: Ballinger.

1991. "Constructing an Organizational Field as a Professional Project: U.S. Art Museums, 1920–1940." Pp. 267–292 in *The New Institutionalism in Organizational Analysis*, edited by Paul J. DiMaggio and Walter W. Powell. Chicago: University of Chicago Press.

DiMaggio, Paul J. and Walter W. Powell. 1983. "The Iron Cage Revisited: Institutional Isomorphism and Collective Rationality in Organizational Fields." *American Sociological Review* 48:147–160.

Domini, Amy L. and Peter D. Kinder. 1984. *Ethical Investing*. Reading, MA: Addison-Wesley.

Douglas, William. 2001. "Who's Who in Codes of Conduct." http://128.121.176.141/CodesofConduct1-02-01.html. Retrieved July 1, 2014.

Drake, Pamela Peterson and Frank J. Fabozzi. 2010. *The Basics of Finance: An Introduction to Financial Markets, Business Finance, and Portfolio Management*. New York: John E. Wiley & Sons.

Drucker, Peter. 1984. "The New Meaning of Corporate Social Responsibility." *California Management Review* 26(winter):53–63.

Durkheim, Emile. 1895/2014. *The Rules of Sociological Method: And Selected Texts on Sociology and Its Method*. New York: Simon and Schuster.

DVFA. 2008. "KPIs for ESG: Key Performance Indicators for Environmental, Social and Governance Issues." www.rwe.com/web/cms/mediablob/de/405414/data/0/7/DVFA-Kriterien-fuer-Non-Financials.pdf. Retrieved October 17, 2013.

Eccles, Neil and Suzette Viviers. 2011. "The Origins and Meanings of Names Describing Investment Practices that Integrate a Consideration of ESG Issues in the Academic Literature. *Journal of Business Ethics* 104(3):389–402.

Eccles, Robert G. and Aldo Sesia. 2009. *"CalPERS' Emerging Equity in the Markets Principle."* Cambridge, MA: Harvard Business School.

Eccles, Robert G., George Serafeim, and Michael P. Krzus. 2011. "Market Interest in Nonfinancial Information." *Journal of Applied Corporate Finance* 23(4): 113–127.

Eccles, Robert G. and Michael P. Krzus. 2010. *One Report: Integrated Reporting for a Sustainability Strategy*. New York: Wiley & Sons.

Eccles, Robert G., Michael P. Krzus, Jean Rogers, and George Serafeim. 2012. "The Need for Sector-Specific Materiality and Sustainability Reporting Standards." *Journal of Applied Corporate Finance* 24(2): 65–71.

Edwards, Michael and David Hulme. 1995. "NGO Performance and Accountability in the Post-Cold War World." *Journal of International Development* 7(6):849–856.

Eikenberry, Angela M. 2009. "Refusing the Market: A Democratic Discourse for Voluntary and Nonprofit Organizations." *Nonprofit and Voluntary Sector Quarterly* 38(4):582–596.

Eikenberry, Angela M. and J. D. Kluver. 2004. "The Marketization of the Nonprofit Sector: Civil Society at Risk?" *Public Administration Review* 64(2):132–140.

Elders, Gregory and Barbara Evans. 2011. "Finding Fundamental Value." Pp. 4–5 in *ESG USA 2011: Investing For a Sustainable Economy Magazine*. www.responsible-investor.com/images/uploads/reports/ESG_USA_2011_Mag.pdf. Retrieved June 12, 2014.

Elmore, Richard F. 2007. *School Reform from the Inside Out: Policy, Practice, and Performance*. Cambridge, MA: Harvard Education Press.

Emerson, Jed and Fay Twersky, eds. 1996. *New Social Entrepreneurs: The Success, Challenge and Lessons of Non-Profit Enterprise Creation*. San Francisco: Roberts Foundation.

Emerson, Jed, Jay Wachowicz, and Suzi Chun. 2000. "Social Return on Investment: Exploring Aspects of Value Creation in the Nonprofit Sector." Pp. 131–173 in *Social Purpose Enterprises and Venture Philanthropy in the New Millennium, Volume 2*. San Francisco: The Roberts Foundation.

Emerson, Jed with Mark Cabaj. 2000. "Social Return on Investment." *Making Waves* 11(2):10–14.

Emerson Jed, Melinda T. Tuan, and L. Dutton. 1998. "The Roberts Enterprise Development Fund: Implementing a Social Venture Capital Approach to Philanthropy." Stanford University Graduate School of Business. S-E-45, October.

Emirbayer, Mustafa, and Victoria Johnson. 2008. "Bourdieu and Organizational Analysis." *Theory and Society* 37(1):1–44.

Enhanced Analytics Initiative. 2008. "Research Centre Stage: For Years of the Enhanced Analytics Initiative." www.onvalues.ch/images/publications/08–12_EAI_4-year_review.pdf. Retrieved August 3, 2014.

Entine, Jon. 2003. "The Myth of Social Investing: A Critique of Its Practice and Consequences for Corporate Social Performance Research." *Organization & Environment* 16(3): 1–17.

Epstein, Paul D. 1992. "Get Ready: The Time for Performance Measurement is Finally Coming!" *Public Administration Review* 52(5):513–519.

Escopil. 2013. "Mensagem Do PCA Da Escopil Internatcional, LDA." www.escopil.co.mz/. Retrieved October 25, 2013.

Espeland, Wendy and Michael Sauder. 2007. "Rankings and Reactivity: How Public Measures Recreate Social Worlds" *American Journal of Sociology* 113(1):1–40.

Espeland, Wendy Nelson and Mitchell L. Stevens. 2008. "A Sociology of Quantification." *European Journal of Sociology* 49(03):401–436.

1998. "Commensuration as a Social Process." *Annual Review of Sociology* 24:313–343.

Esping-Andersen, Gosta. 1990. *Three Worlds of Welfare Capitalism*. Princeton, NJ: Princeton University Press.

Etzion, Dror and Fabrizio Ferraro. 2010. "The Role of Analogy in the Institutionalization of Sustainability Reporting." *Organization Science* 21(5):1092–1107.

Etzioni, Amitai. 1999. "The Good Society." *The Journal of Political Philosophy* 7(1):88–103.

European Union. 2001. "Green Paper: Promoting a European Framework for Corporate Social Responsibility." http://eur-lex.europa.eu/smartapi/cgi/sga_doc?smartapi!celexplus!prod!DocNumber&lg=en&type_doc=COMfinal&an_doc=2001&nu_doc=366. Retrieved August 30, 2012.

Evaluation Exchange. 1998. "An Interview with Harry Hatry and Joseph Wholey." *The Evaluation Exchange*. IV(1). www.gse.harvard.edu/hfrp/eval/issue10/qanda.html. Retrieved February 2, 2014.

Eyal, Gil. 2013. "For a Sociology of Expertise: The Social Origins of the Autism Epidemic." *American Journal of Sociology* 118(4):863–907.

Fair Labor Association. 2014. "Improving Workers' Lives Worldwide." fla.org. Retrieved February 13, 2014.

Ferguson, James. 1990. *The Anti-Politics Machine: "Development," Depoliticization, and Bureaucratic Power in Lesotho*. Cambridge: Cambridge University Press.

Ferranti, David De and Anthony J. Ody. 2007. *Beyond Microfinance: Getting Capital to Small and Medium Enterprises to Fuel Faster Development*. New York: Brookings Institute.

Filene, Edward A. 1922. "A Simple Code of Business Ethics." *Annals of the American Academy of Political and Social Sciences* 101(May):223–228.

Financial Accounting Standards Board. 1980. "Qualitative Characteristics of Accounting Information." Statement of Financial Accounting Concepts No. 2. www.fasb.org/

cs/BlobServer?blobcol=urldata&blobtable=MungoBlobs&blobkey=id&blobwhere=1175820900526&blobheader=application%2Fpdf. Retrieved March 3, 2015.

Financial Crisis Inquiry Commission. 2011. *"The Financial Crisis Inquiry Report."* Washington, DC: US Government Printing Office.

Fligstein, Neil. 2001. "Social Skill and the Theory of Fields." *Sociological Theory* 19(2):105–125.

Fligstein, Neil and Doug McAdam. 2012. *A Theory of Fields*. Oxford: Oxford University Press.

Fombrun, Charles J. 1998. "Indices of Corporate Reputation: An Analysis of Media Rankings and Social Monitors' Ratings." *Corporate Reputation Review* 1(4):327–340.

Forbes. 2013. "The 50 Largest U.S. Charities." www.forbes.com/companies/united-way/. Retrieved August 2, 2014.

Forbes, David P. 1998. "Measuring the Unmeasurable." *Nonprofit and Voluntary Sector Quarterly* 27(2):183–202.

Ford Foundation. 1967. *New Options in the Philanthropic Process*. New York: Ford Foundation.

Foucault, Michel. 1994. *The Order of Things: An Archeology of the Human Sciences*. New York: Vintage Books.

1979. *Discipline & Punish: The Birth of Prison*. New York: Vintage Books.

Foundation Center. 2014. "Tools and Resources for Assessing Social Impact." http://trasi.foundationcenter.org/search_results.php. Retrieved March 23, 2014.

Fourcade, Marion. 2011. "Cents and Sensibility: Economic Valuation and the Nature of 'Nature.'" *American Journal of Sociology* 116:1721–77.

Fourcade, Marion and Kieran Healy. 2007. "Moral Views of Market Society." *Annual Review of Sociology* 33:285–311.

Frankel, Emil. 1926. "Standardization of Social Statistics." *Social Forces* 5(2):243–247.

Freeman, Robert E. 1984. *Strategic Management: A Stakeholder Approach*. Boston: Pitman/ Ballinger.

Fremont-Smith, Marion R.. 2004. "Pillaging of Charitable Assets: Embezzlement and Fraud." *Exempt Organization Tax Review* 46(3): 333–346.

Friedland, Roger and Robert Alford. 1991. "Bringing Society Back In: Symbols, Practices and Institutional Contradictions." Pp. 232–263 in *The New Institutionalism in Organizational Analysis*, edited by Walter W. Powell and P. J. DiMaggio. Chicago: University of Chicago Press.

Friedman, Milton. 1970. "The Social Responsibility of Business is to Increase Profits." *New York Times Magazine* September 13.

1962. *Capitalism and Freedom*. Chicago: University of Chicago Press.

Frumkin, Peter. 2002. *On Being Nonprofit*. Cambridge, MA: Harvard University Press.

FTSE. 2011. "Integrating ESG into Investments and Stewardship." London: FTSE.

Fulton, Brad, Bruce M. Kahn, and Camilla Sharples. 2012. "Sustainable Investing: Establishing Long-Term Value and Performance." New York: Deutsche Bank Climate Change Advisors. https://institutional.deutscheawm.com/content/_media/Sustainable_Investing_2012.pdf. Retrieved June 11, 2014.

G20. 2010. "The G20 Seoul Summit Leaders' Declaration." www.g20.utoronto.ca/2010/g20seoul.html. Retrieved March 28, 2013.

Gair, Cynthia. 2009. "*SROI Act II: A Call to Action for Next Generation SROI.*" San Francisco: REDF.

——— 2002. "*A Report from the Good Ship SROI.*" San Francisco: REDF.

Galaskiewicz, Joseph and Sondra N. Barringer. 2012. "Social Enterprises and Social Categories." Pp. 47–80 in *Social Enterprises: An Organizational Perspective*, edited by Benjamin Gidron and Yeheskel Hasenfeld. New York: Palgrave-Macmillan.

Galbraith, John K. 1967. *The New Industrial State.* Boston: Houghton Mifflin.

Garz, H., F. Schnella and R. Frank. 2010. "KPIs for ESG. A Guideline for the Integration of ESG into Financial Analysis and Corporate Validation. Version 3.0." www .effas-esg.com/wp-content/uploads/2011/07/KPIs_for_ESG_3_0_Final.pdf. Retrieved June 14, 2014.

Garud, Raghu. 2008. "Conferences as Venues for the Configuration of Emerging Organizational Fields: The Case of Cochlear Implants." *Journal of Management Studies* 45(6):1061–1088.

Gates, Bill. 2008. "Making Capitalism More Creative." *Time Magazine* 31.

Gendron, Yves. 2013. "Accounting Academia and the Threat of the Paying-Off Mentality." *Critical Perspectives on Accounting* 26:168–176.

Gereffi, Gary and Miguel Korzeniewicz, eds. 1994. *Commodity Chains and Global Capitalism.* Santa Barbara, CA: ABC-CLIO.

GIIN. 2015a. "For Investors." www.impactbase.org/info/investors. Retrieved August 13, 2014.

——— 2015b. "ImpactBase." www.impactbase.org/info/about-impactbase. Retrieved August 13, 2014.

——— 2015c. "Sample Profile." www.impactbase.org/sites/all/themes/ib1/samples/110118b_ sample_profile.pdf. Retrieved August 12, 2014.

——— 2014. "IRIS Metrics." http://iris.thegiin.org/iris-standards. Retrieved April 3, 2014.

GIIRS. 2012. "The Company Impact Rating." http://giirs.org/companies/companies. Retrieved June 18, 2013.

——— 2011. *Assessment 101.* Berwyn: B Lab.

Gittell, Ross, Matt Magnusson, and Michael Merenda. 2012. *The Sustainable Business Case Book*, v. 1.0. Washington, DC: Flat World Knowledge.

Gjølberg, Maria. 2009. "The Origin of Corporate Social Responsibility: Global Forces or National Legacies?" *Socio-Economic Review* 4:605–637.

Glaser, Barry G. and Anselm L. Strauss. 1967. *The Discovery of Grounded Theory: Strategies for Qualitative Research.* Chicago: Aldine.

Glickman, Lawrence B. 2009. *Buying Power: A History of Consumer Activism in America.* Chicago: University of Chicago Press.

Global Reporting Initiative. 2013. "The GRI Sustainability Reporting Guidelines Main Features of G4." www.globalreporting.org/resourcelibrary/main-features-of-g4 .pdf. Retrieved March 22, 2015.

——— 2012a. "Non-Governmental Organizations." www.globalreporting.org/reporting/ sector-guidance/ngo/Pages/default.aspx. Retrieved July 16, 2012.

——— 2012b. "Sustainability Disclosure Database." http://database.globalreporting.org/. Retrieved July 16, 2012.

Glynn, Mary Ann and Michael Lounsbury. 2005. "From the Critics' Corner: Logic Blending, Discursive Change and Authenticity in a Cultural Production System." *Journal of Management Studies* 42:1031–1055.

Godeke, Steven with Doug Bauer. 2008. *Philanthropy's New Passing Gear: Mission-Related Investing. A Policy and Implementation Guide for Foundation Trustees.* New York: Rockefeller Philanthropic Advisers.

Goede, Marieke de. 2005. *Virtue, Fortune, and Faith: A Geneaology of Finance.* Vol. 24. Minneapolis: University of Minnesota Press.

Good Capital. 2012. "Frequently Asked Questions." www.goodcap.net/faqs.php#A1. Retrieved August 8, 2012.

Goldman, Michael. 2005. *Imperial Nature: The World Bank and Struggles for Social Justice in the Age of Globalization.* New Haven: Yale University Press.

Gordon, C. Wayne and Nicholas Babchuk. 1959. "A Typology of Voluntary Associations." *American Sociological Review* 24:22–29.

Gore, Albert. 1998. *Reaching Public Goals: Managing Government for Results: Resource Guide.* DIANE Publishing.

Gourevitch, Peter. 2011. "The Value of Ethics: Monitoring, Normative Compliance in Ethical Consumption Markets." Pp. 86–105 in *The Worth of Goods: Valuation and Pricing in the Economy,* edited by Jens Beckert and Patrick Aspers. London: Oxford University Press.

Gourevitch, Peter A. and James Shinn. 2005. *Political Power and Corporate Control: The New Global Politics of Corporate Governance.* Princeton: Princeton University Press.

Gourevitch, Peter A., David A. Lake, and Janice Gross Stein. 2012. *The Credibility of Transnational NGOs: When Virtue is Not Enough.* London: Cambridge University Press.

Government of Nigeria 2010, *Nigerian Oil and Gas Industry Content Development Bill,* 2010 *Explanatory Memorandum.* www.nogicjqs.com/NOGICD_Act_2010 .pdf. Retrieved July 17, 2013.

Graddy-Reed, Elizabeth, Dawn Trembath, and Maryann Feldman. 2012. "A Report on North Carolina's Social Innovation: Innovation at Work for Carolina Communities." http://maryannfeldman.web.unc.edu/files/2013/09/SI-Report_.pdf. Retrieved May 3, 2014.

Graham, Benjamin. 2006. *The Intelligent Investor.* New York: Collins Business Essentials.

Gray, Hillel. 1983. *New Directions in the Investment and Control of Pension Funds.* Washington, DC: Investor Responsibility Research Center.

Greenhouse, Steven. 1996. "A Crusader Makes Celebrities Tremble." *New York Times* June 18, B4.

Greenwood Royston, Roy Suddaby, and C. R. Hinings 2002. "Theorizing Change: The Role of Professional Associations in the Transformation of Institutionalized Fields." *Academy of Management Journal* 45:58–80.

Greyston Bakery. 2012. "Social Mission." www.greystonbakery.com/social-mission/. Retrieved August 6, 2012.

GS Sustain. 2009. "GS SUSTAIN: Challenges in ESG Disclosure and Consistency." www.sseinitiative.org/files/GS_SUSTAIN__Challenges_in_ESG_disclosure_and_ consistency.pdf. Retrieved March 5, 2015.

Guay, Terrence, Jonathan D. Doh, and Graham Sinclair. 2004. "Non-Governmental Organizations, Shareholder Activism, and Socially Responsible Investments: Ethical, Strategic, and Governance Implications." *Journal of Business Ethics* 52(1):125–139.

Guidestar. 2014. "Welcome to Charting Impact." www.guidestar.org/rxg/update-non
profit-report/charting-impact.aspx. Retrieved September 2, 2014.

Gunningham, Neil, Robert A. Kagan, and Dorothy Thornton. 2004. "Social License and
Environmental Protection: Why Businesses Go Beyond Compliance." *Law & Social
Inquiry* 29(2):307–341

Haas, Peter M. 1992. "Introduction: Epistemic Communities and International Policy
Coordination." *International Organization* 46(1):1–35.

Hagerman, Lisa A. and Janneke Ratcliffe. 2009. "Increasing Access to Capital: Could
Better Measurement of Social and Environmental Outcomes Entice More Institutional Investment Capital into Underserved Communities?" *Community Development Investment Review* 6(1):43–64.

Hahn, Rüdiger. 2012. "Inclusive Business, Human Rights and the Dignity of the Poor:
A Glance Beyond Economic Impacts of Adapted Business Models." *Business Ethics:
A European Review* 21(1):47–63.

Halberg, Kristin. 2000. *A Market-Oriented Strategy for Small and Medium Scale
Enterprises*. Washington, DC: The World Bank.

Hall, Matthew, Yuval Millo, and Emily Barman. 2015. "Who and What Really Counts?
Stakeholder Prioritization and Accounting for Social Value." *Journal of Management Studies* 52(7):907–934.

Hall, Peter Dobkin. 1992. *Inventing the Nonprofit Sector and Other Essays in Philanthropy, Voluntarism, and Nonprofit Organization*. Baltimore: Johns Hopkins
University Press.

Hallett, Tim. 2010. "The Myth Incarnate Recoupling Processes, Turmoil, and Inhabited
Institutions in an Urban Elementary School." *American Sociological Review*
75(1):52–74.

Halme, Minna, Sara Lindeman, and Paula Linna. 2012. "Innovation for Inclusive
Business: Intrapreneurial Bricolage in Multinational Corporations." *Journal of
Management Studies* 49(4):743–784.

Hamilton, Sally, Hoje Jo, and Meir Statman. 1993. "Doing Well While Doing good?
The Investment Performance of Socially Responsible Mutual Funds." *Financial
Analysts Journal* 49(6):62–66.

Handler, Joel F. and Yeheskel Hasenfeld. 2007. *Blame Welfare, Ignore Poverty and
Inequality*. Cambridge, UK: Cambridge University Press.

Hansmann, Henry B. 1980. "The Role of Nonprofit Enterprise." *The Yale Law Journal*
89(5):835–901.

Harji, Karim and Edward Jackson. 2012. *Accelerating Impact Investing*. New York:
Rockefeller Foundation.

Hart, Stuart L. 2005. *Capitalism at the Crossroads: The Unlimited Business Opportunities
in Solving the World's Most Difficult Problems*. New York: Pearson Education.

Harvard University. 1971. *Report of the Committee on University Relations with
Corporate Enterprise*. Cambridge: Harvard University

Harvey, David. 2005. *A Brief History of Neoliberalism*. New York: Oxford University
Press.

Harvey, Pharis, Bama Athreya, and Terry Collingsworth. 2000. *Developing Effective
Mechanisms for Implementing Labor Rights in the Global Economy*. Washington,
DC: International Labor Rights Fund.

Hasenfeld, Yeheskel and Eve E. Garrow. 2012. "Nonprofit Human-Service Organizations, Social Rights, and Advocacy in a Neoliberal Welfare State." *Social Service Review* 86(2):295–322.

Hatry, Harry P. 1999. *Performance Measurement: Getting Results*. Washington, DC: The Urban Institute.

——— 1978. "The Status of Productivity Measurement in the Public Sector." *Public Administration Review* 38(1):28–33.

——— 1977. *How Effective Are Your Community Services?: Procedures for Monitoring the Effectiveness of Municipal Services*. Washington, DC: The Urban Institute.

——— 1970. "Measuring the Effectiveness of Nondefense Public Programs." *Operations Research* 18(5):772–784.

——— 1961. "Economic Analysis in the Selection of Space Systems," General Electric Company, Technical Military Planning Operation (TEMPO), SP-130, April.

Hatry, Harry and Linda Lampkin. 2001. *An Agenda for Action: Outcome Measurement in Nonprofit Organizations*. Washington, DC: Urban Institute.

Hatry, Harry P., Louis H. Blair, Donald Fisk, and Wayne Kruimie. 1976. *Program Analysis for State and Local Government*. Washington, DC: Urban Institute.

Hatry, Harry P., Richard E. Winnie, Donald M. Fisk, and Louis H. Blair. 1981. *Practical Program Evaluation for State and Local Governments*. Washington, DC: The Urban Institute.

Hatry, Harry P., Theresa van Houten, Margaret C. Plantz, and Martha T. Greenway. 1996. *Measuring Program Outcomes: A Practical Approach*. Alexandria, VA: United Way of America.

Hayek, Friedrich A. 1960. *The Constitution of Liberty*. London: Routledge.

Heald, Morris. 1977. *The Social Responsibilities of Business: Company and Community 1900–1960*. New York: Transaction Publishers.

Healy, Kieran. 2006. *Last Best Gifts: Altruism and the Market for Human Blood and Organs*. Chicago: University of Chicago Press.

Hebb, Tessa, ed. 2012. *The Next Generation of Responsible Investing*. Vol. 1. New York: Springer.

Heimer Carol, 1985. *Reactive Risk and Rational Action: Managing Moral Hazard in Insurance Contracts*. Berkeley, CA: University of California Press.

Helgesson, Claes Fredrik and Fabien Muniesa. 2014. "Valuation Is Work." *Valuation Studies* 2:1–4.

Hendricks, Michael, Margaret C. Plantz, and Kathleen J. Pritchard. 2008. "Measuring Outcomes of United Way-Funded Programs: Expectations and Reality." Pp. 13–35 in *Nonprofits and Evaluation: New Directions*, edited by Joanne G. Carman and Kimberly A. Fredericks. New York: John Wiley & Sons.

Herbert, Bob. 1997. "In America: Mr. Young Gets It Wrong." *New York Times* June 27:A27.

Heuts, Frank and Annemarie Mol. 2013. "What is a Good Tomato? A Case of Valuing in Practice." *Valuation Studies* 1(2):125–145.

Hirschman Albert O. 1982. "Rival Interpretations of Market Society: Civilizing, Destructive, or Feeble?" *Journal of Economic Literature* 20:1463–1484.

Hitch, Charles Johnston and Roland N. McKean. 1960. *The Economics of Defense in the Nuclear Age*. Cambridge: Harvard University Press.

Ho, Virginia Harper. 2010. "'Enlightened Shareholder Value': Corporate Governance Beyond the Shareholder – Stakeholder Divide" *The Journal of Corporation Law* 36:59–112.

Holstein, W. J. 1996. "Santa's Sweatshop." U.S. News and World Report December 16:50–60.

Holt, Glen E. and Donald Elliott. 2003. "Measuring Outcomes: Applying Cost-Benefit Analysis to Middle-Sized and Smaller Public Libraries." *Library Trends* 51(3): 424–440.

Hood, Christopher. 1991. "A Public Management for All Seasons?" *Public Administration* 69.1:3–19.

Hope Consulting. 2010. *Money for Good: The US Market for Impact Investments and Charitable Gifts from Individuals and Investors.* hopeconsulting.us/pdf/Money%20for%20Good_Final.pdf. Retrieved August 5, 2014.

HopeLab. 2012. "About Us." www.hopelab.org/about-us/. Retrieved August 6, 2012.

Hopkins, Bruce R. 2011. *The Law of Tax-Exempt Organizations.* Vol. 5. New York: John Wiley & Sons.

Hopwood, Anthony and Peter Miller. 1994. *Accounting as Social and Institutional Practice.* Vol. 24. Cambridge: Cambridge University Press.

Horrigan, James O. 1968. "A Short History of Financial Ratio Analysis." *Accounting Review* 43(2):284–294.

Hudson, Julie, Hubert Jeaneau, and Eva Tiffany Zlotnicka. 2012. "UBS Investment Research Q-Series: What is 'Integrated Reporting'?" www.theiirc.org/wp-content/uploads/2012/06/UBS-What-Is-Integrated-Reporting.pdf. Retrieved October 11, 2013.

Hufbauer, Gary Clyde and Jeffrey J. Schott. 2013. *Local Content Requirements: A Global Problem.* Vol. 102. Washington, D.C.: Peterson Institute for International Economics.

Hutton, R. Bruce, Louis D'Antonio, and Tommi Johnsen. 1998. "Socially Responsible Investing." *Business & Society* 37(3):281–304.

Hwang, Hokyu and Walter W. Powell. 2009. "The Rationalization of Charity: The Influences of Professionalism in the Nonprofit Sector." *Administrative Science Quarterly* 54(2):268–298.

Hylton, Maria O'Brien. 1992. "Socially Responsible" Investing: Doing Good versus Doing Well in an Inefficient Market." *American University Law Review* 42(1):1–52.

Ianchovichina, Elena and Susanna Lundstrom. 2009. "*What is Inclusive Growth?*" Washington, DC: The World Bank.

Institute for Social Entrepreneurs. 2008. "Evolution of the Social Enterprise Industry: A Chronology of Key Events." Dallas: Institute for Social Entrepreneurs.

Interfaith Center on Corporate Responsibility. 2014. "About Us." www.iccr.org/about-iccr. Retrieved July 26, 2014.

1975. "Corporate Examiner." 4(10).

International Business Leaders Forum. 2005. "Business Action for Development." http://europeandcis.undp.org/guides/poverty/spd/ras/01_Business_action_for_Development_May2005.pdf#! Retrieved November 26, 2013.

International Federation of Accountants. 2012. "Investor Demand for Environmental, Social and Governance Disclosures: Implications for Professional Accountants in Business." www.hesabras.org/Portals/_Rainbow/images/default/download/report%20%20%28ESG%29.pdf. Retrieved March 15, 2013.

International Finance Corporation. 2012. *The Business Case for Sustainability.* Washington, DC: International Finance Corporation

2007. "Developing SMEs through Business Linkages." www.ifc.org/wps/wcm/con nect/topics_ext_content/ifc_external_corporate_site/ifc+sustainability/publications/ publications_handbook_developingsmes. Retrieved October 20, 2013.

International Integrated Reporting Committee. 2013. "Consultation Draft of the International <IR> Framework." www.theiirc.org/wp-content/uploads/Consultation-Draft/Consultation-Draft-of-the-InternationalIRFramework.pdf. Retrieved October 17, 2013.

2011. "Towards Integrated Reporting: Communicating Value in the Twenty-First Century." http://theiirc.org/wp-content/uploads/2011/09/IR-Discussion-Paper-2011_spreads.pdf. Retrieved October 17, 2013.

Internal Revenue Service. 2014a. "Compliance Guide for 501(c)(3) Public Charities." www.irs.gov/pub/irs-pdf/p4221pc.pdf. Retrieved March 17, 2014.

2014b. "Tax Exempt Status for Your Organization: Publication 557." www.irs.gov/ pub/irs-pdf/p557.pdf. Retrieved March 17, 2014.

Investor Responsibility Research Center. 1987. "News for Investors." XIV(2).

IRIS. 2015. "Welcome to IRIS." https://iris.thegiin.org/guide/getting-started-guide. Retrieved February 6, 2015.

2013. "About Us." www.thegiin.org/cgi-bin/iowa/aboutus/index.html. Retrieved March 2, 2013.

2011. *"Data Driven: A Performance Analysis for the Impact Investing Industry."* New York: GIIN and IRIS.

James, Estelle. 1993. "Why Do Different Countries Choose a Different Public-Private Sector Mix of Educational Services?" *Journal of Human Resources* 28.571 92.

Javitz, Carla. 2008. *"REDF's Current Approach to SROI."* San Francisco: REDF.

Jeacle, Ingrid and Chris Carter. 2011. "In TripAdvisor We Trust: Rankings, Calculative Regimes and Abstract Systems." *Accounting, Organizations and Society* 36(4):293–309.

Jenkins, Rhys. 2005. "Globalization, Corporate Social Responsibility and Poverty." *International Affairs* 81(3):525–40.

2001. *Corporate Codes of Conduct: Self-regulation in a Global Economy.* Geneva: United Nations Research Institute for Social Development.

Jensen, Michael C. and William H. Meckling. 1976. "Theory of Firm – Managerial Behavior, Agency Costs and Ownership Structure." *Journal of Financial Economics* 3:305–360.

Johnson, Victoria. 2008. *Backstage at the Revolution: How the Royal Paris Opera Survived the End of the old Regime.* Chicago: University of Chicago Press.

Jones, Candace, Massimo Maoret, Felipe G. Massa, and Silviya Svejenova. 2012. "Rebels with a Cause: Formation, Contestation, and Expansion of the De Novo Category "Modern Architecture," 1870–1975." *Organization Science* 23(6): 1523–1545.

J.P. Morgan. 2013. "Survey Shows Market Growth in Impact Investments and Satisfaction among Investors." www.jpmorgan.com/cm/cs?pagename=JPM_redesign/ JPM_Content_C/Generic_Detail_Page_Template&cid=1320509594546&c=JPM_ Content_C. Retrieved January 15, 2014.

2011. *Insight into the Impact Investment Market: An In-Depth Analysis of Investor Perspectives and over 2,200 Transactions.* New York: J.P. Morgan.

Kalberg, Stephen. 1980. "Max Weber's Types of Rationality: Cornerstones for the Analysis of Rationalization Processes in History." *American Journal of Sociology* 85(5):1145–1179.

Kanani, Rahim. 2011. "The Global Impact Investing Network (GIIN): An Interview with CEO Luther Ragin, Jr." *Forbes* October 30. www.forbes.com/sites/rahimkanani/2011/10/30/the-global-impact-investing-network-giin-an-interview-with-ceo-luther-ragin-jr/. Retrieved March 3, 2015.

Kanter, Rosabeth M. and David V. Summers. 1987. "Doing Well while Doing Good: Dilemmas of Performance Measurement in Nonprofit Organizations and the Need for a Multiple-Constituency Approach." Pp. 154–166 in *The Nonprofit Sector: A Research Handbook*, edited by Walter W. Powell. New Haven: Yale University Press.

Kaplan, Robert S. and D. P. Norton. 1992. "The Balanced Scorecard – Measures That Drive Performance." *Harvard Business Review* (January–February):71–79.

Kaplan, Sarah and Fiona Murray. 2010. "Entrepreneurship and the Construction of Value in Biotechnology." *Research in the Sociology of Organizations* 29: 107–147.

Karnani, A. 2007. "The Mirage of Marketing to the Bottom of the Pyramid." *California Management Review* 49(4):90–111.

Karoly, Lynn A. 2008. *Valuing Benefits in Benefit-Cost Studies of Social Programs.* Santa Monica: Rand Corporation.

Karpik, Lucien. 2010. *Valuing the Unique: The Economics of Singularities.* Princeton: Princeton University Press.

Kates, Robert W., Thomas M. Parris, and Anthony A. Leiserowitz. 2005. "What is Sustainable Development? Goals, Indicators, Values, and Practice." *Environment* 47(3):8–21.

Keck, Margaret E. and Kathryn Sikkink. 1998. *Activists Beyond Borders.* Ithaca, NY: Cornell University Press.

Kerlin, Janelle, ed. 2009. *Social Enterprises: A Global Comparison.* Lebanon: University Press of New England.

Kernaghan, Charles. 1996. "Behind Closed Doors." *The US in Haiti: How to Get Rich on 11¢ an Hour.* Washington, DC: National Labor Committee Education Fund. www.globallabourrights.org/reports/html-file/abstract-51.html. Retrieved August 8, 2014.

Kershaw, David and Jerilyn Fair. 1977. *The New Jersey Income-Maintenance Experiment.* New York: Academic Press.

Kettl, Donald. 1997. "The Global Revolution in Public Management: Driving Themes, Missing Links." *Journal of Policy Analysis and Management* 16(3): 446–462.

Kinder, Peter D. 2005. *Socially Responsible Investing: An Evolving Concept in a Changing World.* Boston: KLD Research & Analytics, Inc.

Kinder, Peter, Steven D. Lydenberg, and Amy Domini. 1994. *Investing for Good: Making Money while Being Socially Responsible.* New York: HarperCollins.

King, Brayden G. and Nicholas A. Pearce. 2010. "The Contentiousness of Markets: Politics, Social Movements, and Institutional Change in Markets." *Annual Review of Sociology* 36:249–267.

Knutsen, Wenjue Lu and Ralph S. Brower. 2010. "Managing Expressive and Instrumental Accountabilities in Nonprofit and Voluntary Organizations: A Qualitative Investigation." *Nonprofit and Voluntary Sector Quarterly* 39(4):588–610.

Kopytoff, Igor. 1998. "The Cultural Biography of Things: Commoditization as Process." Pp. 64–91 in *The Social Life of Things: Commodities in Cultural Perspective*, edited by Arjun Appadurai. Cambridge: Cambridge University Press.

Kozlowski, Lori. 2012. "Impact Investing: The Power of Two Bottom Lines." October 10, 2012. www.forbes.com/sites/lorikozlowski/2012/10/02/impact-investing-the-power-of-two-bottom-lines/. Retrieved April 13, 2013.

KPMG. 2013. "International Survey of Corporate Responsibility Reporting 2013." www.kpmg.com/Global/en/IssuesAndInsights/ArticlesPublications/corporate-responsibility/Documents/kpmg-survey-of-corporate-responsibility-reporting-2013.pdf. Retrieved June 2, 2013.

———. 2012. "Integrated Reporting: Performance Insight through Better Business Reporting." www.kpmg.com/Global/en/IssuesAndInsights/ArticlesPublications/Documents/road-to-integrated-reporting.pdf. Retrieved October 13, 2013.

Kramer, Mark and Sarah Cooch. 2006. *Investing for Impact: Managing and Measuring Proactive Social Investments*. Boston: Foundation Strategy Group.

Kramer, Ralph M. 1981. *Voluntary Agencies in the Welfare State*. Berkeley: University of California Press.

Kramer, Roderick M., Charles G. McClintock, and David M. Messick. 1986. "Social Values and Cooperative Response to a Simulated Resource Conservation Crisis." *Journal of Personality* 54(3):576–592.

Krause, Monika. 2014. *The Good Project: Humanitarian Relief NGOs and the Fragmentation of Reason*. Chicago: University of Chicago Press.

Krippner, Greta R. 2011. *Capitalizing on Crisis*. Cambridge, MA: Harvard University Press.

Kristol, Nicholas D. 1985. "Social-Issue Funds Growing: South Africa a Big Factor." *New York Times* August 17: 35.

Krogh, Matt. 2009. *Channeling Investment for Impact*. Wayne, PA: B-Lab.

Kurtz, Lloyd, Steve Lydenberg, and Peter Kinder. 1992. "The Domini Social Index: A New Benchmark for Social Investors." *Social Investment Almanac: A Comprehensive Guide to Socially Responsible Investing*, edited by Amy Domini, Peter Kinder, and Steven Lydenberg. New York: Henry Holt & Co.

Lafaye, C. and L. Thévenot. 1993. "Une Justification Ecologique? Conflits Dans L'ame Nagement De La Nature." *Revue Francaise De Sociologie* 34(4):495–524.

Lamont, Michèle. 2012. "Toward a Comparative Sociology of Valuation and Evaluation." *Annual Review of Sociology* 38(21):201–221.

———. 2009. *How Professors Think*. Cambridge, MA: Harvard University Press.

Langbein, J. H. and R. A. Posner. 1980. "Social Investing and the Law of Trusts." *Michigan Law Review* 79(1):72–112.

Laufer, William S. 2003. "Social Accountability and Corporate Greenwashing." *Journal of Business Ethics* 43(3):253–261.

Lele, Sharachchandra M. 1991. "Sustainable Development: a Critical Review." *World Development* 19(6):607–621.

LeRoux, Kelly and Nathaniel S. Wright. 2010. "Does Performance Measurement Improve Strategic Decision Making? Findings from a National Survey of Nonprofit Social Service Agencies." *Nonprofit and Voluntary Sector Quarterly* 39(4): 571–587.

Letts, Christine, William P. Ryan, and Allen Grossman. 1997. "Virtuous Capital: What Foundations Can Learn from Venture Capitalists." *Harvard Business Review*, March/April:2–7.

Levin, Peter. 2008. "Culture and Markets: How Economic Sociology Conceptualizes Culture." *The Annals of the American Academy of Political and Social Science* 619:114–129.

Lewis, Michael. 2004. *Moneyball: The Art of Winning an Unfair Game*. New York: WW Norton & Company.

Lieberson, Stanley. 1991. "Small N's and Big Conclusions: An Examination of the Reasoning in Comparative Studies Based on a Small Number of Cases." *Social Forces* 70(2):307–320.

Liou, Y. Thomas and Robert C. Stroh. 1998. "Community Development Intermediary Systems in the United States: Origins, Evolution, and Functions." *Housing Policy Debate* 9(3):575–594.

Lohmann, Roger A. 1999. "Has the Time Come to Reevaluate Evaluation? or, Who Will Be Accountable for Accountability?" *Nonprofit Management and Leadership* 10(1):93–101.

London, Ted. 2009. "Making Better Investments at the Base of the Pyramid." *Harvard Business Review* 87(5):106–113.

Longstreth, Bevis and H. David Rosenbloom. 1973. *Corporate Social Responsibility and the Institutional Investor: A Report to the Ford Foundation*. New York: Praeger.

Lydenberg Steve, J. Rogers, and David Wood. 2010. *From Transparency to Performance: Industry-Based Sustainability Reporting on Key Issues*. The Hauser Center for Nonprofit Organizations at Harvard University.

MacKenzie, Donald and Yuval Millo. 2003. "Negotiating a Market, Performing Theory: The Historical Sociology of a Financial Derivatives Exchange." *American Journal of Sociology* 109:107–145.

Mackey, John and Rajendra Sisodia. 2013. *Conscious Capitalism: Liberating the Heroic Spirit of Business*. Cambridge, MA: Harvard Business Review.

Madan, Renu. 2007. *"Demystifying Outcome Measurement in Community Development."* Cambridge, MA: Joint Center for Housing Studies of Harvard University.

Maguire, Steve, Cynthia Hardy, and Thomas B. Lawrence. 2004. "Institutional Entrepreneurship in Emerging Fields: HIV/AIDS Treatment Advocacy in Canada." *Academy of Management Journal* 47:657–679.

Mansbridge, Jane. 1998. "On the Contested Nature of the Public Good." Pp. 3–19 in *Private Action and the Public Good*, edited by Walter W. Powell and Elisabeth Clemens. New Haven: Yale University Press.

Margolis, Joshua D. and James P. Walsh. 2003. "Misery Loves Companies: Rethinking Social Initiatives by Business." *Administrative Science Quarterly* 48(2):268–305.

Markowitz, Harry. 1952. "Portfolio Selection." *The Journal of Finance* 7(1):77–91.

Markowitz, Linda, Denise Cobb, and Mark Hedley. 2012. "Framing Ambiguity: Insider/Outsiders and the Successful Legitimation Project of the Socially Responsible Mutual Fund Industry." *Organization* 19:3–23.

Martin, Josh. 1986. "Happy Returns for Do-Gooders." *Financial World* March 18.

Martin, Roger L. 2011. *Fixing the Game: Bubbles, Crashes, and what Capitalism can Learn from the NFL*. Cambridge, MA: Harvard Business Press.

Martin, Roger L. and Sally Osberg. 2007. "Social Entrepreneurship: The Case for Definition." *Stanford Social Innovation Review* 5(2): 28–39.

Marx, Jerry, and Christie Davis. 2012. "Nonprofit Governance: Improving Performance in Troubled Economic Times." *Administration in Social Work* 36(1):40–52.

Marx, Karl. 1867/1992. *Capital: Volume 1: A Critique of Political Economy.* London: Penguin Classics.

Mason, David E. 1996. *Leading and Managing the Expressive Dimension: Harnessing the Hidden Power Source of the Nonprofit Sector.* San Francisco: Jossey-Bass, Inc.

Massarsky, Cynthia and Samantha L. Beinhacker. 2002. *Enterprising Nonprofits: Revenue Generation in the Nonprofit Sector.* Englewood Cliffs, NJ: Yale School of Management and the Goldman Sachs Foundation Partnership on Nonprofit Ventures.

McMillen, A. W. 1930. *Measurement in Social Work: A Statistical Problem in Family and Children Welfare and Allied Fields.* Chicago: University of Chicago Press.

Melkers, Julia, and Katherine Willoughby. 2005. "Models of Performance-Measurement Use in Local Governments: Understanding Budgeting, Communication, and Lasting Effects." *Public Administration Review* 65(2):180–190.

Mendoza, Ronald U. and Nina Thelen. 2008. "Innovations to Make Markets More Inclusive for the Poor." *Development Policy Review* 26(4):427–458.

Meyer, John and Brian Rowan. 1977. "Institutionalized Organizations: Formal Structure as Myth and Ceremony." *American Journal of Sociology* 83:333–63.

Meyer, John W., William R. Scott, D. Strang, and A. L. Creighton. 1994. "Bureaucratization without Centralization: Changes in the Organizational System of U.S. Public Education, 1940–1980." Pp. 179–205 in *Institutional Environments and Organizations: Structural Complexity and Individualism,* edited by William R. Scott and John W. Meyer. Thousand Oaks, CA: Sage.

Miles, Matthew B. and A. Miles Huberman. 1994. *Qualitative Data Analysis: A Sourcebook of New Methods,* second edition. Beverley Hills, CA: Sage.

Mill, John Stuart. 1950. *Philosophy of Scientific Method,* edited by Ernest Nagel. New York: Hafner.

Miller, Alan Jay. 1991. *Socially Responsible Investing: How to Invest with Your Conscience.* New York: New York Institute of Finance.

Miller, Peter. 2001. "Governing by Numbers: Why Calculative Practices Matter." *Social Research* 68(2):379–396.

Miller, Robin Lin and Valerie Caracelli. 2013. "The Oral History of Evaluation: The Professional Development of Joseph Wholey." *American Journal of Evaluation* 34(1):120–131.

Milligan, Katherine and Miriam Schoning. 2011. "Taking a Realistic Approach to Impact Investing." *Innovations Journal* September: 161–172.

Mills, John Stuart. 1861/2007. *Utilitarianism, Liberty & Representative Government.* Rockville, MD: Wildside Press.

Milward, H. Brinton, and Keith G. Provan. 2000. "Governing the Hollow State." *Journal of Public Administration Research and Theory* 10(2):359–380.

Mintzberg, Henry. 1994. *Rise and Fall of Strategic Planning.* New York: Simon and Schuster.

Mishan, Edward J. and Euston Quah. 2007. *Cost Benefit Analysis.* New York: Routledge.

Mitchell, George E. 2012. "The Construct of Organizational Effectiveness: Perspectives from Leaders of International Nonprofits in the United States." *Nonprofit and Voluntary Sector Quarterly* 42(2):324–345.

Mizruchi, Mark S. 2013. *The Fracturing of the American Corporate Elite.* Cambridge, MA: Harvard University Press.

Monitor Institute. 2009. *Investing for Social and Environmental Impact*. New York: Monitor Institute.

Moody, Michael. 2008. "Building a Culture: The Construction and Evolution of Venture Philanthropy as a New Organizational Field." *Nonprofit and Voluntary Sector Quarterly* 37:324–352.

Moore, Mark Harrison. 1995. *Creating Public Value: Strategic Management in Government*. Cambridge: Harvard University Press.

Morduch, Jonathan. 1999. "The Microfinance Promise." *Journal of Economic Literature* 37(4):1569–1614.

Morley, Elaine, Elisa Vinson, and Harry P. Hatry. 2001. *Outcome Measurement in Nonprofit Organizations: Current Practices and Recommendations*. Washington, DC: Urban Institute.

Moxham, Claire and Ruth Boaden. 2007. "The Impact of Performance Measurement in the Voluntary Sector: Identification of Contextual and Processual Factors." *International Journal of Operations & Production Management* 27(8):826–845.

Mulgan, Geoff. 2010. "Measuring Social Value." *Stanford Social Innovation Review* Summer 38–43.

Nader, Ralph and Mark J. Green. 1973. *Corporate Power in America*. New York: Grossman Publishers.

Nadvi, Khalid and Frank Wältring. 2001. *Making Sense of Global Standards (Draft IDS-INEP working paper)*. Sussex: Institute for Development Studies.

Narain, Saurabh and Joseph Schmidt. 2009. "NCIF Social Performance Metrics: Increasing the Flow of Investments in Distressed Neighborhoods through Community Development Banking Institutions." *Community Development Investment Review* 6(1):65–75.

National Center for Charitable Statistics. 2014. "National Taxonomy of Exempt Entities." http://nccs.urban.org/classification/NTEE.cfm. Retrieved August 24, 2014.

National Information Bureau. 1958. *Safeguard We Must the Contributor's Trust*. New York: National Information Bureau.

Nelson, Jane. 2003. "Economic Multipliers: Revisiting the Core Responsibility and Contribution of Business to Development." IBLF Policy Paper No. 4.

Nelson, Jane and Dave Prescott. 2008. *Business and the Millennium Development Goals: A Framework for Action*, second edition. London: International Business Leaders Forum.

Nestlé Peru and WBCSD/SNV. 2011. "Nestle Peru and the WBCSD-SNV Alliance for Inclusive Business: 'Bienestar en Casa': Measuring the Impact of an Innovative Distribution Business Model for Nutritional Food in Peru." www.inclusivebusiness.org/nestle_peru_measuring_impact_march2011.pdf. Retrieved November 15, 2014.

New Economics Foundation. 2007. *Measuring Real Value: A DIY Guide to Social Return on Investment*. London: New Economics Foundation.

New York Times. 1982. "In Stocks, All the Saints Are Sinners." February 7: 3

Nicholls, Jeremy, Ellis Lawlor, Eva Neitzert, and Tim Goodspeed. 2009. *A Guide to Social Return on Investment*. London: Office of the Third Sector, The Cabinet Office.

Novick, David, ed. 1967. *Program Budgeting: Program Analysis and the Federal Budget*. Cambridge, MA: Harvard University Press.

O'Connor, Rory. 1989. "Clean vs. Dirty." *Mother Jones Magazine* June: 56–57.

OECD. 2007. Promoting Pro-Poor Growth: Policy Guidance for Donors. www.oecd
.org/dac/povertyreduction/promotingpro-poorgrowthpolicyguidancefordonors
.htm. Retrieved January 2, 2015.

2004. "Accelerating Pro-Poor Growth through Support for Private Sector Development:
An Analytical Framework." www.gsdrc.org/document-library/accelerating-pro-poor-
growth-through-support-for-private-sector-development/. Retrieved January 11, 2015.

Olsen, Sara and Brent Galimidi. 2008. *Catalog of Approaches to Impact Measurement.*
San Francisco: Social Ventures Technology Group.

Olson, Mancur. 1965. *Logic of Collective Action: Public Goods and the Theory of
Groups.* Cambridge, MA: Harvard University Press.

Orlitzky, Marc, Frank L. Schmidt, and Sara L. Rynes. 2003. "Corporate Social and
Financial Performance: A Meta-Analysis." *Organization Studies* 24.3:403–441.

O'Rourke, Dara. 2005. "Market Movements: Nongovernmental Organization Strategies to Influence Global Production and Consumption." *Journal of Industrial
Ecology* 9:115–28.

2003. "Outsourcing Regulation: Analyzing Nongovernmental Systems of Labor
Standards and Monitoring." *Policy Studies Journal* 31(1):1–29.

Ortega, Bob. 1995. "Conduct Codes Garner Goodwill for Retailers: But Violations
Go On." *Wall Street Journal* July 3: 1.

Osborne, David and Ted Gaebler. 1992. *Reinventing Government: How the Entrepreneurial Spirit is Transforming the Public Sector.* Reading, MA: Addison-Wesley.

O'Sullivan, Mary. 2001. *Contests for Corporate Control: Corporate Governance and
Economic Performance in the United States and Germany.* London: Oxford
University Press.

Owens, Patricia. 2013. "From Bismarck to Petraeus: The Question of the Social and
the Social Question in Counterinsurgency." *European Journal of International
Relations* 19(1):139–161.

Oxfam International. 2009. "Oxfam Poverty Footprint: Understanding Business
Contribution to Development." *Briefings for Business* 4. Oxford, UK: Oxfam
International Secretariat.

Padgett, J. F. and C. K. Ansell. 1993. "Robust Action and the Rise of the Medici,
1400–1434." *American Journal of Sociology* 98:1259.

Paine, Lynn, Rohit Deshpandé, Joshua D. Margolis, and Kim Eric Bettcher. 2005.
"Up to Code: Does Your Company's Conduct Meet World-Class Standards?"
Harvard Business Review 83(12):122–135.

Panel on the Nonprofit Sector. 2005. *Strengthening Transparency, Governance,
Accountability of Charitable Organizations: A Final Report to Congress and the
Nonprofit Sector.* Washington, DC: Independent Sector.

Parmelee, Maurice. 1920. *Poverty and Social Progress.* New York: The Macmillan
Company.

Parmenter, David. 2011. *Key Performance Indicators: Developing, Implementing, and
Using Winning KPIs.* New York: John Wiley & Sons, Inc.

Pattberg, Philipp H. 2007. *Private Institutions and Global Governance: The New
Politics of Environmental Sustainability.* New York: Edward Elgar Publishing.

Pax World Investments. 2014. "A Leader in Sustainable Investing." www.paxworld
.com. Retrieved March 21, 2014.

Perlmann, Joel and Mary Waters. 2002. *The New Race Question: How the Census
Counts Multiracial Individuals.* New York: Russell Sage Foundation.

Peters, Thomas J. and Robert H. Waterman, Jr. 1982. *In Search of Excellence.* New York: Harper.

Pettijohn, Sarah L. 2013. *The Nonprofit Sector in Brief: Public Charities, Giving, and Volunteering, 2013.* Washington, DC: Independent Sector.

Pike, Alan. 1989. "Survey of Charities (2): Shell: Grants Are Good Business – The Importance of Corporate Support." *Financial Times,* December 11.

Piller, Charles, Edmund Sanders, and Robyn Dixon. 2007. "Dark Cloud over Good Works of Gates Foundation." *The Los Angeles Times January* 7:A1.

Pine Street Inn. 2014. "iCater: Corporate Catering for a Cause." www.pinestreetinn .org/social_enterprise/icater. Retrieved December 16, 2014.

Plantz, Margaret C., Martha T. Greenway, and Michael Hendricks. 1997. "Outcome Measurement: Showing Results in the Nonprofit Sector." Pp. 15–30 in *Using Performance Measurement to Improve Public and Nonprofit Programs,* edited by Kathryn E. Newcomer. San Francisco: Jossey-Bass.

Podger, Pamela. 1986. "Principal Meets Principle; Morals Aren't Mortgaged with Socially Responsible Funds." *American Banker* May 20. 151.

Poland, Orville F. 1974. "Program Evaluation and Administrative Theory." *Public Administration Review* 34(4):333–338.

Polanyi, Karl. 1957. "The Economy as Instituted Process." Pp. 243–270 in *Trade and Market in the Early Empires,* edited by Karl Polanyi, C. M. Arensberg and H. W. Pearson. London: Collier Macmillan.

1944. *The Great Transformation.* New York: Rinehart.

Porter, Michael E. and Mark R. Kramer. 2011. "Creating Shared Value." *Harvard Business Review* 89(1/2): 62–77.

Porter, Theodore M. 1995. *Trust in Numbers: The Pursuit of Objectivity in Science and Public Life.* Princeton, N.J.: Princeton University Press.

1994. "Making Things Quantitative." Pp. 36–56 in *Accounting and Science, Natural Inquiry and Commercial Reason,* edited by Michael Power. New York: Cambridge University Press.

Poverty Cure. 2014. "Malik Fal – Advocacy for Small-Medium Enterprises." www.povertycure.org/voices/malik-fal/. Retrieved August 3, 2014.

Power, Michael. 1994. *The Audit Explosion.* London: Demos.

Powers, Charles W. 1971. *Social Responsibility & Investments.* Nashville: Abingdon Press.

Prahalad, C. K. 2004. *The Fortune at the Bottom of the Pyramid.* Philadelphia: Wharton School Publishing.

Prasad, Monica. 2006. *The Politics of Free Markets: The Rise of Neoliberal Economic Policies in Britain, France, Germany, and the United States.* Chicago: University of Chicago Press.

Pressman, Jeffrey L. and Aaron B. Wildavsky. 1973. *Implementation: How Grert Expectations in Washington Are Dashed in Oakland; Or, Why It's Amazing that Federal Programs Work at All …* Berkeley: University of California Press.

Principles for Responsible Investment. 2014. "The Six Principles." www.unpri.org/ about-pri/the-six-principles/. Retrieved August 28, 2014.

2013a. "Building the Capacity of Investment Actors to Use Environmental, Social and Governance Information." http://ec.europa.eu/enterprise/policies/sustainable-business/files/reporting-disclosure/7-building-esg-capacity_en.pdf. Retrieved July 1, 2013.

2013b. "Integrated Analysis: How Investors Are Addressing Environmental, Social and Governance Factors in Fundamental Equity Valuation." www.unpri.org/viewer/?file=wp-content/uploads/Integrated_Analysis_2013.pdf. Retrieved August 3, 2013.

2011. "5 Years of PRI: Report on Progress." www.unpri.org/viewer/?file=wp-content/uploads/annual_report2011.pdf. Retrieved January 13, 2014.

Privcap. 2012. "Sign Here for Responsible Investing." www.privcap.com/sign-here-for-responsible-investing/. Retrieved September 3, 2013.

Proffitt, W. Trexler and Andrew Spicer. 2006. "Shaping the Shareholder Activism Agenda: Institutional Investors and Global Social Issues." *Strategic Organization* 4(2):165–190.

Putnam, Robert D. 2000. *Bowling Alone: The Collapse and Revival of American Community.* New York: Simon & Schuster.

PWC. 2013. "Integrated Reporting: Going Beyond the Financial Results." www.pwc.com/us/en/cfodirect/publications/point-of-view/integrated-reporting-pov.jhtml. Retrieved October 12, 2013.

Quinn, Sarah. 2008. "The Transformation of Morals in Markets: Death, Benefits, and the Exchange of Life Insurance Policies." *American Journal of Sociology* 114(3): 738–780

Radin, Beryl A. 2006. *Challenging the Performance Movement: Accountability, Complexity, and Democratic Values.* Washington, DC: Georgetown University Press.

Radin, Margaret. 2001 *Contested Commodities: The Trouble with Trade in Sex, Children, Body Parts, and Other Things.* Cambridge, MA: Harvard University Press

Ralph, Georgia. 1915. *Elements of Record Keeping for Child Helping Organizations.* New York: Survey Associates.

Ramani, Shyama V. and Vivekananda Mukherjee. 2014. "Can Breakthrough Innovations Serve the Poor (BOP) and Create Reputational (CSR) Value? Indian Case Studies." *Technovation* 34(5): 295–305.

Ramirez, Jaime. 2011. "Economic Empowerment through Enterprise." *Innovations* 6(3):107–115.

Ramey, Joanna. 1997. "Textile, Apparel Importers Set up PAC." *Women's Wear Daily* November 25:13–14.

Rasche, Andreas and Georg Kell, eds. 2010. *The United Nations Global Compact: Achievements, Trends and Challenges.* New York: Cambridge University Press.

Rawls, John. 1971. *A Theory of Justice.* Cambridge: Belknap Press.

Reay, Trish, Golden-Biddle Karen, and Kathy Germann. 2006. "Legitimizing a New Role: Small Wins and Microprocesses of Change." *Academy of Management Journal* 49:977–998.

REDF. 2000. "Social Return on Investment (SROI) Collection." www.redf.org/learn-from-redf/publications/119. Retrieved February 6, 2011.

Reich, Adam D. 2014. "Contradictions in the Commodification of Hospital Care." *American Journal of Sociology* 119(6):1576–1628.

Reinecke, Juliane and S. Ansari. 2012. "*The Politics of Values and Value Creation.*" Academy of Management Best Paper Proceedings.

Reis, Tom. 2003. "Blurred Boundaries and Muddled Motives: A World of Shifting Social Responsibilities." www.wkkf.org/knowledge-center/resources/2003/12/Blurred-Boundaries-And-Muddled-Motives-A-World-Of-Shifting-Social-Responsibilities.aspx. Retrieved October 13, 2012.

Rivlin, Alice M. 1971. *Systematic Thinking for Social Action*, Vol. 3. New York: Brookings Institution Press.

Rivlin, Alice M. and Joseph S. Wholey. 1969. "Education of Disadvantaged Children." *Socio-Economic Planning Sciences* 2(2):373–380.

Robeco Group and Booz & Co. 2008. *Responsible Investing: A Paradigm Shift from Niche to Mainstream*. New York: Robeco Group.

Rockefeller Philanthropy Advisors. 2010. *Solutions for Impact Investors: From Strategy to Implementation*. New York: Rockefeller Philanthropy Advisors.

2006. *Finding Philanthropy's New Sweet Spot: Powerful and Innovative Ideas for Grantmakers, Investors, and Nonprofits*. New York: Rockefeller Philanthropy Advisors.

Rockness, Joanne and Paul F. Williams. 1988. "A Descriptive Study of Social Responsibility Mutual Funds." *Accounting, Organizations and Society* 13(4):397–411.

Rosato, Donna. 1997. "Critics: Apparel Pact Is Wrinkled." *U.S.A. Today* April 14:B3.

Rose, Nikolas. 1993. "Government, Authority and Expertise in Advanced Liberalism." *Economy and Society* 22(3):283–299.

Rosenstiel, Thomas B. 1983. "Making Money Work: Ethical Investing: A Way to Put Your Money Where Your Conscience Is." *Los Angeles Times* October 30:E2.

Rossman, Gabriel. 2014. "Obfuscatory Relational Work and Disreputable Exchange." *Sociological Theory* 32(1): 43–63.

Rossi, Peter, Mark W. Lipsey, and Howard E. Freeman. 2004. *Evaluation: A Systematic Approach*. Thousand Oaks, CA: Sage Publications.

Roy, Ananya. 2010. *Poverty Capital: Microfinance and the Making of Development*. New York: Routledge.

Saith, Ashwani. 2006. "From Universal Values to Millennium Development Goals: Lost in Translation." *Development and Change* 37(6):1167–1199.

Salamon, Lester M., ed. 2012. *The State of Nonprofit America*. New York: Brookings Institution Press.

1993. "The Marketization of Welfare: Changing Nonprofit and For-Profit Roles in the American Welfare State." *The Social Service Review* 67(1):16–39.

1987. "Of Market Failure, Voluntary Failure, and Third-Party Government: Toward a Theory of Government-Nonprofit Relations in the Modern Welfare State." *Nonprofit and Voluntary Sector Quarterly* 16(1–2):29–49.

Salesforce. 2012. "Health and Human Services." www.salesforce.com/solutions/public-sector/health-human-services.jsp. Retrieved January 2, 2012.

Salvation Army. 1916. *Yearbook*. London: Salvation Army.

Samuelson, Paul A. 1954. "The Pure Theory of Public Expenditure". *Review of Economics and Statistics* 36(4):387–389.

Sand, Jess. 2010. "Beyond the Sweatshop: Poverty Footprints and Supply Chains." *Guardian* October 26. www.theguardian.com/sustainable-business/beyond-sweatshop-supply-chain-assessment. Retrieved July 15, 2014.

Sandel, Michael J. 2012. *What Money Can't Buy: The Moral Limits of Markets*. New York: Macmillan.

Sassen, Saskia. 2007. *A Sociology of Globalization*. New York: W.W. Norton & Company, Inc.

Sawhill, John C. and David Williamson. 2001. "Mission Impossible? Measuring Success in Nonprofit Organizations." *Nonprofit Management and Leadership* 11(3):371–386.

Schatz, Robin. 1985. "When Conscience Rules." *New York Times* October 13:F14

Schlegelmilch, Bodo B. 1997. "The Relative Importance of Ethical and Environmental Screening: Implications for the Marketing of Ethical Investment Funds." *International Journal of Bank Marketing* 15(2):48–53.

Schlesinger, Jacob M. 1984. "Investing Based on Social Issues is Gaining Adherents Among the Children of the '60s." *The Wall Street Journal* July 11, 1984.

Schlesinger, Mark, Shannon Mitchell, and Bradford H. Gray. 2004. "Restoring Public Legitimacy to the Nonprofit Sector: A Survey Experiment using Descriptions of Nonprofit Ownership." *Nonprofit and Voluntary Sector Quarterly* 33(4):673–710.

Schneiberg, Marc and Elisabeth S. Clemens. 2006. "The Typical Tools for the Job: Research Strategies in Institutional Analysis." *Sociological Theory* 24(3):195–227.

Schneider, Anne and Helen Ingram. 1993. "Social Construction of Target Populations: Implications for Politics and Policy." *American Political Science Review* 87(02):334–347.

Schueth, Steve. 2003. "Socially Responsible Investing in the United States." *Journal of Business Ethics* 43(3):189–194.

Scrivner, George N. 2001. "A Brief History of Tax Policy Changes Affecting Charitable Organizations." Pp. 126–142 in *The Nature of the Nonprofit Sector*, edited by J. S. Ott. Boulder, CO: Westview.

Seelos, Christian and Johanna Mair. 2005. "Social Entrepreneurship: Creating New Business Models to Serve The Poor." *Business Horizons* 48:241–246.

Seidman, Gay W. 2007. *Beyond the Boycott: Labor Rights, Human Rights, and Transnational Activism*. Ithaca, NY: Cornell University Press.

Sen, Amartya. 1999. *Development as Freedom*. New York: Anchor Books.

——— 1979. "Utilitarianism and Welfarism." *The Journal of Philosophy* 76(9):463–489.

Sewell, William H. 1996. "Three Temporalities: Toward an Eventful Sociology," Pp. 245–80 in *The Historic Turn in the Human Sciences*, edited by Terrence J. McDonald. Ann Arbor: University of Michigan Press.

——— 1992. "A Theory of Structure: Duality, Agency, and Transformation." *American Journal of Sociology* 98(1):1–29.

Shamir, Ronen. 2008. "The Age of Responsibilization: On Market-Embedded Morality." *Economy and Society* 37(1):1–19.

Shane, Philip B. and Barry H. Spicer. 1983. "Market Response to Environmental Information Produced Outside the Firm." *The Accounting Review* 58(3):521–538.

Shapiro, Harvey. 1983. "Doing Well While Doing Good." *New York Times* August 7:F17.

Shapiro, Joan. 1992. "The Movement since 1970." *Social Investment Almanac: A Comprehensive Guide to Socially Responsible Investing*, edited by Amy Domini, Peter Kinder, and Steven Lydenberg. New York: Henry Holt & Co.

Sheehan, Robert M. 1996. "Mission Accomplishment as Philanthropic Effectiveness: Key Findings from the Excellence in Philanthropy Project." *Nonprofit and Voluntary Sector Quarterly* 25(1):110–123.

Siha, Samia. 1998. "Physician Outcome Measurement: Review and Proposed Model." *International Journal of Health Care Quality Assurance* 11(6):193–203.

Silby, Wayne, 2011. "Impact Investing: Frontier Stories." *Innovations Journal* September: 17–22.

Simmel, Georg. 1907/1990. *The Philosophy of Money*, edited by D.P. Frisby. London: Routledge.

Simon, Herbert A. 1956. "Rational Choice and the Structure of the Environment." *Psychological Review* 63(2):129–138.

Simon, John, and Julia Barmeier. 2011. *More than Money: Impact Investing for Development*. Washington, DC: Center for Global Development.

Simon, John, Charles W. Powers, and Jon P. Gunneman: 1972. *The Ethical Investor: Universities and Corporate Responsibility*. New Haven: Yale University.

Smith, Adam. 1776/2012. *The Wealth of Nations*. New York: Simon & Brown.

Smith, Charles W. 2007. "Markets as Definitional Mechanisms: A Robust Alternative Sociological Paradigm." *Canadian Journal of Sociology* 32(1):1–39.

Smith, Steven Rathgeb 2010. "Nonprofits and Public Administration: Reconciling Performance Management and Citizen Engagement." *The American Review of Public Administration* 40(2):129–152.

Smith, Steven Rathgeb and Michael Lipsky. 1993. *Nonprofits for Hire: The Welfare State in the Age of Contracting*. Cambridge, MA: Harvard University Press.

Social Accountability International. 2014. "SAI8000 Standard." www.sa-intl.org/index .cfm?fuseaction=Page.ViewPage&pageId=1365. Retrieved August 3, 2014.

Social Enterprise Alliance. 2012. "What is Social Enterprise?" www.se-alliance.org/ what-is-social-enterprise. Retrieved August 16, 2012.

Social Investment Forum Foundation. 2010. "*2010 Report on Socially Responsible Investing Trends in the United States.*" Washington, DC: Social Investment Forum Foundation.

  1995. "After South Africa: The State of Socially Responsible Investing in the United States." www.ussif.org/files/Publications/95_trends_Report.pdf. Retrieved July 25, 2014.

Social Solutions. 2012. "Human Services Software." www.socialsolutions.com/eto-impact-non-profit-software.aspx. Retrieved January 2, 2012.

Soederberg, Susanne. 2009. "The Marketisation of Social Justice: The Case of the Sudan Divestment Campaign." *New Political Economy* 14(2):211–229.

Solenberg, Edwin D. 1909. "The Essentials of an Annual Report." Proceedings. National Conference of Charities and Corrections.

Somers, Margaret R. and Fred Block. 2005. "From Poverty to Perversity: Ideas, Markets, and Institutions over 200 Years of Welfare Debate." *American Sociological Review* 70(2):260–287.

Soros, George. 2000. *The Open Society: Reforming Global Capitalism*. New York: Public Affairs Press.

Soule, Sarah A. 2009. *Contentious and Corporate Social Responsibility*. Cambridge, UK: Cambridge University Press.

Spar, Debora L. 2013. *The Baby Business: How Money, Science, and Politics Drive the Commerce of Conception*. Cambridge, MA: Harvard Business Press.

Speckbacher, Gerhard. 2003. "The Economics of Performance Management in Non-profit Organizations." *Nonprofit Management and Leadership* 13(3):267–281.

Stark, David. 2011. *The Sense of Dissonance*. Princeton: Princeton University Press.

Steinberg, Richard and Walter W. Powell. 2006. "Introduction." Pp. 1–12 in *The Nonprofit Sector: A Research Handbook*, edited by Richard Steinberg and Walter W. Powell. New Haven: Yale University Press.

Steinmetz, George. 1993. *Regulating the Social: The Welfare State and Local Politics in Imperial Germany*. Princeton, NJ: Princeton University Press.

Stiglitz, Joseph. 2002. *Globalization and its Discontents*. New York: W.W. Norton & Co.

  1989. "Markets, Market Failures, and Development." *The American Economic Review* 79(2):197–203.

Stiglitz, Joseph E. and Andrew Charlton. 2005. *Fair Trade for All: How Trade Can Promote Development*. Oxford: Oxford University Press.

Stone, Melissa Middleton, Mark A. Hager, and Jennifer J. Griffin. 2001. "Organizational Characteristics and Funding Environments: A Study of a Population of United Way-Affiliated Nonprofits." *Public Administration Review* 61(3):276–289.

Stout, Lynn A. 2012. *The Shareholder Value Myth: How Putting Shareholders First Harms Investors, Corporations, and the Public*. San Francisco: Berrett-Koehler Publishers.

Straf, Miron L. 1996. "Discussion." Pp. 35–40 in *Proceedings of the Census Bureau Annual Research Conference and Technology Interchange*. www.census.gov/prod/2/gen/96arc/istraf.pdf. Retrieved March 1, 2014.

Strang, David, and John W. Meyer. 1993. "Institutional Conditions for Diffusion." *Theory and Society* 22(4):487–511.

Sturges Judith E. and Kathleen J. Hanrahan. 2004. "Comparing Telephone and Face-to-Face Qualitative Interviewing: A Research Note." *Qualitative Research* 4:107–118.

Suchman, Edward. 1967. *Evaluative Research: Principles and Practice in Public Service and Social Action Programs*. New York: Russell Sage.

Suchman, Mark C. 1995. "Managing Legitimacy: Strategic and Institutional Approaches." *Academy of Management Review* 20(3):571–610.

Suddaby, Roy and Royston Greenwood. 2005. "Rhetorical Strategies of Legitimacy." *Administrative Science Quarterly* 50(1):35–67.

Suleiman, Ezra N. 2013. *Dismantling Democratic States*. Princeton, NJ: Princeton University Press.

SustainAbility. 2010. "Rate the Raters Phase Two: Taking Inventory of the Ratings Universe." London: SustainAbility.

Sustainability Accounting Standards Board. 2013. "Conceptual Framework of the Sustainability Accounting Standards Board." www.sasb.org/wp-content/uploads/2013/10/SASB-Conceptual-Framework-Oct-3.pdf. Retrieved October 21, 2013.

Sustainability Asset Management. 2012. "*Corporate Sustainability Assessment Methodology Measuring Intangibles*." Zurich: Sustainability Asset Management.

2008. *The Sustainability Yearbook 2008*. Zurich: Sustainability Asset Management.

Swidler, Ann. 1986. "Culture in Action: Symbols and Strategies." *American Sociological Review* 51:273–86.

Swoboda, Frank. 1992. "Levi Strauss to Drop Suppliers Violating Its Worker Rights Rules." *Washington Post* March 13:D1.

Taylor, Martha E. and Russy D. Sumariwalla. 1993. "Evaluating Nonprofit Effectiveness: Overcoming the Barriers." Pp. 93–116 in *Governing, Leading and Managing Nonprofit Organizations*, edited by Dennis R. Young, Robert M. Hollister, and Virginia Ann Hodgkinson. San Francisco: Jossey Bass.

Thomson, Dale E. 2010. "Exploring the Role of Funders' Performance Reporting Mandates in Nonprofit Performance Measurement." *Nonprofit and Voluntary Sector Quarterly* 39(4):611–629.

Thompson, Frank J. and Norma M. Riccucci. 1998. "Reinventing Government." *Annual Review of Political Science* 1:231–257.

Thomson Reuters. 2014. "Corporate Responsibility Indices." http://thomsonreuters.com/corporate-responsibility-indices/. Retrieved April 4, 2014.

Thornton, Patricia H., William Ocasio, and Michael Lounsbury. 2012. *The Institutional Logics Perspective: A New Approach*. London: Oxford University Press.

Tilly, Charles. 1986. "European Violence and Collective Action since 1700." *Social Research* 53(1):159–184.

Titmuss, Richard.1971. *The Gift Relationship: From Human Blood to Social Policy.* New York: Vintage.

Tocqueville, Alexis De. (1835) 1966. *Democracy in America.* New York: Harper & Row.

Tolbert, Patricia S. and Lynn G. Zucker. 1996. "Institutionalization of Institutional Theory." Pp. 175–190 in *The Handbook of Organization Studies*, edited by Stewart Clegg, Cynthia Hardy, and Walter R. Nord. Thousand Oaks, CA: Sage.

Townley, Barbara. 1997. "The Institutional Logic of Performance Appraisal." *Organization Studies* 18(2):261–285.

     1993. "Foucault, Power/Knowledge, and Its Relevance for Human Resource Management." *Academy of Management Review* 18(3):518–545.

Trausch, Susan. 1981. "Ethical Investing." *Boston Globe* April 14:35.

Tuan, Melinda. 2008. *"Measuring and/or Estimating Social Value Creation."* Seattle: Bill and Melinda Gates Foundation.

     2002. *"REDF: Reflections on Five Years of Venture Philanthropy Implementation."* Washington, DC: Venture Philanthropy Partners, Inc.

Tuan, Melinda and Jed Emerson. 1999. "The Roberts Enterprise Development Fund: A Case Study on Venture Philanthropy." Pp. 1–12 in *Social Purpose Enterprises and Venture Philanthropy in the New Millennium.* San Francisco: The Roberts Foundation.

Tullis, Paul. 2011. "Bloomberg's Push for Corporate Sustainability." *Fast Company* April 1.

Turco, Catherine. 2012. "Difficult Decoupling: Employee Resistance to the Commercialization of Personal Settings." *American Journal of Sociology* 118(2): 380–419.

UBS. 2011. "Socially Responsible Investments: Introducing Impact Investing." *Wealth Management Research* August 11.

U.K. Parliament. 2006. *Cabinet Office.* www.legislation.gov.uk/ukpga/2006/46/con tents. Retrieved August 1, 2014.

Unilever. 2010. "Sustainable Living Plan." www.unilever.dk/Images/UnileverSustaina bleLivingPlan_tcm112-219379.pdf. Retrieved October 23, 2014.

Unitarian Universalist Association. 2014. "History of SRI and the UUA." www.uua.org/finance/investment/sri/57458.shtml. Retrieved February 28, 2014.

United Nations. 2002. *Report of the International Conference on the Financing for Development.* New York: United Nations.

     2000. *United Nations Millennium Declaration.* New York: United Nations.

United Nations Development Programme. 2010. *"The MDGs: Everyone's Business."* Geneva: United Nations Development Programme.

     2008. *"Creating Value for All: Strategies for Doing Business with the Poor."* Geneva: United Nations Development Programme.

     2004. *"Unleashing Entrepreneurship: Making Business Work for the Poor."* Geneva: United Nations Development Programme.

     2003. *"Business and the Millennium Development Goals: A Framework for Action, first edition."* Geneva: United Nations Development Programme.

     1990. *"Human Development Report 1990: Concept and Measurement of Human Development."* Geneva: United Nations Development Programme.

United Nations Environmental Programme Finance Initiative. 2007. "Demystifying Responsible Investment Performance: A Review of Key Academic and Broker Research on ESG Factors." www.unepfi.org/fileadmin/documents/Demystifying_ Responsible_Investment_Performance_01.pdf. Retrieved June 12, 2014.

United Nations Environmental Programme Finance Initiative Asset Management Working Group. 2006. "Show Me the Money: Linking Environmental, Social and Governance Issues to Company Value." www.unepfi.org/fileadmin/docu ments/show_me_the_money.pdf. Retrieved June 28, 2014.

2004. "The Materiality of Social, Environmental and Corporate Governance Issues to Equity Pricing." www.unepfi.org/fileadmin/documents/amwg_materiality_equity_ pricing_report_2004.pdf. Retrieved June 28, 2014.

United Nations Environmental Programme Finance Initiative and Freshfields Bruckhaus Deringer. 2005. *Legal Framework for the Integration of Environmental, Social and Governance Issues into Institutional Investment.* New York: United Nations Environment Program Finance Initiative.

United Nations Global Compact. 2014. *UN Global Compact Participants.* New York: United Nations Global Compact Office.

2012. *What is the UN Global Compact?* New York: United Nations Global Compact.

2010. *A Global Compact for Development.* New York: United Nations Global Compact Office.

2007. *UN Global Compact Annual Review: 2007 Leaders Summit.* New York: United Nations Global Compact Office.

2004. *Who Cares Wins: Connecting Financial Markets to a Changing World.* New York: United Nations Global Compact Office.

United Nations Trade and Development. 2011. *Investment and Enterprise Responsibility: Analysis of Investor and Enterprise Policies on Corporate Social Responsibility. New York: United Nations.* New York: United Nations Trade and Development.

United States Department of Education. 1998. *National Assessment of Educational Progress.* Washington, DC: United States Department of Education.

United States General Accounting Office. 2004. *Results-Oriented Government.* Washington, DC: Government Accounting Office.

1997. "Performance Budgeting: Past Initiatives Offer Insights for GPRA Implementation." Letter Report, March, 27, 1997, GAO/AIMD: 97–46.

United States National Performance Review. 1993. *Creating a Government that Works Better and Costs Less: The Report of the National Performance Review.* Washington, DC: Government Printing Office.

United States Securities and Exchange Commission. 2012. "Commission Guidance Regarding Disclosure Related to Climate Change." www.sec.gov/rules/interp/ 2010/33–9106. Retrieved September 12, 2014.

2008. "Draft Final Report of the Advisory Committee on Improvements to Financial Reporting to the United States Securities and Exchange Commission." 1www.sec .gov/about/offices/oca/acifr/acifr-dfr-071108.pdf. Retrieved September 14, 2015.

United Way of America. 1996. *"Measuring Program Outcomes: Training Kit."* Alexandria, VA: United Way of America.

US SIF. 2012. "Report on Sustainable and Responsible Investing Trends in the United States." www.ussif.org/files/Publications/12_Trends_Exec_Summary.pdf. Retrieved July 3, 2013.

Useem, Michael. 1993. *Executive Defense: Shareholder Power and Corporate Reorganization*. Cambridge, MA: Harvard University Press.

Vance, Stanley C. 1975. "Are Socially Responsible Corporations Good Investment Risks?" *Management Review* 64:18–24.

Varley, Pamela, ed. 1998. *The Sweatshop Quandary: Corporate Responsibility on the Global Frontier*. Washington, DC: Investor Responsibility Research Center.

Viscusi, W. Kip, and Joseph E. Aldy. 2003. "The Value of a Statistical Life: A Critical Review of Market Estimates throughout the World." *Journal of Risk and Uncertainty* 27(1):5–76.

Vogel, David. 2006. *The Market for Virtue: The Potential and Limits of Corporate Social Responsibility*. New York: Brookings Institution Press.

1978. *Lobbying the Corporation*. New York: Basic Books.

Wach, Eli. 2012. "Measuring the Inclusivity of 'Inclusive' Business." *IDS Practice Paper* 12(9). Brighton: IDS.

Wackernagel, Mathis and William E. Rees. 1996. *Our Ecological Footprint: Reducing Human Impact on the Earth*. Gabriola Island, BC: New Society Publishers.

Waddock, Sandra. 2008a. "Building A New Institutional Infrastructure for Corporate Responsibility." *The Academy of Management Perspectives* 22(3):87–108.

2008b. *The Difference Makers: How Social and Institutional Entrepreneurs Created the Corporate Responsibility Movement*. Sheffield, UK: Greenleaf Publishing.

Waddock Sandra and Samuel B. Graves. 1997. "The Corporate Social Performance-Financial Performance Link." *Strategic Management Journal* 18:303–19.

Waghorn, Terry. 2014. "Joseph Keefe: Sustainable Investing." *Forbes Magazine* May 1. www.forbes.com/sites/terrywaghorn/2014/05/01/joseph-keefe-sustainable-investing/. Retrieved August 22, 2014.

Walzer, Michael. 1983. *Spheres of Justice: A Defense of Pluralism and Equality*. New York: Basic Books.

Warren, Janice, and Mark Thomsen. 2012. "The Case for Corporate Responsibility Reporting: Valuing and Communicating the Intangibles." www.one-report.com/wp_request.html. Retrieved February 4, 2014.

Weber, Max. 1922. *Economy and Society*, edited by M. Rheinstein. New York: Simon and Schuster.

Weber, Klaus, Hetal Patel, and Kathryn L. Heinze. 2013. "From Cultural Repertoires to Institutional Logics: A Content-Analytic Method." *Research in the Sociology of Organizations* 39:351–382.

Weisbrod, Burton A. 1988. *The Nonprofit Economy*. Cambridge, MA: Harvard University Press.

1977. *The Voluntary Nonprofit Sector*. Lexington: Lexington Books.

Weiss, Carol H. 1972. *Evaluative Research: Methods of Assessing Program Effectiveness*. New York: Prentice Hall.

White, Harrison C. 2002. *Markets from Networks: Socioeconomic Models of Production*. Princeton: Princeton University Press.

Wholey, Joseph S. 2012. "Using Evaluation to Improve Program Performance and Results." Pp. 261–266 in *Evaluation Roots: A Wider Perspective of Theorists' Views and Influences*, edited by Marvin C. Alkin. New York: Sage Publications.

1983. *Evaluation and Effective Public Management*. New York: Little, Brown.

1979. *Evaluation: Promise and Performance*. Washington, DC: Urban Institute.

Wholey, Joseph S. and Harry Hatry. 1992. "The Case for Performance Monitoring." *Public Administration Review* 52(6):604–610.

Wildavsky, Aaron. 1966. "The Political Economy of Efficiency: Cost-Benefit Analysis, Systems Analysis, and Program Budgeting." *Public Administration Review* 26(4): 292–310.

Willis, Alan. 2003. "The Role of the Global Reporting Initiative's Sustainability Reporting Guidelines in the Social Screening of Investments." *Journal of Business Ethics* 43(3):233–237.

Wood, David and Belinda Hoff. 2007. "*Handbook on Responsible Investment across Asset Classes.*" Boston: Boston College Center for Corporate Citizenship.

Woolford, Andrew and Amelia Curran. 2011. "Neoliberal Restructuring, Limited Autonomy, and Relational Distance in Manitoba's Nonprofit Field." *Critical Social Policy* 31(4):583–606.

World Bank. 2004a. "*Monitoring & Evaluation: Some Tools, Methods, and Approaches.*" Washington, DC: The World Bank.

2004b. *The World Development Report, 2004: Making Services Work for the Poor.* Washington, DC: World Bank Group.

2001. *World Development Report 2000/2001: Attacking Poverty.* New York: Oxford University Press.

1991. *World Development Report 1991: The Challenge of Development*, New York: World Bank/Oxford University Press.

1990. *World Development Report 1990.* Washington, DC: World Bank Group.

World Business Council for Sustainable Development. 2013a. "Measuring Social Value Creation at *Saipem*'s Karimun Island Fabrication Yard in Indonesia." www.wbcsd .org/Pages/EDocument/EDocumentDetails.aspx?ID=15365&NoSearchContextKey= true. Retrieved March 1, 2014.

2013b. "Measuring Socio-Economic Impact: A Guide for Business." www.wbcsd .org/Pages/EDocument/EDocumentDetails.aspx?ID=13357&NoSearchContextKey= true. Retrieved February 23, 2014.

2008a. "Measuring Impact: Beyond the Bottom Line." www.wbcsd.org/pages/edocu ment/edocumentdetails.aspx?id=206. Retrieved February 23, 2014.

2008b. "Measuring Impact Framework Methodology." www.wbcsd.org/pages/edocu ment/edocumentdetails.aspx?id=205&nosearchcontextkey=true. Retrieved February 23, 2014.

2005. "Business for Development: Business Solutions in Support of the Millennium Development Goals." www.wbcsd.org/web/publications/biz4dev.pdf. Retrieved June 3, 2014.

World Business Council for Sustainable Development/SNV. 2008. "Inclusive Business: Profitable Business for Successful Development." www.inclusivebusiness.org/2008/ 03/new-alliance-br.html. Retrieved February 13, 2014.

World Commission on Environment and Development. 1987. *Our Common Future.* Oxford: Oxford University Press.

World Economic Forum. 2011. "*Accelerating the Transition towards Sustainable Investing.*" Geneva: World Economic Forum.

2005. "*Private Investment for Social Goals: Building the Blended Value Capital Market.*" Geneva: World Economic Forum.

2003. "*Philanthropy Measures Up: Benchmarking Philanthropy Report.*" Geneva: World Economic Forum.

World Intellectual Capital Initiative. 2010. "Concept Paper on WICI KPI in Business Reporting ver. 1" https://circabc.europa.eu/webdav/CircaBC/FISMA/markt_consultations/Library/accounting/Non-financial-reporting/registered_organisations/BE_WICI2_en.pdf. Retrieved March 21, 2015.

Wright, Karen. 2001. "Generosity vs. Altruism: Philanthropy and Charity in the United States and the United Kingdom." *Voluntas* 12:399–416.

Wright, Laurence A., Simon Kemp, and Ian Williams. 2011. "'Carbon Footprinting': Towards a Universally Accepted Definition." *Carbon Management* 2(1):61–72.

Wright, Peter, and Stephen P. Ferris. 1997. "Agency Conflict and Corporate Strategy: The Effect of Divestment on Corporate Value." *Strategic Management Journal* 18(1):77–83.

Young, Dennis. 2003. "New Trends in the US Non-profit Sector: Towards Market Integration?" Pp. 61–136 in *The Non-Profit Sector in a Changing Economy*, edited by *Antonella Noya and Corinne Nativel*. Paris: OECD.

Young, Dennis and Lester Salamon. 2002. "Commercialization, Social Ventures, and For-Profit Competition." Pp. 423–446 in *The State of Nonprofit America*, edited by Lester Salamon. Washington, DC: Brookings Institution Press.

Yunus, Muhammad. 1999. *Banker to the Poor: Micro-Lending and the Battle against World Poverty*. New York: Public Affairs.

Zelizer, Viviana. 2009. *The Purchase of Intimacy: Pin Money, Paychecks, Poor Relief, and Other Currencies*. Princeton, NJ: Princeton University Press.

1997. *The Social Meaning of Money*. New York: Basic Books.

1985. *Pricing the Priceless Child: The Changing Social Value of Children*. Princeton: Princeton University Press.

1983. *Morals and Markets: The Development of Life Insurance in the United States*. New Brunswick, NJ: Transaction Books.

Zimmermann, J. M. and B. W. Stevens. 2006. "The Use of Performance Measurement in South Carolina Nonprofits." *Nonprofit Management & Leadership* 16(3):315–327.

Zuckerman, Ezra W. 1999. "The Categorical Imperative: Securities Analysts and the Illegitimacy Discount." *American Journal of Sociology* 104(5):1398–1438.

Index

Printed in the United States
By Bookmasters